Keywords in Literature and Culture

The books in this series present keywords for individual literary periods in an easily accessible reference format. More than a dictionary, each volume is written by a leading scholar and consists of an engaging collection of short essays, which consider the ways in which words both register and explore historical change. Indebted to the work of Raymond Williams, the series identifies and documents keywords as cultural analysis, taking the reader beyond semantic definition to uncover the uncertainties, disagreements, and confrontations evident in differing usages and conflicting connotations.

Published:

Anglo-Saxon Keywords	Allen J. Frantzen
Modernism: Keywords	Melba Cuddy-Keane, Adam Hammond, and Alexandra Peat

Forthcoming:

Middle English Keywords	Kellie Robertson
British Literature 1660-1789: Keywords	Robert DeMaria Jr.
Romanticism: Keywords	Frederick Burwick

Modernism: Keywords

Modernism: Keywords

Melba Cuddy-Keane
Adam Hammond
Alexandra Peat

WILEY Blackwell

This edition first published 2014
© 2014 Melba Cuddy-Keane

Registered Office
John Wiley & Sons, Ltd, The Atrium, Southern Gate, Chichester, West Sussex, PO19 8SQ, UK

Editorial Offices
350 Main Street, Malden, MA 02148-5020, USA
9600 Garsington Road, Oxford, OX4 2DQ, UK
The Atrium, Southern Gate, Chichester, West Sussex, PO19 8SQ, UK

For details of our global editorial offices, for customer services, and for information about how
to apply for permission to reuse the copyright material in this book please see our website at
www.wiley.com/wiley-blackwell.

The right of Melba Cuddy-Keane to be identified as the author responsible for this work has been asserted in
accordance with the UK Copyright, Designs and Patents Act 1988.

Library of Congress Cataloging-in-Publication Data

Cuddy-Keane, Melba.
  Modernism keywords / Melba Cuddy-Keane, Adam Hammond and Alexandra Peat. – First Edition.
    pages   cm. – (Keywords in literature and culture (KILC).)
  Includes index.
  ISBN 978-1-4051-8655-1 (hardback)
1. English language–Etymology.   2. English language–Glossaries, vocabularies, etc.   3. Modernism (Literature)
4. Social structure–Terminology.   5. Culture–Terminology.   6. Sociolinguistics.   7. Vocabulary.   I. Title.
  PE1580.C794 2014
  820.9'11203–dc23

                                    2013038470

A catalogue record for this book is available from the British Library.

Cover design by E&P Design

Set in 9.75/13pt BellGothic by SPi Publisher Services, Pondicherry, India
Printed in Malaysia by Ho Printing (M) Sdn Bhd

1   2014

Contents

Credits and Acknowledgments   viii
Introduction: Unsettling Modernism   x
Note on References   xviii

A
Advertising   1
Atom, Atomic   6
Avant-Garde   11

B
Best Seller   15
Bigness, Smallness   20
Biography, New Biography   26

C
Common Man   34
Common Mind, Group Thinking   40
Conventional, Conventionality   45
Coterie, Bloomsbury   49

D
Democracy   56
Difficulty, Obscurity   63

E
Einstein   70
Empire, Imperialism   77

Contents

F

Fascism 85

Form, Formalism 91

G

God, Gods 99

H

Hamlet 107

Highbrow, Middlebrow, Lowbrow 111

Hygiene 119

I

Impression, Impressionism 125

International, Internationalism 129

M

Manifesto 136

Modern, Modernism 139

N

Negro, New Negro 147

P

Personality, Impersonality 155

Primitive 162

Propaganda 170

Q

Queer, Gay 177

R

Race 184

Readers, Reading 191

Reality, Realism 196

Rhythm 203

S

Sentimental, Sentimentality 210

Shock, Shell Shock 214

Contents

U

Unconscious   223
Universal   231

W

Woman, New Woman   238
Words, Language   246

Index of Modernist Authors   254
Index of Modernist Keywords   263

vii

Credits and Acknowledgments

Our thanks go first and foremost to the Social Sciences and Humanities Research Council of Canada (SSHRC) for a Standard Research Grant that supported much of our work and to the University of Toronto Excellence Awards, which supported Claire Marie Stancek as an undergraduate assistant for two summers. We are indebted as well to the excellent services at the research and rare book libraries at the University of Toronto, and in the Metropolitan Toronto Public Library system, and to the numerous online sites that have made available digitized versions of modernist books and periodicals. We owe a particular debt of gratitude to colleagues and students at the University of Toronto and Franklin University Switzerland who commented on our entries and to modernist scholars everywhere – especially to colleagues in the Modernist Studies Association – whose rich discussions and illuminating scholarship simulated our thinking and encouraged our work.

The production of this work as a collaborative effort makes it impossible to assign specific credit for individual portions of it. All members of the team contributed substantially to the research and most also commented on draft entries and suggested approaches to structure. The graduate students employed by the project inevitably varied in the length of time they could be involved in the project, as reflected in their different roles, but the project is greatly indebted to them all. Members of the research team included collaborating writer Marybeth Curtin; collaborating contributors Glenn Clifton and Rohanna Green; contributors Claire Battershill, Kimberly Fairbrother Canton, and Daniel Harney; and research assistants Tania Botticella, Stewart Cole, and Sarah Copland. Rohanna Green and Adam Hammond provided invaluable assistance in establishing our collaborative websites. Special thanks are also due to Claire Marie Stancek for her excellent research, recordings of our meetings, and commentaries on numerous entries.

Credits and Acknowledgments

Primary responsibility for the project was undertaken as follows: Melba Cuddy-Keane was project director and senior editor, and Alexandra Peat served for many years as project manager. Marybeth Curtin and Adam Hammond joined Cuddy-Keane and Peat on an editorial team in the spring of 2010, all four collaborating as writers until Curtin graduated and took up a government research position in June 2011. Cuddy-Keane, Hammond, and Peat continued as co-writers; in the last phase of the project, Cuddy-Keane and Hammond revised and expanded the text, developing and completing the remaining entries, the bibliography, and the keyword index; Peat provided editorial assistance. All three co-authors collaborated in copyediting and proofreading.

This project would never have been realized without Wiley Blackwell's Commissioning Editor Emma Bennett, who first proposed the idea for this book, and without the patient guidance of Project Editor Ben Thatcher and all the Wiley Blackwell staff. We are indebted to SPi Global for their help with copy-editing, to Mary Newberry for producing the author index using TExtract, and to EndNote for its indispensable bibliographic software. Thanks go finally to many wonderful friends and family members who were inspirational in their unwavering support.

Introduction: Unsettling Modernism

Spanning the "long" modernist period, from roughly 1880–1950, *Modernism: Keywords* tracks words used with frequency and urgency in "written modernism." The approach takes its inspiration from Raymond Williams's *Keywords: A Vocabulary of Culture and Society* (1976), which argued that we can best understand the character and thought of an era not through its dominant beliefs, but through the problems and debates inadvertently revealed in its words. Differing from periodizations that try to identify an era's dominant ideology, or "the spirit of the age," a keywords approach identifies controversial words that mattered enough to become magnets of cross-talk and exchange. Unlike dictionaries and glossaries, Keywords focuses on words that cannot be easily and summarily defined: words with unstable meanings and conflicting implications, which testify to culture as an active and living thing. Unlike historical dictionaries, Keywords goes further than quotation to analyze relationships and to probe the issues or forces underlying ambiguous words. Keywords attempts to discover cultural processes at work.

Aims and Approach

While adopting Williams's combination of cultural analysis and close reading, *Modernism: Keywords* responds as well to the revolutionary changes in research techniques since his time. By his own account, Williams's resources consisted primarily of *The Oxford English Dictionary* (the OED) and his own reading over an approximately 25-year span. Today, electronic databases and online searching have vastly increased the number of texts readily available, while the range of accessible materials extends to forms such as popular journalism, advertisements, and (often posthumously published) letters and diaries. In addition, while Williams focused his study on British culture and society, the research offered here embraces the transatlantic and, where possible, the larger English-speaking

Introduction: Unsettling Modernism

world. The new scope requires vast quantities of material and the technologies to make it available; the present work could not have been written without electronic databases, internet searching, and the wide reading of a collaborative research team. As a result, the evidence we present differs from the original *Keywords* as well. Williams, for the most part, offered generalized broad summaries about the meaning of terms; *Modernism: Keywords* documents usage with specific quotations, citing, from a much larger bibliography of works consulted, over 1100 primary texts.

To assist manageability, however, this volume has a more specific focus than Williams's work: our subject is *written* modernism and our audience is, first and foremost, a readership engaged in the study of English Literature. Although emphasizing the nineteenth century, Williams's coverage ranged from earliest usages to the mid-1970s; the present work limits itself to seventy years, concentrating on a period particularly noted for radical change. Furthermore, whereas Williams's approach was broadly cultural and sociological, the approach here always considers the relevance of its "interdisciplinary" usages – in, for example, psychology, sociology, and science – for understandings pertinent to the discipline of literature.

A word should be said too about ideology. As a Marxist, Williams was accused – notably by William Empson (1977) – of political partisanship, although we believe that a careful reading of his *Keywords* reveals it to be remarkably fair. Williams himself, however, drew attention to the inescapability of bias, noting the prevalence in the OED of "orthodox opinion," and the way that his own "positions and preferences" inevitably seep through. The present work certainly aspires to ideological fairness, on the assumption that we can recover a sense of on-going conversation only by giving all voices equal chance to speak. We pursue, in this light, a comment by Williams himself: "an 'enlightened Radical or Liberal' ought, as Mill said of Coleridge, 'to rejoice over such a Conservative' as Eliot" for the way he "raised questions which those who differ from him politically must answer, or else retire from the field" (1956). We take inspiration as well from a critic speaking from the liberal-humanist side: as F. R. Leavis stated, "finding essential insight in work about which one has to have critical reserves is a most important order of educational experience" (1969). Those who contributed research for this volume represent a wide range of interests, beliefs, and political allegiances, and these collaborative voices helped us to listen carefully to the range of voices in the works that we read. Yet, finally, even a study of vocabulary makes ethical judgments at certain points. While we have tried, for example, to present the reasons why some writers used words such as fascism or imperialism in positive ways, we still expose the ethical problems in endorsements of these terms.

Theoretical Implications

A keywords approach implies a methodological and theoretical departure from most critical books being written today. First, not only does it focus on words rather than ideas – or rather, it accesses ideas *through* words – but it also relies on what words meant to the modernists rather than what they mean to us now. It may seem like a simple process of leaping over current assumptions, but – as we have learned – it is not as easy as it sounds. Second, our entries seek out diversity, even messiness, rather than resolution, so that contrary to the usual scholarly demand for original and singular interpretations, forestalling over-arching interpretation has been our goal. Keywords thus resonates with current dissatisfactions with linear histories, as expressed, for example, in Michael Levenson's turn to "adjacencies." Arguing an approach to modernism through "the simmering of conversation, the unstoppable circulation of jokes and curses, critical dicta and common-readerly buzz" (2011: 677), Levenson advocates a historicism based on "a network of heterogeneous manifestations" "which needn't be elevated to "frameworks" or "metanarratives" (2011: 676, 675). Keywords also aligns with Michael Whitworth's view that returning to "the full historical context" can "unearth associations and implications which complicate meaning," with the result that "historicism can reopen texts, and that reopening can place the past in new dialogues with the present" (2012: 22).

But the project of "opening history" urges us to go beyond juxtaposition to interaction. *Modernism: Keywords* envisions a mobile history through the trope of "the bounce," conceiving the words of the past as bouncing against each other as well as out to us. Imagine a field full of multiple players hitting multiple bouncing balls, which spring up from the ground, ricochet off each other, pass from hand to hand, and bounce out to the spectators too. The balls seem to be propelling themselves by their own volition, yet almost invisible hands animate them, speeding them on their way. Like these bouncing, colliding balls, words carry the imprint of previous touch, since communicative power depends on communal speech. Like the watchers, we, as readers and critics, influence the course of the motion, our changing perceptions bringing multiple patterns into play. By focusing our attention, we bring one ball or one word or one text into the foreground and place others in the background, but by frequently shifting focus, we activate a continual alternation between what is foreground (text) and what background (context). Our vision is most likely limited to a series of rapid still shots of partial aspects, but long exposure and slow watching help us imaginatively to glimpse the whole. The bounce is simply a suggestive metaphor and not meant exactly to replicate the way words work. It will be useful if it offers possibilities for glimpsing, if not fully apprehending, a total field of motion, and capturing the mobile, dynamic, noncentric interaction of keywords at work.

Conceiving history as motion also means infusing history with doubt. As art historian Richard Shiff said in a recent interview: "Theorizations are hypotheses to be tested – they're pragmatic guesses, often guesses quite in the dark. Belief in your own theory eliminates the capacity to doubt" (Siegel, 2008, Web.) At times, these entries will ask you to set aside your own point of view, even to read from the enemy's position. Although this doesn't mean abandoning judgments about value and ethics, it does involve trying to understand the other's view in its own terms. If we do then return to our initial theories, they will have accumulated depth and complexity along the way.

Modernists and Modernism

While this book does not seek to engage current debates about modernism, the method itself inevitably challenges ideas about modernists and modernism that, in the latter half of C20, became ensconced. A keywords approach makes it more difficult to label a writer's thought, or to place writers definitively in opposite camps, since, in a relational network, utterances often overlap with those of apparent opponents, or expose the insecurity and uncertainty under-lying fixed meanings and views. Theories about segregated cultures, about "divides" between "highbrow" and "middlebrow," or between serious art and popular culture, simply become more difficult to maintain. And the plurality inherent in a keywords approach challenges any single idea of modernism itself. Modernism is coming to signify in the way "romanticism" now does: it can be understood as an identifiable transhistorical style, approach, or response (although one with internal variations and disagreements); alternatively, it can be simply a period, or an era, delimited somewhat arbitrarily and yet meaning-fully by certain dates. From scholars who take the latter approach, a new com-prehensive version of historical modernism is emerging, rather like the modernists' own sense of "atmosphere," in which boundaries are porous and ideas circulate – as they began to do literally on radio – through the air. Perhaps, indeed, our greatest departure from Williams lies in our proffered view of mod-ernism itself, since Williams, somewhat ironically, contributed to its labeling when he defined modernism as "metropolitan" art (1989). Our project, con-versely, seeks not to settle modernism; in charting what unsettled modernists, we unsettle the idea of modernism as possible to define. The modernist period was a vibrant time of broadly circulating difference, evidencing neither an ultimate messiness nor an ultimate cohesion; its heartbeat sounded in an ongoing engagement of many people, in many of the same things, at the same time. Modernists also had no certain idea of what modernism was or how its debates would end. Nor perhaps do we.

A Note on the Words

Our materials encompass all forms of writing in the modernist period, or by writers whose work falls primarily within our dates. Our sources range from vernacular prose to experimental literary forms, including books, periodical literature, newspapers, songs, even advertising. We mix canonical works with noncanonical, conservative with radical thinkers, "serious" with "popular" culture, generalist with specialist discourse, paying equal attention to all. While our selection is guided by the anticipated use of this book by literary students and scholars, here "fictive" or "imaginative" works inhabit a mixed universe, immersed in the larger textual world. Since our subject is written, not visual or musical, modernism, with a concentration on works written in English, references to the nonverbal arts and to European writers are minimal, limited to works that had significant impact on written English at the time. Our examples derive primarily from British and American writers, although where possible we have included writers from Australia, Canada, the Caribbean, India, New Zealand, and South Africa.

The words in this book are of several kinds: new words that were coined during the modernist period ("fascist," "Hamletize"); words that were changing/ shifting in meaning or connotation ("propaganda," "hygiene"); words that were being used frequently but in conflicting and contradictory ways ("realism," "woman"); and "word clusters" indicating emerging ideas, for which no single word was consistently used ("common mind/group thinking/super-cortex"). As the evidence emerged from our data, the results were often not what we expected to find. Many words associated now with modernism ("avant-garde") were, on their home turf, surprisingly thin; words we expected to be disappearing ("God") were in strong circulation, or being translated into other terms. And words that seem later to have settled into one dominant usage ("coterie," "form") were, in the modernist period, translucent and prismatic, reflecting many different sides.

We omitted words easily to be understood by consulting the OED; and we avoided words whose definition can be found in handbooks of literary terms, unless they were part of a larger conversation involving divergent interpretations and usages. Nor have we included foreign terms not yet translated into English (like Walter Benjamin's "aura"), or critical terms that became established after the mC20 to discuss modernist texts ("cultural capital" or "free indirect discourse"). Our focus is always on words that modernists were using, and the dynamics and complexities of that use.

A Note on Methodology

Identifying keywords depends on both objective database searching and interpretive judgment. Keywords must be in wide circulation, and they must exhibit uncertainty and variation in use. Frequency of use is not the only criterion, so that statistical counts, even if we had all relevant texts in an electronic data-base, would not suffice; keywords always embody some underlying dynamic tension, or some significant process of change, and identifying those features depends on the critical mind. Two important resources are thus needed for this task: the availability of extensive print and digitized materials, and a collaborative research team.

Inevitably, projects begin with what we know, and with a research group extending, over the years, to twelve people, most of them graduate students, we were aided by the reasonably large database of a collective mind. But the scope of the enterprise required us to go far beyond our own knowledge and our own critical frames. By responding to the results of our searches, as opposed to what we sought, we were frequently prompted to new understandings and new views. As scholars, we tend to store in our memories what we select as most important and significant; keyword searches of electronic archives, however, don't distinguish between important and insignificant usages – they simply return every "hit." What human memory could recall one of the earliest cultural references to modernism in a *Cosmopolitan* advertisement for "Rubdry towels"? Our numerous databases were fully part of the collaboration, especially in uncovering unpredictable use.

Research on such a grand scale depends on massive resources; we were assisted both by excellent libraries and by the increasing amount of material available online. Our materials included digitized books (through Project Gutenberg, Open Alliance, Google Books, the HathiTrust Digital Library, and especially Internet Archive); early journals and periodicals (the *TLS* Historical Archive; the Modernist Journals Project; *JSTOR*; UNZ.org and numerous other newspaper and periodical databases); anthologies of modernism; bibliographies in scholarly works; scholarship on modernism, and a wide range of print materials from the modernist time.

We became alert as well to the potential problems of internet resources: OCR recognition (translation from scanned printed text to searchable electronic form) is strikingly imperfect: "Racism" in a Google Book turned out to be an erroneous transcription of "Itacism"; in another transcribed text, the original word was "Ostracism." A publication listed from the United Nations in 1911 was clearly an error; the actual date was 1981. Further, as the creators of the Google Ngram Viewer have explained, "some metadata providers assign any book whose date is unknown the date 1899; others use 1905; still others use different dates" (Michel *et al.*, 2011). The internet is also full of misattributions, and once the misattribution occurs on one website, it is picked up and repeated on numerous other sites as well. Online searching, we discovered, needs to be complemented by reading that returns to the original, either the facsimile or the actual printed page.

Using This Book

Modernism: Keywords is designed for advanced undergraduates, graduate students, teachers, and advanced scholars of literature in English, with the hope that it will be of interest to broad interdisciplinary and general audiences as well. In its nature, this book falls between a dictionary and a book of criticism; it can be approached by reading a single entry, reading from cover to cover, starting with one entry and following the "see also" suggestions to track related ideas, or ferreting out entries relating to a specific topic of interest or research. Collectively, the entries offer a wealth of information, but they are best understood as an accompaniment and guide to further work. Many of the entries pair well with readings we consider "keywords in action" – novels, poems, plays that may not use the actual words we discuss, or use them only infrequently, but that nevertheless participate in the underlying debates. It is hard to think of a work that wouldn't pair with entries such as modern/modernism, readers/reading, reality/realism, and words, but more specific pairings can be used as well. To cite a few possibilities:

Dark Princess (W. E. B. Du Bois) with empire/imperialism, internationalism, universal

Death Comes for the Archbishop (Willa Cather) with propaganda, bigness/smallness, universal

Heart of Darkness (Joseph Conrad) with convention, empire/imperialism, primitive

The Heat of the Day (Elizabeth Bowen) with fascism, democracy, shock/shell shock

Jacob's Room (Virginia Woolf) with bigness/smallness, biography, common man

Mrs. Warren's Profession (George Bernard Shaw) with conventional, sentimental/sentimentality, woman/New Woman

Passing (Nella Larsen) with queer, personality/impersonality, unconscious

The Sound and the Fury (William Faulkner) with Hamlet (Quentin's chapter), race

Vile Bodies (Evelyn Waugh) with coterie/Bloomsbury, shock shell shock

The Waste Land (T. S. Eliot) with common mind, difficulty/obscurity, God/gods

While these examples list some of the works most frequently read in the classroom, the references at the end of each entry frequently cite less well-known works as well. Readers will also, we think, be surprised to discover how frequently these words appear in writings not cited here; our examples were many more than we could include, or fully track. The richness of these words will be discovered through further reading, and further reading will undoubtedly discover more keywords.

Future Directions

Modernism: Keywords is only a beginning in the larger project of using language to track the full modernist network of discussion and debate. The Table of Contents offers a relatively small selection, although additional words appear in the Index of Keywords. The keywords we have selected are significant, but modernism's significant words do not end with our list. We hope to cover additional words in future publication; we also hope, as did Williams, that others will join this collaborative task (indeed, several recent monographs use the approach of investigating a particular word.) For the future, more could be done to increase the international scope, to recognize the way foreign words were enriching the English language, and to complement this study with similar work in the nonwritten arts. Ideally, such work could move to a digital environment, with possibilities for incorporating feedback and submitted contributions; the web of meaning could then become a scholarly web as well. We should remember, however, that a keywords approach is designed not to replace but to mix with more traditional scholarship. This book will serve its function if it increases alertness to words and their changing meanings, and if it stimulates the reading of modernist texts for the meanings that were circulating at that time. Whether or not our readers take up a keywords approach for themselves, we hope they will all find their readings changed by reading *Modernism: Keywords*.

References

Empson, William (1977). "Compacted Doctrines." Rev. of *Keywords: A Vocabulary of Culture and Society* by Raymond Williams. *The New York Review of Books* (October 17), 21–22.

Leavis, F. R. (1969). *English Literature in Our Time and The University*. The Clarke Lectures, 1967. London: Chatto & Windus.

Levenson, Michael (2011). "Novelty, Modernity, Adjacency." *New Literary History* 42.4: 663–680.

Michel, Jean-Baptiste *et al.* (2011). "Quantitative Analysis of Culture Using Millions of Digitized Books." *Science* 331 (January): 176–182.

Siegel, Katy (Interviewer) (2008). "Richard Shiff with Katy Siegel." *The Brooklyn Rail: Critical Perspectives on Arts, Politics, and Culture* (May 8): Web.

Whitworth, Michael (2012). "Woolf, Context, and Contradiction." In *Contradictory Woolf: Selected Papers from the Twenty-First Annual International Virginia Woolf Conference* (eds. Derek Ryan and Stella Bolaki). Clemson: Clemson University Press. 11–22.

Williams, Raymond (1956). "Second Thoughts I: T. S. Eliot on Culture." *Essays in Criticism* 6.3: 302–318.

Williams, Raymond (1976). *Keywords: A Vocabulary of Culture and Society*. London: Fontana/Croom Helm.

Williams, Raymond (1989). *The Politics of Modernism*. Edited with Introduction by Tony Pinkney. London: Verso.

Note on References

Every effort has been made to cite the earliest publication or circulation of our keywords in the modernist period. Original publication dates, where they differ, appear after the title (for novels, this includes dates of serial publication). If the work was written significantly earlier than the date of publication, the date of composition is presented in square brackets, as are variant titles and dates for different previous versions of a text or, for works in translation, their original language publication. Unless otherwise indicated, translations from non-English works are ours.

A complexity of modernist bibliography worth mentioning is the frequency of simultaneous publication by different, and sometimes multiple, presses on both sides of the Atlantic. We have generally followed the practice of listing the publisher in the country where the writer resides, unless the work itself carries the imprint of different publishers. Our approach of weaving together different "national literatures," however, finds support in the publishing evidence that modernist readers were encountering these books in precisely that way.

Advertising

In *A Hope for Poetry* (1934), the poet Cecil Day Lewis lists "advertisement and cheap publicity" among the "'gross and violent stimulants' that are reducing the modern mind 'to a state of almost savage torpor.'" Likening advertising to numbing intoxicants, Day Lewis quotes William Wordsworth's attacks, in his Preface to the 1802 edition of *Lyrical Ballads*, on the numerous forces in *his* society serving "to blunt the discriminating powers of the mind." The irony, however, is that, in the first edition of *Lyrical Ballads* (1798), Wordsworth's introductory remarks were headed not "Preface," but "Advertisement." Day Lewis thus unwittingly signals a significant semantic shift: from its early neutral meaning of notification and information, "advertising" by the modernist period had come to name an industry, a rhetoric of persuasion, and a competing art form.

Citizens of modernity were exposed to advertising in a dazzling variety of forms. Skywriting, neon signs, billboards, posters, newspaper ads, window displays, sandwich boards, throwaways (flyers), and jingles had become elements of daily life. The ubiquity of advertising led French journalist Louis Chéronnet to remark in 1927, "The composition of the air has changed. To the oxygen and nitrogen we breathe we have to add Advertising. [. . .] It surrounds us, envelops us, it is intimately mingled with our every step, in our activities, in our relaxation, and its 'atmospheric pressure' is so necessary to us that we no longer feel it." Indeed, as early as 1913, *Maclean's Magazine* declared, "We live in the Advertising Age."

ABCDEFGHIJKLMNOPQRSTUVWXYZ

Modernism: Keywords, First Edition. Melba Cuddy-Keane, Adam Hammond, and Alexandra Peat.
© 2014 Melba Cuddy-Keane. Published 2014 by John Wiley & Sons, Ltd.

Advertising

As might be expected, many modernist works exhibit strong antipathy to advertising, often contrasting dishonest, sensational, hoax-prone advertising with disinterested "pure" art. H. G. Wells's *Tono-Bungay* (1908) satirically depicts the aggressive marketing of a "slightly injurious" bogus tonic (loosely based on Coca-Cola), in contrast to the serious but nonlucrative art of the narrator's alter-ego Bob Ewart. The advertisements (illustrated in the first edition) temporarily make the family's fortune, but the narrator retrospectively describes the process as "the giving of nothing coated in advertisements for money." In George Orwell's *Keep the Aspidistra Flying* (1936), Gordon Comstock – recognizing the "beastly irony in the fact that he, who wanted to be a 'writer,' should score his sole success in writing ads for deodorants" – similarly confronts the reality that it is advertising, not pure art, that pays. More threateningly, advertising reflects the reductiveness of totalitarian discourse in Stephen Spender's *Vienna* (1934): the Executive (the Fascist Dollfuss regime in Austria) say of the Unemployed, "We can read their bodies like advertisements/On hoardings, shouting with common answers."

Yet such outright attacks were countered by arguments in advertising's defense. In *Nuntius: Advertising and its Future* (1926), Gilbert Russell sought to convince an "ill-informed or misinformed public" that advertising was not only an economic necessity but an "educative" and "civilising" force as well. Advertising, he argued, helped to maintain manufacturing quality, alerted consumers to safer and healthier products, and increased exposure to culture, prompting people to read more widely. In its most positive guise, advertising connoted creativity. According to André Billy, the French poet Guillaume Apollinaire "found a source of inspiration in prospectuses, [. . .] catalogues, posters, advertisements of all sorts," and named advertising "the poetry of our epoch" (1912). In a similarly positive vein, the Austrian-born philologist and critic Leo Spitzer took the coinage of "sunkist" for "oranges" as typifying advertising's ability to inject beauty and poetry into an overly rational world, and he argued further that this advertisement's playfully ironic overtones prompted its audience to reflect critically on the differences between reality and dream (1949). Whether advertising is imaginative art or humbug plays out in the polarized responses to circus entrepreneur P. T. Barnum. In 1910, the trade journal *The Printers' Ink* marked the 100th anniversary of Barnum's birth by disclaiming any relation between Barnum's notorious sensationalism and modern business practices, noting that his "advertising ability," though "interesting as a starting point of the profession," was "lamentably gross and misrepresentative of the modern development of it." Conversely, in 1940, Yale professor William Lyon Phelps linked advertisement positively with the arts by calling Barnum "the Shakespeare of advertising" (Wallace, 1959).

A similar division of attitudes surrounded the question of advertising's style. Hostile responses cast its rhetoric as the obverse of the literary, with charges ranging from its goal of coercion to its mode of desperation. Q. D. Leavis and Wyndham Lewis portrayed advertising as an ideological tool productive of unreflecting conformity. "It is more than difficult, it is next to impossible," wrote Leavis, "for the ordinary uncritical man to resist when, whichever way he looks in the street, from poster and hoarding, and advertisement in bus and tramcar [. . .] the pressure of the herd is brought to bear on him" (1932). Lewis interpreted advertising as mind control, arguing that the masses had been "hypnotized into a sort of hysterical imbecility by the mesmeric methods of Advertisement" (1927). Evelyn Waugh associated advertising with the fetishization of the new: claiming that "no serious writer has ever been shy of an expression because it has been used before," he accused "the writer of advertisements" of "always straining to find bizarre epithets for commonplace objects" (1946).

Other modernist usages positioned advertising as a literary genre – one from which more traditional genres could learn. While one view, as we have seen, attributed a literary character to advertising due to its poetic creativity, another approach, valuing economy and precision, extolled the rhetoric of advertising as a desirable element in literary form. Aldous Huxley called advertising "one of the most interesting and difficult literary forms" – adding the qualified term "applied literature," however, for those benighted readers "who still believe[d] in the romantic superiority of the pure, the disinterested, over the immediately useful" (1920). Huxley himself praised the "elegance and economical distinction" of advertising prose; reflecting on its "honest man-to-man style" – "lucid and simple enough to be understood by all" – he concluded, "the art of advertisement writing has flowered with democracy." In "The Advertisement is Literature" (1926), Dashiell Hammett called the advertiser a "literary worker" since he "must set his idea on paper in such a form that it will have the effect he desires on those who read it"; like Huxley, Hammett suggested that literature could learn from advertising by replacing "the needlessly involved sentence, the clouded image" with the concision, clarity, and efficiency of good ad copy.

Yet in modernist literature overall, the prevailing treatment of advertising was less clear-cut. In the penultimate chapter of Henry James's *The Ambassadors* ([1903]1909), when Chad Newsome – a Jamesian "American abroad" – announces his discovery that advertising is "the great new force" which is "infinite like all the arts," his words waver between the chilling suggestion that he is reverting to his family's economic materialism and the complicating possibility that a new, dynamic energy is infusing his habitually passive demeanor. In F. Scott Fitzgerald's *The Great Gatsby* (1925), the faded billboard picturing the pale eyes and gigantic spectacles of the vanished oculist Doctor T. J. Eckleburg initially suggests the disappearance of God in an ethically weak capitalist society: after the catastrophic accident, when George Wilson looks up at the billboard and intones, "God sees everything," "That's an advertisement" is his friend's curt rejoinder. Yet Eckleburg's human counterpart – nicknamed "Owl Eyes" because of his "enormous owl-eyed spectacles" – is the one character other than the narrator who responds to Gatsby with perception and compassion, an oddity suggesting that the billboard

3

can be read as a text about human witnessing as well. In Jean Rhys's *Voyage in the Dark* (1934), advertising is initially a force of social hypnosis. The narrator Anna, transplanted to London from the Caribbean, hears a jingle for Standard Bread which, despite her resistance, plays "over and over again" in her head: "It's the tune that's so awful; it's like blows." Yet in a climactic moment, Anna's childhood memory of "a picture advertising the Biscuits Like Mother Makes" leads to a crucial insight: the depiction of "a little girl in a pink dress" with "a shiny pale-blue sky" near enough to touch exposes the Empire's utopian marketing of England as a "cosy" and happy place where God is always near, while the "high, dark wall" behind her signifies the inaccessibility of this dream for the colonized outsiders.

James Joyce's *Ulysses* (1922), a novel littered with slogans, posters, throw-aways, and sandwich boards, captures the ambiguity of advertising as simultaneously a playful, creative art and an insidiously dominating form. Protagonist Leopold Bloom – himself an ad canvasser and practitioner of what one character calls "the gentle art of advertisement" (with a subtle ironic play on the well-known expression "the gentle art of persuasion") – subverts such coercive intent when he uses "Plumtree's Potted Meat" as a springboard to free associate everything from the sexual act to a buried corpse. Nonetheless, as Bloom goes to sleep at the end of the novel, he fantasizes about "the infinite possibilities hitherto unexploited of the modern art of advertisement" and he dreams of creating a totalizing advertisement with the power "to arrest involuntary attention, to convince, to decide." The tension between regulation and freedom is similarly embodied in the famous skywriting scene in Virginia Woolf's *Mrs. Dalloway* (1925). As an airplane flies over central London, skywriting ragged and rapidly dissolving letters in smoke, scattered pedestrians are both uniformly held in a moment of coerced attention and loosely combined in a participatory act of group seeing. The ambiguous skywriting produces a scene of modernist reading, eliciting interpretations ranging from the mystical to the mundane. What Septimus Smith interprets, in aesthetic rapture, as a sign from the beyond, other onlookers collectively decipher as a message about something to eat: "they were advertising toffee."

Advertising thus exhibited a double voicedness, as both a dominating, manipulative rhetoric and a cultural sign to be creatively produced, read, and used. As concerns about standardization and mass marketing grew, however, educators and cultural theorists gravitated to the uniformly negative readings of Lewis and Leavis. Marshall McLuhan, for his part, wavered in his sentiments, expressing concerns that "the business of the advertiser is to see that we go about our business with some magic spell or tune or slogan throbbing quietly in the background of our minds" (1953), yet, only one year later, "blessing" "advertising art" for "its pictorial VITALITY and verbal CREATIVITY" (1954). For Northrop Frye, however, advertising was straightforwardly an "anti-art" – a form of propaganda with a dangerous propensity to "stun and demoralize the critical

4

consciousness with statements too absurd or extreme to be dealt with seriously" (1967). Such powerful critiques served to entrench modernism and advertising as an oppositional binary; crosscurrents within the modernist period, however, show "advertisement" functioning in plural and controversial ways.

SEE ALSO: *Best Seller; Form; Propaganda; Readers, Reading*

References

(1910). "Barnum and Advertising." *The Printers' Ink* (July 14), 193.

(1913). "New Profession for Girls: Posing for Illustrations in Advertisements has Now Become a Regular Business." *Maclean's Magazine* (May), 135–136.

Billy, André (1912). "Comme je suis devenu poête." *Les Soirées de Paris* (October 1), 276–280.

Chéronnet, Louis (1927). "La Publicité, Art du XXe Siècle [Advertising, Art of the Twentieth Century]." *L'Art vivant* 3 (March): 192.

Day Lewis, Cecil (1934). *A Hope for Poetry.* Oxford: Basil Blackwell.

Fitzgerald, F. Scott (1925). *The Great Gatsby.* New York: Charles Scribner's Sons.

Frye, Northrop (1967). *The Modern Century.* Toronto: Oxford University Press.

Hammett, Dashiell (1926). "The Advertisement is Literature." *Western Advertising: A Magazine for the Buyer and Seller of Advertising* (October), 35–36.

Huxley, Aldous (as Autolycus) (1920). "Marginalia." *The Athenaeum* (September 17), 378. Rpt. as Aldous Huxley, "Advertisement." In *On the Margin: Notes and Essays.* London: Chatto & Windus, 1923. 127–133.

James, Henry (1909). The Ambassadors. [1903]. In *The Novels and Tales of Henry James.* New York Edition. 26 vols. New York: Charles Scribner's Sons. Vol. 21–22.

Joyce, James (1922). *Ulysses.* Paris: Shakespeare and Co.

Leavis, Q. D. (1932). *Fiction and the Reading Public.* London: Chatto & Windus.

Lewis, Wyndham (1927). *Time and Western Man.* London: Chatto & Windus.

McLuhan, Marshall (1953). "The Age of Advertising." *Commonweal* (September 11), 555–557.

McLuhan, Marshall (1954). *Counterblast.* Toronto: Marshall McLuhan.

Orwell, George (1936). *Keep the Aspidistra Flying.* London: Victor Gollancz; Secker and Warburg.

Rhys, Jean (1934). *Voyage in the Dark.* London: Constable.

Russell, Gilbert (1926). *Nuntius: Advertising and its Future.* To-Day and To-Morrow. London: Kegan Paul, Trench, Trubner.

Spender, Stephen (1934). *Vienna.* London: Faber and Faber.

Spitzer, Leo (1949). "American Advertising Explained as Popular Art." originally given as the Third Annual Smith College Lecture Series, delivered on February 19. In *A Method of Interpreting Literature.* Northampton: Smith College. 102–149.

Wallace, Irving (1959). *The Fabulous Showman: The Life and Times of P. T. Barnum.* New York: A. A. Knopf.

Waugh, Evelyn (1946). "Fan-Fare." *Life* (April 8), 53–54, 56, 58, 60.

Wells, H. G. (1908). *Tono-Bungay.* New York: Duffield; London: Odhams.

Woolf, Virginia (1925). *Mrs. Dalloway.* London: Hogarth.

Wordsworth, William (1798). *Lyrical Ballads with a Few Other Poems.* Bristol: printed by Biggs and Cottle for T. N. Longman, Paternoster-Row, London, 1798.

Atom, Atomic

When Karl Pearson published his third edition of *The Grammar of Science* (1911), he added a Preface warning against assumptions of permanent scientific truth. The contemporary physicist, he admonished, might be in danger of treating the electron, as he did the "old unchangeable atom," as "a reality of experience," forgetting "that it is only a construct of his own imagination," "certain to be replaced by a wider concept as his insight expands." Atom was truly a powerful imaginative construct in both scientific and general discourse, although subject to rapid change and varying use. The mysteries, multiplicities, and contradictoriness of the atom, however, constituted a large part of its imaginative appeal.

Until almost the end of C19, the atom was considered the smallest unit of the physical universe. The following half-century subjected the atom to two revolutionary turns: the discovery of subatomic particles named electrons and protons, and the construction and detonation, in 1945, of the atomic bomb. Metaphorical uses of atom often lagged, in knowledge, behind scientific research, yet they captured the implications of the new physics in at least three significant ways: (i) the idea or experience of being a minute particle, especially in the expanded scale and heightened speed of the modern world; (ii) an uncertainty and even radical doubt about a knowable, meaningful universe; and (iii) an increased reverence for the new forces unlocked by science, along with a horror at the appalling destruction now possible to inflict upon living bodies and the planet itself.

For much of the period, literary and popular references to the atom generally assumed the earlier sense of smallest imaginable unit, but now in the context of new dimensions in scale. Overawed by the sky, Virginia Woolf's Miss Anning thinks humbly of herself and her companion as "atoms, motes . . . and their lives . . . as long as an insect's and no more important" ([1925?] 1944); conversely, Tom Sefton's poem "Incarnation" forges a link between the tiny self and cosmic space: a "glimpse" in the "sub-conscious mind" leads him to affirm, "I am a part/Of one vast pulsing heart;/An atom of a comprehensive whole" (1912). Atom could also suggest the minute individual in a vast social scheme. In *Memoirs of a Social Atom* (1903), W. E. Adams – the son of a plasterer and the editor of a local weekly – described himself as "a small speck on the surface of society"; nonetheless, he asserted that a record of "the hopes and aspirations of the common people" would not "lack interest on that account." Atom indeed conveys a new literary attentiveness to the small, in writers as different as F. T. Marinetti and Virginia Woolf: Marinetti, seeking to overpass what he considered the obsessively human, called upon writers to fuse "the infinite smallness that surrounds us, the imperceptible, the invisible, the agitation of atoms" with the "infinitely great" ([1913]1973). Virginia Woolf's appeal in "Modern Fiction" ([1919]1925) for a new literature that "record[s] the atoms as they fall upon the mind" was a testimony to the value of common, everyday experience and every sensation and perception that it involves. A note in her diary records her commitment, too, to the smallest particle of time: "what I want now to do," she wrote, "is to saturate every atom [...] to give the moment whole" ([1928]1977–1984).

If modernist responses to the fragment find expression in the single atom, the idea of multiple fragments – as Marinetti's "agitation" and Woolf's falling atoms suggest – finds embodiment in atomic motion. Just as the individual atom could signify significance or insignificance, so the chaotic speed and incessant motion of numerous atoms could instill fear or wonder. In his memoir of his partly fictional self, Henry Adams represented the cataclysmic break with C19 thought by writing that science had catapulted him into "a new universe which had no common scale of measurement with the old" ([1907]1918). Imagining himself not simply "an isolated atom in a hostile universe, but a sort of herring-fry in a shoal of moving fish," Adams conceived this "ocean of colliding atoms" as demolishing any comforting assumptions of "unity," "direction," and "progress" and ushering in a "supersensual world" powered by "chance collisions of movements." Even more fearfully, a character in a John Buchan novel worries about "the danger of splitting into nebulæ of whirling atoms" (1933). Yet for David Lowe, the divisible atom was proof that the earth was "as fluid and fluxible and flexible as thought itself," drawing us "nearer the divine breath" (1909). Similarly, in the self-named "weird fiction" of H. P. Lovecraft, "the feeling that our tangible world is only an atom in a fabric vast and ominous," turns a character into "a searcher for strange realms" seeking something that "would bind him to the stars, and to the infinities and eternities beyond them" ([1927]1938); in another Lovecraft story, the narrator, believing "that human thought consists basically of atomic or molecular motion, convertible into ether waves or radiant energy," sets up telepathic communication with an alternate universe of light (1919). In "Exploring the Atom," Edward Free explained the new scientific vision to a lay audience: "Beneath the visible structure of the universe there exists, we have discovered, another universe almost infinitely finer in grain. Solid objects like a block of lead are not really solid at all; they are mostly space. Motionless objects like a grain of sand lying on the table are not really without motion; the sand grain, for example, is a mass of billions of tiny particles all in the most rapid movement, some of them at speeds exceeding 20,000 miles a second" (1924). The broad dissemination of these ideas, and the sense of wonder they could occasion is reflected in Virginia Woolf's *The Years* (1937) when Eleanor looks at a cup of tea and asks, "What [is] it made of? Atoms? And what [are] atoms, and how [do] they stick together?" considering the matter a "marvelous mystery."

The image of multiple atoms also generated metaphors of society, focusing on relations between individuals and the whole. The socialist A. R. Orage attacked individualism as "presuppos[ing] an atomic structure, an infinite multiplicity,

7

a congeries of persons without the necessary addition of the unity amid the diversity" (1907). Similarly, combating "capitalist democracy" with "its atomic conception of social life" and emphasis on "the freedom of citizens," socialist Harold Laski made a "plea for variety in unity" and "a new balance between order and freedom" (1933). The liberal and feminist Dorothy Thompson, commenting on "the America of today," decried "a sterility in human relations" resulting from "an atomization, loneliness, frustration," and she urged a return to "the living, the vital, the human," with "the individual and society, the person and humanity, not in contradiction, but in union, organically united, as the family is, or once was" (1938). T. S. Eliot, for his part, welcomed atomic structure, but its meaning for him was more complex. Finding a remedy for war in the "atomic view of society," he urged the need for each individual to belong to multiple overlapping social groups, so that no one group could again seize a dominant, totalitarian position of power ([1946]1948). Atomic structure, for Eliot, meant an interactive formation of multiple patterns, a paradoxical conjunction of "unity and diversity" that embraces the particle in a fluxible whole.

Beyond such metaphoric employments of physical atoms, increasingly rapid developments in scientific research caused the atom to be literally associated with epistemological and ontological uncertainty. In the negative sense, atomic theory could signify destructive instability. C. A. Ward, reporting "the latest decisions in chemistry," wrote, "Atoms are now said to be infinitely divisible, invisible, imponderable," and offered the pessimistic general reflection, "All this makes one ask what need we have of deciding anything" (1890). In its positive use, however, the divisible atom signified a fruitful decentering of knowledge. D. H. Lawrence celebrated "relativity and quantum theories" for their very uncertainty, making him feel "as if the atom were an impulsive thing always changing its mind" (1929), while for Havelock Ellis, "the very structure of the 'atom' [was] melting into a dream" and the "physical world" was becoming "more impalpable and visionary" (1923). Eugene Jolas wrote, "The atom, once the last reality, has given way to new disintegrations which open up possibilities for tremendous evolutions" (1929). Not all new uses of atom focused on uncertainty, however, since scientific discoveries could also betoken progress, stability, and order. An editorial in the London *Times*, reporting on the Edinburgh meeting of the British Association for the Advancement of Science, referenced Sir Edward Thorpe's vision of "the atom as an ordered system," "a macrocosm of energy in microcosmic space," noting how such "evolution of knowledge" promised a "revolution of thought" (1921). Bart Kennedy interpreted the atom as representing "in miniature" the "macrocosm" of cosmic continuity: "Our world is at one with the shining transplendent whole" (1910). In Eugene O'Neill's *Dynamo* (1929), Reuben both acknowledges the mystery of the divisible atom and reads it as requiring a central organizing force: "The sea is only hydrogen and oxygen and minerals, and they're only atoms, and atoms are only protons and electrons [. . .]. But there must be a center around which all this moves." The narrator of Olaf Stapledon's *Last Men and First* (1930) saw "the tense balance of forces within the atom" as reflecting the "quiescence" of Chinese philosophy, premised on "the perfect balance of mighty forces." For Leo Stein, the divisible atom resolved rather than begat uncertainty: arguing that "the atom was a mystery until it was broken up," he continued, "When we successfully investigate something, it ceases to be mysterious" (1947).

The most controversial usages focused on atomic energy. Before 1945, the potential applications of new atomic knowledge met with mixed speculation. When "atomic energy" entered scientific discourse at the turn of C20, it had positive associations. *The Scientific Monthly* reported that "atomic energy" – "compact and clean," producing "no smoke" and "no dirt" – promised to "greatly ameliorate the conditions of factory life" (1919). The 1921 London *Times* editorial (referenced previously) declared that "the new atomic age" had "opened up a new and inexhaustible source of power for the practical uses of mankind." Writing in *Scientific American*, Haviland Hull Platt protested that "atomic energy is [so thoroughly] the phrase of the hour" that "the possibility of turning to account the vast store of energy contained in the atoms of all matter" was actually obscuring other potential sources for heat (1924). Olaf Stapledon's science fiction *Last Men in London* (1932) envisioned a future in which humans wore "flying-suits [. . .] studded with minute sources of sub-atomic energy on the soles of the feet." Yet H. G. Wells's *The World Set Free* (1914) offered sober reflection on atomic technology: speculating on the "social possibilities of the atomic energy" and the political consequences of the "atomic bomb," he argued that the future would be one of "atomic destruction" unless a "world government" could be formed to "ensure [. . .] universal pacification." While A. E. R. in *The New Age* declared Wells's pessimism "atomic bombast" (1914), fear of the applications of atomic technology was widespread. In Talbot Mundy's *Om* (1924), the Lama says of "the men of the West," "Wait until they have learned how to explode the atom, and then see what they will do to one another." Harold Nicolson warned, "We must now assume that a single atomic bomb is capable of destroying all matter within a circumference of seventy to eighty miles from the point of explosion" (1932). Atomic age, coined in the 1920s at a moment of optimism, came into widespread use only after 1945, with associations of impending disaster. In her "Three Poems for the Atomic Age" (1948), Edith Sitwell described how the bombs dropped on Hiroshima and Nagasaki had "squeezed the stems/Of all that grows on the earth," concluding, "There was no more hating then,/And no more love: Gone is the heart of Man." Leo Stein read the explosion of the atomic bomb as an indictment of Western civilization, arguing that the "atomic bomb" put "thunderous emphasis on the fact that the culture of the past is not good enough" (1947).

9

Atom, Atomic

Cultural employments of atom were thus motivated by scientific developments, yet went far beyond science. Atom signified a new modernist perception of the fragment, balancing the minuteness of individual monads against the vastness and complexity of the chaotic patterns formed from the motion of the whole. Rising to prominence in public discourse, atom betrayed the tensions between isolation and interconnectedness, between anxiety about the dissolution of secure grounds of knowledge and excitement about new possibilities and freedoms, and between the potential for improving human life and the danger of destroying the planet. But possibly the greatest appeal of the atom was its very nature as an imaginative construct. Writers used atom when they meant minute particle or chaotic motion, not only because the image captured the imagination so much better than abstract terms but also because the atom suggested something partly unknowable, something in excess of normal perception, and something participant in profound and fundamental change. In its uncertainty and instability, atom was a crucial image for the modernist world.

SEE ALSO: *Bigness, Smallness; Common Mind, Group Thinking; International; Unconscious; Personality, Impersonality; Reality, Realism*

References

10

(1919). "The Disintegration of Atoms and Atomic Energy." *Scientific Monthly* (December), 587–589.

(1921). "The British Association." Editorials/Leaders. *The Times* (London) (September 15), 9; col E.

Adams, Henry (1918). *The Education of Henry Adams*. Privately printed, Washington, 1907. Boston and New York: Houghton Mifflin.

Adams, William Edwin (1903). *Memoirs of a Social Atom*. London: Hutchinson.

A.E.R. [Alfred E. Randall] (1914). Rev. of *The World Set Free* by H. G. Wells. *The New Age* 15.3 (May 21): 66.

Buchan, John (1933). *A Prince of Captivity*. London: Hodder and Stoughton.

Eliot, T. S. (1948). "Appendix: Broadcasts 1946." In *Notes Towards the Definition of Culture*. London: Faber and Faber. 110–124.

Ellis, Havelock (1923). *The Dance of Life*. Boston: Houghton Mifflin.

Free, Edward (1924). "Exploring the Atom." *The Forum* (October), 505–514.

Jolas, Eugene (1929). "Notes on Reality." *transition: An International Quarterly for Creative Experiment* 18 (November): 13–20.

Kennedy, Bart (1910). "Days." *The New Age* 6.23 (April 7): 535–536.

Laski, Harold (1933). *Democracy in Crisis*. London: George Allen.

Lawrence, D. H. (1929). "Relativity." In *Pansies: Poems*. London: Martin Secker. 116.

Lovecraft, H. P. (1919). "Beyond the Wall of Sleep." *Pine Cones* 1.6 (October): 2–10.

Lovecraft, H. P. (1938). "The Descendant" [1927]. *Leaves* 2: 107–110. Published by R. H. Barlow

Lowe, David (1909). "A Visit from Killermont." *The New Age* 5.11 (July 8): 216.

Marinetti, F.T. (1973). "Destruction of Syntax–Wireless Imagination–Words-in-Freedom." 1913. Trans. R. W. Flint. In *Futurist Manifestos* (ed. U. Apollonio). Boston: MFA Publications. 95–106.

Mundy, Talbot (1924). *Om: The Secret of Ahbor Valley*. Indianapolis: Bobbs-Merrill; New York: A. L. Burt.

Nicolson, Harold (1932). *Public Faces*. London: Constable.

O'Neill, Eugene (1929). *Dynamo*. New York: H. Liveright.

Orage, A. R. (1907). "Towards Socialism III." *The New Age* 1.25 (October 17): 393–394.

Pearson, Karl (1911). *The Grammar Of Science*. 3rd rev. and enl. ed. London: Adam and Charles Black.

Platt, Haviland Hull (1924). "Atmospheric Heat as a Source of Power: A Suggestion of a Means by Which This Reservoir Might Ultimately be Tapped." *Scientific American* (August), 120.

Sefton, Tom (1912). "Incarnation." *The New Age* 10.10 (January 4): 220.

Sitwell, Edith (1948). "Dirge for the New Sunrise." In *The Song of the Cold*. New York: Vanguard.

Stapledon, Olaf (1930). *Last and First Men: A Story of the Near and Far Future*. London: Methuen.

Stapledon, Olaf (1932). *Last Men in London*. London: Methuen.

Stein, Leo (1947). *Appreciation: Painting, Poetry and Prose*. New York: Crown/Random House.

Thompson, Dorothy (1938). *Dorothy Thompson's Political Guide: A Study of American Liberalism and Its Relationship to Modern Totalitarian States*. New York: Stackpole Sons.

Ward, C. A. (1890). "Books, Libraries, and Reading." *The Bookworm* 3: 20.

Wells, H. G. (1914). *The World Set Free: A Story of Mankind*. New York: E. P. Dutton; London: Macmillan.

Woolf, Virginia (1925). "Modern Fiction" ["Modern Novels," 1919]. In *The Common Reader*. London: Hogarth. 184–195.

Woolf, Virginia (1937). *The Years*. London: Hogarth.

Woolf, Virginia (1944). "Together and Apart" [1925?]. In *The Haunted House*. London: Hogarth. 115–121.

Woolf, Virginia (1977–1984). Diary entry, November 28, 1928. In *The Diary of Virginia Woolf* (ed. Anne Olivier Bell). 5 vols. London: Hogarth. Vol. 3: 209.

11

Avant-Garde

In its original sense, an avant-garde was the furthest advanced part of an army, whose role it was to clear territory for other troops. During the French Revolution, the Jacobins departed from the term's strictly military meaning by describing themselves as a political avant-garde. Many C19 socialist groups adopted this usage, often calling on artists to assist in their political work. The artist character in Olinde Rodrigues's dialogue "L'artiste, le savant et l'industriel" (1825) describes socialist artists as representing an "avant-garde" who "spread new ideas among men," "exerting a positive influence on society" by "throwing themselves ahead [*en avant*] of all the intellectual faculties." The modernist notion of a radical aesthetic avant-garde began with F. T. Marinetti, who called "Futurism, in its overall program, [. . .] an atmosphere of the avant-garde" ([1913]2006). Registering the term's military and radical inheritance, Marinetti depicted Futurism as "an inexhaustible machine gun pointing at the army of the dead, of the gouty and the opportunists, whom we want to strip of their authority and subject to the bold and creative young."

As a revolutionary term, avant-garde appears rarely, however, in English literary texts of the modernist period. E. Sutton's war poem "The Drum" (1914) employs avant-garde in a military but also patriotic way: the eponymous Drum says admiringly of some passing canons, "Avant-garde am I to these Lords of dreadful revelries." Although Wyndham Lewis's *The Tyro* has been regarded as an exemplary avant-garde magazine, the word avant-garde appears in it only in an advertisement for another journal, *De Stijl*, which promises to gather "all the avant garde activities of Holland" (1922). In "Vital English Art" (1914b), a Futurist document first published in English, Marinetti and C. R. W. Nevinson employed the English rather than the French term, calling for the creation of "a powerful advance guard" to "save English Art." (The Italian and French versions respectively read "*una grande avanguardia futurista*" (1915) and "*une grande avant-garde futuriste*" (1914a).) The Paris-based journal *transition* likewise employed the English term in a preview of contents promising "WORKS OF CONTINENTAL ADVANCE GUARD" (1929), suggesting a primary association of avant-garde with continental European art. Alain Locke used advance-guard as well but with a deliberately nonviolent intent: the American New Negro's ability to resist confronting prejudice with "counter-hate," he argued, was due in part to the inspiriting "consciousness of acting as the advance-guard of the African peoples in their contact with Twentieth Century civilization" (1925). Avant-garde *does* appear in reference to film. Writing in the cinema journal *Close Up*, Bryher (Annie Winifred Ellerman) invoked avant-garde's radical associations when she argued that the "New American Cinema" needed to be "more avant-garde," "to attack the formula and not tolerate it" (1931). Describing his film *Borderline*, Kenneth Macpherson emphasized the territorial, military sense: it was "perhaps the only really 'avant-garde' film ever made," he said, adding that critics complained of its "obscurity" only because it "travers[ed] new ground" (1930).

Around mC20, avant-garde became a term in literary and art criticism but with a broader scope than its etymological origins. A number of articles by American critics associated with the *Partisan Review* introduced ideas of historical diversity in avant-garde movements and roles. Clement Greenberg located the origins of the C20 avant-garde in the revolutionary "bohemian" culture of the 1840s but distinguished two further phases in which the avant-garde was first threatened by the popularity of kitsch, by which he meant the watering down and commodification of art which became the "culture of the masses" (1939), and then by absorption into the American middle-class and middlebrow professionalism and academicism (1948). Paul Goodman divided the C20 avant-garde into three historical phases: 1900–1920, "Naturalism"; 1920s, "The Revolution of the Word"; and 1930s, "Social Solidarity" (1951). Richard Chase considered the avant-garde a "permanent movement" in the arts since the breakdown of the aristocracy in C17; his avant-garde included Wordsworth, Coleridge, Melville, and Whitman, and he defined "modernism" as the particular "phase" of the avant-garde between 1912 and 1950 (1957). The move, in all these critics, to identify diverse avant-garde phases reflects a response to the perceived end of the modernist phase with hope for a rebirth of the avant-garde in a new form.

All three critics defined the avant-garde less by a style than by a relation to an audience, conceiving the role of the avant-garde broadly as challenging stultifying norms, provoking change, and promoting life. Chase called the avant-garde artist an "insurgent intellectual" and argued that "far from being merely the isolated band of highbrows and sterile academicians many Americans think it is," the avant-garde was "a necessary part of the cultural economy." Goodman saw the avant-garde's relation to its audience as paradoxically "loving and hostile," both a reaching out and a "forcing of unwanted attention" for the purpose of reforming the public's values.

Avant-garde was also associated with alienation, but the latter was understood as a product of the culture and the time, rather than an attitude willfully adopted by the artists. While for Greenberg the C19 avant-garde deliberately alienated itself from the bourgeois in order to "keep culture moving," he argued that by C20, the masses, in turning to kitsch, had alienated themselves from the avant-garde. Greenberg is also the likely source of the designations of "high" versus "low" cultural forms, but his "low" was not popular culture, but the "predigest[ed]" reduction of "genuine" art in kitsch. Yet he placed blame for the ubiquitous acceptance of kitsch not on the masses, but on both capitalist and communist totalitarian systems, which left ordinary people too exhausted to have the time or energy for active engagement with serious art.

Goodman, too, approached alienation as inherent in the overall culture, which he declared to be "'alienated' from itself, from its own creative development." For him, while both artist and audience were alienated, the avant-garde artist was more conscious of alienation and so sought in his work "to disgorge the alien culture." Acceptance or rejection of the avant-garde was also seen as reflecting the level of anxiety in the audience. Goodman posited a "golden age" in the 1920s, when the avant-garde artist was matched with a buoyancy and hope in the audience, in contrast to the period following WWII, where intense but also unacknowledged anxiety caused the "shell-shocked" audience to withdraw from the avant-garde. Chase in particular argued against polarized and isolated views of the avant-garde artist, agreeing with William Phillips that "any movement to line

13

him up on one side or another over-simplifies his role and limits his creative function."
For Chase, the history of art was a series of alternations between avant-garde and
"integrated" artists, each of whom performed crucial roles. He argued further
that this dialectic exists *within* the best artists, who "embody the contradictions
of their culture" or, in Lionel Trilling's words, "the yes and the no of their culture,"
in their own work. In like fashion, Chase argued, flexible critics and readers can be
open to both forms: why should we not enjoy, he questioned, "*both* Wallace Stevens
and Sherwood Anderson," "*both* [Ezra] Pound and [Van Wyck] Brooks"?

SEE ALSO: *Coterie, Bloomsbury; Highbrow, Middlebrow, Lowbrow;
Manifesto; Modern, Modernism; Readers, Reading*

References

(1922). Advertisement. *The Tyro* 2: Back Advertisements: adv5–adv6.
(1929). [Promotional Flyer]. *transition: An International Quarterly for Creative Experiment*
16–17 (June): Insert.
Bryher (1931). "The Hollywood Code II." *Close Up* 8.4 (December): 280–282.
Chase, Richard (1957). "The Fate of the Avant-Garde." *The Partisan Review* 24.3
(Summer): 363–375.
Goodman, Paul (1951). "Advance-Guard Writing in America; 1900–1950." *The Kenyon
Review* 13.3 (Summer): 357–380.
Greenberg, Clement (1939). "Avant-Garde and Kitsch." *The Partisan Review* 6.5 (Fall):
34–49.
Greenberg, Clement (1948). "The State of American Writing: A Symposium." *The Partisan
Review* 15.8 (August): 870–875.
Locke, Alain (1925). "Enter the New Negro." *Survey Graphic*. Harlem: Mecca of the New
Negro (March), 631–639.
Macpherson, Kenneth (1930). "As Is." *Close Up* 7.5 (November): 293–298.
Marinetti, F. T. (2006). "An Open Letter to the Futurist Mac Delmarle" ["Lettera aperta
al futurista Mac Delmarle," 1913]. Trans. Doug Thompson. In *Critical Writings*
(ed. Günther Berghaus). New York: Farrar, Straus and Giroux. 104–106.
Marinetti, F. T. and C. R. W. Nevinson (1914a). *Contre l'art anglais*. Milan: Stab. Tip.
Taveggia.
Marinetti, F. T. and C. R. W. Nevinson (1914b). "Vital English Art." *The Observer* (June 7), 7.
Marinetti, F. T. and C. R. W. Nevinson (1915). "Manifesto Futurista." *Lacerba* 2.14
(July 15): 210–211.
Saint-Simon, Henri comte de [Olinde Rodrigues] (1825). "L'artiste, le savant, et
l'industriel." In *Opinions littéraires, philosophiques, et industrielles*. Paris: Galérie de
Bossange Père. 331–392.
Sutton, E. (1914). "The Drum." *Scribner's Magazine* (November), 645.

Best Seller

Best seller was a modernist coinage and a subject of controversy throughout the whole of the modernist age. In 1891, *The Bookman* (UK) began to report on "Sales of Books During the Month," identifying "the best selling books." *The Bookman* (US) followed by reporting on book sales by city beginning in 1895, adding a composite list of the "Best-Selling Books" in 1900, reprinted in *Publishers' Weekly* starting in 1906. The coinage "best seller" developed more gradually, evolving from a reference to an individual book that sold well to the designation of a genre, the latter clearly in place by the time of O. Henry's short story "The Best Seller" (1909). Measures for identifying best sellers, however, were varied and nonstandardized: the word could refer to the number of books sold, or the ranking given by selected bookstores, or simply the popularity of the book. As for genre, O. Henry's story engages the further idea that best sellers are all of a kind: idealistic and unrealistic. As one character complains, "You don't see or hear of any such didos or capers in real life"; but O. Henry's famous twist comes when that character's life turns out to mimic the plot of the best seller he has deplored.

The emergence of best sellers was accompanied by deep-seated suspicion, as readers, publishers, and critics worried about the difference between the "best books" and "the books people liked best" (Melcher, 1945). In his 1932 autobiography, the American lawyer Clarence Darrow expressed his contempt plainly,

ABCDEFGHIJKLMNOPQRSTUVWXYZ

writing "It may seem absurd that I should be trying to write about myself in an age when only a mystery story has any chance as a best-seller," adding, "I can think of nothing about myself to distort into any such popular fiction." In her obituary for *Chicago Tribune* columnist Bert Leston Taylor, Harriet Monroe singled out for particular praise his ability "to set some clamorous best-seller in its place" (1921). Negative attitudes toward best sellers were so pervasive that they were sometimes incorporated into advertisements for works aspiring to what Arthur Beverly Baxter called "the doubtful altitude of best-sellership" (1920): a *Scribner's Magazine* ad, for example, declared that Basil King's *The Street Called Straight* "[stood] out above the mass of recent fiction" and promised "to have more than the brief vogue of the best seller" (1912). Yet the best seller had defenders as well as critics. While many argued that best sellers were potentially harmful to both readers and writers, others considered the new phenomenon beneficial to society, artistically worthwhile, and worthy of serious consideration. And while these debates tended to pit the best seller against "serious" literature, many of the most "serious" and challenging modernist works defied this antithesis by appealing to broad publics and appearing on best-seller lists.

Q. D. Leavis's *Fiction and the Reading Public* (1932) was the major modernist work to tackle the question of the social significance of the best seller. Leavis provided a thorough taxonomy of modernist attitudes toward best sellers, highlighting negative attitudes, and particularly those of "serious" readers. If "'best seller' [had become] an almost entirely derogatory epithet among the cultivated" of her time, Leavis argued, it was due to the perception that best sellers were socially dangerous. Publishers seeking high sales followed a logic of "giving the Public what it wants," which entailed "providing fiction that require[d] the least effort to read" and that "set the reader up with a comfortable state of mind." Such fiction "[got] in the way of genuine feeling and responsible thinking" by "creating cheap mechanical responses" and "throwing [its] weight on the side of social, national, and herd prejudices." Since challenging a reader's attitudes might hurt sales, Leavis argued, the aim of the best-selling novel became simply "to persuade the ordinary prosperous citizen that life is fun, he is living it at its fullest, and there are no standards in life or art other than his own." Leavis also leveled the charge that best sellers led to social stratification and fragmentation. Arguing that publishers "target" best sellers at a particular social/intellectual class (the lower classes, the less educated), she claimed the best seller caused leading publishers to create "several publics" each with a "standardize[d]" "level [. . .] of taste."

Regarding the effects on readers and writers, many modernists agreed that the best seller was dangerous. A pervasive argument was that best sellers duped or tricked readers in order to take their money. In the most extreme formulation, Leavis argued that best sellers functioned like narcotics and that "novel-reading is now largely a drug-habit." George Bowling, the narrator of George Orwell's *Coming Up for Air*, described himself as "what you might call the typical Boots Library subscriber" – easily susceptible to the coercion of publishers: "I always fall for the best-seller of the moment" (1939). In "The Mystery of the Best Seller," Granville Hicks explained the (to him) perplexing success of Hervey Allen's massive novel *Anthony Adverse* – the #1 year-end US best seller for 1933 and 1934 – by blaming it on an "extraordinary advertising campaign" that succeeded in confusing readers' economic and aesthetic values, and convincing them that "1224 pages for three dollars is a good buy" (1934). *The Journal of Marketing* agreed that the main factor in determining whether a book would become a best seller was "an extensive and unusual advertising campaign"; "best-sellerdom," it concluded, belonged in "the realm of social behavior characterized by fads [and] fashions" (1943). Even serious experimental writing could be seen as complicit in best-sellerdom. Harrison S. Morris called the shocking techniques of "highbrow" modernist literature a sales ploy which traded in good taste for public appeal: "Throw away tradition; deride taste and beauty, desert domestic life, join the nudists of art and literature, and you will be a big bold self-conscious and naughty best-seller" (1935). In contrast, confronting the early difficulties of finding a printer willing to publish James Joyce's *A Portrait of the Artist as a Young Man*, Harriet Shaw Weaver targeted the obverse prerequisites for "best-sellerdom": "orthodox Morality" combined with "a furtive salaciousness" (1916). The "accepted recipe for the creation of the 'best-seller,'" she argued, was "ultra-lofty sentiments" combined with "heated sensual suggestions," while honest, "cool analysis" of sex was "regarded as an enormity of peculiarly brazen and heartless nature." Joyce, she continued, refusing to censor himself or to "bring his work a little nearer the popular level," "found that no publisher would touch his book." Joyce tellingly serialized his next novel, *Ulysses*, in *The Little Review*, which called itself "A Magazine of the Arts – Making No Compromise with the Public Taste" – its disdain for best-sellership perhaps explained by the fact that all issues containing sections of *Ulysses* were banned as obscene in the US, while the book version of *Ulysses* was for over a decade banned in all English-speaking countries.

The furthest Q. D. Leavis would go in defending the best seller was to note that it deserved serious attention: in *Fiction and the Reading Public*, she quoted I. A. Richards's statement (1924) that "best-sellers" are "worthy of very close study" because they "exemplify [. . .] the most general levels of attitude development"; later, she argued that since best sellers were "read with pleasure by so many," they could "tell us something important about the formation of taste" ([1965]1983). Many writers were more categorical in their support of best sellers – though they tended to express this support by attacking the condescending assumptions of "serious" critics. In 1915, *Scribner's* published "The Best Seller," a short story by Gordon Hall Gerould about a "highbrow" author with limited sales who decides to write a best seller. Although he "detest[s] what the populace wants," he resolves to put his aesthetic sensibilities aside ("Art can go hang!") for the financial wellbeing of his family. When the novel is rejected by his publisher as mere cliché, the wife of the would-be best seller reassures him, "You've only shown that [. . .] you can't do something not worth your while," adding, "I doubt whether you'd be very much good about digging ditches, either." When, however, an unexpected legacy saves the family from financial distress and produces "an illogical happy ending," the couple find themselves (with echoes of the O. Henry story) ironically "living the unrealities of sensational fiction" which they had abhorred. In case the moral of the story was missed, *Scribner's* printed a "Point of View" in their next issue, declaring, "Nothing is more absurd than the belief of the High-Brow that the authors of Best-Sellers are 'writing down' to the public. That, in fact, is just what these authors are not doing" (1915).

The view that the best seller, far from being inartistic, should be regarded as a literary genre in its own right was shared by Aldous Huxley – himself a best-selling author – who emphasized that, like "all literature," "the Best Seller must be sincere," although he added a cautionary proviso: "Only a person with a Best-Seller mind can write Best-Sellers; and only someone with a mind like Shelley's can write *Prometheus Unbound*" (1926). In Edith Wharton's *The Gods Arrive* (1932), Vance Weston repudiates his first best-selling historical fiction, fantasizing (erroneously) that his real calling is to write "high-brow" poetry: "Using words to tell stories," he declares, "is like paving the kitchen floor with diamonds. [. . .] Supposing Keats had used his words to write best-sellers with?" Wharton herself, a many times over best-selling novelist, wrote of "that odd form of literary fame" in more sympathetic terms: Henry James, she proposed, had "secretly dreamed of being a 'best seller,'" having suffered "a life-long disappointment at his lack of popular recognition" (1934).

But while many modernist debates turned on the absolute distinction between best sellers and "serious" literature, in practice the division was not at all clear. Although *The Little Review* later made contempt for "public taste" its guiding principle, it printed lists of best sellers in its early issues; indeed, its second issue reviewed Leona Dalrymple's *Diane of the Green Van*, the #2 best seller that month, concluding, "Not all 'best sellers' have as much real charm as this one" (1914). A more serious challenge to the perceived split came from the names on the best-seller lists. While Q. D. Leavis lamented that "The best sellers of the twentieth century do not change their courses because D. H. Lawrence, Virginia Woolf, or James Joyce has written" (1932), each of these writers were best sellers at particular times. Among "serious" writers to feature on the annual US best-seller lists in *Publishers' Weekly* were Joseph Conrad (*Arrow of Gold*, 1919), Eugene O'Neill (*Strange Interlude*, 1928), Rebecca West (*The Thinking*

Reed, 1936), Virginia Woolf (*The Years*, 1937), and Ernest Hemingway (*For Whom the Bell Tolls*, 1941 and 1942), while Lawrence's *Lady Chatterly's Lover* (1928) appeared on the list in its first unexpurgated edition in 1959. The commercial popularity of "serious" modernist literature arguably reached its peak in 1933–1934: appearing on best-seller lists were Woolf's *Flush* (*PW* November 11, 1933), Gertrude Stein's *Autobiography of Alice B. Toklas* (*PW* October 14, 1933), and Joyce's *Ulysses*, finally available following a well-publicized obscenity trial (*PW* March 10, 1934). Both Stein and Joyce were featured on the cover of *Time* in this period – although *Time*'s article "Ulysses Lands" (1934) commented, "Censorship rather than sound criticism has spread [the book's] reputation." In "The Apotheosis of Miss Stein," *Vanity Fair*, noting the "huge sales" of Joyce's "master-work" and the massive success of Stein ("we doubt if any one – even Miss Stein herself – ever envisaged a time when a Stein book would, month after month, grace the best seller lists"), concluded, "But this is 1934, and the twin miracles have happened" (1934). Later, during WWII, Woolf's *The Years* (1937) was published in an Armed Services edition (1945), its dust jacket informing its primary audience of soldiers that the volume was both a "best seller" and "one of Mrs. Woolf's finest novels." (*The Years* peaked at #1 in *PW* July 10, 1937 and appeared on the *New York Times* list for a total of 16 weeks.)

From a publisher's viewpoint, Geoffrey Faber argued that "without the best-seller it is a safe bet that the publisher cannot, in these days, possibly survive if the main part of his business is the supply of *new general literature*," since "the best-seller scoops the pool and other books become more and more difficult to sell"; Faber concluded if "some energetic member of the Oxford University English Club" would "start an Anti-Best-Seller League," he would "be delighted to become a subscribing member"(1934). From the viewpoint of readership, however, best-seller lists from the modernist period contributed less to the compartmentalization of popular and serious writers than later academic attributions of canonical/noncanonical status. Modernist sales figures indicate both that many reputedly highbrow modernist authors produced works accessible to a popular audience and that popular audiences often reacted with curiosity to work that challenged the status quo. Furthermore, in the expanded scale of mass readership, Compton Mackenzie leaves us with an intriguing thought: "It is impossible to-day, when the potential number of readers is so much vaster than it was a generation ago, that a novelist or a book can become a best-seller without reaching beyond the class of readers to whom it appeals" (1933).

SEE ALSO: *Advertising; Coterie, Bloomsbury; Highbrow, Middlebrow, Lowbrow; Readers, Reading*

19

References

(1891). "Sales of Books During the Month." *The Bookman* (UK) (October), 31.

(1895). "Sales of Books During the Month." *The Bookman* (US) (February), 64–65.

(1900). "The Best Selling Books." *The Bookman* (US) (January), 508.

(1906). "Best Selling Books in April." *The Publishers' Weekly: The American Book Trade Journal* (May 5), 1335.

(1912). Advertisement. *Scribner's Magazine* (October), 12.

(1914). "A $10,000 Novel." *The Little Review* 1.2 (April): 39–40.

(1915). "The Point of View." *Scribner's Magazine* (November), 640–642.

(1934). "The Apotheosis of Miss Stein, 1934." *Vanity Fair* (May), 21.

(1934). "Ulysses Lands." *Time Magazine* (January 29), 49–51.

Berreman, Joel V. (1943). "Advertising and the Sale of Novels." *The Journal of Marketing* 7.3 (January): 234–240.

Beverly Baxter, Arthur (1920). *The Parts Men Play.* Toronto: McClelland and Stewart.

Darrow, Clarence (1932). *The Story of My Life.* New York: Charles Scribner's Sons.

Faber, Geoffrey Cust (1934). *A Publisher Speaking.* London: Faber and Faber.

Gerould, Gordon Hall (1915). "The Best-Seller." *Scribner's Magazine* (September), 325–335.

Henry, O. (1909). "The Best Seller." *Munsey's Magazine* (April), 18–23.

Hicks, Granville (1934). "The Mystery of the Best Seller." *The English Journal* 23.8 (October): 621–629.

Huxley, Aldous (1926). "Sincerity in Art." *Vogue* (Late April), 65, 92.

Leavis, Q. D. (1932). *Fiction and the Reading Public.* London: Chatto & Windus.

Leavis, Q. D. (1983). "A Glance Backwards, 1965." In *Collected Essays* (ed. G. Singh). Cambridge: Cambridge University Press. Vol. 1: 10–11.

Mackenzie, Compton (1933). *Literature in My Time.* London: Rich & Cowan.

Melcher, Frederic G. (1945). "Foreword." In *Fifty Years of Best Sellers, 1895–1945* (ed. Alice Payne Hackett), New York: Bowker. vi–vii.

Monroe, Harriet (1921). "The Death of B. L. T." *Poetry: A Magazine of Verse* 18.2 (May): 97–98.

Morris, Harrison S. (1935). "The Revolt Against Taste." *Proceedings of the American Philosophical Society* 75.4: 275–280.

Orwell, George (1939). *Coming Up for Air.* London: Secker and Warburg.

Richards, I. A. (1924). *Principles of Literary Criticism.* London: Kegan Paul, Trench, Trubner.

Weaver, Harriet Shaw (1916). "Views and Comments." *The Egoist* 3.3 (March): 33–35.

Wharton, Edith (1932). *The Gods Arrive.* New York: D. Appleton.

Wharton, Edith (1934). *A Backward Glance.* New York: D. Appleton-Century.

Woolf, Virginia (1945). *The Years.* 1937. Armed Services Edition, Vol. 772. New York: Harcourt, Brace and Co..

Bigness, Smallness

The modernist period was one of shifting scales. On the one hand, developments in technology were making things bigger: bigger cities, bigger machines, bigger economies. Politics too was becoming bigger, as electorates in democratic countries grew to include larger numbers of voters and as new techniques of persuasion sought to convince ever-growing numbers of people of the "right" views. On the other hand, all this growing and expansion brought about a reorientation of scale, as what had previously seemed big seemed to shrink in size. The pervasive emphasis on the new bigness, however, made many writers increasingly aware of, and respectful of, what was small.

Bigness, in the modernist period, frequently reveals a tension between the power of the cities and the lure of open space. A Whitmanesque celebration of industrial vibrancy and energy continues in the poetry of Carl Sandburg, who hailed Chicago as "City of the Big Shoulders" (1914); yet, like many romantic poets, modernists located bigness in nature – in North America, frequently in the prairies and the mid-West of the "new world." In Zane Grey's *Wildfire* (1917), the heroine Lucy has a traditionally romantic experience of the sublime prompted by the immensity of the landscape of the American West – "a sense of the bigness, the openness of this valley," whose "wildness and strangeness" appears "vaster, higher, and stranger" even than the Egyptian pyramids. In the poetry of Charles Erskine Scott Wood, bigness signifies the barrenness and silence of the Oregon desert. In his *The Poet in the Desert* (1915), the speaker is initially overwhelmed by the scale of the landscape, "frightened of [the desert's] bigness and its indifference" and "afraid of [his own] littleness." Yet, in a manner reminiscent of Whitman's "cosmic consciousness," the speaker moves toward integration with "Life in its fullest immensity"; taking inspiration from the "Desert-warbler" who is "Unafraid of the solitude; undismayed in the bigness of the universe," he comes to feel simultaneously his "own littleness" and his "own greatness" as both "one with the mole" and one "with the limitless sky." In contrast, the loss of natural bigness is mourned in Emmy Veronica Sanders's "Into These Things" (1922), which describes the transformation of countryside into industrial space ("Bigness went/To steel and stone/ . . . /Furnaces, steel towers, engines, cities") and the corresponding spiritual diminution of industrial workers ("Their little souls,/Their cowardly cramped souls").

21

Increasingly, concepts of the sublime became attached to the bigness of what was man-made – the bigness of cities, of industry, of commerce, of war. In contrast to Sandburg, Henry James found serious writing impossible in Chicago, being overwhelmed by "the *muchness* of space and distance and time (consumed) and above all of people (consuming)" and the "huge, *infinite*" city, with its railways "of maddening complexity and gigantic length" and its manifestations of "*power*, huge and augmenting power (vast mechanical, industrial, social, financial) everywhere!" ([1905]1920). For her part, Eleanor H. Porter's Susan is rendered speechless by the bigness of WWI: "the whole awful frightfulness of it an' the bigness of it seemed to swallow me up"; she says, "I knew then't was too big for me. I didn't try to write no more" (1919). Reflecting on the sinking of the Titanic,

Bigness, Smallness

Joseph Conrad lamented what he saw as the spurious worship of technological and financial bigness – the tendency of many people to "put their trust in mere bigness, in the reckless affirmations of commercial men and mere technicians" (1912). Conrad warned, "the mere increase of size is not progress"; "bigness is mere exaggeration." In *English Journey* (1934), J. B. Priestley described an "enormous round white tower" (which he later learned was "a new gasometer") as "bigger than anything else in sight" in the Black Country landscape and of such size that it had "no dimension that could be measured," making it an apt symbol for the new veneration of man-made enormity: "You could think of it, without unduly straining your fancy, as the temple of some horrible new religion."

In a secular commercial world, big became synonymous with money and success, as indicated in the emergence, primarily in the US, of such phrases as big business, big name, big stick, and big wheel. Indeed, the transformation from the natural to the economic sublime informs the plot of Jack London's *Martin Eden* (1909). At first, Martin, an aspiring young writer from the working class, yearns to express the "big things, the spirit of beauty that was like a fire in him," to capture the way the "breath of the universe" is in "the scent of grass." Yet when Martin becomes entangled in the commercial world, receiving an advance contract from a publisher who is "going in on this thing big" and later making "a bigger strike" "in point of sales," he senses the "beginning of the little thing that was soon to become the big thing": the fatal disillusionment consequent on being lionized by the bourgeois adulation of money and fame. The narrator of Booth Tarkington's *The Turmoil* (1915) similarly posits "Bigness" as "the god of all good American hearts," exposing the ubiquity of big in commercial language: "the biggest skyscraper," "the biggest builder," "one of the biggest men," "show me a bigger deal," and "your department's got to go bigger." The Americans' "profound longing for size" echoes in the refrain, "We must be Big! We must be Bigger! Bigness means Money!" F. Scott Fitzgerald's "The Diamond as Big as the Ritz" (1922) likewise challenged the valuation of economic bigness: the Washington family owns a diamond so large and so valuable that there is not "enough gold in the world to buy a tenth part of it"; it must be hidden from the authorities because word of its existence would collapse financial markets. When it is discovered, Mr. Washington attempts to bribe God with "the greatest diamond in the world" but is refused and decides to blow up his diamond rather than yield it to others.

In political terms, bigness was widely associated with notions of collectivity, eliciting polarized responses. Many welcomed the expanding size of electorates as a symbol of increasing political unity and brotherhood. Toward the end of Sherwood Anderson's *Marching Men* (1917), the narrator speaks of the numerical as well as the moral bigness of the working classes, prophesying that the Labor movement would "make the world see – see and feel its bigness at last": "Men were come to the end of strife," he says, "men united – Marching! Marching!

Marching!" Jane Harrison saw in much modern writing a democratic impetus to go beyond "mere individual emotion" and "to aim at something bigger, more bound up with a feeling towards and for the common weal": "The art of Arnold Bennett," she argued, achieved "bigness" and "collectivity" as "generation after generation rolls by in ceaseless panorama," and "after a vision so big, to come back to the ordinary individualistic love-story is like looking through the wrong end of a telescope" (1913). Contrasting this positive association of bigness with democracy was the sense that the increasing size of democratic institutions was making them paradoxically less democratic. In his 1949 Labor pamphlet *Small Man: Big World*, Michael Young argued that active democratic decision-making worked best in small units such as the family; "the great dilemma of modern society," he argued, was that its democratic ideals demanded larger units which gave individual citizens less ability to decide. Writing to his brother Henry, William James made a similar point even more emphatically: "The day of 'big'ness – big national destinies, political parties, trade combines, newspapers, is sweeping every good principle and quality out of the world" ([1899]1992–2004); in another letter, to Sarah Wyman Whitman, he wrote, "I am against bigness and greatness in all their forms; and with the invisible molecular forces that work from individual to individual [...]. The bigger the unit you deal with, the hollower, the more brutal, the more mendacious is the life displayed" ([1899]1920).

Reactions against bigness directed attention to smallness instead. Twenty years after *Marching Men* was published, Sherwood Anderson expressed his disillusionment with an America in which "the idea of accumulation of possessions [was] all mixed up with the ideas of happiness." Where bigness meant not collective unity but rather an individual's "getting to be something big in the world," Anderson expressed his preference for "the idea of smallness as opposed to bigness" ([1939]1947). A competition between bigness and smallness plays out in Lawrence Perry's short story "A Question of Bigness" (1915), in which Sam Trowbridge, a wealthy New York railwayman, tries to convince his childhood friend William Hardy – a pillar of his small-town community – to move to the city and join his enterprise. Trowbridge expresses his desire to "take William out of Bolton and make a big man of him"; but Hardy's wife Mary rejects this definition of "big," telling Trowbridge, "William Hardy is a bigger man than you," and asserting, "There are big things in life, yes. [...] But there are little things, too."

Mary Hardy was not alone in arguing for the relativity of concepts of big and small in the modernist period. Like her, Mina Loy sought, in her "Aphorisms on Futurism" (1914), a reorientation of scale whereby moral and imaginative bigness was located in the common person: "the smallest people live in the greatest houses./BUT the smallest person, potentially, is as great as the universe." Modern technology was a particularly powerful force in complicating relationships of size: by making things bigger and bigger, it made what was previously thought big seem small. As opposed to testimonies to the immensity of the modern city, the speaker of David O'Neil's "The Ascent" (1917) shows how an aerial perspective can make even the city seem small: "With following the paths that ascend," he says, he has "Lost the sense of city's bigness/As it dwindles to mosaics." Further, by making it easier and faster to move from place to place, modern technology relativized the notion of distance. *The Dawn of a World-Order* (1932), a League of Nations-inspired book on internationalism, demonstrated in quantitative terms the modernist reconfiguration of scale: the shift from stagecoach to airplane meant that "the distance, measured in time," between Rome and London was "at least sixfold smaller than in 1834"; communications technologies like the telephone and radio had similarly reduced "the shrinking world" to approximately one sixth of its former size. Western modernists were acquiring a new sense of their own relative smallness in the wider world. Harriet Monroe, reviewing the Indian poet Rabindranath Tagore, argued that he "show[ed] us how provincial we are": "England and America are little recently annexed corners of the ancient earth, and their poets should peer out over sea-walls and race-walls and pride-walls, and learn their own littleness and the bigness of the world" (1913). In Virginia Woolf's *The Voyage Out* (1915), the passengers on the ship Euphrosyne look back at England and see it as "a shrinking island in which people were imprisoned"; in *The Years* (1937), Eleanor similarly comments, on returning to England from travel abroad, "It was small; it was smug; it was petty after Spain." The protagonist of D. H. Lawrence's *Aaron's Rod* (1922), recently arrived in Italy, reflects, "There was something big and exposed about it all. No more the cosy English ambushed life, no longer the cosy littleness of the landscape. A bigness – and nothing to shelter the unshrinking spirit."

A new sense of littleness did not necessarily mean diminishment; it could lead to enriched awareness and appreciation of the small. Following an automobile journey to the country in E. M. Forster's *Howards End* (1910), Margaret "recapture[s] the sense of space which the motor had tried to rob from her," avoiding the "phantom of bigness, which London encourages" by "remember[ing] [...] that ten square miles are not ten times as wonderful as one square mile, that a thousand square miles are not practically the same as heaven." Many modernist critics saw appreciation of the small as a distinguishing trait of modernist literature. Erich Auerbach in *Mimesis* ([1946]1953) perceived in the writing of Woolf, Proust, and Joyce an attention to "minor, unimpressive, random events." In "Modern Fiction," Virginia Woolf cautioned, "Let us not take for granted that life exists more in what is commonly thought big than what is commonly thought small" ([1919]1925); in *A Room of One's Own* (1929), she described the sensibility of her fictional female writer as "light[ing] on small things and show[ing] that perhaps they were not small after all." W. H. Hudson recalled a chance meeting in a business hotel with a commercial traveler who falsely assumed

Hudson was an agricultural salesman: "You are a traveller in little things," he told Hudson, whereas he himself – working in "big towns" – was "a traveller in something very large." Hudson chose not to correct the man's mistake nor to challenge the association of power and importance with what is big; instead, quietly thinking that the man had transgressed "an unwritten law" among "Commercials" – "The big and the little man, once inside the hostel, [. . .] are on an equality" – Hudson with some wry amusement acknowledged himself "grateful" to find his work as a writer so "accurately and aptly described" and chose *A Traveller in Little Things* for the title of his book.

SEE ALSO: *Atom, Atomic; Biography, New Biography; Common Man; Democracy; Form, Formalism*

References

Anderson, Sherwood (1917). *Marching Men*. New York: John Lane.

Anderson, Sherwood (1947). "A Writer's Conception of Realism." Limited Publication, 1939. In *The Sherwood Anderson Reader* (ed. Paul Rosenfeld). Boston: Houghton Mifflin. 337–347.

Auerbach, Erich (1953). *Mimesis: The Representation of Reality in Western Literature.* [*Mimesis: Dargestellte Wirklichkeit in der abendländischen Literatur*, 1946]. Trans. Willard R. Trask. Princeton: Princeton University Press.

Conrad, Joseph (1912). "Some Reflexions, Seamanlike and Otherwise, on the Loss of the Titanic." *The English Review* 11 (May): 304–315.

Fitzgerald, F. Scott (1922). "The Diamond as Big as the Ritz." *The Smart Set* 68.2 (June): 5–29.

Forster, E. M. (1910). *Howards End*. London: Edward Arnold.

Grey, Zane (1917). *Wildfire*. New York: Harper and Brothers.

Harrison, Jane Ellen (1913). *Ancient Art and Ritual*. London: Williams and Norgate.

Hudson, W. H. (1921). *A Traveller in Little Things*. New York: E. P. Dutton.

James, Henry (1920). Letter to Edward Warren, 19 March 1905. [1905]. In *The Letters of Henry James* (ed. Percy Lubbock). 2 vols. New York: Charles Scribner's Sons. 2: 31–32.

James, William (1920). Letter to Mrs. Henry Whitman, 7 June 1899. [1899]. In *The Letters of William James* (ed. Henry James). 2 vols. Boston: Atlantic Monthly Press. Vol. 2: 90.

James, William (1992–2004). Letter to Henry James Jr., 20 February 1899. [1899]. In *The Correspondence of William James* (eds. Ignas K Skrupskelis and Elizabeth M. Berkeley). 12 vols. Charlottesville: University Press of Virginia. Vol. 3: 50.

Lawrence, D. H. (1922). *Aaron's Rod*. New York: Thomas Seltzer.

London, Jack (1909). *Martin Eden*. New York: Macmillan.

Loy, Mina (1914). "Aphorisms on Futurism." *Camera Work* 45 (January [pub. June]): 13–15.

Monroe, Harriet (1913). "The New Beauty." *Poetry: A Magazine of Verse* 2.1 (April): 22–25.

O'Neill, David (1917). "The Ascent." *Poetry: A Magazine of Verse* 11.2 (November): 76.

Perry, Lawrence (1915). "A Question of Bigness." *Scribner's Magazine* (September), 353–362.

Porter, Eleanor H. (1919). *Dawn*. Boston: Houghton Mifflin.

Priestley, J. B. (1934). *English Journey*. London: W. Heinemann.

Sandburg, Carl (1914). "Chicago." *Poetry* 3.6 (March): 191–192.

Sanders, Emmy Veronica (1922). "Into These Things." *Poetry* 20.6 (September): 301–302.

Smith, Nowell Charles and J. C. Maxwell Garnett (1932). *The Dawn of World-Order: An Introduction to the Study of the League of Nations*. London: Oxford University Press.

Tarkington, Booth (1915). *The Turmoil*. New York: Grosset and Dunlap.

Wood, Charles Erskine Scott (1915). *The Poet in the Desert*. Portland, Oregon: F. W. Baltes.

Woolf, Virginia (1915). *The Voyage Out*. London: Duckworth.

Woolf, Virginia (1925). "Modern Fiction." ["Modern Novels," 1919]. In *The Common Reader*. London: Hogarth. 184–195.

Woolf, Virginia (1929). *A Room of One's Own*. London: Hogarth.

Woolf, Virginia (1937). *The Years*. London: Hogarth.

Young, Michael (1949). *Small Man: Big World*. London: Labour Publications Department.

Biography, New Biography

Biography is an ancient form. In 1927, critic James Chapman Johnston reminded his audience that The Gospels and "Lives of the Caesars" by Suetonius – both C1 – were among its earliest examples and that St. Augustine's "Confessions" (C5) was the "prototype" for "most of our present-day autobiographic forms." But biography (and Biographia) did not appear in written English until lC17, and autobiography emerged roughly 100 years later, coined but rejected by William Taylor, who marginally favored Isaac D'Israeli's less "pedantic" use of self-biography instead (1797). By C20, however, biography had evolved into a specialized literary term. Historian James Truslow Adams hailed Johnston's work as "the first elaborate effort to establish [biography] as a separate [form] worthy of critical analysis and study," noting, from the slightness of Johnston's secondary sources, that "almost nothing has been written about biography as an art" (1927). The new critical interest was paralleled by an increasing appetite among readers – especially following WWI – for stories of "real lives." According to *The Publishers' Weekly*, between 1920 and 1939, 11,382 biographies were published in the US alone (1941), while Thomas Seccombe, writing in 1919, claimed, "there seems to be more biographic tinder lying about for sparks to alight on in England than in any other country." Biography and autobiography were often grouped together, but there was growing recognition of a wide diversity of forms: Johnston appended a 14-page glossary of variant terms, such as Anecdotes, Apology, Diary, Epitaph, Journal, Memoir, Letters, Life, Obituary, and Reminiscences, plus two new compound terms – Biographical Fiction and Novelized Biography. Not surprisingly, Seccombe described "Biographical literature" as "a maze without a plan," and Adams asserted, "It is high time that someone should attempt to treat the biographical, and to clarify both the philosophy and technique of what is rapidly becoming one of the most popular and prolific of all literary forms."

Controversy, rather than clarification, however, dominated eC20 discussions of biographical writing, with the greatest clash of opinion circulating around the "modern" or "new." The idea that biography was changing came dramatically to the fore with the publication of Lytton Strachey's short, irreverent portraits of four *Eminent Victorians* (1918). Distinguishing his work from the Victorian "Standard Biographies" of "two fat volumes" commemorating the dead, Strachey cast himself as "the modern inquirer" writing for "the modern eye," exercising both "a becoming brevity" and the "freedom [. . .] to lay bare the facts." Strachey's approach, however, aroused strikingly opposite critical sentiments. Summing up his achievement, Edmund Wilson highlighted Strachey's success in "blast[ing] once and for all the pretensions of the Victorian age" and concluded, "Something had been punctured for good" (1932). Leonard Woolf acknowledged the contrary view: while stating that Strachey was "the dominating influence upon the intellectuals of his generation," Woolf noted both "the admiration and the hostility" that Strachey's biographies aroused, admitting that they sometimes betrayed "an almost contemptuous, if not unscrupulous, disregard of accuracy in detail" (1932).

The mixed response to Strachey's approach reflects the most salient questions being debated about biography itself: was modern biography really new and, more pertinently, was it critically respectable? In "The New Biography" (1927), Virginia Woolf firmly associated the genre with change, writing positively of "the new school of biographies," "the new attitude to biography," and "this new phase of the biographer's art." But while Woolf proclaimed, "the days of Victorian biography are over," by new, she did not mean never encountered before. A revolution had already occurred, Woolf explained, at the end of C18: James Boswell's *The Life of Samuel Johnson* established a new human relation between both biographer and subject and biographer and audience, largely through Boswell's "speaking in his natural voice." Yet further change, she protested, was needed, since in C19, "the convention which Boswell had destroyed settled again." Glossing biography as "*The Literature of Personality*," James Chapman Johnston advanced a similar view, stating that "the so-called 'new biography,' with its eminently proper emphasis on interpretation, is successful to the extent to which it utilizes Boswell's methods." Assessing "New Biography" (1928), Milton Byron also positively judged that the five biographies under his consideration were "anything but the conventional, cut-and-dried 'lives' that one too often associates with the word biography." Yet reviewer Arthur Colton declared "Modern Biography" "an unsatisfactory term," arguing that "what M. Maurois calls 'Victorian Biography' is perhaps as prevalent now as it was fifty years ago"; Colton doubted that "Strachey's 'Victoria' is any more 'truthful' than Trevelyan's 'Macaulay,' or that a reticence is more misleading than a slant" (1930). J. T. Adams went much further to assert, "If there is any word which more than another is coming to send a shiver down the susceptible spine of a man who has an historical background, it is the word 'new,' so sweated in literary shops, the 'new history,' the 'new freedom,' the 'new biography.'" Launching a yet more scathing attack, in "This New Biography" (1932), Frances Winwar judged Violet Hunt's *The Wife of Rossetti* possibly acceptable "as highly-colored fiction" but argued that "since it appears as biography, based on truth, or at least, fact," it must be held accountable for its "formidable amount of wilful distortion of fact, garbled quotation and misrepresentation," "in justice to Dante Gabriel Rossetti who, through Miss Hunt's zeal for her 'heroine,' stands condemned."

Attitudes toward biography thus divided over the question of "newness" and over the strengths and the weaknesses of putatively new forms. The controversies over biography furthermore significantly mirrored the general debates in the modernist period about writing itself. If biography was now an art, what was the art of the modernist age? If biography now centered on personality, what did personality mean? Whose lives mattered enough to be written about, and what should be considered a significant "event"? And if morality now condoned a new frankness and openness, were there still limits that ethical responsibility must respect? What is the writer's responsibility to tell the truth – but then, what is truth? In numerous ways, biography served as a testing ground for larger issues about art and life.

Positive descriptions of the new biography welcomed its revolutionary challenge to conventional values. While acknowledging that Strachey's followers copied many of his worst features and put them to "infamous use," Mary Butts celebrated the way Strachey himself "took the triple tombstone, the old three-volume Life and Letters, smashed it to bits, and showed once and for all how to reassemble its fragments" ([1936]1998). Noting aesthetic qualities that much resembled those of the new modernist fiction, Butts further commended Strachey for "illustrat[ing] the overwhelming importance of rhythm, design, a point of view, and above all, of scale." Similarly applauding the new nonheroic approach for "reduc[ing] these nineteenth-century phantoms to human scale," Virginia Woolf humorously declared, "The respectable union between us and British biography has been broken" by "this lapse into biographic immorality" (1920). Whereas C19 biography had elevated the "Victorian worthies" to figures "almost always above life size," in "this new phase of the biographer's art," Woolf explained, the "point of view" is "altered," and the biographer relates to his subject as "an equal," not a slavish follower (1927). In "The Art of Biography" (1939), she further asked, "what is greatness? And what smallness?" Biography was pushing its readers to revisit fundamental assumptions about hierarchical values.

Respect for the small appears in numerous titles, highlighting ordinariness in *Memoirs of a Social Atom* (W. E. Adams, 1903) and *One of the Multitude* (Acorn,

1911), dispossession in *Autobiography of a Super-Tramp* (Davies, 1908) and *Up From Slavery: An Autobiography* (Washington, 1901), and the nonheroic in *Alger: A Biography Without a Hero* (Mayes, 1928) and *Lives of Twelve Bad Men*, stories of "eminent scoundrels" from C16-C19 (Seccombe, 1894). Introducing himself as the "ordinary person," W. E. Adams declared that, as a "Social Atom," he had "mingled with no great people, been admitted to no great secrets, met with no great adventures, witnessed no great events, taken part in no great transactions," yet he judged himself as worthy as anyone "to write a book of recollections." Virginia Woolf similarly defended "The Lives of the Obscure" (1924), commenting elsewhere, "It is much to be regretted that no lives of maids [. . .] are to be found in the Dictionary of National Biography" (1938). Milton Byron commended the "real sympathy and understanding" emerging from the relation of equals "in which Alger is just plain 'Horatio' to his biographer" (1928). And, although he himself wrote about famous subjects such as Balzac, Lenin, and George Washington, Emil Ludwig defended the use of the small detail in "historical portraiture," noting that formerly "accounts of a man's daily habits" were regarded "shamefacedly, and as though with a lowering of professional dignity," while today, "the most trivial habit" reveals "some major trait of character, and the accredited anecdote becomes an epigram" (1927). Commending a developing frankness in moral respects, Thomas Seccombe opened his volume by declaring, "The practice of whitewashing has proved as injurious to biography as the worst taint of bigotry or partisanship in the pages of history," explaining his aim as "the rehabilitation of the bad man in his native badness." Noting the positive change from the "time when autobiographies were only written by the old" to the present "era of autobiographies written by those still young in years," Iolo Aneurin Williams additionally observed that WWI brought a new honesty about brutality: Vera Brittain's *Testament of Youth*, he judged, committed "no failure of taste" in "its unshrinking frankness" as "a testimony to the horror and waste of war" (1933). Modern biography gave expression to the ordinary person, the ordinary detail, and the less glorious side of life.

29

Attitudes toward such developments were not, of course, uncomplicated. Although Harold Nicolson wrote biographies about conventional subjects such as Tennyson and King George V, his book *Some People* was a highly unconventional series of factual–fictional sketches that were composite portraits of various "ordinary" people in Nicolson's life. While, in *The Development of English Biography* (1927), Nicolson insisted on the separation between "pure" and "impure" biography, demanding from the former an "absolute detachment" that eschews both "hagiography" and "didacticism," Virginia Woolf judged that *Some People* went "a step" beyond Strachey by combining "the artistry of fiction" with irreverent laughter: as Nicolson laughs at Lord Curzon, the Foreign Office, and also, crucially, himself, "the attitude of the bribed and docile official" is "blown to atoms" (1927). Openness about personal life was controversial as well: while Edmond Gosse very early recommended, "the first theoretical object of the biographer should be indiscretion, not discretion" (1903), thirty years later, Ernest Boyd rather more cynically remarked, "the overemphasis of the sex element in contemporary biography doubtless explains in large part the current vogue of that branch of writing" (1932). When it came to writing homosexual life, however, as late as 1938, James G. Southworth declared, "With conditions as they are, it is useless to expect from the ordinary biography anything but superficial facts, and even those facts are worthless because a sympathetic and understanding interpretation of them is lacking." On the traditional side, J. T. Adams again voiced the orthodox critique: "No great biography can be written about a small man," but "many modern biographers [. . .] choose subjects unimportant and uninteresting in themselves merely because they can rake out of their careers enough episodes to sell their books." Psychoanalytic approaches, too, were for Adams another disreputable "new fad": "If we are to write biographies in terms of unconscious complexes and the subconscious," he asked, "why not in terms of biology, of chemistry, or even in terms of the aggregate dance of atoms which constitute the 'physical' John Smith?"

Those for whom personality did resemble a "dance of atoms," however, sought more flexibility and indeed hybridity in biographical forms. As Colton explained, a "characteristic of modern biography" was "the greater sense of the complexity and mobility of human beings and a lesser emphasis on their unity." André Maurois wrote that Proust, "reduces the whole idea of personality to dust," offering "only a succession of states and feelings, grouped, but not united," and representing the self as "a colony of feelings, a coral-reef of diverse personalities" (1929). Virginia Woolf linked such multiplicity to multiple images: suggesting that *Some People* was a form of relational autobiography, she wrote, "each of the supposed subjects holds up in his or her small bright diminishing mirror a different reflection of Harold Nicolson" (1927). She also linked multiple mirrors with candid photography: "in an age when a thousand cameras are pointed [. . .] at every character from every angle," biography might "enlarge its scope by hanging up looking-glasses at odd corners" (1939).

Biography's new multiplicity was reflected in the coinage of new compound words. Franklin Fearing referred to "the new psychobiography" as "a development of the last fifteen years" (1927), and Gamaliel Bradford – regarded as the American Strachey – chose the term "psychography" to describe his own "modification of biographical method" (1925): differing from the portrait in its effort to grasp not one moment but as many as possible, from standard biography in not being bound to chronological sequence of events, and from psychology in dealing with individuals not general principles (1917). For Bradford, psychography, while not new, was the best way to convey the "two things chiefly notable about

30

biography, first its lack of finality, second its charm," for "the biographer's one object is to catch something of the fluidity, the mobility, the versatility of the human spirit." Other coinages reflected the blending of biography with fiction: Ford Madox Ford's "novelized biography" (1929) and Stephen Reynolds's more striking "Autobiografiction" (1906). The echoing of authors' names in titles signaled experiment in third-person autobiographies, as in Henry Adams, *The Education of Henry Adams* (1918), and Edward Bok, *The Americanization of Edward Bok* (1920). Bok claimed the third person as "the most effective method of writing an autobiography," explaining that the public Bok "has had and has been a personality apart from my private self" (1920). Christopher Isherwood's fictionalized third-person autobiography *Christopher and His Kind* (1976) over-lapped with his biographical fiction *Goodbye to Berlin* (1939), in which he asserted, "the 'I' of this narrative" (named Christopher Isherwood) is "a conve-nient ventriloquist's dummy nothing more." Other forms of ventriloquist auto-biography included Gertrude Stein's *The Autobiography of Alice B. Toklas* (1933) and *Everybody's Autobiography* (1937), while imaginative creation flowered in fantastic biographies, such as Woolf's *Orlando: A Biography* and *Flush: A Biography* (of Elizabeth Barrett Browning's dog).

Yet biography was caught in a conflict because, as Colton wrote, "truth is something solid, and personality something flickering and intangible" – clearly echoing Woolf's formulation of "truth as something with granite-like solidity" and "personality as something with rainbow-like intangibility," with biography strug-gling "to weld these two into one seamless whole" (1927). And the tension led to differing concepts of biography as a genre; as Maurois so pertinently asked, "Ought biography to be an art or a science?" Whereas Maurois believed "that art and science can be reconciled," Lord David Cecil noted that "for the typical modern biographer literature comes first" (1936), while J. W. Slaughter stressed the need for "biography makers" to "recognize the fact that biography is scientific as well as literary" (1911). Harold Nicolson argued, "Were biography generally accepted as an important branch of psychology, the high standards inherent in that science would impose their own discipline and sanctions" (1927), while Bernard DeVoto proposed that "literary people should not be permitted to write biography," since its "first condition is absolute, unvarying, unremitted accuracy" (1933). Critics and historians were in general urging more sober treatment, while, in practice, literary biographers were inventing highly creative and often light-hearted, new forms.

Seemingly unresolvable conflicts in biography's aims, however, did not constrain biography's future. "Biography does not, as yet, possess a distinct identity," Nicolson claimed, naming it an "elastic Category" (1927). Virginia Woolf wrote further that if "the facts of science" – "facts that can be verified by other people" – do not mix with "facts as an artist invents them," there are other facts the biographer can employ: facts that are "subject to changes of opinion [. . .] as the times change" and, most important of all, "the creative fact; the fertile fact; the fact that suggests and engenders" (1939). By incorporating both truth and personality, biography, she predicted, would someday achieve "that high degree of tension which gives us reality."

SEE ALSO: *Atom, Atomic; Bigness, Smallness; Common Man; Form; Modern, Modernism; Personality, Impersonality; Queer, Gay; Rhythm; Reality, Realism; Unconscious*

References

(1941). *The Publishers' Weekly: The American Book Trade Journal* (January 18), 232.

Acorn, George [pseud.] (1911). *One of the Multitude*. London: W. Heinemann.

Adams, James Truslow (1927). "Biography as an Art." Rev. of *Biography: The Literature of Personality* by James Chapman Johnston. *The Saturday Review of Politics, Literature, Science, and Art* (November 12), 297–298.

Adams, William Edwin (1903). *Memoirs of a Social Atom*. London: Hutchinson.

Bok, Edward (1920). *The Americanization of Edward Bok: the Autobiography of a Dutch Boy Fifty Years After*. New York: Charles Scribner's Sons.

Boyd, Ernest (1932). "Sex in Biography." *Harper's Magazine* (November), 753–756.

Bradford, Gamaliel (1917). *A Naturalist of Souls: Studies in Psychography*. New York: Dodd, Mead.

Bradford, Gamaliel (1925). "The Art of Biography." *The Saturday Review of Literature* (May 23), 769–770.

Butts, Mary (1998). "Bloomsbury." [1936]. Eds. Camilla Bagg and Nathalie Blondel. *Modernism/modernity* 5.2 (April): 32–45.

Byron, Milton (1928). "New Biography." *The Outlook* (April 11): 596.

Cecil, Lord David (1936). Introduction. In *An Anthology of Modern Biography*. London: Thomas Nelson & Sons. ix–xvi.

Colton, Arthur (1930). "Modern Biography." Rev. of *Aspects of Biography* by Andre Maurois. *The Saturday Review of Politics, Literature, Science, and Art* (January 18), 649.

Davies, William Henry (1908). *Autobiography of a Super-Tramp*. London: A. C. Fyfield.

DeVoto, Bernard (1933). "The Sceptical Biographer." *Harper's Magazine* (January), 184–192.

Fearing, Franklin (1927). "Psychological Studies of Historical Personalities." *Psychological Bulletin* 24.9: 521–539.

Ford, Ford Madox (1929). *The English Novel*. Philadelphia: J. B. Lippincott.

Gosse, Edmund (1903). "The Ethics of Biography." *The Cosmopolitan* (July), 317–323.

Isherwood, Christopher (1939). *Goodbye to Berlin*. London: Hogarth.

Isherwood, Christopher (1976). *Christopher and His Kind: 1929–1939*. New York: Farrar, Straus, Giroux.

Johnston, James C. (1927). *Biography: The Literature of Personality*. New York: The Century Co.

Ludwig, Emil (1927). "Introduction: 'On the Writing of History'". In *Genius and Character*. New York: Harcourt, Brace, and Co. 3–9.

Maurois, André (1929). *Aspects of Biography.* Trans. Sydney Castle Roberts. New York: D. Appleton.

Mayes, Herbert R. (1928). *Alger: A Biography Without a Hero.* New York: Macy-Masius.

Nicolson, Harold (1927). *The Development of English Biography.* London: Hogarth.

Reynolds, Stephen (1906). "Autobiografiction." *Speaker,* New Series 15.366: 28, 30.

Seccombe, Thomas (1894). Preface. *Lives of Twelve Bad Men: Original Studies of Eminent Scoundrels by Various Hands* (ed. Thomas Seccombe). New York: G. P. Putnam's Sons. xvii–xx.

Seccombe, Thomas (1919). "The Reading of Biography." *The Living Age* 300 (February 15): 435–437.

Slaughter, John Willis (1911). *The Adolescent.* London: George Allen and Unwin.

Southworth, James G. (1938). "Wystan Hugh Auden." *The Sewanee Review* 46.2 (April–June): 189–205.

Strachey, Lytton (1918). *Eminent Victorians.* London: Chatto & Windus.

[Taylor, William] (1797). "Art. IV." Rev. of *Miscellanies; or, Literary Recreations* by I. D'Israeli. *Monthly Review* 2.24: 374–379.

V. W. [Virginia Woolf] (1920). "A Character Sketch." Rev. of *Frederick Locker-Lampton: A Character Sketch* (ed. Augustine Birrell). *The Athenaeum* (August 13), 201–202.

Washington, Booker T. (1901). *Up From Slavery: An Autobiography.* Garden City: Doubleday.

[Williams, Iolo Aneurin] (1933). Rev. of *Testament of Youth: An Autobiographical Study of the Years 1900–1925* by Vera Brittain. *TLS* (August 31), 571.

Wilson, Edmund (1932). "Lytton Strachey." *The New Republic* (September 21), 146–148.

Winwar, Frances (1932). "This New Biography." Rev. of *The Wife of Rossetti* by Violet Hunt. *The Saturday Review of Politics, Literature, Science, and Art* (December 17), 327.

Woolf, Leonard (1932). "Lytton Strachey." *The New Statesman and Nation* (January 30), 118–119.

Woolf, Virginia (1924). "The Lives of the Obscure." *The London Mercury* (January), 261–268. Reprinted slightly revised in *The Common Reader* (London: Hogarth, 1925): 146–167.

Woolf, Virginia (1927). "The New Biography." Rev. of *Some People* by Harold Nicolson. *The New York Herald Tribune* (October 30), Section 7, Books: 1, 6.

Woolf, Virginia (1938). *Three Guineas.* London: Hogarth.

Woolf, Virginia (1939). "The Art of Biography." *The Atlantic Monthly* (April), 506–510.

Common Man

Rejecting Henry R. Luce's designation of the present age as the "American Century," American Vice-President Henry A. Wallace urged a global alternative: "The century which will come out of this war [. . .] can be and must be the century of the common man" (1943). More confidently, a 1911 editorial in *Scribner's* "boast[ed]," "to-day is the day of the common man," adding that "Lincoln said that God must love the common people, because he made so many of them." A burgeoning interest in the common man surfaces in the proliferating expressions used to describe him, from the plebian "man-in-the-street" to the cosmopolitan "*l'homme moyen sensuel*" – a term apparently originating in Matthew Arnold's identification of Paris as the city of "*l'homme sensuel moyen, the average sensual man*" (1873). The common man could be John and Jane Doe (C14); John Bull (C18); John Chinaman or John Confucius (C19); Johnny and Janey Canuck (Can. C19, C20); Joe College (US 1932), or Joe Blow (US military 1941). Everyman, a character in a C15 morality play, became, in 1906, a name for the vast reading public to be educated by Everyman's Library. In 1922, a cartoonist for the *Chicago Daily News* created the hugely popular John Q. Public, whose income was taxed and whose opinions were surveyed and analyzed. The common man acquired a new public role. Alternately heroic and homely, powerful and passive, valorized and vilified, he transformed from a figure lost in the crowd to a rallying cry and a slogan.

ABC**C**DEFGHIJKLMNOPQRSTUVWXYZ

Modernism: Keywords, First Edition. Melba Cuddy-Keane, Adam Hammond, and Alexandra Peat.
© 2014 Melba Cuddy-Keane. Published 2014 by John Wiley & Sons, Ltd.

Such widely divergent attitudes can be attributed at least in part to different constructions of what common meant. Both Wallace and the Scribner's editor used common to refer to human characteristics broadly shared – Wallace, to argue that the outcome of WWII must be a greater commitment to "social justice" to achieve "freedom from want" throughout the whole world, while the Scribner's editor used "Our Common Lot" of eventual death to promote the value of "real, every-day, common place human life" against signs of "hostility to ordinary life" and the "frenetic search for luxury." Arnold's focus was less on what we all share than on what we could all arguably acquire: a development of "the senses, the apparent self, all round, in good faith," "confidently and harmoniously," "equally and systematically." All three usages emphasize shared humanity, but common could also designate a distinct stratum of society: commoners as opposed to Lords, lower as opposed to upper class. Complaining that "the British Army is officered by the British upper classes," the military commentator for *The New Age*, "Romney," contrasted the "refinements" of the aristocrats and their consequent failure to grasp "the real meaning of the word 'work'" to the "virtues of the common man" – "crude, clumsy, blundering, but strong" (1913). Praising the Indiana dialect poet James Whitcomb Riley, Albert J. Beveridge argued that "the aristocrat may [. . .] state high truths in austere beauty" but "only the brother of the common man can tell what the common heart longs for and feels" (1908). Common could thus mean anyone or the lower classes; further ambiguity surrounded its cognate average, which could range in meaning from everyday, straightforward, and balanced to typical, or worse, mediocre. The common man could signify compassion and commonsense versus ambition and privilege or, conversely, standardization and mediocrity versus noteworthy achievement and respect for individual lives.

Given such diversification, the common man could be championed from a variety of positions on the political spectrum. G. K. Chesterton, a "Little-Englander" committed to the preservation of small, local communities, argued that "progress has been merely the persecution of the Common Man," blaming "liberal economics" for giving a few "the liberty to grow richer," and "emancipated ethics and politics" for banishing "common sense" (1936). Conceding his great difference as a "Socialist" from Chesterton, H. G. Wells nevertheless affirmed that they were "on the same side of the [present] great political and social cleavage," aligning "with the interests of the mass of common men as against that growing organisation of great owners who have common interests directly antagonistic to those of the community and State" (1908). Expanding from the national to the international community, socialist and President of PEN Margaret Storm Jameson wrote, in a message distributed around the world, that "any word, any act, any treaty which debases the dignity and freedom of the common man is evil and to be rejected" (1940). Liberal humanist E. M. Forster, writing on the eve of WWII, identified the common man's enemy as political rather than economic coercion, deploring "the Great Man" or "dictator-hero" who "produce[s] a desert of uniformity around [him]" and advocating instead "different kinds of small men"; rather than using common man, however, Forster proposed a revolutionary redefinition of aristocracy (wondering at the same time "if a democrat may use [that word]"): "Not an aristocracy of power, based upon rank and influence, but an aristocracy of the sensitive, the considerate and the plucky," coming from "all nations and classes" and representing "the true human tradition, the one permanent victory of our queer race over cruelty and chaos" ([1938]1939). Although Forster aligned "small men" against war, in popular sentiment the world wars highlighted the common man's sacrifices in battle; following the recommendation of Peyton Thomas, a chaplain with the British army in WWI, both Britain and France unveiled monuments to the "Unknown Warrior" in 1920, and other nations promptly followed suit. During WWII, American composer Aaron Copland wrote "Fanfare for the Common Man" (1942), commissioned by the Cincinnati Symphony Orchestra, which the conductor honored by placing its premiere at income tax time (1984).

The increasing prominence of the common man in C20, however, was accompanied by criticism of his limited conceptions and "average" abilities. Wells argued that, as a socialist, he had "to ram right into" the common man's "circle of ideas," until engrained attachments to private property were replaced with more enlightened ideas of public ownership (1908). A more extreme skepticism concerned the common man's capacity for political involvement; in 1944, G. B. Shaw suggested a special "Everyman Congress" where the common man's interest might be heard while the real business of government was performed by the "politically competent." Even while urging measures to break "the monopoly of mass culture," Joseph Wood Krutch nevertheless questioned whether it were possible to have "an Age of the Common Man without making it an Age of the Common Denominator" (1953). Both economically and politically, the common man was thus seen as distressingly vulnerable to manipulation. Pitting "vested interests," or "those who control the conditions of work," against "the common man," or "those others who have the work to do," Thorstein Veblen argued that "the great distinguishing mark of the common man is that he is helpless within the rules of the game" (1919), while Helmut Kuhn was not alone in suggesting that manipulation of the common man enabled the rise of fascism in Mussolini's Italy and Hitler's Germany, "where the common man rose and showed a fiendish countenance" (1944). George Orwell, while celebrating author Henry Miller as "a voice from the crowd [. . .] from the ordinary, non-political, non-moral, passive man," nonetheless wrote, "Within a narrow circle (home life, and perhaps the trade union or local politics) [the ordinary man] feels himself master of his fate, but against major events he is as helpless as against the elements" (1940).

By describing Miller as an "ordinary man" whose writing gave "the 'average sensual man' [. . .] the power of speech," Orwell implied no contradiction with Miller's offering a "viewpoint" that was "individualistic." The words common and average posed more difficulty, especially for novelists interested in individual character. For Aldous Huxley, the "average" man was a "purely mythical being," for "none of us are average; we are all individuals" (1924). Evelyn Waugh protested that "the Common Man does not exist" since "there is no such thing as normality," arguing as well that "a novelist has no business with types; they are the property of economists and politicians and advertisers and the other professional bores of our period" (1946). As D. H. Lawrence put it, the "Average Man" represents "the reduction of the human being to a mathematical unit"; Lawrence argued further that this "standard" was "never intended to be worshipped" and that, in our adulation for this abstracted "man-in-the-street," we have "made prime fools of ourselves" (1919; 1936). Such aggregate terms were seen to strip people of their individuality and reduce their diversity to an average mean.

Poems, plays, and novels of this era, however, brought a useful complexity to this abstraction. The paradoxes of the common man as both small and heroic, both individual and humanly representative, are at the heart of *Johnny Johnson: The Biography of a Common Man* (1936), a play by Paul Green set to music by Kurt Weill (1937). Initially pacifist, the titular Johnny is persuaded by WWI propaganda to go off to war, where a German he captures named Johann explains, "It means John – in English." Reflecting that Americans and Germans are praying to the same God, Johnny renews his pacifist efforts after the war but is ostracized by a community bent on military celebration. Here the common man goes against the crowd yet does so for the sake of shared humanity. A character in Miles Franklin's novel *Back to Bool Bool* (1931) rails against the "common man" as "only so much clay in the hands of the uncommon man," raising the question, "who shall fashion the herd, the militant and predatory groups, or the idealists." Others accuse the speaker, however, of being "unpatriotic" – working for an American firm, he is planning to give up his Australian citizenship – yet later in the novel, he comes "to appreciate Bool Bool's pioneers, tamers of the wilderness, battling against primitive conditions, rearing immense families without conveniences." The plight of the common man was perhaps most famously espoused by the American dramatist Arthur Miller, notably in *Death of a Salesman* (1949a) and its companion essay, "Tragedy and the Common Man" (1949b). Here Miller argued that those "who are without kings" can more positively look to "the heart and spirit of the average man" for the heroic subject of tragedy. Miller's tragic hero is common in being "lowly" in status rather than "well-placed" or "exalted" but uncommon in protesting his fate and "the scheme of things that degrades [him]," exceptional in his readiness "to lay down his life"

37

in fighting for "his whole due as a personality," and finally representative in embodying "the indestructible will of man to achieve his humanity."

In the full range of literary works, the common man appears in numerous guises, from the struggling human being victimized by propaganda and suppressed by hegemonic discourse to the touchstone for the values of daily life. He appears variously in Ezra Pound's "L'Homme Moyen Sensuel" (1917), W. H. Auden's "The Unknown Citizen" (1939), Carl Sandburg's "The people is Everyman, everybody" (1936), and e. e. cummings's "anyone lived in a pretty how town" (1940). Ezra Pound praised James Joyce's Leopold Bloom as "the basis of democracy," "the man in the street," "the next man," "l'homme moyen sensuel," and "Everyman," still finding individuality, however, in the way "Joyce's characters not only speak their own language, but they think their own language" (1922). Virginia Woolf regendered the common man as "Mrs. Brown" (1924), unclassed the common man as the "common reader" (1925), and detailed the lives of "Ordinary People" – a provisional title for her novel *The Years* (1937). Sherwood Anderson's *Winesburg, Ohio* portrayed a series of "grotesques" to capture "what is understandable and lovable" in "what are called very common people" (1919), and Thornton Wilder described *Our Town* (1938) as "an attempt to find a value above all price for the smallest events in our daily life." Prophecies of the Age of the Common Man continued to resound. Veblen warned "the vested interests" of signs that the "common man" within the UK, at least judged by the Labor Party, had "reached the limit of tolerance" and more broadly noted "the IWW" [International Workers of the World] as "a vanguard of dissent" ushering in that "dread word," "Syndicalism" (1919). Toward the end of the period, Orwell wrote, "I myself believe, perhaps on insufficient grounds, that the common man will win his fight sooner or later, but I want it to be sooner and not later – some time within the next hundred years, say, and not some time within the next ten thousand years. That was the real issue of the Spanish war, and of the last war, and perhaps of other wars yet to come" ([1943]1953).

38

SEE ALSO: *Bigness, Smallness; Biography, New Biography; Common Mind, Group Thinking; Democracy; Highbrow, Middlebrow, Lowbrow*

References

(1911). "The Point of View." *Scribner's Magazine* (February), 250–253.

Anderson, Sherwood (1919). *Winesburg, Ohio*. New York: B. W. Huebsch.

Arnold, Matthew (1873). *Literature and Dogma: An Essay Towards a Better Apprehension of the Bible*. London: Smith, Elder.

Auden, W. H. (1939). "The Unknown Citizen." *The Listener* (August), 215.

Beveridge, Albert J. (1908). "James Whitcomb Riley – Poet of the People." In *The Meaning of the Times and Other Speeches*. Indianapolis: Bobbs-Merrill. 254–259.

Chesterton, G. K. (1936). "Persecuting the Common Man." *The American Mercury* (January), 67–71.

Copland, Aaron and Vivian Perlis (1984). *Copland: 1900 through 1942*. New York: St. Martin's/Marek.

cummings, e. e. (1940). "anyone lived in a pretty how town." In *50 Poems*. New York: Grosset and Dunlop. 29 [verso and recto].

Forster, E. M. (1939). *What I Believe*. ["Two Cheers for Democracy," 1938]. London: Hogarth.

Franklin, Miles [Stella Maria Sarah] (as Brent of Bin Bin) (1931). *Back to Bool Bool, a Ramiparous Novel with Several Prominent Characters and a Hantle of Others Disposed as the Atolls of Oceana's Archipelagoes*. Edinburgh: William Blackwood and Sons.

Green, Paul (1936). *Johnny Johnson: The Biography of a Common Man, in Three Acts*. New York: S. French.

Huxley, Aldous (1924). "By Their Speech Ye Shall Know Them." *Vanity Fair* (December), 72, 104.

Jameson, [Margaret] Storm, President *et al*. International PEN. Club, London Center (1940). "For Freedom and Conscience." *The Nation* (July 27), 80.

Krutch, Joseph Wood (1953). "Is Our Common Man Too Common?" *The Saturday Review of Literature* (January 10), 8–9, 35–37.

Kuhn, Helmut (1944). "The Common Man on Trial." *The Review of Politics* 6.1 (January): 18–35.

Lawrence, D. H. (1936). "Democracy: I. The Average." 1919. In *Phoenix: The Posthumous Papers of D. H. Lawrence*. Edited with an Introduction by Edward D. McDonald. London: W. Heinemann. 699–704.

Miller, Arthur (1949a). *Death of a Salesman*. New York: Viking.

Miller, Arthur (1949b). "Tragedy and the Common Man." *The New York Times* (February 27), X1.

Orwell, George (1940). "Inside the Whale." In *Inside the Whale and Other Essays*. London: Victor Gollancz. 131–188.

Orwell, George (1953). "Looking Back on the Spanish War." [1943 (i–iv)]. In *Such, Such Were the Joys*. New York: Harcourt, Brace. 129–153.

Pound, Ezra (1917). "L'Homme Moyen Sensuel." *The Little Review* 4.5 (September): 8–16.

Pound, Ezra (1922). "Paris Letter." *The Dial* 72.6 (June): 623–629.

Romney (1913). "Military Notes." *The New Age* 14.2 (November 13): 38–39.

Sandburg, Carl (1936). *The People, Yes*. New York: Harcourt, Brace and Co.

Shaw, Bernard (1944). *Everybody's Political What's What?* New York: Dodd, Mead and Company; London: Constable.

Veblen, Thorstein (1919). *The Vested Interests and the Common Man*. New York: B. W. Huebsch.

Wallace, Henry A. (1943). *The Century of the Common Man*. New York: Reynal and Hitchcock.

Waugh, Evelyn (1946). "Fan-Fare." *Life* (April 8), 53–54, 56, 58, 60.

Wells, H. G. (1908). "About Chesterton and Belloc." *The New Age* 2.11 (January 11): 209–210.

Wilder, Thornton (1957). "Preface." In *Three Plays: "Our Town"; "The Skin of Our Teeth"; "The Matchmaker."* New York: Harper and ROW. vii–xiv.

Woolf, Virginia (1924). *Mr Bennett and Mrs Brown*. London: Hogarth.

Woolf, Virginia (1925). *The Common Reader*. London: Hogarth.

Woolf, Virginia (1937). *The Years*. London: Hogarth.

39

Common Mind, Group Thinking

Community, as Raymond Williams states, was increasingly used in C19 as a more intimate term than state or society. In 1887, the distinction was influentially theorized by Ferdinand Tönnies ([1887]1955) as *Gemeinschaft* (community, or instinctual ties based on kinship, shared place, or shared belief) versus *Gesellschaft* (society, or associations based on shared forms of self-interest). Although Tönnies argued the necessary mixture of the two forms, believing that community could reinvigorate and redeem society, his categories were most frequently invoked in the early modernist period to decry the community's perceived demise. New media with increasingly rapid transmission, mass communication harnessed for advertising and propaganda, increasing travel and the sense of a shrinking globe – all threatened the existence of community as intimate relations transpiring face-to-face. Alongside efforts to revive traditional *Gemeinschaft*, however, a host of alternative perceptions arose, offering new ways to imagine community in modern, mass terms, with expanded dimensions of scale. Just as there was wide diversity in views, however, so there was no consensus about applicable terms. Reimaginings of community appear in a sizeable keyword cluster, including collective mind, herd mentality, group thinking, *la vie unanime*, supercortex, common mind, life in common, Universal Mind, and World Brain.

40

Communal terms with negative connotations targeted the way instinctual energy can be mobilized into blind conformity. Gustave Le Bon's pioneering study *The Crowd* (1896) (*La psychologie des foules* [1895]) analyzed a "collective mind" that dangerously enabled a charismatic leader, himself under the spell of his idea, to impart to the crowd illusions of invincible power while simultaneously reducing its members to a "servile flock." Furthering the sociological study of group psychology, Wilfred Trotter used herd mentality to describe the process by which the individual will succumbs to the will of the group (1916). Drawing on Trotter's analysis of rationalization as the process by which we justify our uncritical adherence to beliefs of the group, psychoanalyst John T. MacCurdy conceived an "antagonism between individual, intellectual activity and acceptance of 'group thinking'"; associating primitive societies with group consciousness (with both positive and negative effects) and civilization with independent thinking, MacCurdy expressed concerns that his contemporaries were "stultify[ing] individual intelligence to gain the unanimity essential to herd life" (1922). Sigmund Freud's *Massenpsychologie*, translated as *Group Psychology*, allowed for the positive element in a group's selfless sacrifice for an ideal, but also highlighted the dangers of a leader's functioning as an ego ideal and the bolstering of bonds within one social group by excluding and scapegoating groups that lie outside ([1921]1922, 1930). By his own confession, Leonard Woolf devoted three books and 31 years to the analysis of what he termed communal psychology

(1967), warning that Europe confronted a choice between "a civilized community of freemen" and "a community of soldiers disciplined to be a blind instrument of power in the hands of a dictator" (1939). Wryly dismissing the intellectual quality of early Christian theological discussions, Rebecca West similarly inveighed against "the depreciation of thought by the hasty and facile processes inevitable in group-thinking" (1933). Focusing specifically on business and political organizations, William H. Whyte, Jr., an editor of *Fortune* magazine, coined the term "Groupthink" to argue that imposed conformity of thought in the prevailing business model suppressed useful critical views (1952).

Another cluster of terms, however, associated collective life with noncoercive and expansive modes of perception, taking the individual beyond a limited sense of self and tapping into a larger social or spiritual reality. In the 1910s, *Unanimisme*, a literary movement in France founded by Jules Romains, attracted interest on both sides of the Atlantic for its vision of *la vie unanime* [unanimous life] and *les unanimes* – moments of semimystical, semipsychological consciousness, transpiring in ordinary places like a theatre or café or at a funeral and embodying the experience of "collective reality" (1926). In the dedicatory letter, addressed to Roger Fry, for his cotranslation of Romains's novel *Le Mort de Quelqu'un* (1911) as *The Death of a Nobody* (1914), Desmond MacCarthy noted the similarity of Romains's style to "Post-Impressionism" in art and related Romains's representation of "composite consciousness" to Emile Durkheim's "group consciousness," while E. M. Forster compared the ending of Virginia Woolf's *The Voyage Out* to the "atmosphere" of Romains's novel (1915). Leonard Woolf explained Romains's interest in "the feelings of persons, not as individual characters, but as members of groups" and the growth of "a kind of consciousness of the group in addition to that of each individual of the group" (1913). The Cambridge myth-ritualist Jane Ellen Harrison, who posited the origins of art in the "collective emotion" of the old "Choral Dance," wrote of the *Unanimistes* as a "hopeful sign" of art's return to its social function, in line with what she remarked as Science's turn to "something strangely like a World-Soul" (1913). Ezra Pound, less in favor of what he considered the "soft" as opposed to "hard" element in Romains's poetry, described Unanimism as "the adoration of the group unit or something of that sort" (1913), yet Pound still credited Romains with the ability to make "poetry out of crowd psychology" and "metropolitan conditions" (1918a), thus generating "the fullest statement of the poetic consciousness of our time" (1918b). In 1928, under the terms of an undergraduate prize awarded at Trinity College, Dublin, Samuel Beckett wrote an essay on Unanimism, which he simultaneously parodied in a fictional work on an imaginary movement named Le Concentrisme, founded by a poet to whom Beckett gave his own date of birth ([1920s]2011). Romains's anonymous Quelqu'un (literally "Someone," but translated "Nobody") was echoed

41

in a similar collective term in James Joyce's "Here Comes Everybody" (1925), later HCE in *Finnegans Wake* (1939).

Although references to Unanimism diminish after WWI, the search to articulate positive collective experience continues in numerous ways. Concerned with the inadequacies and slowness of the individual neural cortex when confronting "the more complex forms of [modern] experience," Rebecca West posited the existence of a supercortex as a mental capacity that is "collective and partially external" (1928). Supercortical activity, she hypothesized, synthesizes experience "pooled among those who share [the individual's] environment" and is operative in both science and art; "empathy," in the latter, or our power of "projecting ourselves into the destiny of others" enables an interactive blend. Unlike reductive group thinking, which West deprecated, supercortical activity involves a constant modification of experience as it circulates among individuals, modifying them in turn. West's close friend Winifred Holtby considered such collective activity the basis of "our corporate action" and applied the Biblical phrase "members one of another" to social and political realms. This phrase from Holtby's Preface to her novel *South Riding* (1936) is repeated by one of her characters, who continues, "We cannot escape this partnership. This is what it means – to belong to a community. This is what it means, to be a people." In a possible allusion to the communal pageant that ends Holtby's novel, Woolf has one of her characters reductively but also pertinently sum up the pageant in *Between the Acts* (1941): "We are members one of another. Each is part of the whole."

In numerous ways, models of collectivity shifted from the town or village to the mind. Carl Jung posited that, in addition to a personal unconscious, we possess a collective unconscious or "a second psychic system of a collective, universal, and impersonal nature" which we inherit genetically as members of the human race ([1934]1959). Referring to Ira Progoff's intensive journaling method, Anaïs Nin described diary writing as "going inside of a well and digging down and down" and so "reach[ing] the water that everyone shares, the universal water, the collective unconscious," which she also termed "a collective emotional identity" (1975). One of Virginia Woolf's early diary entries records her perception, in reading, of the way our minds are "all threaded together," creating a "common mind" that links "the whole world" ([1903]1992); a later essay suggests that "great writers" find "an atmosphere in which they work best, a mood of the great general mind which they interpret and discover" (1917). Using, like Nin, an image of water, Woolf referred metaphorically to the common mind as a common pool ([1929]1985), writing as well that "masterpieces are not single and solitary births" but "the outcome of many years of thinking in common, so that the experience of the mass is behind the single voice" (1929). Focusing on a more factual level, H.G. Wells pursued models of world knowledge along the lines of a networked brain, conceiving an encyclopedic global knowledge, a World Brain working somewhat like a mammoth computer. In his view, "a widespread world intelligence conscious of itself" (1938) would provide a bulwark against dictators and class rule, and he looked forward to "a more and more conscious co-operating unity [. . .] informing without pressure or propaganda, directing without tyranny" (1936).

Positive articulations of collective experience, however, struggled for ways to incorporate individuality into the mass. D. H. Lawrence inveighed against the popular belief in a "Universal Mind," equating the idea with a mesmerized audience at the cinema, yet he also wrote passionately to Katherine Mansfield about his desire to create a "life in common" among a few people who, while still preserving their singularity, could unite in "a unanimous blossoming" ([1915]1932). The American Mary Parker Follett, a pioneer in community organization and management theory, addressed this basic tension by distinguishing between the crowd and the group. Against "the crowd fallacy" and the fear that "collective action" requires "annihilation of the individual," Follett argued that the group "fulfills, not wipes out [. . .] individuality," and she extended her theory to a model of democratic education that fosters "individual initiative that has learned how to be part of a collective initiative" (1918). Later in the period, T. S. Eliot responded to the devastating effects of imposed uniformity in Germany and Italy by advocating a new national and international model based on multiple, overlapping groups. Arguing that a uniform world culture would be "no culture at all," Eliot advocated instead "a common world culture, which will yet not diminish the particularity of its constituent parts"; each person, Eliot envisioned, would belong to "a constellation of cultures," on the basis that "a people should be neither too united nor too divided" ([1946]1948). Recognizing "the difficulties, the practical impossibility, of its realization," Eliot nonetheless urged loyalty to "an unimaginable world culture" as an ideal.

43

As a whole, modernist terms for collectivity expose the era's pervasive concern with negotiating "Unity and Diversity," the title of two of Eliot's chapters. The proliferation of terms evidences the diversity in approach, varying between, on the one hand, a pervasive fear that mass consciousness involves blind adherence to an undeviating faith and, on the other, a belief that massification can be resisted either by flexible group affiliations that preserve individualism or through multiple, overlapping groups within the mass. The individualism for which modernism is more generally known thus emerges as a corrective to coercive group thinking and as a crucial element incorporated into models of community imagined in pluralist rather than monolithic ways.

SEE ALSO: *Democracy; God, Gods; International; Primitive; Readers, Reading; Unconscious; Universal*

References

Beckett, Samuel (2011). "'Le Concentrisme' and 'Jean du Chas': Two Extracts." [1920s?]. Ed. John Pilling. *Modernism/modernity* 18.4 (November): 883–886.

Eliot, T. S. (1948). "Appendix: Broadcasts 1946." [1946]. In *Notes Towards the Definition of Culture*. London: Faber and Faber. 110–124.

Follett, M. P. (1918). *The New State: Group Organization, the Solution for Popular Government*. New York: Longman, Green and Co.

Forster, E. M. (1915). Rev. of *The Voyage Out* by Virginia Woolf. *Daily News and Leader* (April 8), 7.

Freud, Sigmund (1922). *Group Psychology and the Analysis of the Ego*. [*Massenpsychologie und Ich-Analyse*, 1921]. Trans. James Strachey. London: Hogarth.

Freud, Sigmund (1930). *Civilization and its Discontents*. [*Das Unbehagen in der Kultur*, 1930]. Trans. Joan Riviere. London: Hogarth Press.

Harrison, Jane Ellen (1913). *Ancient Art and Ritual*. London: Williams and Norgate.

Holtby, Winifred (1936). *South Riding*. London: Collins.

Joyce, James (1925). "From Work in Progress." ["Here Comes Everybody"]. In *Contact Collection of Contemporary Writers* (ed. Robert McAlmon). Paris: Contact Editions and Three Mountains Press, 1925. 133–136.

Joyce, James (1939). *Finnegans Wake*. London: Faber and Faber.

Jung, C. G. (1959). "The Archetypes and the Collective Unconscious." ["Über die Archetypen des kollektiven Unbewussen," 1934]. Trans. R. F. C. Hull. In *Collected Works of C. G. Jung* (eds. Sir Herbert Read, Michael Fordham and Gerhard Adler). London: Routledge and Kegan Paul; Princeton: Princeton University Press. Vol. 9, Part 1: 3–41.

Lawrence, D. H. (1932). Letter to Katherine Mansfield, 12 December 1915. [1915] In *The Letters of D. H. Lawrence* (ed. Aldous Huxley). London: W. Heinemann. 288–290.

Le Bon, Gustave (1896). *The Crowd: A Study of the Popular Mind* [*La psychologie des foules*. Paris, F. Alcan, 1895.]. London: T. F. Unwin; New York: Macmillan.

MacCarthy, Desmond (1914). Dedication. In *The Death of a Nobody*, by Jules Romains. Trans. Desmond MacCarthy and Sydney Waterlow. New York: B.W. Huebsch; London: Howard Latimer. iii–vii.

MacCurdy, John T. (1922). *Problems in Dynamic Psychology: A Critique of Psychoanalysis and Suggested Formulations*. New York: MacMillan.

Nin, Anaïs (1975). "The Personal Life Lived Deeply." In *A Woman Speaks: The Lectures, Seminars and Interviews of Anais Nin* (ed. Evelyn J. Hinz). Chicago: Swallow Press. 148–180.

Pound, Ezra (1913). Rev. of *Odes et Prieres* by Jules Romains. *Poetry: A Magazine of Verse* 2.5 (August): 187–189.

Pound, Ezra (1918a). "The Hard and the Soft in French Poetry." *Poetry: A Magazine of Verse* 11.5 (February): 264–271.

Pound, Ezra (1918b). "Jules Romains." *The Little Review* 4.10. A Study of French Modern Poets (February): 54–61.

Romains, Jules (1926). *La vie unanime: poèmes, 1904–1907*. Paris: Gallimard.

Tönnies, Ferdinand (1955). *Community and Association*. [Gemeinshaft und Gesellschaft, 1887].Trans. Charles Price Loomis. London: Routledge and Paul; *Community and Society*. Trans. Charles Price Loomis. East Lansing: Michigan State University Press, 1957.

Trotter, W. (1916). *Instincts of the Herd in Peace and War*. London: Fisher Unwin; New York: Macmillan.

Wells, H. G. (1936). *The Idea of a World Encyclopedia*. A lecture delivered at the Royal Institution, November 28, 1936. London: Hogarth.

Wells, H. G. (1938). *World Brain*. London: Methuen and Co.

West, Rebecca (1928). "The Strange Necessity." In *The Strange Necessity: Essays and Reviews*. London: Jonathan Cape. 31–198.

West, Rebecca (1933). *St. Augustine*. London: Peter Davies; New York: D. Appleton and Co.

Whyte, William H., Jr. (1952). "Groupthink." *Fortune* (March), 114–117, 142, 146.

Woolf, Leonard (1913). Rev. of *Les Copains* by Jules Romains. *TLS* (August 7), 330.

Woolf, Leonard (1939). *Barbarians at the Gate*. New York: Harcourt, Brace and Co.

Woolf, Leonard (1967). *Downhill all the Way: An Autobiography of the Years 1919–1939*. London: Hogarth.

[Woolf, Virginia] (1917). "The Old Order." Rev. of *The Middle Years* by Henry James. *TLS* (October 18), 497–498.

Woolf, Virginia (1929). *A Room of One's Own*. London: Hogarth.

Woolf, Virginia (1941). *Between the Acts*. London: Hogarth Press.

Woolf, Virginia (1985). "The Fascination of the Pool." [1929]. In *The Complete Shorter Fiction* (ed. Susan Dick). London: Hogarth. 220–221.

[Woolf, Virginia] Stephen, Virginia (1992). "The Country in London." [1903]. In *A Passionate Apprentice: The Early Journals, 1897–1909* (ed. Mitchell A. Leaska). London: Hogarth. 177–179.

Conventional, Conventionality

Summing up Isabel Archer's fate, Ralph Touchett laments, "You wanted to look at life for yourself – but you were not allowed [. . .]. You were ground in the very mill of the conventional!" (Henry James, *The Portrait of a Lady* [1880–1881] 1908). The crushing of Isabel's imaginative freedom by "appearance" and "propriety" epitomizes the way conventional and conventionality had become, by the modernist period, highly pejorative terms. In Edith Wharton's *The Age of Innocence* (1920), spontaneous and honest conversation is inhibited by being "imprisoned in the conventional"; in Grant Allen's *The Woman Who Did* (1895), the New Woman heroine chooses "a blameless union of pure affection" over "bondage to the conventional lies and the conventional injustices" of marriage; in Joseph Conrad's *Under Western Eyes* (1911), Razumov wonders with some horror whether he might possibly have "a conventional conscience." The reaction against conventionality was pervasive and closely tied to a reaction against the middle class. In Conrad's *Chance*, the narrator reflects that de Barral, seeking a governess for his daughter, might have found "a model of all the virtues, or the repository of all knowledge, or anything equally harmless, conventional, and middle class" ([1913]1914), and in F. Scott Fitzgerald's *This Side of Paradise* (1920), when Amory's mother asks whether he has had a "horrible" two years away at school, he responds, "I adapted myself to the bourgeoisie. I became conventional."

Since mC19, the social customs and manners of the genteel middle class had been under attack for conformity, artificiality, and even hypocrisy. The modernists,

45

however, were impelled by a new and distinctively modern belief in the need for frank expression: much of their reaction against convention was fueled by a desire to be able to speak openly about the body and sex. Conventionality became synonymous with a censorship that was both legislated and imposed by public opinion. While S. P. Mais in the *Daily Express* praised James Joyce for defying "conventional reticences" in *Ulysses* (1922), D. H. Lawrence worried that *Lady Chatterley's Lover* was "so improper, according to the poor conventional fools, that it'll never be printed" ([1927]1932). When Harold Nicolson was prohibited from mentioning either Lawrence or Joyce on the BBC, the *New Statesman and Nation* cast the BBC as a group of "old men" who were "out of touch with modern thought" and whose "policy of fear and conventionality" prevented the public from "coming into contact with the chief formative influences of the day" (1931). Then too, a heightened emphasis on the importance of thinking for oneself, in the face of increasing standardization, prompted critiques of the way conventions induce passivity and self-repression. Lawrence urged the need to "break the automatism of ideals and conventions" (1922), and Virginia Woolf speculated, in a fictionalized scenario, that her difficulty in reading a nonconventional novel was perhaps due to being "merely lazy minded and conventional into the bargain" (1929).

46

Conventions were also critiqued for imposing the norms of masculinity and heterosexuality. Bernard Shaw's Vivie Warren, protesting the silence surrounding her mother's profession (prostitution), complains, "there is nothing I despise more than the wicked convention that protects these things by forbidding a woman to mention them" ([1893]1898). Virginia Woolf argued that since "men are the arbiters of [the] convention" that establishes "an order of values" in life and "since fiction is largely based on life," those values prevail in fiction as well (1929). Suggesting that convention was restrictive of homosexual relations, Israel Solon wrote of Joyce's play *Exiles* that the "two men who are in love with each other" were "bound by the letter of conventional morality more completely than most men" at the same time as they were denied "the disguises winked at by organised society" (1919). A lighthearted, male-authored article in the *Atlantic Monthly* proposed that "woman is much less conventional than man" and thus "more interesting": "unconsciously she seeks a more liberal atmosphere, while man is nearly always contented with the atmosphere that is" (1915). Marianne Moore imaged such a woman "rustling in the storm/of conventional opinion" and wielding her body and exotic dress as either "weapons or scalpels" to "dissect destiny" (1917).

Conventionality could equally signal repression in matters of literary form and approach, with unconventional writing promising more honesty, interest, and a broader range of life. F. L. Pattee, writing on the American short story, praised the *Atlantic Monthly* for selecting "the best that America could produce" and keeping "its pages free from the sentimental and the conventional" (1923). Ezra Pound extolled Joyce's *Dubliners* as the work of a realist who was "not bound by the tiresome convention that any part of life, to be interesting, must be shaped into the conventional form of a 'story'" (1914). Turning similarly against traditional plots, Mina Loy charged that the conversion of suffering into fame was merely "conventional for the heroic," and she made a plea for the lowly unfortunate whose "common tragedy is to have suffered/without having 'appeared'" (1962). At the end of WWI, Arthur Waugh welcomed a new generation of "young realists" notable for their "determination to speak the truth about the ugly things of life," rejecting "the concealing veils of sentimentality and pretence" with "an almost universal distrust of conventional consolation" (1918). Waugh foresaw "an entire revolution in the conventions of the British novel, clearing away a vast burden of traditional cant, and establishing a fresh and decent relation between the essential facts of life and their artistic revelation." Perhaps most famously, Woolf's "Mr. Bennett and Mrs. Brown" claimed that, while the narrative approach of Edwardian writers "worked admirably" for that "age and generation," for the Georgians of her own time, "those conventions are ruin, those tools are death" (1924).

Yet modernists could also be quick to criticize the hollowness of unconventionality pursued for its own sake and so, paradoxically, conventional was sometimes applied to new ways. Lascelles Abercrombie, in reviewing Lawrence's *Love Poems*, found an "admirable power" in their language but charged that their rhythmic "daring" seemed "to be really a fear of being conventional" (1913). Describing a fictionalized Bloomsbury, Mary Butts charged that despite the array of "arty" allegiances the fashionable Curtin siblings professed, they moved "in as rigid a convention as any other" (1932). But convention and unconventionality could also be more finely nuanced. E. M. Forster's *A Room with a View* exposes the way unconventionality can be either affected or authentic: Eleanor Lavish's vociferous flaunting of unconventionality – she loudly professes to "detest conventional intercourse" and to fly "in the face of conventions" – contrasts with Lucy Honeychurch's quieter struggle to honor "the emotions of which the conventions and the world disapprove" (1908). Wharton's May Welland is portrayed as "no less conventional" than her mother, yet the daughter nonetheless holds "more tolerant views" (1920). Somerset Maugham contrasts a painter-cum-stockbroker's sincere disregard of convention with the fashionable yet safe unconventionality of others, noting "it is not difficult to be unconventional in the eyes of the world when your unconventionality is the convention of your set" (1919).

Despite all the controversies, conventions were frequently recognized as essential. Refuting the claims of literary naturalism, Arnold Bennett argued that "all plots" are necessarily "a conventionalization of life," for one needs some structure in order to make sense of "unsystematized observation" (1914). Even James's Isabel Archer asks, "What's language at all but a convention?" and she

47

Conventional, Conventionality

praises Madame Merle for having "the good taste not to pretend [. . .] to express herself by original signs" ([1880–1881]1908). Woolf explained that "[a] convention in writing is not much different from a convention in manners"; together they serve the crucial function of "bridging the gulf between the hostess and her unknown guest on the one hand, the writer and his unknown reader on the other"; when relations between people change, however, "convention ceases to be a means of communication between writer and reader, and becomes instead an obstacle and an impediment" (1924). The challenge for the modernists was then to devise their own conventions, to find the right forms for their time. Whether the issue was fashion or expression, Elizabeth Bowen wisely advised, "convention is a good guide, but a deadening ruler" (1956).

SEE ALSO: *Biography, New Biography; Form, Formalism; Realism, Reality; Sentimental, Sentimentality; Shock, Shocking; Woman, New Woman*

References

22222

(1931). "The Battle of Savoy Hill." *The New Statesman and Nation* (December 12), 736–737.
Abercrombie, Lascelles (1913). "Poetry." *The Blue Review* (June): 117–122.
Allen, Grant (1895). *The Woman Who Did*. London: John Lane.
Bennett, Arnold (1914). *The Author's Craft*. New York: George H. Doran; Hodder and Stoughton.
Bowen, Elizabeth (1956). "How to Be Yourself – But Not Eccentric." *Vogue* (July), 54–55.
Butts, Mary (1932). "In Bloomsbury." In *Several Occasions*. London: Wishart.
Conrad, Joseph (1911). *Under Western Eyes*. London: Methuen.
Conrad, Joseph (1914). *Chance*. (50 copies privately printed 1913). London: Methuen.
Fitzgerald, F. Scott (1920). *This Side of Paradise*. New York: Charles Scribner's Sons.
Forster, E. M. (1908). *A Room with a View*. London: Edward Arnold.
George, W. L. [Walter Lionel] (1915). "Notes on the Intelligence of Woman." *The Atlantic Monthly* (December), 721–730.
James, Henry (1908). *The Portrait of a Lady*. [1880–1881]. *The Novels and Tales of Henry James*. New York Edition. New York: Charles Scribner's Sons. Vol. 3–4.
Lawrence, D. H. (1922). *Fantasia of the Unconscious*. New York: Thomas Seltzer.
Lawrence, D. H. (1932). Letter to The Hon. Dorothy Brett, 8 March 1927. [1927]. In *The Letters of D. H. Lawrence* (ed. Aldous Huxley). London: W. Heinemann. 679–681.
Loy, Mina (1962). "Untitled.". *Between Worlds* 2.1 (Fall–Winter): 27.
Maugham, Somerset (1919). *The Moon and Sixpence*. London: W. Heinemann.
Moore, Marianne (1917). "Those Various Scalpels." *Lantern* 25 (Spring): 50–51.
Pattee, Fred Lewis (1923). *The Development of the American Short Story*. New York: Biblo and Tannen.
Pound, Ezra (1914). "Dubliners and Mr James Joyce." *The Egoist* 1 (July 15): 267.
S.P.B.M. [Mais, S. P.] (1922). "Odd Contrasts." *The Daily Express* (March 25), 4.
Shaw, Bernard (1898). *Mrs. Warren's Profession*. [1893]. In *Plays Pleasant and Unpleasant*. 2 vols. London: G. Richards. The first volume, containing three Unpleasant Plays: 163–244.

Solon, Israel (1919). "Exiles: A Discussion of James Joyce's Plays." *The Little Review* 5 (January): 22–23.

Waugh, Arthur (1918). "War Poetry (1914–1918)." *The Quarterly Review* (October), 380–400.

Wharton, Edith (1920). *The Age of Innocence*. New York: D. Appleton.

Woolf, Virginia (1924). *Mr Bennett and Mrs Brown*. London: Hogarth.

Woolf, Virginia (1929). "Women and Fiction." *The Forum* (New York) (March), 179–183.

Coterie, Bloomsbury

Coterie has been commonly identified with modernism, most frequently in unsympathetic terms. The pejorative connotations were crystallized by the critic Van Wyck Brooks in his 1941 talk at Columbia University entitled "Primary Literature and Coterie Literature." Modernist cosmopolitan intellectuals, Brooks charged, had lost touch with the literary mainstream's commitment to national culture and positive moral values, isolating themselves in a small, special-interest elite. Coterie's previous connotations, however, had been multiple and complex. Derived from the French word for associations of *cotiers* or tenants of humble cottages, the first English usages of coterie (rhymed by Byron with lottery) referred either to political factions, generally revolutionary or bound by religious affiliations, or to friends and acquaintances in high society, often congregating at a fashionable lady's salon. The word's social history thus incorporated a tension between banding together for a common, often minority, cause and belonging to a privileged in-group. As C19 saw the increasing formation of small groups of artists and writers, criticism of the privilege and exclusiveness in social coteries bled over easily to attacks on aesthetic coteries. Yet, at the same time, coterie maintained its earlier sense of marginalized groups, relevant to writers barred from traditional venues for publication due to prevailing censorship and the expectations, in mass culture, for easily marketable texts. In the modernist period, coterie thus bore various and contradictory implications. With underlying meanings spanning social prestige, hedonism, intellectual and sexual freedom, and free speech and publishing, coterie and its cognates are some of modernism's most controversial terms.

As a label, coterie was used in three different ways: for people, for literary magazines and small presses, and, more broadly as Van Wyck Brooks employed it, for linguistic and/or cultural form. In the first, most literal and narrow usage, coterie applied to groups of friends or artists who could be identified by a collective name. The groups themselves, however, were strikingly unlike: putative coteries included C19 socialite groups like "the grand set" and "the smart set," described as "two totally different sections of the best London Society" (Hamilton [1885]1972); subcultures as diverse as Rupert Brooke's pastoral Neo Pagans and the London-oriented Bright Young Things; and a broad range of intellectual and aesthetic groups such as the Bloomsbury Group, Gertrude Stein's or Paulette Nardal's Parisian salons, the Greenwich Village Bohemians, the Birmingham Group of working-class writers, and the numerous "schools" of artists identified by "isms." Perhaps no group, however, came to "stand" for coterie more than "Bloomsbury"; attitudes toward Bloomsbury, furthermore, capture the general ambiguity of coterie as an evaluative term.

"Bloomsbury" refers to a group of writers, artists, and intellectuals whose association began in informal Thursday evening gatherings organized by Virginia (Stephen) Woolf's brother Thoby around 1905 and expanded, with the notable inclusions of Roger Fry and T.S. Eliot, as a Memoir Club in 1920. Yet, as Mary Butts stated, "'Bloomsbury' [...] as a collective noun" came "to stand for something" larger – something that aroused "a complicated reaction, including envy and dislike" ([1936]1998). "Say 'Bloomsbury'," she wrote, and such associations will arise as "the Intelligentsia in excelsis," "those barren leaves," "mental hermaphrodites," and "brittle intellectuals." Just why Bloomsbury came to be such a powder-keg term is difficult to say. Wyndham Lewis, one of the more rebellious leaders in the attack, used his character Pierpoint in *The Apes of God* to castigate Bloomsbury as "a select and snobbish club" and a "new cosmopolitan Bohemia," who represented the "monied middleclass descendents of victorian [sic] literary splendor" (1930). In the conservative *Library Review*, Stanley Snaith led an equally emotional charge against Bloomsbury as a clique (1931). Yet the vehemence of these negative views suggests deeper causes: for Butts, "the English shame and fear before the fact of intelligence," plus, in Lewis, the "exceedingly male" contempt, bolstered by the "neuroticism of virility," for the "intricacies" of "feminine elements" and "the snobberies, the pedantries of culture." Virginia Woolf herself blamed sexual antagonism, describing *The Apes of God* – which her press nonetheless offered to publish – as Lewis's "Bloomsbury Black Book in which every sod[omite] and every Saph[ist] is to be pilloried" ([1930]1975–1980). Yet reviewer Stanley Snaith inadvertently revealed something more fundamental at stake: the nature indeed of "reality." Snaith, seeking to return literature to "its old sanity and stature," credited Woolf with "an obviously sincere search for reality," yet opted himself for the alternative "bracing tang of reality" in novels by Wells and Bennett, claiming "reality" to be something with which Bloomsbury had "lost touch." Bloomsbury was not of course the only putative coterie representing a contentious other way of seeing the world: coteries were to be found in the privileged center as well. Reacting against the privilege of the male insiders' elite, Dorothy Richardson protested that "the feminist point of view" had been excluded by "the man modiste, the pub, and the club" (1925). Evelyn Waugh's *Decline and Fall* (1928) satirized the aristocrats of the Bollinger Club (a fictionalized version of the exclusive Oxford Bullingdon Club, noted for drunkenness) who destroy a Matisse, a grand piano, a poem, and the career of the middle-class Paul Pennyfeather, while remaining protected by their moneyed positions.

The extent to which informal associations were really discrete groups was also part of the debate, the labels generally being taken less seriously by putative members than by the public and the press. "Neo Pagans" began as a kindly but slightly mocking term used by Virginia Woolf for a younger group clustered around Rupert Brooke ([1911]1975–1980); "Bloomsbury" derived from Molly MacCarthy's light coinage "Bloomsberries," referring to their meeting in the Bloomsbury area of London (WC1) (Bell, 1956); Evelyn Waugh recalled that it was "the newspapers who dubbed us 'the bright young people' and spoiled our fun" (1964). Even the term postimpressionist was apparently a response to a media request. Desmond MacCarthy recollected that, at the time of the first exhibition, Roger Fry was so pressured by a journalist to provide a name that he said, "Oh, let's just call them post-impressionists; at any rate, they came after the impressionists" (1945). Although Leonard and Virginia Woolf used Bloomsbury as an affectionate term for close friends and family, they dismissed the notion that it was an exclusive and unified group. Virginia Woolf described Bloomsbury to a Harvard student as "a word that stands for very little," being "largely a creation of the journalists" ([1932]1975–1980). Leonard Woolf commented that "Bloomsbury" "never existed in the form given to it by the outside world," which he considered obsessed with the fiction of "a largely imaginary group of persons with largely imaginary objects and characteristics" (1964). Viewed from inside, groups were porous and diverse; from outside, they seemed unified and discrete.

Positively viewed, coteries were defended for their role in bringing like-minded writers together and creating safe enclaves where artistic freedom could flourish and marginalized voices could be heard. Edith Wharton celebrated "the famous French 'Salon'" as "the best school of talk and of ideas that the world has ever known" (1919). In her unfinished novel about the Neo Pagans, Gwen Raverat wrote that though "each of us alone might still doubt his powers," as a group "all the possibilities of the world seemed open to us" ([1916]2003). Although T. S. Eliot acknowledged the value of an artist who is "not a member of a family or of a caste or of a party or of a coterie," he also defended groups as "easier to find, easier to talk about" and "more inspiring to watch than the silent struggles of a single man" (1919). Alain Locke affirmed the importance of "a new group psychology" for African American intellectuals to foster "a more positive self-respect and self-reliance" (1925). Writing to Marshall McLuhan, Ezra Pound called for "a widening of the northern coterie" to encourage the production and publication of Canadian poetry (1951). Coterie formation also allowed freedom of expression in a time of censorship: Maynard Keynes asserted that the Apostles at Cambridge (a secret society devoted to open discussion) "repudiated entirely customary morals, conventions, and traditional wisdom," and Natalie Barney's *Academie des*

51

Femmes – the prototype for the lesbian salon in *The Well of Loneliness* (1928) – supported Radclyffe Hall when her novel was charged with obscenity. In Paris of the 1930s, the Martinican sisters Paulette and Jane Nardal founded a literary salon, which, as reported by Michel Fabre (1973), Paulette preferred to call a "cercle d'amis" to distance it from the bourgeois social salons; here, as Léopold Senghor recalled, "African Negroes, West Indians, and American Negroes used to get together" ([1960]1974), creating an international foundation for the négritude movement in France.

Beyond its reference to social groups and friendships, coterie designated writers and artists who published in the same small-circulation magazines or who were published by the same small press. Here, class antagonism aimed at the powerful and wealthier segments of society carried over into antagonism toward the perceived power of coterie publication. Frank Swinnerton condemned the "coterie system" of book reviews as "partial and mean," "full of little jealousies, little favouritisms, little snobberies, and little retaliations for past affronts" (1932). R. G. Cox, commenting on the state of English periodicals, decried the "mushroom growth of 'little magazines'," asserting that they "represent small groups more or less out of touch with each other and with any common centre of critical opinion," so that "a new writer achieves a coterie reputation and a market value without ever once coming up against any other standards than those of his group" (1946). Yet coterie publication brought together writers who sought both the freedom to write unhampered by prevailing norms and social mores and a source of income for their work. An article by "B. L." about chapbook publishing and the Scottish Literary Renaissance wrote of the need for "a sufficiently good little group of local writers and artists capable of an expression of themselves on a certain level, and with such a significance in their work as is distinctively local, or at least regional" (1921). Suggesting that coteries are not limited to the well-off or highbrow, T. S. Eliot noted their practical value, arguing that "a group is even a useful thing" for "advertisement": "a dozen people can attract more attention together than dispersedly; and if they can attract enough attention, some of them may be able to make a living" (1919). Various small-circulation magazines defended the need for alternative publishing venues while protesting the label of coterie: Gwyn Jones, editor of *The Welsh Review*, asserted his periodical was "not the mouthpiece of a coterie" nor was he "a steam-roller appointed to flatten out the styles and opinions of his contributors," noting as well that "next month's poems are strikingly different from this month's" (1939). Explaining the policies of the journal *transition*, Eugene Jonas stated that it was "never conceived [. . .] to be the review of a narrow group, clique, chapelle" or "movement"; it sought "to develop organically," to give voice merely to "certain parallel tendencies among the fresh elements of various nations" (1928). Ironically, Chaman Lall, the editor of the literary periodical *Coterie* (1919–1921), named for a wartime group of

Oxford undergraduates who met to read poetry, quoted an attack on its not being *enough* of a coterie: a review in the *Daily Herald* had stated, whereas "'coterie' signifies 'a set of persons associated by exclusive interests'," "the ineffectiveness of this quarterly is due to the individualism of its contributors," "its lack of collective significance," and its failure to be "a coherent group-movement" (1920–1921). Lall juxtaposed these remarks to the *Manchester Guardian*'s contrasting description of *Coterie* as an "enterprising quarterly" and pointed out the absurdity of expecting a publication to be only one thing.

The broadest meaning of coterie designated intellectual or poetic language as coterie speech, shared by writers and their limited audiences. T. S. Eliot's *The Waste Land* was derided for being "incomprehensible" to the "general reader," the poet's "suffering inscrutable to all but a chosen coterie of his similars" (Munson, 1924). Gertrude Stein's work was likewise accused of being impossible for anyone who did "not belong to her coterie" to understand (Flanner, 1940). A diatribe derived from his talk at Columbia appeared in Brooks's autobiographical novel *The Opinions of Oliver Allston*, where his mouthpiece Allston descries modernist "coterie-writers" as an elite, urban group, cut off from "the life that is natural to mankind" and writing "in a private language of personal friends" (1941). For Dorothy Livesay, the problem with "speak[ing] to a coterie" was that, as she noted of her fellow Canadian A. J. M. Smith's poetry, it resulted in a "lack of range" (1944). Reacting against Stephen Spender's recollection that he had been treated, by Auden, as one of "the Gang" and finding in John Maynard Keynes's Bloomsbury self-identification proof that "the triumph of the social-personal (or 'club,' we may now call it) principle is complete," F. R. Leavis condemned "that coterie influence, which pervaded the literary world at large" and replaced "real standards" with "personal and coterie considerations" (1951). The Canadian critic Pelham Edgar, while sympathetic to Virginia Woolf's work, worried that she would find "a more limited audience than her talent deserves": "her doom is the coterie" (1933).

Lurking behind criticisms of coterie as private language was a larger debate about the state of modern culture. Van Wyck Brooks's talk spurred a critical protest in the pages of the left-leaning *Partisan Review*. William Phillips asserted that "modern art" "could not have come into being except through the formation by the intelligentsia of a distinct group culture," as the only way "to resist being absorbed by the norms of belief and behavior" (1941). Dwight Macdonald defended the right of coterie writers "to be skeptical and critical" and mocked the idea that "they perversely prefer to isolate themselves from 'humanity,'" claiming that their audiences were small only because "popular cultural values are debased" (1941). Macdonald also castigated Van Wyck Brooks's call for literature on the "great themes" of "courage, justice, mercy, honor, love" as a reflection of "totalitarian cultural values," exemplary of "the drift towards totalitarianism" in the

53

US; W. H. Auden joined the fray by proposing, "The Masses resent 'coterie' art, not for its real vice, which is a failure to attain an all-inclusive vision of the age, but for its real virtue, which is a refusal to accept fully the contemporary illusion," democratically adding however, "Whenever the word Masses is used we must read the words 'myself in my weaker moments'" (1942). Such proponents of modernism added significantly to an understanding of how and why coterie literature came about; nonetheless, they were possibly as significant for alienating audiences as for winning support. Defending skepticism, pessimism, and alienation from traditional values, they reinforced the idea of modernism as coterie art by deflecting attention away from modernism's intense engagement with its time.

SEE ALSO: *Common Mind, Group Thinking; Democracy; Difficulty, Obscurity; Highbrow, Middlebrow, Lowbrow; Readers, Reading; Queer, Gay; Reality, Realism*

References

Auden, W. H. (1942). "La trahison d'un clerc." *Perspectives* 5.2 (January): 12.

B. L. (1921). "The World of Books, A Literary Causerie." *The Montrose Review* (June 3): 6.

Bell, Clive (1956). *Old Friends: Personal Recollections*. London: Chatto & Windus.

Brooks, Van Wyck (1941a). *The Opinions of Oliver Allston*. New York: E. P. Dutton.

Brooks, Van Wyck (1941b). "What is Primary Literature?" Shortened version of "Primary Literature and Coterie Literature," a talk presented at Columbia University, 10 September 1941. *The Yale Review* (September): 25–37.

Butts, Mary (1998). "Bloomsbury." [1936]. Eds. Camilla Bagg and Nathalie Blondel. *Modernism/modernity* 5.2 (April): 32–45.

Cox, R. G. (1946). "Mixed Currency." Rev. of *The Mint: A Miscellany of Literature, Art and Criticism* (ed. Geoffrey Grigson). *Scrutiny* 14.1 (Summer): 59–61.

Edgar , Pelham (1933). *The Art of the Novel from 1700 to the Present Time*. New York: Macmillan.

Eliot, T. S. (1919). "The Post-Georgians." *The Athenaeum* (April 11), 171.

Fabre, Michel (1973). "Autour de Maran." *Présence africaine* 86 (2nd trimester): 165–172.

Flanner, Janet (1940). "History Tramps Down the Champs Elysées." Rev. of *Paris, France* by Gertrude Stein. *The New York Herald Tribune* (June 23), 1.

Hamilton, E. W. (1972). "Diary entry, 20 May, 1885." [1885]. In *The Diary of Sir Edward Walter Hamilton* (ed. Dudley W. R Balhman). 2 vols. Oxford: Clarendon. Vol. 2: 867.

Jolas, Eugene (1928). "Notes." *transition: An International Quarterly for Creative Experiment* 14 (Fall): 180–185.

Jones, Gwyn (1939). "Editorial." *The Welsh Review* 1.1 (February): 2–3.

Lall, Chaman (1920–1921). "Editorial." *Coterie* 1.6/7 (Winter): 3–5.

Leavis, F. R. (1951). "Keynes, Spender, and Currency Values." Rev. of *World Within World* by Stephen Spender and *The Life of John Maynard Keynes* by R. F. Harrod. *Scrutiny* (June): 45–55.

Lewis, Wyndham (1930). *The Apes of God*. London: Arthur.

Livesay, Dorothy (1944). Rev. of *News of the Phoenix and Other Poems*, by A. J. M. Smith. *First Statement* 2.6 (April): 18–19.

Locke, Alain (1925). "Enter the New Negro." *Survey Graphic*, Harlem: Mecca of the New Negro (March), 631–639.

MacCarthy, Desmond (1945). "The Art Quake of 1910." *The Listener* (February 1), 123–124, 129.

Macdonald, Dwight (1941). "Kulturbolschewismus is Here." *The Partisan Review* 8 (November–December): 442–451.

Munson, Gorham B. (1924). "The Esotericism of T. S. Eliot." *1924* 1 (July 1): 3–10.

Phillips, William (1941). "The Intellectuals' Tradition." *The Partisan Review* 8 (November–December): 481–490.

Pound, Ezra (1951). Letter to Marshall McLuhan, 20 June 1951. H. Marshall McLuhan Fonds. National Archives of Canada, Ottawa. MG 31, D 156, Vol. 34.

Raverat, Gwen (2003). "Two Excerpts from an Unfinished Novel." In *Virginia Woolf and the Raverats: A Different Sort of Friendship* (ed. William Pryor). Bath: Clear. 29–31.

Richardson, Dorothy (1925). "Women in The Arts: Some Notes on the Eternally Conflicting Demands of Humanity and Art." *Vanity Fair* (May), 47, 100.

Senghor, Léopold Sédar (1974). "Letter of February 1960." [1960]. Trans. Ellen Conroy Kennedy. In *Black Writers in French* (ed. Lilyan Kesteloot). Philadelphia: Temple University Press. 55–56.

Snaith, Stanley (1931). "Picnic in Bloomsbury." *Library Review: A Magazine on Libraries and Literature* 19 (Autumn): 105–110.

Swinnerton, Frank. (1932). "Reviewers." In *Authors and the Book Trade*, London: Gerald Howe. 103–122.

Waugh, Evelyn (1928). *Decline and Fall*. London: Chapman and Hall.

Waugh, Evelyn (1964). *A Little Learning: The First Volume of an Autobiography*. London: Chapman and Hall.

Wharton, Edith (1919). *French Ways and Their Meaning*. New York: D. Appleton.

Woolf, Leonard (1964). *Beginning Again*. London: Hogarth.

Woolf, Virginia (1975–1980). Letter to Clive Bell, 18 April 1911. [1911]. In *The Letters of Virginia Woolf* (eds. Nigel Nicolson and Joanne Trautmann). 6 vols. London: Chatto & Windus. Vol. 1: 460.

Woolf, Virginia (1975–1980). Letter to Harmon H. Goldstone, 16 August 1932. [1932]. In *The Letters of Virginia Woolf* (eds. Nigel Nicolson and Joanne Trautman). 6 vols. London: Chatto & Windus. Vol. 5: 90–91.

Woolf, Virginia (1975–1980). Letter to Vanessa Bell, 27? October 1930. [1930]. In *The Letters of Virginia Woolf* (eds. Nigel Nicolson and Joanne Trautman). 6 vols. London: Chatto & Windus. Vol. 4: 235–238.

Democracy

In the modernist period, problems with defining democracy begin, rather than end, with the attainment of universal franchise, or the right to vote. As Raymond Williams explains, in C19, democracy was still a revolutionary term signifying popular power (from *demos* (people) and *kratos* (rule)), although its meaning was gradually shifting from the predominantly negative connotations of anarchic mob rule to the positive sense of a form of ordered government in which the body of the people has participatory rights. With the increasing empowerment of elected representatives and the extension of the vote, at least in theory, to all adult citizens – working-class men (UK 1867), African American men (US 1870), and women (Australia 1902; Canada 1917; UK 1918, 1928; Southern Rhodesia 1919; US 1920) – democracy came increasingly to signify representative democracy (as opposed to direct democracy) and, by eC20, to be accepted by almost all political parties as a positive belief. After "winning the vote," controversies over democracy shifted to the problems of acquiring functional democracy in the modern contexts of social and economic inequalities in the electorate, the vast scale of mass society, and mass communication as a disseminating mode.

Democracy was interpreted so variously, however, that T. S. Eliot concluded it was "a term that needed to be, not only defined, but illustrated, almost every time" it was used ([1946]1948). Democratic could describe a form of government, a philosophical belief, or social, economic, or cultural practices. Democracy might

ABC*D*EFGHIJKLMNOPQRSTUVWXYZ

Modernism: Keywords, First Edition. Melba Cuddy-Keane, Adam Hammond, and Alexandra Peat.
© 2014 Melba Cuddy-Keane. Published 2014 by John Wiley & Sons, Ltd.

signify an ideal to be pursued, or the actual functioning of existing democratic states. Putative democracies could appear as anti-democratic in practice, and what was democratic in one view could seem anti-democratic in another. Praise or support for democracy varies according to what writers take it to mean, but as Eliot indicates, that meaning is not always self-evident in the single word.

Fundamentally different interpretations animated a 1931 series of BBC broadcasts by Leonard Woolf and Lord Eustace Percy on the topic "Can Democracy Survive?" (Adams, 1933). Woolf, beginning from philosophical and ethical first principles, defined democracy as the belief that "the everyday happiness of ordinary people" is as important as the happiness of the military and aristocratic classes, and he argued the corollaries of equal access to education, economic equality, independence of thought, and freedom of choice. Woolf further defined democratic ideals by identifying antithetical forces: (i) nationalism, imperialism, communism, and fascism, all of which depend on centralized authority; (ii) capitalism, which concentrates wealth in the hands of a few; and (iii) "standardization," which conditions individuals to follow leaders like sheep. Percy countered with an economic approach, analyzing the existing conditions of "modern industrial democracy." Democracy, he argued, came about in C19 because people wanted "the freedom to accumulate wealth," and he claimed that the current loss of faith in democracy – that "vague word" – had been caused by the failure of profits from production to match demands for income. Identifying the problem as living on "promissory notes," both technically in sense of the nation's borrowed money and attitudinally in terms of living in expectation of increased future income, Percy urged two lessons from Fascist Italy: self-sacrifice rather than self-interest and self-reliance based on acquired skills. Woolf and Percy agreed on the need for parliamentary government and the importance of thinking for oneself; however, while Woolf ended by urging the extension of democratic principles to minorities within European states and to the whole of the British Empire, so that democratic principles would cease to be "a perpetual monopoly of the white race," Percy concluded with the need for both England and the individual to learn to take care of themselves.

The BBC debate captures one of the basic tensions in democracy: equal opportunity versus individual rights. Democracy in the first view was closely linked to democratic education, combining opportunities for broad personal growth and social justice. In the US, John Dewey's *Democracy and Education* (1916) argued that democracy is "more than a form of government": it is "a mode of associated living, of conjoint communicated experience," and democratic education must therefore unite individual growth with cooperative pluralist understanding and readiness for social change. W. E. B. Du Bois, like Woolf beginning from first principles, defined democracy as "a method of realizing the broadest measure of justice for all human beings," and he consequently argued

57

the need to educate "generation after generation" in "the whole experience of the [human] race for the benefit of the future," not excluding "women or Negroes or the poor or any class" ([1912]1920). In the UK, similar views appear in writings for the Workers' Educational Association: R. H. Tawney's outline for "Democratic Education" argued the workers' right to study for the purposes of a "reasonable and humane conduct of life" (1914); the labour historian G. D. H. Cole argued that working-class students deserved a new model of education, "an essentially democratic and co-operative method of give and give between tutors and students" (1923).

As the BBC debate indicates, however, democracy could signify either the duty to promote equal opportunity and inclusive culture or the right to individual freedom and self-determination. The latter meaning informs C. Hugh Douglas's *Economic Democracy*, serialized in *The New Age* and enthusiastically reviewed by Ezra Pound. Rejecting "ballot-box" democracy, the banking system, and existing capitalism as various forms of locating power in the hands of a few, Douglas proposed both return of profits to employees and the issuing of debt-free credit in the form of national dividends "to obtain effective distribution of the results and to restore personal initiative" (1920b). Claiming that taxation is "legalised robbery" (1931), Douglas argued that "genuine democracy" means not "the 'rights' of majorities" but conditions in which "the will of all individuals shall prevail over their own affairs" (1920a). Known as Social Credit, Douglas's approach spawned political parties in Canada and New Zealand, but it transformed into broader cultural critique in the hands of Ezra Pound. Adamant himself about the perniciousness of usury and the international financial industry, which he claimed supported wars to make money from debt, Pound advocated economic democracy as "an alternative to bloody and violent revolutions" (1920). Yet his support for democracy in this particular form became entangled with another, more common, and yet more slippery, usage: democracy as cultural attitude.

Applied to culture, democracy was used in highly idiosyncratic and individual ways, bending to serve a writer's particular stance or belief. Thus, while Pound championed economic democracy for its stance against the "sacrifice of the individual intelligence" to "external organization" (1920), he called on the artist "to defy the subversive pressure of commercial advantage" and the "mediocre spirit which is the bane and hidden terror of democracy" (1915). In the latter use, democracy refers to American culture, its cultured gentility, and indeed its censorship of the revolutionary arts. The artist, whose "chance for existence," Pound claimed, "is equal to that of the bushman," has "dabbled in [this kind of] democracy long enough" (1914). Writing, however, in the same journal in which Pound reviewed Douglas, Mina Loy proclaimed a new "Democracy of The Spirit," which she defined as "government by creative imagination" (1921). Alike with Pound in opposing "the Dummy Public, originated by the Press, financed by the Capitalist," and above all militarism, Loy nonetheless coined the term, "Psycho-Democracy," placing cultural democracy and the artist on the same side. Advocating "intellectual heroism as a popular ideal in place of physical heroism" and "individual psychology in place of mob-psychology," Loy focused optimistically on the power of an active minority to transform the social system. D. H. Lawrence offered a third possibility: bifurcating democracy into two differing material and cultural forms. Lawrence stated that "Democracy and Socialism rest upon the Equality of Man, which is the Average" (1919; 1936), a principle that he accepted as "sound enough" as long as provisions for such equality focused on material needs. In all other ways, Lawrence argued, the individual is a pure singularity: never to be merged into "Oneness," never even to be "comprehended by any other self." At this level, there can be no question of equality, which depends on comparison: "There is no comparing or estimating. There is only the strange recognition of *present otherness*." And yet he named this mystical perception "Democracy, the new order" ([1919]1936).

The slipperiness, indeed messiness, of democracy emerges even more strongly in disparate views of democratic writing, pertaining to both content and style or, as Louis Untermeyer put it, "a democracy of spirit and a democracy of speech" (1919). Democratic spirit, however, could mean celebrating the "common man" or including everyone: Untermeyer found Whitman's "wider aspect of democracy" in poetry that rejected "little salons and erudite groups" in favor of "a glorification of the ordinary man" (1921), whereas Virginia Woolf suggested that "the art of a truly democratic age" would emerge with the eradication of the class system and its privileging of middle-class writers, making the act of writing accessible to every walk of life (1928). Harriet Monroe used democratic to imply reaching the broadest readership: the poet, she wrote, "must speak for the many," and the many "must not only hear but understand," or "modern democracy must go uninspired" (1914). Democratic style was conceived even more varyingly, applying indeed to fully opposite forms. In an interview in *The New York Times* by Joyce Kilmer, entitled "Free Verse Hampers Poets and Is Undemocratic," writer Josephine Preston Peabody stated that "Whitman was a democrat in principle, but not in poetic practice" since his free verse "lacked strongly stressed, intelligible, communal music"; arguing that "the most democratic thing" is "the rhythm of the heart-beat," Peabody defended "traditional" forms that reach "the hearts of the people" (1916). Louis Untermeyer similarly praised poets who focused on "the casual and commonplace" and used "ordinary speech," and he labeled those poets "aristogogues" who sought only "to see, to record or create beautiful and precious things" (1919). Yet for others, democratic "speech" meant precisely the freedom to break away from traditional conventions and to think and feel in new ways. Both Ezra Pound and William Carlos Williams enthusiastically quoted a review celebrating the "revolutionary" character of the poetry in the magazine *Others*: J. B. Kerfoot had called it "the expression of a democracy of feeling rebelling against an aristocracy of form" – the latter referring to the same traditional forms that Peabody found democratic (1915). H. L. Mencken, less convinced by the "highly dubious rumble-bumble about the 'inherent Americanism' and soaring democracy of the movement," nevertheless praised *Others*'s originality and freshness, lauding the free verse movement for "an effective war on the cliché," which purged "the verse of the nation of much of its old banality in subject and phrase" (1919). Gertrude Stein drew a stronger parallel between democratic egalitarianism and style, claiming that she "threw away punctuation" in order to get "this evenness of everybody having a vote" (Haas [1946]1962– 1964). Virginia Woolf united egalitarianism in speech and freedom in spirit: words are "highly democratic" in their belief that "one word is as good as another" (1937), while "the precious prerogatives of the democratic art of prose" are "its freedom, its fearlessness, its flexibility" (1927).

Democratic writing could thus be defined as addressing the majority or being diverse and eclectic enough to represent all. It could ground itself in the common and traditional or it could be a reforming, revolutionary force. Despite divided opinions about these questions – often within writers themselves – all these references to democratic writing, whether achieved or envisioned, signify something good. In contrast, a rising tide of dissatisfaction with functioning democracy signaled a crisis of disillusionment and disbelief.

60

Defined initially against its "external" enemy, aristocracy, democracy became an increasingly conflicted term, undermined internally by what came to be called, after James Russell Lowell (1884), democracy's "disease." The conservative humanist Irving Babbitt blamed America's "standardized mediocrity" for "inferior types of leadership," positing the "danger of producing in the name of democracy one of the most trifling brands of the human Species that the world has yet seen," and reminding his readers of "Byron's definition of democracy as an 'aristocracy of blackguards'" (1924). The radical Sinclair Lewis offered a similar critique through his fictional character coincidentally named George Babbitt, whose stereotypical middle-class membership in a small town's "Good Citizens' League" aligns him with the belief "that American Democracy did not imply any equality of wealth, but did demand a wholesome sameness of thought, dress, painting, morals, and vocabulary" (*Babbitt*, 1922). The too easy slippage from democracy to "tyranny" was the basis of Lewis's *It Can't Happen Here* (1935), in which a president elected by popular vote on a platform resembling Social Credit turns America into a Fascist regime; in the eyes of the protagonist, the true culprit is less "Big Business" than "advocates of Democracy" who have no "notion what the word ought to mean," and "the conscientious, respectable, lazy-minded" ordinary citizens who "let the demagogues wriggle in." Similarly locating democracy's fault line in its tendency to centralized authority, Wyndham Lewis railed against the "farce" of democracy and the "subjugation" imposed by "The Democratic

Educationalist State," in which "the imposition of the will of the ruler through the press and other publicity channels" makes a mockery of the "free citizen" (1926). In a more trenchant analysis, Walter Lippmann posited the source of the problem in an "image of democracy" that was "derived from the self-contained village" and fundamentally unworkable in the new mass scale. In his analysis, modernity redefines democracy, making it vulnerable to "the manufacture of consent," the inadequacy of the press as "a Court of Public Opinion," and above all, "the failure of self-governing people to transcend their casual experience and their prejudice" (1922). Urging a need to abandon "the original dogma of democracy" with its "theory of the omnicompetent citizen," Lippmann argued, "Never has democratic theory been able to conceive itself in the context of a wide and unpredictable environment" and that "dangerous crises are incompatible with democracy," because "to act quickly a very few must decide and the rest follow rather blindly" (1922). While such critiques were aimed at existing, not ideal, democracy, the crisis of disbelief targeted fundamental contradictions at democracy's core.

Democracy was increasingly torn between the ideal of government by the people and the need, again in modern conditions of scale, for specialization and expertise. As India moved toward independence, tensions arose between efforts to eradicate the inequities of the caste system and the complexities of C20 governance. Sarvepalli Radhakrishna, a future Prime Minister of India, contrasted the initially positive response to democracy "as a release from autocratic rule" with "the growing realization that government is a technical art and only those skilled in it can be the rulers," concluding, "Democracy in its actual working rarely permits a country to be governed by its ablest men" (1929). Yet another tension lay between democracy and minorities. Given democracy's etymological roots in rule of the people, Beatrice Webb asked, "Who are 'the people?'" For minorities living under majority rule, she argued, "a democratically elected Government" might seem "as tyrannous as an autocratic monarch" (1933).

Given such conflicting uses of democracy, the modernist period confronted an overwhelming paradox. Following Woodrow Wilson's famous declaration, "The world must be made safe for democracy" (1917), democracy became the slogan justifying involvement in the two World Wars and the following Cold War; yet the ironic realization that wartime conditions meant suspensions of democratic rights and freedoms led to further, profound critiques of the anti-democratic operations of putatively democratic states. The impasse was captured in Winston Churchill's definition of democracy as "the worst form of government, except for all the other forms that have been tried" (1947) and E. M. Forster's limiting his "cheers" for democracy to two but not three, reserving his highest allegiance for "Love, the beloved Republic" as the one true determiner of ethical relations with others in the world ([1938]1939). Yet there were signs of new directions as well. T. S. Eliot argued that "the modern question as popularly put is: 'democracy is dead; what is to replace it?' whereas it should be: 'the frame of democracy has been destroyed: how can we, out of the materials at hand, build a new structure in which democracy can live?''' (1928). Sinclair Lewis's *It Can't Happen Here* ends with a muted hope for a "Revived Traditional Democracy," spurred by "a new feeling" and a revival of the "free, inquiring, critical spirit." And Leonard Woolf ended his broadcast by replacing the BBC's proposed question "Can democracy survive?" with the pungent rejoinder: "Can the modern world survive at all without democracy?"

SEE ALSO: *Atom, Atomic; Common Man; Common Mind, Group Thinking; Fascism; Readers, Reading*

References

Adams, Mary (ed.) (1933). *The Modern State*. By Leonard Woolf, Lord Eustace Percy, Mrs. Sidney Webb, Professor W. G. S. Adams, and Sir Arthur Salter. London: George Allen and Unwin.

Babbitt, Irving (1924). *Democracy and Leadership*. Boston: Houghton Mifflin.

Churchill, Winston (1947). Speech, November 11. The Official Report, House of Commons (5th Series), Vol. 444, cc 206-07.

Cole, G. D. H. (1923). "Workers' Education: Achievements–Needs–Prospects, I and II." *The Highway: A Monthly Review of Adult Education and the Journal of the Workers' Educational Association,* (April), 97–98; (May), 114–115.

Dewey, John (1916). *Democracy and Education: An Introduction to the Philosophy of Education*. New York: Macmillan.

Douglas, C. H. (1920a). *Credit-Power and Democracy*. London: Cecil Palmer.

Douglas, C. H. (1920b). *Economic Democracy*. London: Cecil Palmer.

Douglas, C. H. (1931). *Warning Democracy* London: C. M. Grieve.

Du Bois, W. E. B. (1920). "Of the Ruling of Man: the Call." ["Disenfranchisement," Speech to the National American Woman Suffrage Association, November 24, 1912.] In *Darkwater: Voices from Within the Veil*. New York: Harcourt, Brace, and Howe. 134–162.

Eliot, T. S. (1928). "The Literature of Fascism." *Criterion* 8.31 (December): 280–290.

Eliot, T. S. (1948). "Appendix: Broadcasts 1946." [1946]. In *Notes Towards the Definition of Culture*. London: Faber and Faber. 110–124.

Forster, E. M. (1939). *What I Believe*. ["Two Cheers for Democracy," 1938]. London: Hogarth Press.

Haas, Robert. B (1962–1964). "Gertrude Stein Talking: A Transatlantic Interview." [1946]. *Uclan Review* Part I. 8.2 (Summer 1962): 3–11. Part II. 9.1 (Spring 1963): 40–48. Part III. 9.2 (Winter 1964): 44–48.

Kerfoot, J. B. (1915). "The Latest Books." *Life* (September 23), 568.

Kilmer, Joyce (1916). "Free Verse Hampers Poets and Is Undemocratic: An Interview with Josephine Preston Peabody." *The New York Times Magazine* (January 23), 14.

Lawrence, D. H. (1936). "Democracy IV: Individualism" [1919]. In *Phoenix: The Posthumous Papers of D. H. Lawrence*. Edited with an Introduction by Edward D. McDonald. London: W. Heinemann. 713–718.

Lawrence, D. H. (1936). "Democracy: I. The Average" 1919. In *Phoenix: The Posthumous Papers of D. H. Lawrence*. Edited with an Introduction by Edward D. McDonald. London: W. Heinemann. 699–704.

Lewis, Sinclair (1922). *Babbitt.* New York: Harcourt, Brace and Co.; P. F. Collier; Grosset and Dunlap.

Lewis, Sinclair (1935). *It Can't Happen Here.* New York: Doubleday, Doran.

Lewis, Wyndham (1926). *The Art of Being Ruled.* London: Chatto & Windus.

Lippmann, Walter (1922). *Public Opinion.* New York: Harcourt, Brace and Co.

Lowell, James Russell (1884). *On Democracy.* An address delivered in the Town Hall, Birmingham, on the 5th of October. Birmingham: Cond Brothers.

Loy, Mina (1921). "Psycho-Democracy: A Movement to Focus Human Reason on the Conscious Direction of Evolution." *The Little Review* 8.1 (Autumn): 14–19.

Mencken, H. L. (1919). "New Poetry Movement." In *Prejudices: First Series.* New York: A. A. Knopf. 83–96.

Monroe, Harriet (1914). "The Audience: II." *Poetry: A Magazine of Verse* (October): 31–32.

Pound, Ezra (1914). "The New Sculpture–I-II." *The Egoist* 1.4 (February): 67–68.

Pound, Ezra (1915). "The Renaissance III." *Poetry: A Magazine of Verse* (May): 84–91.

Pound, Ezra (1920). Rev. of *Economic Democracy* by Major C. H. Douglas. *The Little Review* 6.11 (April): 39–42.

Radhakrishna, Sarvepalli (1929). *Kalki: Or the Future of Civilization.* London: Kegan Paul, Trench, Trubner.

Tawney, R. H. (1914). "An Experiment in Democratic Education." *Political Quarterly* 2 (May): 62–84.

Untermeyer, Louis (1919). "Introduction 'The New Spirit'." In *The New Era in American Poetry.* New York: Henry Holt and Co. 3–14.

Untermeyer, Louis (1921). "Preface." In *Modern American Poetry* (rev. and enl.). New York: Harcourt, Brace; London: Jonathan Cape. xvii–xlvii.

Untermeyer, Louis (1923). *American Poetry Since 1900.* New York: Henry Holt and Co.

Webb, Beatrice (1933). "The Drawbacks of Democracy." In *The Modern State* (ed. Mary Adams). London: George Allen and Unwin. 182–195.

Wilson, Woodrow (1917). Speech, April 2. 65th Congress, 1st Session, Senate Document No. 5, Serial No. 7264, Washington, DC, 3–8.

Woolf, Virginia (1927). "Poetry, Fiction and the Future." *The New York Herald Tribune* (August 14), Section 6, Books: 1, 6–7;(August 21), Section 6, Books: 1, 6.

Woolf, Virginia (1928). "The Niece of an Earl." *Life and Letters* (October), 356–361.

Woolf, Virginia (1937). "Craftsmanship." *The Listener* (May 5): 868–869.

63

Difficulty, Obscurity

In his conclusion to *The Use of Poetry and the Use of Criticism* (1933), T. S. Eliot conceded that "something should be said about the vexed question of obscurity and unintelligibility." But in stating that "modern poetry is supposed to be difficult," he meant not that modern poetry *should* be difficult, but that it was generally *thought* (supposed) to be so. In outlining the "several reasons" for this common view, Eliot attributed one to writing, two to reading, and one to writing and reading combined. Regarding the writer, Eliot noted that "there may be personal causes which make it impossible for a poet to express himself in any but an obscure way," adding "while this may be regrettable, we should be glad, I think, that the man has been able to express himself at all." Turning to readers, he considered two possible factors. First, "difficulty may be due just to novelty" – clearly a temporary effect, given that the currently popular poet Robert Browning "was the first to be *called* difficult." Second, Eliot considered the effect of "the reader's having been told, or having suggested to himself, that the poem is going to prove difficult." Instead of reading in "a state of sensitivity," the "ordinary reader" then "obfuscates his senses by the desire to be clever and to look very hard for something, he doesn't know what – or else by the desire not to be taken in." Finally, Eliot addressed a feature of modernist style: leaving out. Not finding what he expects, "the reader, bewildered, gropes about for what is absent, and puzzles his head for a kind of 'meaning' which is not there, and is not meant to be there." While akin to novelty, this last reason relates to a form that replaces authorial "message" with textual gaps that solicit the readers' participatory role. While Eliot's reasons do not of course cover all possible explanations of difficulty, his analysis highlights two significant points: that modernists recognized there was a problem, and that it derived from a combination of readers and texts.

Eliot's identification of the varieties of difficulty was reflected in modernist response as a whole. Difficulty was frequently linked with novelty and explained as a temporary effect of the shock of encountering radically new ways of seeing the modern world. Mina Loy held that the "seeming strangeness" of "Modern Poetry" was the "inevitable" result of the modernist artist's "independent contact with nature" and "new manner" of perception (1925). Gertrude Stein explained that the "genius" of Picasso lay in his ability to set aside conventional modes of perception conditioned by "habits, schools, daily life, reason, necessities of life, indolence" and "see things in a new way that is really difficult"; "another vision than that of all the world," she said, "is very rare" (1938). Describing the reaction to his "avant-garde" film *Borderline*, Kenneth Macpherson argued that critics complained of its "obscurity" only because it "travers[ed] new ground" (1930). Difficulty was also explained as reflecting the difficult nature of modern reality itself. William Carlos Williams, in an article on Joyce's *Work in Progress*, shifted attention to the matter that difficulty conveyed: "I see no other approach [. . .] to the difficulties [of] modern literary styles," he wrote, "than to endeavor to find what truth lies in them" (1927). Addison Hibbard proposed that modernist artists were "saying things in a different way because of a new mood," and he justified this strangeness on the grounds that "life *has* become more complex; science *has* broadened our knowledge and taught us a scattered interest; [and] unity *has* departed from a civilization wracked with the warring attitudes of fascism, communism, and democracy" (1939). Difficulty was further associated with increasing individual differences and the mounting challenge of accessing the private experiences of others. In *Principles of Literary Criticism* (1924), I. A. Richards presented the "general communicative difficulty" of modern poetry as a symptom of an age in which "thought and feeling" are increasingly "special and peculiar to the individual man." F. R. Leavis critiqued Auden's poetry for dealing with "private neuroses and memories," inadvertently, however – given Auden's outlawed homosexuality – supporting Eliot's comment that there might be private reasons why a writer is obscure (1936).

Another approach to difficulty focused, like Eliot's, on questions of audience, often with an eye to the rapidly expanding reading public. Some modernists – it was charged – responded by seeking smaller, more select audiences, and so courted difficulty as a deliberately alienating device. Horace Gregory saw "obscurity" as a snobbish effort to keep the common reader at bay – a "counter-attack" against the average reader's growing interest in, and putative encroachments upon, poetry (1933). Wyndham Lewis rejected justifications for the "superhuman *difficulty*" of modernist writing, arguing that modernists themselves had "propagat[ed]" the myth of difficulty in order to explain away their own "mediocrity, or smallness of output" (1934). Pamela Hansford Johnson argued that literary writing had become a "private game [. . .] played at a private party," the fruits of which the "ordinary cultivated reader" found "arid, unenjoyable, and not infrequently incomprehensible" (1949). Yet other readers and critics dismissed or diminished the notion of difficulty as a defining trait. Louis Untermeyer's and Carter Davidson's *Poetry: Its Appreciation and Enjoyment* (1934) rejected the idea that "the modern world" was "being mirrored in cerebral poetry of increasing sensibility, indecisive rhythms and obscure inner conflicts," recommending "among the finest expressions of this age, the untroubled clarity of Robert Frost, the clean craftsmanship of Elinor Wylie and the simple, straightforward lyricism of A. E. Housman." (Their anthology included no poetry by Eliot.) A reader of Isabel Paterson's regular "Turns with a Bookworm" column objected to her comment that William Carlos Williams was hard to understand, adding "not that I pretend always to understand him, but I'm not always sure which of us is to blame" (1928). Paterson responded that she was justifiably giving "a hint to the author to be a little more explicit next time," but she also categorized modernist authors very differently as far as difficulty was concerned: Marcel Proust ("no difficulty"), André Gide ("incomprehensible"), and Virginia Woolf ("easy enough"). Responses to difficulty also varied widely, from alienation and befuddlement to engagement and excited interest. A *Saturday Review of Literature* review of the initial issue of *transition* noted how, to different readers, difficulty could mean different things: Gertrude Stein's "feats of word legerdemain" possessed "strange powers" since "some minds were fascinated by her scrambled sentences," while "others [were] driven to wails and cursings"; *Ulysses* was "praised by some of the discriminating" who genuinely enjoyed its "controvers[ial]" "execution," as well as by those

65

"who delight in art in proportion to its obscurity, and detest the very name of common sense" ("Gyring and Gimbling" 1927).

Perhaps most frequently, modernist difficulty was associated with a prolific use of allusion. R. C. Trevelyan's *Thamyris: or, Is There a Future of Poetry* (1925) blamed modernist poets like Eliot for the perceived decline in the popularity of poetry, naming "obscurity" their "most frequent fault" and tracing it to "an Alexandrine love of recondite allusions." Eliot himself acknowledged the difficulties posed by the allusiveness of *The Waste Land*, both supplying notes and prefacing them with the suggestion that reading Jessie L. Weston's *From Ritual to Romance* would "elucidate the difficulties of the poem much better than [his] notes" (1922). Yet difficulty could also be attributed not to a heavier reliance on allusion, but to the lack of a common cultural background, so that many readers did not know to what the allusions referred. Using a historical example, Yeats argued that while many C20 readers found Shakespeare difficult, in his own time, "Shakespeare's art was public [. . .] because poetry was a part of the general life of his people, who had been trained by the Church to listen to difficult words" (1917). I. A. Richards saw "allusion" as "the most striking" of the ways that modern poetry suffered from a loss of shared cultural experience: "tak[ing] into its service elements and forms of experience which are not inevitable to life but need to be acquired," modernist allusion presented for Richards a "special instance of the general communicative difficulty" of the period itself. Difficulty could also be attributed to false or unnecessary expectations. Clement Greenberg attributed the perceived "obscurity" of modernist poetry to "the new [academic] stress on exegesis," or the determining of "overt meaning"; while not denying the "benefits" brought about by "'close' reading," Greenberg argued that "the drift and shape of an 'obscure' poem or novel can be grasped for the purposes of art without being 'worked out'" ([1950, 1956]1961). Similarly, when Eliot cautioned against the reader's "grop[ing]" for "meaning" which is "not there," he added, "the more seasoned reader [. . .] does not bother about understanding" (1933). For himself, Eliot confessed, "I know that some of the poetry to which I am most devoted is poetry which I did not understand at first reading; some is poetry which I am not sure I understand yet." Ezra Pound, responding to complaints about the inclusion of untranslated foreign phrases in his work, declared it "All tosh about *foreign languages* making it difficult": "Skip anything you don't understand and go on till you pick it up again," he counseled; "The quotes are all either explained at once by repeat or they are definitely *of* the things indicated" – *not* allusions to something outside the poem. Admitting, however, that "there are a couple of Greek quotes [. . .] that can't be understood without Greek," Pound suggested that another possible use of allusion was educating the reader: "*If* I can drive the reader to learning at least that much Greek, she or he will indubitably be filled with a durable gratitude" ([1934]1950).

Difficulty was indeed often conceived as a stimulus for the reader, since it provoked a more creative and participatory engagement in the literary work. In their *Survey of Modernist Poetry* (1927), Laura Riding and Robert Graves accepted difficulty as a defining trait of the poetry under consideration ("poetry not characteristically 'modernist' presents no difficulty to the plain reader") but supported the potentially beneficial challenge to the reader: because it "demands a [. . .] vigorous imaginative effort," they argued, modernist literature required "the plain reader [to] make certain important alterations in his critical attitude." Not surprisingly, the reading of difficult work was often described with words or images relating to physical effort or struggle. Distinguishing between "the temptation of a popular art, which yields itself easily and flamboyantly" and the "stony, steep, and winding" "paths" presented by the poetry of Marianne Moore, Glenway Wescott argued, "The artful reader must decide at once whether he can endure the strain, whether he honestly wishes to pursue a delight so hard to get, whether he will pay her price" (1923). D. H. Lawrence argued that "to read a really new novel will *always* hurt," because it demands "the struggle with and replacing of old connexions"; as opposed to the "alcoholic sort of pleasure" in "re-acting old relationships," innovative art demands "a new relatedness," and "There will always be resistance" before "acquiescence" (1925). Isabel Paterson compared her response to "the Gertrude Stein-e.e. cummings-James-Joyce method of using words" to the effect of "falling down the cellar stairs with a lemon pie in [her] hands," though she admitted that "some folks do seem to derive nourishment from these experiments" and "Morley Callaghan certainly found them inspiring" (1929). Virginia Woolf – one of the modernists Paterson found most accessible – argued that it was a wager that great artists necessarily took. Noting that "the great writers [. . .] often require us to make heroic efforts," Woolf argued, "the writers who have most to give us often do most violence to our prejudices" and thus require all the reader's "imagination and understanding" (1931). Lecturing on *Ulysses* and *Finnegans Wake*, Joyce Cary similarly defended "difficulty" as a "necessary device which an artist may use to break the crust of a too-practised, in fact a bored audience": "it is as if one offered to the knife of the mind not a bundle of cotton wool in which the blade only seems to penetrate, but a firm skin which resists the blade, and demands an effort of pressure, so that when the blade does cut it goes deep by its own impetus; it gets somewhere" ([1948–1953]1983).

While the subject of difficulty remained controversial, the varying usages together make a valuable point: difficulty resides not in writing or reading alone, but in the communicative network linking them, including the personal and cultural background each participant brings to the text. Whether it surprised readers with new perceptions, confronted them with the intricate modernist world, fenced them out from the area of "high" art, or made them participants in literary creation, difficulty reflects modernism's deep engagement with the difficult relation between writer and audience. "Returning to the question of obscurity," Eliot proposed a possible answer: the "most useful poetry" would "cut across all the present stratifications of public taste" and, like Shakespeare's, be challenging but accessible to all readers by appealing to them on different levels (1933). The difficulty of thus overcoming difficulty might be an insurmountable task for the writer – "but," he admitted, "one must experiment as one can."

SEE ALSO: *Coterie Bloomsbury; Democracy; Form Formalism; Highbrow, Middlebrow, Lowbrow; Propaganda; Readers, Reading*

References

(1927). "Gyring and Gimbling (or Lewis Carroll in Paris)." Editorial. *The Saturday Review of Literature* (April 30), 777, 781.

Cary, Joyce ([1948–1953]). Untitled TS with holograph adds. Cary Papers. Bodleian Library, Oxford. MS Cary 238. Quoted in Melba Cuddy Creelman, "Beyond Modernism: Critical Attitudes in Some Unpublished Joyce Cary Materials," *Contemporary Literature* 24.1 (Spring 1983): 13–29.

Eliot, T. S. (1922). *The Waste Land*. New York: Boni and Liveright.

Eliot, T. S. (1933). *The Use of Poetry and the Use of Criticism*. London: Faber and Faber.

Greenberg, Clement (1961). "T. S. Eliot: A Book Review." [1950, 1956]. In *Art and Culture: Critical Essays*. Boston: Beacon. 239–244.

Gregory, Horace (1933). "Poetry in America." *New Verse*. 4 (July): 11–16.

Hibbard, Addison (1939). "The Road to Modernism." *The Saturday Review of Literature* (January 21), 3–4, 16.

I. M. P. [Isabel Paterson] (1928). "Turns with a Bookworm." *New York Herald Tribune* (June 17), Books XII: 19.

I. M. P. [Isabel Paterson] (1929). "Turns with a Bookworm." *New York Herald Tribune* (April 14), Books XII.

Johnson, Pamela Hansford (1949). "The Sick-room Hush over the English Novel." *The Listener* 42 (August 11): 235–236.

Lawrence, D. H. (1925). "Morality and the Novel." *The Calendar of Modern Letters* 2 (December): 269–274.

Leavis, F. R. (1936). "Mr. Auden's Talent." Rev. of *Look, Stranger!* by W. H. Auden and *The Ascent of F.6* by W. H. Auden and Christopher Isherwood. *Scrutiny* 5.3 (December): 323–327.

Lewis, Wyndham (1934). *Men Without Art*. London: Cassell.

Loy, Mina (1925). "Modern Poetry." *Charm* 3.3 (April): 16–17.

Macpherson, Kenneth (1930). "As Is." *Close Up* 7.5 (November): 293–298.

Pound, Ezra (1950). Letter to Sarah Perkins Cope, 15 January 1934. [1934]. In *The Letters of Ezra Pound: 1907–1941* (ed. D. D. Paige). New York: Harcourt, Brace. 250–251.

Richards, I. A. (1924). *Principles of Literary Criticism*. London: Kegan Paul, Trench, Trubner.

Riding, Laura and Robert Graves (1927). *A Survey of Modernist Poetry*. London: W. Heinemann.

Stein, Gertrude (1938). *Pablo Picasso.* London: B.T. Batsford.

Trevelyan, R. C. (1925). *Thamyris: or, Is there a Future for Poetry?* London: Kegan Paul, Trench, Trubner.

Untermeyer, Louis and Carter Davidson (1934). *Poetry: Its Appreciation and Enjoyment.* New York: Harcourt, Brace and Co.

Wescott, Glenway (1923). "Miss Moore's Observations." In Marianne Moore, *Marriage by Marianne Moore.* Manikin Series. New York: Monroe Wheeler. 4-page Insert.

Williams, William Carlos (1927). "A Note on the Recent Work of James Joyce." *transition: An International Quarterly for Creative Experiment* 8 (November): 149–154.

Woolf, Virginia (1931). "The Love of Reading." In *Company of Books: A Selected Booklist for the Coming Year, 1931–32.* Northampton: Hampshire Bookshop. 3–5.

Yeats, W. B. (1917). "Note on 'At The Hawk's Well'." In *The Wild Swans at Coole, Other Verses, and a Play in Verse.* Churchtown: Cuala. 42–47.

Einstein

After Albert Einstein published his special (1905) and general (1916) theories of relativity and his theories received widely publicized verification by Arthur Stanley Eddington (in 1919), the word Einstein transcended the world of science and began to take on a life of its own. The founding of the American magazine *Popular Science Monthly* in 1872 signaled a broad concern with disseminating new scientific ideas to an audience composed primarily of educated laypeople, an effort that became strikingly notable in numerous later attempts to explain relativity in accessible ways: Herbert Dingle's *Relativity for All* (1922); Clement V. Durrell's *Readable Relativity: A Book for Non-Specialists* (1926); Sir Oliver Lodge's *Relativity, A Very Elementary Exposition* (1926); James Rice's *Relativity, An Exposition Without Mathematics* (1928); and not forgetting Einstein's own *Relativity: The Special and General Theory: A Popular Exposition* (1920). But apart from such general understandings offered of scientific relativity, Einstein captured the public imagination as a signifier of revolutionary thought. Whether betokening genius, complexity, uncertainty, paradox, mystery, incomprehensibility, apocalypse, or world peace, Einstein frequently stood for a version of modernism itself.

Einstein was of course inseparable from relativity but, quite apart from the theory, his name had a meaningful circulation in the public imagination. Expressions such as "an Einstein" (T. S. Eliot, 1923) or "he is no Einstein"

ABCD**E**FGHIJKLMNOPQRSTUVWXYZ

Modernism: Keywords, First Edition. Melba Cuddy-Keane, Adam Hammond, and Alexandra Peat.
© 2014 Melba Cuddy-Keane. Published 2014 by John Wiley & Sons, Ltd.

(Ogden Nash, 1942) reflect an up-to-date word for genius. A corollary of the genius equation, however, was that Einstein also meant "difficult to understand." As Bertrand Russell stated in *ABC of Relativity* (1925), "Everybody knows that Einstein has done something astonishing, but very few people know exactly what it is that he has done." Yet for some, the inscrutability of the theory was Einstein's main charm. In his poem "Relativity" (1929), D. H. Lawrence wrote, "I like relativity and quantum theories/Because I don't understand them/and they make me feel as if space shifted/about like a swan that can't settle,/refusing to sit still and be measured." When the Canadian humorist Stephen Leacock described a lecture tour of England, during which he was preceded by a lecture on relativity, he told the chairman, "Surely this kind of audience couldn't understand a lecture like that!"; the chairman apparently replied, "No [. . .] they didn't understand it, but they all enjoyed it" (1922). A 1930 headline in *The Literary Digest* proclaimed, "We May Not 'Get' Relativity, but We Like Einstein."

The vagueness or imprecision of lay understandings of relativity, however, did not interfere with speculations about its momentous significance, in both physical and metaphysical realms. An article on "The Disintegration of Atoms and Atomic Energy" in *The Scientific Monthly* stated that "relativity, though based on physical observations and mathematical equations, seems to carry us into a metaphysical region remote from our normal interests" (1919); writing in *The New Age*, Major Clifford Hugh Douglas (C. H. D.) concurred, arguing that "Dr. Einstein's research work" had "an interest far wider than its apparent bearing," addressing "philosophical issues" by making it "almost possible to assert as a physical proposition that which has always been claimed by the metaphysician[:] that all existence is one; differing only in form and consciousness" (1919). Indeed, for Rosicrucian Elworth Pound, the metaphysical implications supported a mystical apprehension of the universe: linking Einstein to Richard Bucke's *Cosmic Consciousness*, Pound hailed the birth of a new religion: "Time and space are about to fall: witness, Einstein!" (1920). Exposing the rampant trivializing of such high-flown theories, a character in Aldous Huxley's satirical *Crome Yellow* regards Einstein as auguring the collapse of her little civilization: "This Einstein theory. It seems to upset the whole starry universe. It makes me so worried about my horoscopes" (1921). More seriously, Jeanette Marks considered that Einstein had implications for aesthetics, arguing that the "theory of Einstein-refraction" meant that "some things comfortably fixed in beauty and truth and goodness are not at all in the position in which they are thought to be," adding, "it is even conceivable that beauty has a fourth dimension" (1922). In contrast, Alfred E. Randall (A. E. R.), writing in *The New Age*, resoundingly dismissed "the famous 'fourth dimension,' about which so much mystical nonsense has been talked" as "humbug" (1921).

71

More scientifically grounded approaches circumscribed Einstein's unknowability by acknowledging his theory's limits and specific applicability. Bertrand Russell objected to popular exaggerations and misunderstandings: "The theory does not say that *everything* is relative; on the contrary, it gives a technique for distinguishing what is relative from what belongs to a physical occurrence in its own right" (1925). And, as A. E. R. succinctly reported, "Einstein has succeeded in separating far more completely than hitherto the share of the observer and the share of external nature in the things we see happen," elucidating the difference between "*measured space*" – including "the space of everyday perception" – and "the idea of a pre-existing space whose properties cannot be ascertained by experiment" and which is "an Unknowable." Nonetheless, when writing as a drama critic, A. E. R. (here under the pseudonym John Francis Hope) was not averse to calling upon Einstein to puncture Storm Jameson's putative exaltation of the artist in her own image: "Einstein's demonstration of relativity has restored subjectivism to philosophy, perhaps even solipsism" (1921).

Floating thus rather free from scientific foundation, Einstein and relativity became placeholders for the controversial idea that truth could have many sides. J. S. Mackenzie classed Einstein alongside Nietzsche, William James, and Hamlet as thinkers who "hesitate[d] to say that any truth is absolutely true or that any line is absolutely straight" (1923). Herbert Read proposed that "Relativity" represented a more up-to-date name for what "Nietzsche called 'perspectivism'" – the realization that "all is relative to the position of the observer" (1921b). Einstein came thus to stand for a paradigm shift, from the notion of absolute truth to – or perhaps back to – a recognition of truth's plural and unfinalizable nature. In *Fantasia of the Unconscious* (1922), D. H. Lawrence praised Einstein for invalidating the mechanistic Newtonian conception of the physical world and returning a sense of wonder and ungraspability to scientific observation. Stimulated by Einstein, Lawrence reimagined the centric model of the universe, replacing it with a mobile, organic image resembling a dance of atoms in flux: "We are all very pleased with Einstein for knocking the external axis out of the universe. The universe isn't a spinning wheel. It is a cloud of bees flying a veering round." The idea of life as an ongoing fluxible process could be applied to Einsteinian science itself. In Marianne Moore's "The Student" (1932), the speaker asks, "when will your experiment be finished, Doctor Einstein?" and "is pleased" by his response, "science is never finished."

Such readings made for an easy leap from Einstein to modernist art, in discussions of which Einstein could signify as an example of the poetic mind or function as a poetic symbol. Herbert Read quoted Lord Haldane's remark that Einstein was a scientist "with a creative imagination more akin to that of a poet"; Read went one step further, arguing, "there is no poem published in this generation, nor any other so-called work of the imagination, from which such genuine satisfaction is to be derived as from [Einstein's] outline of the general relativity theory" (1921a). In specific poems, Einstein appears as a force either positively paralleling or invasively intruding on nature. William Carlos Williams's "St. Francis Einstein of the Daffodils" (1921), celebrating April as the time of Einstein's first visit to the US, imagines Einstein "shouting/that flowers and men/were created/relatively equal" and promising renewal and growth through "a springtime of the mind." In contrast, Archibald MacLeish's "Einstein" (1926), while seeming to celebrate Einstein's impassioned probing of the secrets of the universe "till swaying time/ Collapses," almost takes comfort in the way the universe refuses to be penetrated by science, "Which seems to keep/Something inviolate. A living something."

The most specific connection between Einstein and art related to conceptions and representations of time. In a broadly sweeping comparison, Harvey Eagleson ventured that "Miss Stein, like Carlyle before her and Einstein with her, is concerned with the problem of Time," noting Stein's specific engagement with "'the continuous present' as she phrases it" (1936). Harold Nicolson, in a famous talk on the BBC in which any mention of *Ulysses* by name was censored, called Joyce "the Einstein of English fiction," whose "method is an innovation destructive of the time-sequence" (1931), while T. S. Eliot similarly likened Joyce's innovations in *Ulysses* to "the discoveries of an Einstein," concluding that "instead of [chronological] narrative method, we may now use mythical method," "manipulating a continuous parallel between contemporaneity and antiquity"(1923). For Wyndham Lewis, however, the modernist tendency to draw on the "'time-lessness' of einsteinian physics, and the time-obsessed flux of Bergson" led deplorably to "a sort of mystical time-cult" (1927). Associating "Einstein with Stein, [Proust's] Swann, [Henri] Bergson, and [Joyce's] Bloom," Lewis disparaged in each a tendency to portray all phenomena as transitory and insubstantial. Other views were more ambivalent. Madeleine B. Stern's "Counterclockwise" – a wide-ranging account of "the flux of time" in Western philosophy and literature, from the earliest writings to the present – culminated with the modernist "subjectivists," offering that "at least in some instances [the ideas] have made for some very good writing" (1936). Quoting from Alexander Moszkowski's conversations with Einstein, however, Stern "commonsensically" balanced such views by noting, "time, which the physicist Einstein has shown to be relative" had "an absolute value for him" when he glanced at his watch. Edmund Wilson, referring to Marcel Proust's *À la recherche du temps perdu*, commented more heroically that Proust "has supplied for the first time in literature an equivalent on the full scale for the new theory of modern physics" (1931). While Proust himself rejected suggestions that Einstein influenced him, or indeed that he influenced Einstein, he acknowledged they had "an analogous manner of distorting Time" ([1921]1992). When a correspondent queried a supposed anachronism in one of his novels, Proust denied the anachronism but

73

added, "Einsteinisons-le si vous voulez pour plus de commodité" ["Let's Einstein-ize it, if that's more convenient for you"] ([1922]1993).

The association with Einstein's concepts of time was invoked as well to defend modernist writing against charges of difficulty. Justifying Joyce's literary complexity through his coinage "the Einstein of English fiction," Nicolson stated, "it is difficult for any reader to follow with confidence the tremendous wavelengths of Mr. Joyce." Eliot likewise supported Joyce's difficulty by allusion to Einstein, referring to "'Finnegans Wake,' which like Einstein's theory, only half a dozen people in the world are supposed to be able to understand" (Hailey, 1950). Madeleine B. Stern, referencing Wyndham Lewis's idea of "Space-Time [as] the einsteinian god," proposed that the "attempt to capture the continuous flow of time" perhaps accounted for Stein's "strange" and "troubling" style (1936). Such explanations surfaced in the popular press as well. A Utah newspaper, reporting on Jeanette Mark's article cited previously in this entry, both enthusiastically quoted her comparison of reading poetry to reading Einstein and used a strong header to urge its main point: "Says Average Reader Willing to Enjoy Poetry but Unwilling to Dig for Meaning" (1922).

A yet more intricate use of Einstein engaged issues of language and form. Emanuel Carnevali used Einstein to argue for scientific clarity: protesting "the involved, long-winded symbolism" of a contemporary Greek poet, Carnevali accused it of being "too much of the old mythological-rhetorical highbrow stuff – too poetical for these days of gas masks and Einstein Theories," which demanded "brevity" and "sharpness" (1920). R. S. Crane used Einstein to mock Cleanth Brooks's obsession with "conventions and formularized techniques for getting 'paradoxical' effects" (1948). For Crane, "Mr. Brooks's criterion for poetic 'structure,' as poetry of synthesis" was no different from "the syntheses of science," offering merely "the formula in which Einstein brought together in a single unified equation the hitherto 'discordant' qualities of mass and energy"; if irony was all that poetry was about, Crane asserted, then "$E = mc^2$" was "the greatest 'ironical' poem written so far in the twentieth century." Edmund Wilson grasped the literary and scientific parallels in more complex interactive fashion, detecting a common conceptual paradigm that balanced multiplicity and change with underlying structure and order. "As Einstein's mathematical apparatus enable us to establish certain relations between the different parts of the universe," he wrote, "so Proust constructs a moral scheme out of the phenomena whose moral values are always shifting"; yet Wilson likened the function of the narrator's grandmother in Proust's multivolume work to the speed of light in Einstein's theories: "the single constant value which makes the rest of the system possible."

As the modernist period progressed, the meaning of Einstein changed with the application of his theories of energy and mass to the atom bomb. After A-bombs destroyed Hiroshima and Nagasaki, a 1946 cover image in *Time* magazine juxtaposed Einstein's image against a flaming mushroom cloud, on which is written $E = mc^2$, all set above the caption "Cosmoclast Einstein." The accompanying article, "Science: Crossroads" (referring to "Operations Crossroads," the nuclear weapons tests), conceded that "Einstein did not work directly on the bomb," but observed that he seemed "to be suffering from blast shock from the bomb he had fathered." In contrast, a report on the 1932 disarmament conference entitled "Einstein in Arms Against Mars" (1933) noted Einstein's long-standing recognition of the destructive potentials of his theory as well as his devotion, from the early 1920s on, to the causes of disarmament, radical pacifism, and world peace. Yet this account exposed the ambiguity of his public image and the divided responses to his idealism as either inspiring or unrealistic: "Dr. Einstein," the article declared, is "a walking delegate of peace, a disarmament conference rolled into one," while a reported conversation at the conference presented the other side: Anatoly Lunacharsky of the Russian delegation apparently scoffed, "A dreamer – a naive dreamer – just because he knows mathematics he thinks he knows everything. We need practical men. Practical men, you understand."

Einstein thus became fully a symbol of the age – its ambivalences as well as its possibilities and potentials – merging the complexities of modernist theory with compassionate concerns about the survival of humanity and indeed of the planet. Choosing three emblematic figures to represent his time, Marshall McLuhan named two artists and one scientist: describing his present world as "the world of Eliot, Stein, and Einstein," McLuhan pointed out the limitation of deriving "emotional organization" from writers like "Kipling, Galsworthy, Shaw and Chesterton" and "the best sellers of yesteryear"(1944). In McLuhan's view, contemporary English and American critics were "provincials," who failed to recognize that "the art of Western Europe" was not "the inevitable fruit of civilization [. . .] dwarfing the art of other places" and correspondingly failed to be "detached in their view of themselves." Conversely, Einstein stood for a desirable "Catholicity of mind" – inclusive, flexible, polyvalent, and able to grasp viewpoints other than its own. Attaining such a global perspective, however, was not assumed to be easy. Emphasizing not ideas but a mode of thought, Einstein himself wrote, introducing an antiracist book for children, "The struggle for an unprejudiced attitude towards the simple and yet so often misunderstood facts of human existence must start at the still flexible mind of the child" (1947). Grasping such "simple" "facts," Einstein suggested, could pose the most difficult challenge of all.

SEE ALSO: *Atom Atomic; Difficulty, Obscurity; Hamlet; International; Modern, Modernism; Readers, Reading*

75

References

(1919). "The Disintegration of Atoms and Atomic Energy." *Scientific Monthly* (December 1), 587–589.

(1922). "Says Average Reader Willing to Enjoy Poetry but Unwilling to Dig for Meaning." *The Deseret News* (July 8), 3: x.

(1930). "We May Not 'Get' Relativity, but We Like Einstein." *The Literary Digest* (December 27), 29.

(1933). "Einstein in Arms Against Mars." *The Literary Digest* (February 4), 28.

(1946). "Cover Image." Credit Ernest Hamlin Baker. *Time* (The Weekly Newsmagazine) (July 1).

(1946). "Science: Crossroads." *Time* (The Weekly Newsmagazine) (July 1), 52.

A. E. R. [Alfred E. Randall] (1921). "Relativity." *The New Age* 28.25 (April 21): 298–299.

C. H. D. [Major Clifford Hugh Douglas] (1919). "Notes of the Week." *The New Age* 26.2 (November 13): 17–19.

Carnevali, Emanuel (1920). Rev. of *Life Immovable* by Kostes Palamas. Trans. by A. E. Phoutrides. *Poetry: A Magazine of Verse* 17.1 (October): 49–51.

Crane, R. S. (1948). "Cleanth Brooks; Or, the Bankruptcy of Critical Monism." *Modern Philology* 45.4 (May): 226–245.

Eagleson, Harvey (1936). "Gertrude Stein: Method in Madness." *The Sewanee Review* 44.2 (April–June): 164–177.

Einstein, Albert (1947). "Foreword." In *All About Us*, by Eva Knox Evans, Vana Earle et al. New York: Capital. 5.

Eliot, T. S. (1923). "Ulysses, Order, and Myth." *The Dial* 75.11 (November): 480–483.

Hailey, Foster (1950). "An Interview with T. S. Eliot." *The New York Times* (April 16), XI.

Hope, John Francis [Alfred E. Randall] (1921). "Drama." *The New Age* 28.12 (January): 141–142.

Huxley, Aldous (1921). *Crome Yellow*. London: Chatto & Windus.

Lawrence, D. H. (1922). *Fantasia of the Unconscious*. New York: Thomas Seltzer.

Lawrence, D. H. (1929). "Relativity." In *Pansies: Poems*. London: Martin Secker. 116.

Leacock, Stephen (1922). *My Discovery of England*. London: John Lane.

Lewis, Wyndham (1927). *Time and Western Man*. London: Chatto & Windus.

Mackenzie, J. S. (1923). "Spiritual Values." *International Journal of Ethics* 33.3 (April): 248–262.

MacLeish, Archibald (1926). "Einstein." In *Streets in the Moon*. Boston and New York: Houghton Mifflin. 43–53.

Marks, Jeanette (1922). "On Reading Poetry To-day." *The North American Review* (June), 827–837.

McLuhan, Marshall (1944). "Wyndham Lewis: Lemuel in Lilliput." In *St. Louis University Studies in Honor of St. Thomas Aquinas*. 3 vols. St. Louis: McMullen Printing Co. Vol. 2: 58–72.

Moore, Marianne (1932). "The Student." *Poetry: A Magazine of Verse* 40.3 (June): 122–126.

Nash, Ogden (1942). *Good Intentions*. Boston: Little, Brown.

Nicolson, Harold (1931). *The New Spirit in Literature*. The Changing World: A Broadcast Symposium. London: British Broadcasting Corporation.

Pound, Elworth (1920). "The Mysterious Great." *The North American Review* (June), 758–767.

Proust, Marcel (1992). Letter to Armand de Guiche, 9 or 10 December 1921. [1921]. In *Correspondance* (ed. Philip Kolb). 21 vols. Paris: Plon. Vol. 20: 577–579.

Proust, Marcel (1993). Letter to Benjamin Crémieux, 5 or 6 August 1922. [1922]. In *Correspondance* (ed. Philip Kolb). 21 vols. Paris: Plon. Vol. 21: 402–403.

Read, Herbert (1921a). "Readers and Writers." *The New Age* 30.6 (December 8): 67–68.

Read, Herbert (1921b). "Readers and Writers." *The New Age* 30.9 (December 29): 103.

Russell, Bertrand (1925). *ABC of Relativity*. London: Kegan Paul.

Stern, Madeleine B. (1936). "Counterclockwise: Flux of Time in Literature." *The Sewanee Review* 44.3 (July–September): 338–365.

Williams, William Carlos (1921). "St. Francis Einstein of the Daffodils." *Contact* 4 (September): 2.

Wilson, Edmund (1931). *Axel's Castle: A Study in the Imaginative Literature of 1870–1930*. New York: Scribner.

Empire, Imperialism

While most official discourse in the modernist period used empire and imperialism in patriotic and celebratory ways, increasing criticism of the practices of Empires caused the terms to be re-evaluated and redefined. The range of imperialism under discussion was broadly historical and widely geographical – including Roman, French, Belgian, and Japanese Empires – but heightening concerns in the English-speaking world turned attention to both a crisis of belief in the British Empire and the gradual shift from political to financial empires as the source of global power. As the course of modernity exposed the injustices of the Victorian Empire, the question of its future developed in two distinct ways: (i) proponents of imperialism looked to science and technology as ways to further the progressive goals of national productivity and international connectivity; (ii) opponents of imperialism tried either to reconceive empire, as in the commonwealth, or to replace it with alternative models of international community, such as the League of Nations. As first doubts about, and then growing horror about, the imperial project exerted a powerful influence on public opinion, empire was condemned for both the delusion of its idealist dreams and the reality of its raw exploitation. Yet many attempted to rehabilitate the terms through redefinition, focusing on the positive possibilities of global community and connectivity.

In positive rhetoric, empire tended to signify not exploration and conquest, but community. Celebrations of the British Empire promoted feelings of shared identity and belonging, and pride in the material accomplishments of the larger whole. Popular support was mobilized by Imperial Exhibitions (beginning with The Great Exhibition 1851) and Empire Day celebrations (inaugurated 1898 in Canada and adopted officially in Britain 1916). The Duke of Devonshire praised the 1924 Wembley Exhibition for imbuing "an immense number of children [. . .] with something of the Imperial spirit" ("Another Year," 1924), while, in Canada, *The Charlottetown Guardian*, honoring the cause of "liberty and justice," asserted

77

that loyalty to the Empire was not "forced sentiment" but "the homage of dutiful children to the Imperial mother who has bequeathed to them this vast and glorious heritage" ("Empire Day," 1928). Promoting such celebrations, the Australian Daisy Bates translated empire to her "aboriginal wards" as "Em-bai-de," and indigenized "the King's Day" as "a day of happy feasting" (1938). In Winifred Holtby's *South Riding* (1936), during the singing of the national anthem at a Jubilee celebration, even the skeptical Sarah is overcome with thoughts of the empire "banded in the unity of mass emotion." Imperial sentiment was also effectively reinforced through propaganda in WWI. British international correspondent A. Maurice Low declared that the Empire "of many races and creeds, but one in its unity" had been "consecrated anew in the blood of its children" (1916), while L. M. Montgomery's Kenneth Ford considers fighting for the British Empire "a family affair" (1921). Such communal feelings were also bolstered through modernization and scientific progress. The Empire Marketing Board (founded 1926) used strikingly modernist posters to further its slogan, "buy empire," and undertook significant financing of scientific research which, according to an item on "Science and Empire Marketing" in the *British Medical Journal*, was distributed "impartially over the Empire" with potential "benefits [to] the whole of civilization" (1929). In the first broadcast Royal Christmas message (written by Rudyard Kipling), King George V praised the wireless as "one of the marvels of modern science" helping to make the "union" of the Empire "closer still" (1932).

Inflated imperial rhetoric was countered, however, by both ironic treatment and direct critique. The narrator in Joseph Conrad's *The Secret Agent* alludes to the popular saying "the sun never sets on the British Empire," wryly noting that the constables watching over the "august spot" at its center (the House of Commons) "did not seem particularly impressed" (1907); Joe Hynes, in James Joyce's *Ulysses*, satirically inverts the saying into the empire "on which the sun never rises" (1922). Virginia Woolf's Richard Dalloway, a heavily satirized figure in *The Voyage Out*, pompously intones that he "can conceive no more exalted aim" than "to be the citizen of the Empire" (1915), while John Flory in George Orwell's *Burmese Days* undercuts imperial rhetoric by demoting empire to "an aged female patient" (1934). Empire was also denounced in outright attack, condemned by George Padmore as "stark imperialist oppression and exploitation" (1936), accused of "tyrannies and swindles" by Ezra Pound (1915), and labeled by Orwell as "dirty work" (1936). The fault lines of empire were increasingly exposed from the perspective of the colonized. Una Marson charged that education in the West Indies was infused with "the old Imperialist propaganda," so that, rather than "useful citizens of their own countries," the schools produced "merely flag-waving little Britishers" (1935). Sardaji, an Indian character in Agnes Smedley's autobiographical novel *Daughter of Earth*, argues that even the English Socialists supportive of the "Indian working class" cannot escape the "machinery of imperialism" by wearing "the garb of ethics," and wonders if the struggle is not just "against the Capitalist system, but of all Asia against the western world" (1929). The narrator of Miles Franklin's *All that Swagger*, commenting on the way a scholarship to Oxford has drawn a young man away from Australia, casts the Empire as a consuming "vampire" enticing "all the ergs of scientific or artistic genius" from its colonies (1936). But advantage could be taken from the position of the colonies too: in her novel *My Career Goes Bung* (1946), Franklin depicted reverse exploitation on the part of "Australia's greatest literary man," a "sizzling imperialist" who turns his "Australian nativity" to "commercial account" by publishing "articles on Australia from an imperial angle" (1946). Economist John A. Hobson exposed imperialism and profit as inextricably mixed in his groundbreaking *Imperialism: A Study* (1902). In Hobson's analysis, the rapid advances, since 1870, of Germany, the US, and Belgium generated a "new Imperialism" whose "taproot" was economics, specifically the "sudden demand for foreign markets for manufactures and for investments." Thus Marlow, in Joseph Conrad's *Heart of Darkness*, notes that the "Company," based in the "whited sepulcher" of Brussels, plans "to run an over-sea empire, and make no end of coin by trade" ([1899]1902), and C. L. R. James condemned the "savagery and duplicity of European imperialism in its quest of markets and raw materials" (1936). For Hobson, such conditions confronted the British with two clear alternatives: an ethical cultivation of the home territory or an unethical exploitation of the world; also sounding a warning bell, George Padmore warned that "the coloured races do not intend to allow the white imperialist nations to trample over them as in the past" (1936).

79

Such clear oppositions were not, however, always so explicitly drawn. Imperialism could also signify mixed motives and mixed effects. Conrad's *Heart of Darkness* probes the entanglement of idealistic aspirations with corruption, as Marlow contemplates "the dreams of men, the seed of commonwealths, the germs of empires." In *Black Lamb and Grey Falcon*, Rebecca West both acknowledges "a certain magnificence about a great empire in being" and counters that "the hideousness outweighs the beauty" (1941), while her one-year cultural history, *1900*, gives the metaphor of the imperial family a contradictory twist: "parenthood at its most enlightened, and parenthood hostile and perverted" (1982). Even more ambiguously, in Christina Stead's *For Love Alone*, empire signifies both personal freedom and colonizing exploitation: the Australian Teresa reads "maps of the British Empire" with "the world strung on a chain of pink" as signifying that "no matter what the colour or kind of men there, nor the customs of the native women, she could get a job, she was a citizen there" (1944).

The double sidedness of empire emerges, though with differing degrees of consciousness, in the writings of colonial administrators as well. Evelyn Baring, Consul General in Egypt from 1883–1907, distinguished "two different Imperial schools of thought": "that of philanthropy" and "the commercial school" (1908). Upholding the first for its "civilising and moralising mission," Baring acknowledged the need, in the second, to "control those defects" arising from "the egotism of the commercial spirit, if it be subject to no effective check." Attributing economic abuses only to "mistakes" and "errors" and not to the system itself, however, Baring continued to endorse "a sound but reasonable" imperialism, devoted to "the self-interest of the subject race" and the commitment "not to enslave, but to liberate from slavery." Yet Baring's imperialism admitted only the colonizer's view: its "moral basis" was "guided by what "we conscientiously think is best for the subject race." In stark contrast, Leonard Woolf's *Imperialism and Civilization* (1928) presented imperialism itself as undermined by inherent contradictions, derived from "a clash of civilizations" with differing values and opposing views. Beyond the claim that the history of India "shows both the merits and demerits of imperialism at its best," Woolf explained "its final impossibility": by supporting "education of Indians on European lines," the government "spread [. . .] those Western ideas of democracy and nationality [. . .] of which imperialism and the Government of India itself were the negation." Woolf's understanding of imperialism furthermore avoided the flaw in Baring's one-sided view: asserting that "a decision must not only be just, it must be seen to be just" and believing that the native Ceylonese had "as good a right to his code of conduct as I had," Woolf declared, "I was not prepared to spend my life doing justice to people who thought my justice was injustice" (1969). The difficulty if not impossibility of determining any single "ethical principle of imperial policy" was broached by Henry Jones Ford, a professor of politics commissioned to report on the Philippines for the Wilson government (1907). Noting that "a counsel to be good" is "not particularly helpful when the very thing to be decided is what is the good course to pursue," and arguing that morals are "subjective concepts and one is no more valid than the other," Ford proposed an alternative model of empire based on what "the biologists call symbiosis, or living together," in which the different countries would "minister each to the other's welfare and derive reciprocal benefits from the vital association."

Reconfiguring empire to ensure equal voices, however, required a new vocabulary. International relations professor Alfred Zimmern urged a reexamination of both "British" and "Empire" as words having "an important bearing on the development of public opinion" (1924), while South African Prime Minister Jan Smuts found it a "pity that the new thing is called by the old name" (1930). The Balfour Declaration (1926) established "the British Commonwealth of Nations," but Canadian John S. Ewart considered the nomenclatures "British Empire" and "British Commonwealth" to be "confusing," and judged that the proper term to recognize Canada's sovereignty would be "that known to international law as a Personal Union" (1927). Since new terms were not easily and universally adopted, empire continued to be used, but in ways that were either qualified – Smuts (1930) and J. W. Eggleston (1936) referred to the commonwealth as the "new Empire" – or modified through composite blendings, such as "imperial cooperation" (Harris, 1929) or "Imperial Federation" (Chandra Pal, 1918). At the same time, a new language was being sought. The Balfour Declaration described the commonwealth as "freely associated," "autonomous communities," "equal in status" (1926); Zimmern wrote that, politically, the "correctest designation" for "what used to be called The British Empire" would be "*the Britannic Entente*" (1924); Whelpley detected a move toward a "Federation" of states (1925); while, writing from South Africa, W. G. Ballinger urged "the ideals of the co-operative commonwealth" (1934). Yet, while T. R. Bavin, Premier of New South Wales, saw the commonwealth as a genuinely different iteration of empire and even "the greatest experiment ever made in human organization" (1929), Smuts worried about the possibility of ongoing "veiled imperialism" (1918), fearing that the changing vocabulary was simply dressing up old imperial ideas in new clothes. In *The Man Who Loved Children* (1940), Christina Stead exposed latent dangers in the new coinages by having the utopian but overbearing and paternalist Samuel Clemens Pollit devise grandiose schemes for a "Federal States of Europe," a "United States of Mankind," and a "Pan-Pacific Comity of Nations": his lofty terms, while promising "world peace, world love, world understanding," belie his agenda for " *Monoman or Manunity*," "in which all differences of nationality, creed, or education will be [. . .] gradually smoothed out," after "weed[ing] out all the misfits and degenerates." Australian Prime Minister William Hughes, for his part, dismissed the linguistic issue, declaring, "Federation-Empire – call it what you might," a strong bond was needed "to ensure the peace of the world," although like Ewart he asserted that "radical" change was necessary to make possible independent declarations of war (1916).

81

Change meant balancing unity with autonomy and accommodating multiple voices and different perspectives. A key question was, as Smuts put it, "how to reconcile unity with multiplicity, freedom with empire" (1930). Bavin similarly conceived the commonwealth as an effort to "unite in common world purpose, communities widely separated" and to negotiate "the two apparently opposing ideas of complete internal autonomy and a single policy" (1929). Redefining empire as belonging to the colonies as much as to the imperial center, Bipin Chandra Pal envisaged a group of nations "each autonomous within itself, and absolutely free," coming together "for purposes of mutual protection and progress" and in "pursuit" of "larger humanitarian ends" (1918), while R. G. Menzies, claiming that Australia saw "no future at all outside the British Empire," added the qualification that he meant "my Empire not merely yours" (1935). Eric W. Harris found "no necessary antagonism between Canadian identity and Imperialism" (1929), while Pal asserted that "both Indian and Imperial evolution" shared a "common ideal-end" (1918). The new vision sought a world model that was multicentric, with Britain being just a part like any other. As J. W. Eggleston argued, Britain, no longer "supreme," was in "a similar relative position to every other nation." The shift in the power structure of empire required "some adjustment of focus," and Eggleston urged Australia to look to the "Pacific basin" rather than to Europe (1936). Uncertainties arose, of course, about the difficulties of such radical transformation: for J. D. Whelpley, "the most interesting question" regarding "the future of the British Empire" was whether it will "continue in the ring" or be content to "leave the more strenuous work of the international arena to younger rivals" (1925).

The old British Empire seemed inevitably at an end, but it was hard to foresee the next stage. In "Thunder at Wembley," Virginia Woolf used the "violent commotion" of a storm disrupting the British Empire Exhibition to signal that "The Empire is perishing" (1924), while Leonard Woolf warned more apocalyptically that "Imperialism, as it was known in the nineteenth century, is no longer possible, and the only question is whether it will be buried peacefully or in blood and ruins" (1928). What might follow such catastrophe was imagined differently too. In Canadian Francis Marion Beynon's *Aleta Dey* (1919), the eponymous and pacifist narrator wonders, in a pessimistic moment, if WWI is not Nature's means for moving "the western nations to self-destruction," bringing about the "disintegration of these vast empires into little states," in order "to lead humanity up to something higher" (1919); in "Shooting an Elephant" (1936), however, while Orwell expressed no regrets that "the British Empire is dying," he feared that it was "a great deal better than the younger empires that are going to supplant it," most likely referring to both Stalinism and Franco's fascism in Spain. Winifred Holtby's *Mandoa, Mandoa!* (1933) – self-described as "a sort of satirical symposium of empire building" ([1931]1936) – leaves us with questions: when Conservative MP Maurice Durrant claims that the British race is "the heart of a vast commonwealth of nations," with "a destiny before it which has not yet been fulfilled," his socialist brother Bill counters, "you can't defeat a living movement by a dead tradition. This Empire business may have won tonight, but to-morrow, the dawn, is ours!" But when Talal – the Lord High Chamberlain of the African state of Mandoa [a fictional Abyssinia] – pledges, at the end of the novel, to take the "city's empty, weed-grown heart" and "build it better," positive hope mingles with uncertainty whether the envisioned new world can ever be sufficiently free from the infiltrated values of materialism and capitalism. Given the difficulties and controversies surrounding empire – both its existence and its demise – there is little doubt why Leonard Woolf predicted that "this movement of 19th-century imperialism and the reaction against it" would be seen in the future "as one of the most important facts in [the modernist] era" (1928).

SEE ALSO: *Democracy; Fascism; International; Race*

References

(1924). "Another Year of Wembley." *The Times* (London) (June 6), 9.

(1926). *Imperial Conference, 1926: Summary of Proceedings*. London: H. M. Stationery Office (Cmd 2768).

(1928). "Empire Day." Editorial. *The Charlottetown Guardian*, (May 24), 4.

(1929)."Science and Empire Marketing." *The British Medical Journal* 2.3579 (August 10): 268.

(1932). "The King to his People." *The Times* (London) (December 27), 10.

Ballinger, W. G. (1934). *Race and Economics in South Africa*. London: Hogarth.

Baring, Evelyn (1908). "The Government of Subject Races." *The Edinburgh Review* (January), 1–27.

Bates, Daisy (1938). *The Passing of the Aborigines: A Lifetime Spent Among the Natives of Australia*. London: J. Murray.

Bavin, the Hon. T. R. (1929). "Empire Citizenship." *The Australian Quarterly* 1.3 (September): 21–25.

Beynon, Francis Marion (1919). *Aleta Dey*. London: C. W. Daniel.

Conrad, Joseph (1902). *Heart of Darkness*. 1899. Edinburgh and London: Blackwood and Sons.

Conrad, Joseph (1907). *The Secret Agent: A Simple Tale*. London: Methuen.

Eggleston, J. W. (1936). "The British Empire, Australia and the Pacific." *The Australian Quarterly* 8.31 (September): 5–11.

Ewart, John S. (1927). "Canada, the Empire, and the United States." *Foreign Affairs* 6.1 (October): 116–127.

Ford, Henry Jones (1907). "The Ethics of Empire." *Political Science Quarterly* 22.3 (September): 498–505.

Franklin, Miles [Stella Maria Sarah] (1936). *All That Swagger*. Sydney: Angus and Robertson.

Franklin, Miles [Stella Maria Sarah] (1946). *My Career Goes Bung: Purporting to be the Autobiography of Sybylla Penelope Melvyn*. Melbourne: Georgian House.

Harris, W. Eric (1929). *Achates, or, The Future of Canada*. To-Day and To-Morrow. London: Kegan Paul; New York: E. P. Dutton.

Hobson, J. A. (1902). *Imperialism: A Study*. London: James Nisbet.

Holtby, Winifred (1933). *Mandoa, Mandoa!: A Comedy of Irrelevance*. London: Collins.

Holtby, Winifred (1936). "Some Letters from Winifred Holtby." Letter to Lady Rhondda, December 1931. *Time and Tide* (April 25): 589.

Holtby, Winifred (1936). *South Riding*. London: Collins.

Hughes, W. M. (1916). *"The Day" – and After: War Speeches of the Rt. Hon. W. M. Hughes, Prime Minister of Australia*. Arranged by Keith A. Murdoch and introduced by the Rt. Hon. Lloyd George. London and Toronto; Melbourne: Cassell.

James, C. L. R. (1936). "Abyssinia and the Imperialists." *The Keys: The Official Organ of the League of Colored Peoples* 3.3 (January–March): 32, 39–40.

Joyce, James (1922). *Ulysses*. Paris: Shakespeare and Co.

Low, A. Maurice (1916). "Nationalism in the British Empire." *The American Political Science Review* 10.2: 223–234.

Marson, Una (1935). Speech to the British Commonwealth League Conference (May 1935). The British Commonwealth League, Sadd Brown Collection. Fawcett Library, Guildhall, London. Qtd. in *The Life of Una Marson, 1905–1965*, by Delia Jarrett-Macauley. Manchester: Manchester University Press; New York: St. Martin's, 1998.

Menzies, the Hon. R. G. (1935). "Australia's Place in the Empire." *Journal of the Royal Institute of International Affairs* 14.4 (July–August): 480–495.

Montgomery, L. M. (1921). *Rilla of Ingleside*. New York: Grosset and Dunlap.

Orwell, George (1934). *Burmese Days: A Novel*. New York: Harper and Bros.

Orwell, George (1936). "Shooting an Elephant." *New Writing* 2 (Autumn): 1–7.

Padmore, George (1936). *How Britain Rules Africa*. London: Wishart Books.

Pal, Bipin Chandra (1918). *Indian Nationalism: Its Principles and Personalities*. Triplicane, Madras: S. R. Murthy.

Pound, Ezra (1915). "Homage to Wilfred Blunt." *Poetry: A Magazine of Verse* 3.6 (March): 222.

Smedley, Agnes (1929). *Daughter of Earth*. New York: Coward-McCann.

Smuts, General the Right Hon. J. C. (1930). "The British Empire and World Peace." *Journal of the Royal Institute of International Affairs* 9.2 (March): 141–153.

Smuts, Jan Christiaan (1918). *The League of Nations: A Practical Suggestion*. London: Hodder and Stoughton.

Stead, Christina (1940). *The Man Who Loved Children*. New York: Simon and Schuster.

Stead, Christina (1944). *For Love Alone*. New York: Harcourt, Brace and Co.

West, Rebecca (1941). *Black Lamb and Grey Falcon: The Record of a Journey Through Yugoslavia in 1937*. 2 vols. London: Macmillan.

West, Rebecca (1982). *1900*. London: Weidenfeld and Nicolson.

Whelpley, J. D. (1925). "The British Empire." *The North American Review* (March), 454–467.

Woolf, Leonard (1928). *Imperialism and Civilization*. London: Hogarth.

Woolf, Leonard (1969). *The Journey not the Arrival Matters: An Autobiography of the Years 1939–1969*. London: Hogarth.

Woolf, Virginia (1915). *The Voyage Out*. London: Duckworth.

Woolf, Virginia (1924). "Thunder at Wembley." *The Nation and Athenaeum* (June 28): 409–410.

Zimmern, Alfred (1924). "The British Empire in 1924." *The Nation and Athenaeum* 35.17 (July 26): 528–529.

Fascism

Fascism entered English usage in 1921, the year Benito Mussolini formed his *Partito Nazionale Fascista*. A mere 25 years later, following a war fought against Fascist regimes, George Orwell concluded that the word was so overused – and its associations, so negative – that it had "no meaning except in so far as it signifies something not desirable" (1946). The word's transformation from heady neologism to common pejorative was both rapid and uneven. When it exited the modernist period, fascism carried violently negative associations with totalitarianism, persecution, and suppression; before it consolidated in this direction, fascism was often positively associated with peace, solidarity, and cooperation. Its precise meaning was throughout a subject of debate.

Fascism derives from the Italian *fascio*, literally a bundle of rods bound around an axe, symbolizing a magistrate's authority in ancient Rome. The root metaphor of the word thus carries the dual meanings of collectivity and centralized power, a paradox that continued to inflect interpretations of the Fascist movement. Positive early employments of the term in English responded consciously to its Italian etymology. In *What is Fascism?* (1929), Harold E. Goad noted that *fascio*, "when applied to men [. . .] means an association or union of individuals co-operating for some purpose," and "Fascism [. . .] means loyalty to that union of purpose." Alexander Robertson similarly conceived fascism as "uniting the workman and the employer, the tenant and the proprietor, the servant and the master, in a common

ABCDE**F**GHIJKLMNOPQRSTUVWXYZ

Modernism: Keywords, First Edition. Melba Cuddy-Keane, Adam Hammond, and Alexandra Peat.
© 2014 Melba Cuddy-Keane. Published 2014 by John Wiley & Sons, Ltd.

brotherhood" (1929). At the same time, for British writers on the left, fascism began to imply the suppression of the individual and the elevation of an elite economic class. Virginia Woolf associated fascism with the "unmitigated masculinity" of "finance," "industry," and "Fascist corporations" (1929); George Bernard Shaw defined "what is now called Fascism" as "a Dictatorship of the Capitalists" (1928). Even Goad recognized that fascism predicated brotherhood on an ethnically uniform nation, stating that "Fascism prefers ethnocracy to democracy."

Fascism's emphasis on social cohesion was interpreted in widely divergent ways: as either a means of achieving peace in the turmoil following WWI or a motive for further militarism. In his early views, Wyndham Lewis argued that the "powerful and stable authority" of fascism might result in "some sort of peace to enable us to work" (1926). J. S. Barnes, the Secretary-General of the *Centre international des études sur le fascisme,* called fascism "the only theory on which a stable state may be built"; while recognizing fascism's "violence" and "intolerant" temper, Barnes nevertheless argued that "greater tolerance [. . .] would spell civil war" (1929). Reversing these implications, however, Harold Blumenfeld argued that "war and Fascism are two aspects of the same thing": "War breeds Fascism – Fascism breeds war" (1937).

Even the underlying politics aroused opposing associations, split in defining fascism's ideological identity as elitist or populist. When W. B. Yeats looked briefly to a Fascist movement in Ireland as "the only end to our troubles," he had in mind "the despotic rule of the educated classes" ([1933]1954); when Ezra Pound celebrated Italian Fascism, however, he called it an "anti-snob movement" ([1933]1936). Fascism's relation to communism was also a subject of debate. Reviewing recent books on fascism, Virginia M. Crawford noted that some portrayed fascism as "a glorious outburst of purest patriotism crushing the disruptive forces of a Lenin-inspired Communism," while others "dr[e]w parallels between the Soviet State and the Fascist State," seeing both as "founded on violence and destruction" (1923). W. Y. Elliot argued that fascism, despite its stated opposition to communism, had "taken over its methods and its general philosophy of government" – specifically, its disdain for the rule of law, its totalitarianism, and its opposition to liberalism (1926). Arguing that both "bully and oppress the individual," Vita Sackville-West stated, "I dislike Communism and Fascism equally," disclaiming "any difference between them, except in their names" (1937).

The imprecision of the term was itself defended and attacked. Ideological vagueness could be construed positively as political pragmatism. Mussolini himself argued that fascism should not be understood as a definite political ideology but rather as a pragmatic response to changing circumstances: "Fascism was not the nursling of a doctrine worked out beforehand," he purportedly said, but "from the beginning practical rather than theoretical" (1933). J. S. Barnes considered fascism "entirely pragmatic," and responded to the accusation that it "changes its methods as it goes along" by stating, "It does and is terribly proud of the fact that it can, without eating a single one of its principles" (1929). But vagueness could also imply irrational, chaotic feelings. T. S. Eliot noted that while few understood its meaning, the word fascism still excited a "vague sentiment of approval," which he worried might reflect a "desire to escape the burden of life and thought" (1928). H. G. Wells saw little to celebrate in this theoretical vacuum, asking, "What is the Nazi movement in Germany? What is Fascism in Italy? Young men who have nothing to do" (1935). Bertrand Russell labeled fascism "anti-rational and anti-scientific" (1945); Frederick Schuman, quoting the Nazi slogan "We think with our blood," described "German Fascism" as "mystical, cloudy, and often not only irrational but consciously anti-rational" (1934).

In designating a form of fascism as specifically "German," Schuman's title reflects growing perceptions of European fascisms as both different and linked. While the Spanish and Italian regimes were generally conflated, as evidenced by the contributions in *Authors Take Sides on the Spanish War*, the question of whether Hitler's National Socialist party counted as "Fascist" was generally unsettled before WWII. The National Socialists – called "Nazis" by the early 1930s – were closely associated with Mussolini's Fascists before 1939, but few writers felt comfortable grouping both under the term "Fascism," which was more often reserved for movements in Italy and Spain. Even during the war, R. G. Collingwood and Bertrand Russell wrote respectively of "Fascists and Nazis" (1940) and "Nazis and Fascists" (1945). Attacking anti-Semitism in Germany, Louis Golding's *A Letter to Adolf Hitler* (1932) used "Nazi" rather than "Fascist"; *The Brown Book of the Hitler Terror* (1933), a widely disseminated early account of crimes committed by Hitler's regime, including its anti-Semitism, referred to "Nazis," "National Socialists," and only once – in the Preface to the English edition – to "Hitler Fascism." A reason for this distinction may have been that anti-Semitism was not perceived as a prominent element of Italian Fascism until the late 1930s; Martin Agronsky stated in January 1939 that the preceding summer's "'race' campaign" in Italy "surprised and puzzled Italians and non-Italians, Jews and non-Jews."

With the approach of WWII, the meaning of fascism hardened and consolidated. What had been welcomed by some as a way forward to a peaceful future became widely decried as a regression into war and violence. Victor Gollancz wrote, "Fascism is culturally and intellectually a species of dementia praecox – a refusal any longer to carry the burden of being human, and a slipping back, happy sometimes but always disgusting, into the primeval slime" (1937). Abraham Magil, pointing to "a new barbarism," warned that "culture may perish under the heels of the fascist hordes; that the civilized world faces an age of book burnings and concentration camps" (1938). In an article on the Spanish Civil War, Leonard Woolf curtly equated "Franco, Fascism, and barbarism" (1937).

As its usage became more uniformly negative, fascism was increasingly seen as antithetical to art. Prior to this period, many had argued – particularly with reference to its Italian incarnation – that fascism shared with modernist art a common source. Roger Fry proposed in 1922 that there was an "aspect of the Italian character which creates Futurism and Fascism." Mussolini himself declared "without Futurism there would never have been a fascist revolution" (De Begnac [1934–1943]1990). When Pound justified his support of Mussolini on the basis "that the Duce will stand not with despots and the lovers of power but with the lovers of ORDER/*to kalon*" ([1933]1936), he conflated politics and aesthetics, equating social order with *to kalon*, Greek for "the beautiful." In the late 1930s and early 1940s, many writers continued to link modernist aesthetics to Fascist politics, although in increasingly negative ways. W. H. Auden argued that Dada and Surrealism "foreshadowed in art the irrational violence which was to emerge politically a few years later as Fascism" (1942). The alternative and growingly pervasive use, however, placed fascism and art on two separate planes. Virginia Woolf, opposing the dominant male voice, wrote that the "Fascist poem" could only be a motherless "abortion" (1928). Introducing *Artists Against Fascism and War*, Aldous Huxley stated, "the whole activity of the self-disciplined artist is a standing protest against war and dictatorship" (1935). John Langdon-Davies went further to state, "Art and anti-Fascism are synonymous" (1937), and Auden considered that a Fascist victory in Spain "would create an atmosphere in which the creative artist and all who care for justice, liberty and culture would find it impossible to work or even exist" (1937). Ernest Hemingway expressed the antagonism in blunt terms: "There is only one form of government that cannot produce good writers, and that system is fascism. For fascism is a lie told by bullies. A writer who will not lie cannot live or work under fascism" (1937).

Hemingway's shifting use of the word, from a specific reference to Fascist governments to a general term for dishonesty and brutality, illustrates the broadest evolution in the word's semantic history. As the term became a linguistic surrogate for totalitarianism, violence, and persecution, it was employed to describe abuses at home as well as abroad. As early as 1926, W. E. B. Du Bois drew a connection between "Fascismo [. . .] in its bold, physical form as it is appearing in Italy and Spain" and "its more spiritual form as it appears in American Fundamentalism," denouncing both "forms of Force." George Seldes contrasted "faraway fascism" and "nearby Fascists," arguing that "the DuPont, Ford, Hearst, Mellon and Rockefeller Empires" represented a "native American

Fascism" that sought to "end the civil liberties of the nation" and "make more money at the expense of a slave nation" (1943). In the UK, Sir Peter Chalmers-Mitchell argued that Germany, Italy, and Spain represented a "more virulent phase" of fascism, as opposed to a "weaker form" in the British government (1937). For many feminists, Fascist regimes in Europe had their counterpart in patriarchal institutions in England. Winifred Holtby attacked Mussolini's call upon women to be "Fascisti" as promulgating the "cult of the cradle" – co-opting women into childbearing as a way of boosting military strength through increased population; the same fixation on woman as "breeder" and "milch cow" rather than "free human being," she argued, pervaded Nazi Germany, France, Southern Ireland, and "all Anglo-Saxon countries," even when not bolstered by government support (1934). Virginia Woolf argued that "the daughters of educated men" were fighting "the same enemy" as those mobilizing "against the Nazi and the Fascist." Yet for her, the term "anti-Fascism" was merely the "jargon of the moment"; women's battle against "Tyrant" and "Dictator" had been waged for a much longer time (1938). Orwell seemingly agreed that over-generalized usage reduced the word's usefulness; nonetheless, a significant record of cultural history resides in the word's semantic change. Although fascism began with the positive connotation of common people banding together for the common good, by the end of the modernist period, antifascism had become a rallying cry on behalf of the oppressed.

SEE ALSO: *Common Mind, Group Thinking; Democracy; Propaganda; Race; Woman, New Woman*

References

Agronsky, Martin (1939). "Racism in Italy." *Foreign Affairs* 17.2 (January): 391–401.

Auden, W. H. (1937). "Answer to 'Spain: The Question'." In *Authors Take Sides on the Spanish War*. London: Left Review. n.p.

Auden, W. H. (1942). "Auden Speaks of Poetry and Total War." *Chicago Sun* (March 14), 14.

Barnes, J. S. (1929). "Fascism." *The Criterion* 8.32 (April): 445–459.

Blumenfeld, Frank B. (1937). *A Blueprint for Fascism: What the Industrial Mobilization Plan Holds for America*. New York: American League Against War and Fascism.

Chalmers-Mitchell, Sir Peter (1937). "Answer to 'Spain: The Question'." In *Authors Take Sides on the Spanish War*. London: Left Review. n.p.

Collingwood, R. G. (1940). "Fascism and Nazism." *Philosophy* 15.58 (April): 168–176.

Crawford, Virginia M. (1923). "The Rise of Fascism and What It Stands For." *Studies: An Irish Quarterly Review* 12.48 (December): 539–552.

De Begnac, Ivon (1990). *Taccuini Mussoliniani* (ed. F. Perfetti). [1934–1943]. Bologna: Il Mulino.

Du Bois, W. E. B. (1926). "The Shape of Fear." *The North American Review* (June–August), 291–304.

Eliot, T. S. (1928). "The Literature of Fascism." *Criterion* 8.31 (December): 280–290.

Elliott, W. Y. (1926). "Mussolini, Prophet of the Pragmatic Era in Politics." *Political Science Quarterly* 41.2 (June): 161–192.

Fry, Roger (1922). "Settecentismo." *Burlington Magazine for Connoisseurs* (October), 158–159.

Goad, Harold E. (1929). *What is Fascism? An Explanation of Its Essential Principles.* 2nd corrected edition. Florence: Italian Mail and Tribune.

Golding, Louis (1932). *A Letter to Adolf Hitler.* The Hogarth Letters. London: Hogarth.

Gollancz, Victor (1937). "Answer to 'Spain: The Question'." In *Authors Take Sides on the Spanish War.* London: Left Review. n.p.

Hemingway, Ernest (1937). "Fascism is a Lie." Speech to the American Writer's Congress, 4 June 1937. *New Masses* 23 (June 22): 4.

Holtby, Winifred (1934). *Women and a Changing Civilization.* London: John Lane, The Bodley Head.

Huxley, Aldous (1935). "Foreword." In *Artists Against Fascism and War.* Catalogue for Artists International Association Exhibition. n.p.

Langdon-Davies, John (1937). "Answer to 'Spain: The Question'". In *Authors Take Sides on the Spanish War.* London: Left Review. n.p.

Lewis, Wyndham (1926). *The Art of Being Ruled.* London: Chatto & Windus.

Magil, Abraham (1938). *The Peril of Fascism: The Crisis of American Democracy.* New York: International Publishers.

Marley, Dudley Leigh Aman (1933). Introduction. In *The Brown Book of the Hitler Terror and the Burning of the Reichstag*, by the World Committee of the Victims of German Fascism. London: Victor Gollancz. 9–10.

Mussolini, Benito (1933). *The Political and Social Doctrine of Fascism.* Trans. Jane Soames. Day to Day Pamphlets. London: Hogarth.

Orwell, George (1946). "Politics and the English Language." *Horizon* (April), 252–265.

Pound, Ezra (1936). *Jefferson and/or Mussolini: Fascism as I Have Seen It.* 1933. London: S. Nott.

Robertson, Alexander (1929). *Mussolini and the New Italy.* 2nd rev. and enl. ed. 1928. London: H. R. Allenson.

Russell, Bertrand (1945). *A History of Western Philosophy and Its Connection with Political and Social Circumstances from the Earliest Times to the Present Day.* New York: Simon and Schuster.

Sackville-West, Vita (1937). "Answer to 'Spain: The Question'." In *Authors Take Sides on the Spanish War.* London: Left Review. n.p.

Schuman, Frederick L. (1934). "The Political Theory of German Fascism." *The American Political Science Review* 28.2 (April): 210–232.

Seldes, George, assisted by Helen Seldes (1943). *Facts and Fascism.* New York: In Fact, Inc.

Shaw, George Bernard (1928). *The Intelligent Woman's Guide to Socialism and Capitalism.* New York: Brentano's.

Wells, H. G. (1935). "Civilization on Trial." *Foreign Affairs* 13.4 (July): 595–599.

Woolf, Leonard (1937). "Answer to 'Spain: The Question'." In *Authors Take Sides on the Spanish War.* London: Left Review. n.p.

Woolf, Virginia (1929). *A Room of One's Own.* London: Hogarth.

Woolf, Virginia (1938). *Three Guineas.* London: Hogarth.

Yeats, W. B. (1954). Letter to Olivia Shakespear, 13 July 1933. [1933]. In *The Letters of W. B. Yeats* (ed. Allan Wade). London: Rupert Hart-Davis. 812.

Form, Formalism

Form has been used ubiquitously in English from at least C13, applied to such various subjects as the body, conversation, government, manners, nature, and printing. In its simplest meaning, form refers to visible or outward appearance, but form also acquired the contrasting sense, in philosophical usage, of shaping principle or inner form. The close tie between the two meanings appears in the use of form for manners or behavior, where form implies both the rules of conduct and the ethical principles from which the rules were derived. John Galsworthy explained the English concept of "good form" as "control of self" grounded on two ideals — "suppression of the ego lest it trample on the corns of other people, and exaltation of the maxim: 'Deeds before words'" ([1917]1919). Recognizing, however, that meaningful inner form can deteriorate into empty outer form, Galsworthy noted that "good form, like any other religion" begins with "a core of virtue" that later becomes "commonised and petrified." Such petrification underlies John Dowell's ironic, self-deprecating comment, at the end of Ford Madox Ford's *The Good Soldier* (1915), that, in a crucial past moment, he repressed an expression of feeling because it "would not be quite English good form." The dwindling of ethical form into mere lifestyle is evidenced when a character in Evelyn Waugh's *A Handful of Dust* (1934), about to visit a country house for the weekend, asks, "What's the form?," and gets the response, "Very quiet and enjoyable."

In the modernist period, form became a focal point in debates about the meaning and value of art, often engaging similar concerns about the inadequacy and "petrification" of inherited models from the past. New ways of seeing or experiencing reality seemed to demand new forms. This approach, however, involved a shift in the understanding of content. Traditionally, content was equated with subject matter or ideas; as Thomas Huxley stated, "the great mass of the literature we esteem is valued, not merely because of having artistic form, but because of its intellectual content" (1883). Content could also be conceived, however, as the emotions, attitudes, and values embodied in formal elements like structure and style. At the end of the modernist period, Mark Shorer thus distinguished between "content" and "the *achieved* content, the form, the work of art as a work of art," arguing that form (or "technique") yields the one means of "discovering, exploring, developing" the experience conveyed in a literary work, and furthermore of "evaluating it" (1948).

In this approach, form is not merely "effective rhetoric"; rather, "form is meaning" (Brooks, 1951). I. A. Richards argued, "the close cooperation of the form with the meaning" means a continuous process of one "modifying" the other and "being modified by it" (1929). May Sinclair defended Imagism as an attempt to merge form and content: "The Image [. . .] is Form. But it is not pure form. It is form *and* substance," offering either "the form of the thing" or "the form of a passion or emotion or mood" (1915). Samuel Beckett read the title "Work in

91

Form, Formalism

Progress" – the early serialized portions of Joyce's *Finnegans Wake* – as a pun referring to both writing and life and thus "a good example of a form carrying a strict inner determination" (1929). Arguing that Joyce presented not the "static lifelessness" of Hell and Paradise but "a continuous purgatorial process at work," Beckett cited "a furious restlessness to the form" that manifested itself in "an endless verbal germination, maturation, putrefaction, the cyclic dynamism of the intermediate" purgatorial state. While emphasizing the importance of form, however, Anglo-American modernists rarely went as far as their European counterparts in narrowing literary scholarship to aesthetic judgment. Victor Erlich stated in 1954 that even claims by the Russian formalists about "disengaging art from society and from the creator" should be read as overstated polemic, motivated by resistance to a "totalitarian" regime; he also noted that "the Formalist influence on Western criticism was until recently almost nil." In 1951, Cleanth Brooks summed up the position of "the so-called 'new critics'" – a group of US scholars emerging in the 1940s devoted to close textual analysis – in an essay entitled "The Formalist Critics"; however, he roundly rejected the "misunderstandings" that formalist critics believed in "cutting [the poem or novel] loose from its author and from his life as a man" or "severing it from those who actually read it." These aspects, he argued, along with formalist criticism, were all part of "the practicing critic['s]" "various jobs."

92

The question of the right form for the modernist age, however, vacillated between desires for tighter and looser shapes. Henry James urged that "form alone *takes*, and holds and preserves, substance – saves it from the welter of helpless verbiage that we swim in as in a sea of tasteless tepid pudding" ([1912]1920), and he elevated "a deep-breathing economy and an organic form" over the "loose baggy monsters" of C19 fiction (1908). Clayton Hamilton also considered the C19 "three-volume novel" "nearly always, in the matter of structure, a slovenly form" (1908). Judging the C19 novel to be too loose even to be considered "a form," T. S. Eliot nonetheless found it an appropriate "expression of an age which had not sufficiently lost all form to feel the need of something stricter"; in contrast, he considered that in abandoning the novel for the "mythical method" in *Ulysses*, James Joyce took "a step [. . .] toward that order and form" capable of "giving a shape and significance to the immense panorama and futility and anarchy that is contemporary history" (1923). H. G. Wells engaged in an alternately friendly and bitter battle with Henry James, in which Wells inveighed against James's elevation of "The Novel" to an "Art Form" and argued that "the novel was about as much an art form as a marketplace or a boulevard" (1934), while James lamented the looseness of form in Wells and Arnold Bennett, making for the "disconnection of method from matter" and "so much truth to be extracted under an equal leakage of its value" (1914). Situated on both sides of the debate, E. M. Forster argued that in an age "when the human race is trying to ride a whirlwind," "form of some kind is imperative" as "the outward evidence of order" (1949), yet he also defended the novel as "that spongy tract," "sogged with humanity," and praised that "untidy novel" *War and Peace* for achieving the "idea to which the novelist must cling": "Not completion. Not rounding off but opening out" (1927). Virginia Woolf sought both heterogeneity and concentrated intensity: seeking a form that would "take the mould of that queer conglomeration of incongruous things – the modern mind" yet also provide "some general shaping power, some conception which lends the whole harmony and force" (1927). Louise Bogan acknowledged the "modern" objections "that form binds" and "that poetic form has become exhausted" yet found in "'modern' poetry as a whole" an "alternate and gradual loosening and tightening of form"; despite the modern poet's "efforts to free poetry from formal restriction," she noted "as much experimentation *in* form as out of it" (1953).

Compounding differences of opinion about the kind of form to be sought, there was no common vocabulary for, or consensus about, what constitutes literary form. In *The Craft of Fiction* (1921), Percy Lubbock lamented the "poverty of our critical vocabulary," and I. A. Richards placed "form" along with "sincerity," "truth," and "meaning" as words that "discharge a cloud of heterogeneous missiles instead of a single meaning" (1929). Form could refer simply to genre, as in epistolary or autobiographic form, or it could refer broadly to all matters of representation, as in Lubbock's references to "whole design," "defined shape," or "the modes of rendering a story." In more specific uses, form was interchangeable with method, technique, and style and was located in such elements as "point of view" (Hamilton, Lubbock) and tone (Richards, Brooks). Cleanth Brooks and the New Critics saw "the essential structure of a poem" as ideally a "pattern of resolved stresses," and held that the poem "triumphs over the apparently contradictory and conflicting elements of experience by unifying them into a new pattern" (1947). R. S. Crane, however, charged Brooks with the "Critical Monism" of reducing all poetry to "the single principle [. . .] which is designated as 'irony' or 'paradox,'" and "deriving the 'structure' of poems [solely] out of their linguistic elements or parts" (1948). While Crane also conceived the literary work as ideally "a complete and ordered whole," he urged an expanded approach to "the plot," going beyond mere "action" to encompass all elements through which experience is "rendered" – much like the Russian formalists' move beyond *fabula* to *sjuzhet* – and he analyzed narrative structure affectively and dynamically as an "interplay of desires and expectations" (1950).

The meaning of form was thus so varied that Erlich could note congruencies between the Russian formalists and critics like Brooks and Richards who "promoted the rigorous discipline of close reading," while F. R. Leavis could praise Richards as "releas[ing criticism] from the thought-frustrating spell of 'Form'" (1969). By form, Leavis meant mere technical analysis, and what he approved in Richards

93

was the linking of imagery, tone, and even sound in poetry to questions about "sensibility" and "perceptive response." Many modernist writers were indeed wary of mere technical analysis: Ezra Pound claimed, "there is a distinct decadence when interest passes from significance – meaning the total significance of a word – into DETAILS of technique" (1938), while E. M. Forster explained that while "principles and systems may suit other forms of art," he had titled his lectures *Aspects of the Novel* "because [aspects] is unscientific and vague" (1927). Clayton Hamilton's *Materials and Methods of Fiction* (an alternate way of saying content and form) had immense popularity in the classroom, being republished in various versions from 1908 to 1940; in a review entitled "The Anatomy of Fiction" (1919), however, Virginia Woolf castigated Hamilton for dissecting fiction like a frog, while Forster's review, "The Fiction Factory," lamented the way the poor hen of the novel had been swooped down upon by "the American eagle" (1919).

Similarly criticizing Lubbock for "appl[ying] his Röntgen rays to the novel," Woolf proposed a possibly startling alternative: "the 'book itself' is not form which you see, but emotion which you feel" (1922). Arguing that "form" "comes from the visual arts," she suggested that a good approach was to read a story and "set down our impressions as we go along, and so perhaps discover what it is that bothers us in Mr. Lubbock's use of the word form." What bothered Woolf was the transportation of a term from a static art to a mobile one, but this was a point strongly made by Lubbock himself. The novel comes to us, he wrote, "not as a single form," "but as a moving stream of impressions," "revealed little by little, page by page" and "withdrawn as fast as it is revealed." As a result, he admitted, "to grasp the shadowy and fantasmal form of a book" is an impossibility, since "nothing, no power, will keep a book steady and motionless before us, so that we may have time to examine its shape and design." Consequently, his goal in analyzing form was to give the reader something to hang on to, enabling the work to "last for longer" in the mind. Many literary discussions of form thus emphasized its effect on the reader, an aspect noted in discussions of "significant form" (Bell, 1914) in the pictorial arts as well. Richards quoted approvingly Roger Fry's comment in *Vision and Design* (1920) (another variant for content and form) that "a work of art was not the record of beauty already existent elsewhere, but the expression of an emotion felt by the artist and conveyed to the spectator" (1924). The long-lasting textbook *Understanding Poetry* (Brooks and Warren, 1938) emphasized that "the arrangement of form [. . .] is directly connected with the concentration and intensity of poetry," and the details "must be so arranged that they will have the greatest effect on the reader." R.S. Crane – in an analysis that caused him to be considered "neo-Aristotelian" – went further to locate form affectively in a text's "distinctive 'working or power,' as the form of the plot in a tragedy [. . .] is the capacity of its unified sequence of actions to effect through pity and fear a catharsis of such emotions" (1950).

Thus, form could mean technique or it could refer to shaped experience, and it was in this latter sense that modernists sought new forms to capture modern perception. Virginia Woolf protested that "for us at this moment the form of fiction most in vogue more often misses than secures the thing we seek" ([1919]1925), and she questioned, "Energy has been liberated, but into what forms is it to flow? To try the accepted forms, to discard the unfit, to create others which are more fitting, is a task that must be accomplished before there is freedom or achievement" (1920). Lucia Trent and Ralph Cheyney claimed that modern poets "ask with justice why grammar must be a fossilized skeleton instead of a living – i.e. changing – form for embodying thoughts. What they want to say is new, different – why not say it with fresh constructions as well as fresh images?" (1934). William Carlos Williams argued that Gertrude Stein made "the 'formal' parts of writing" "the first concern of the moment," enacting "a break-away" from the "dead weight of logical burdens" which form traditionally "dragg[ed] behind" (1930); elsewhere he argued that Marianne Moore's "break through all preconceptions of poetic form" had the liberating power to "ruin" the reader's "whole preconceived scheme of values" (1925).

The perception that form could embody a "scheme of values" gave the search for new forms an ideological and political valency, especially with regard to gender and race. Introducing Dorothy Richardson's *Pointed Roofs* (1915), J. D. Beresford noted "a peculiar difference which is, perhaps, the mark of a new form in fiction," and Virginia Woolf stated that Richardson's *The Tunnel* (1919) "represents a genuine conviction of the discrepancy between what she has to say and the form provided by tradition for her to say it in" (1919). Considering form at the level of both genre and sentence, Woolf elsewhere argued, "there is no reason to think that the form of the epic or of the poetic play suits a woman any more than the sentence suits her" (1929), and she praised Richardson's writing in *Revolving Lights* (1923) for "invent[ing]" or at least "develop[ing]" and apply[ing]" to her own uses, a sentence which we might call the psychological sentence of the feminine gender" (1923). Richardson herself commented that "feminine prose" "should properly be unpunctuated, moving from point to point without formal obstructions" (1938). Raising similar concerns in relation to race, James Weldon Johnson argued that "the colored poet in the United States [. . .] needs to find a form that will express the racial spirit," cautioning, however, against adopting "the mere mutilation of English spelling and pronunciation" and calling for a new "form that is freer and larger than dialect, but which will still hold the racial flavor" (1922).

The possibilities for changing literary form were reinforced by pervasive descriptions of form as "plastic," "elastic," and "flexible." Henry James wrote, "The novel is of all the pictures the most comprehensive and the most elastic. It will stretch anywhere – it will take in absolutely anything [. . .] Its plasticity, its elasticity are infinite" (1899). John Galsworthy claimed, "The beauty of the novel lies in its infinite variety, its elasticity, and its breadth" (1924). Virginia Woolf described Proust as "so porous, so pliable, so perfectly receptive that we realize him only as an envelope, thin but elastic, which stretches wider and wider and serves not to enforce a view but to enclose a world" (1929); and she stated "that it is to express character – not to preach doctrines, sing songs, or celebrate the glories of the British Empire, that the form of the novel, so clumsy, verbose, and undramatic, so rich, elastic, and alive, has been evolved" (1924). Avowing "that poetic form" must be "as plastic as thought itself," Ernest Fenollosa and Ezra Pound looked to "The Chinese Written Character as a Medium for Poetry" (1920), asserting that a language based on the identity of "thing and action" rather than grammatical relationships would fulfill the "one necessity" to "keep words as flexible as possible."

The flexibility welcomed in form carried over into a willingness to engage or consider multiple differing forms. Clayton Hamilton wrote that "style" is "in every case a quality personal to the author who attains it," concluding that "each is right in asserting the value of his own method, and wrong in denying the value of the other's." Virginia Woolf similarly claimed, "any method is right, every method is right," adding that "nothing – no 'method,' no experiment, even of the wildest – is forbidden, but only falsity and pretence" (1925). Welcoming debates concerning "the form of the novel," Henry James wrote, "Art lives upon discussion, upon experiment, upon curiosity, upon variety of attempt, upon the exchange of views and the comparison of standpoints" (1884); for his part, Wells, reflecting back on his quarrel with James, confessed that he had "had a queer feeling that [they] were both incompatibly right" (1934).

SEE ALSO: *Advertising; Impression, Impressionism; Readers, Reading; Rhythm; Modern, Modernism; Propaganda; Words, Language*

References

Beckett, Samuel (1929). "DANTE ... BRUNO. VICO .. JOYCE." *transition: An International Quarterly for Creative Experiment* 16–17 (June): 242–253.

Bell, Clive (1914). *Art.* London: Chatto & Windus.

Beresford, J. D. (1915). "Introduction." In *Pointed Roofs,* by Dorothy Richardson. London: Duckworth.

Bogan, Louise (1953). "The Pleasures of Formal Poetry." *The Quarterly Review of Literature* 7: 176–185.

Brooks, Cleanth (1947). *The Well Wrought Urn.* New York: Harcourt, Brace and Co.

Brooks, Cleanth (1951). "The Formalist Critics." *The Kenyon Review* 13.1 (Winter): 72–81.

Brooks, Cleanth and Robert Penn Warren (1938). *Understanding Poetry.* New York: H. Holt.

Crane, R.S. (1948). "Cleanth Brooks; Or, the Bankruptcy of Critical Monism." *Modern Philology* 45.4 (May): 226–245.

Crane, R. S. (1950). "The Plot of Tom Jones." *The Journal of General Education* 4.2 (January): 112–130.

Eliot, T. S. (1923). "Ulysses, Order, and Myth." *The Dial* 75.11 (November): 480–483.

Erlich, Victor (1954). "Russian Formalism: In Perspective." *The Journal of Aesthetics and Art Criticism* 13.2 (December): 215–225.

Fenollosa, Ernest Francisco and Ezra Pound (1920). "The Chinese Written Character as a Medium for Poetry." 1919. In *Instigations of Ezra Pound*. New York: Boni and Liveright. 357–401.

Ford, Ford Madox (1915). *The Good Soldier* London: John Lane.

[Forster, E. M.] (1919). "The Fiction Factory (by a Novelist)." Rev. of *Materials and Methods of Fiction* by Clayton Hamilton. *Daily News* (April 23), 6.

Forster, E. M. (1927). *Aspects of the Novel*. London: Edward Arnold.

Forster, E. M. (1949). "Art for Art's Sake." *Harper's Magazine* (August), 31–34.

Fry, Roger (1920). *Vision and Design*. London: Chatto & Windus.

Galsworthy, John (1919). "American and Briton" [1917]. In *Another Sheaf*. London: W. Heinemann. 69–87.

Galsworthy, John et al. (1924). "What is a Good Novel? A Symposium." *The Highway: A Journal of Adult Education* 16.3 (Summer): 100–110.

Hamilton, Clayton (1908). *Materials and Methods of Fiction*. New York: Baker and Taylor.

Huxley, Thomas (1883). *On Science and Art in Relation to Education: An Address Delivered in the Liverpool Institute, February 16th, 1883*. An address delivered in the Liverpool Institute, February 16, 1883. Liverpool: D. Marples.

James, Henry (1884). "The Art of Fiction." *Longman's Magazine* 4 (September): 180–186.

James, Henry (1899). "The Future of the Novel." In *The Universal Anthology: A Collection of the Best Literature, Ancient, Mediaeval and Modern, with Biographical and Explanatory Notes* (eds. Richard Garnett, Leon Vallée and Alois Brandl). 33 vols. London: Clarke. Vol. 28: xiii–xxiv.

James, Henry (ed.) (1908). "Preface to *The Tragic Muse*." In *The Novels and Tales of Henry James*. New York Edition. 26 vols. New York: Charles Scribner's Sons. Vol. 7: v–xxii.

James, Henry (1914). "The Younger Generation." *TLS* (March 19), 133–134; (April 2), 157–158.

James, Henry (1920). Letter to Hugh Walpole, 19 May 1912. [1912]. In *The Letters of Henry James* (ed. Percy Lubbock). 2 vols. New York: Charles Scribner's Sons; Macmillan and Co. Vol. 2: 236–238.

Johnson, James Weldon (1922). *The Book of American Negro Poetry*. New York: Harcourt, Brace.

Leavis, F. R. (1969). *English Literature in Our Time and the University*. The Clarke Lectures, 1967. London: Chatto & Windus.

Lubbock, Percy (1921). *The Craft of Fiction*. London: Jonathan Cape.

Pound, Ezra (1938). *Guide to Kulchur*. London: Faber and Faber.

Richards, I. A. (1924). *Principles of Literary Criticism*. London: Kegan Paul, Trench, Trubner.

Richards, I. A. (1929). *Practical Criticism*. London: Kegan Paul, Trench, Trubner.

Richardson, Dorothy (1938). "Foreword." In *Pilgrimage*. 4 vols. New York: A. A. Knopf. Vol. 1: 9–10.

Shorer, Mark (1948). "Technique as Discovery." *The Hudson Review* 1.1 (Spring): 67–87.

Sinclair, May (1915). "Two Notes: I. On H.D. II. On Imagism." *The Egoist* 2.6 (June 1): 88–89.

Trent, Lucia and Ralph Cheyney (ed.) (1934). "What is This Modernism?" In *More Power to Poets*. New York: Henry Harrison. 106–110.

Waugh, Evelyn (1934). *A Handful of Dust*. London: Chapman and Hall.

Wells, H. G. (1934). "Digression about Novels." In *Experiment in Autobiography: Discoveries and Conclusions of a Very Ordinary Brain (Since 1866)*. 2 vols. London: V. Gollancz and Cresset. Vol. 1: 410–415.

Williams, William Carlos (1925). Rev. of *Observations* by Marianne Moore. *The Dial* 78.5 (May): 393–491.

Williams, William Carlos (1930). "The Work of Gertrude Stein." *Pagany: A Native Quarterly* 1.1 (January–March): 41–45.

[Woolf, Virginia] (1919). "The Tunnel." Rev. of *The Tunnel* by Dorothy Richardson. *TLS* (February 13), 81.

[Woolf, Virginia] V. W. (1919). "The Anatomy of Fiction." Rev. of *Materials and Methods of Fiction* by Clayton Hamilton, with an introduction by Brander Matthews. *The Athenaeum* (May 16), 331.

[Woolf, Virginia] (1920). "Men and Women." *TLS* (March 18), 182.

[Woolf, Virginia] (1922). "On Re-Reading Novels." *TLS* (July 20), 465–466.

Woolf, Virginia (1923). "Romance and the Heart." Rev. of *The Grand Tour* by Romer Wilson and *Revolving Lights* by Dorothy Richardson. *The Nation and Athenaeum* (May 19): 229.

Woolf, Virginia (1924). *Mr Bennett and Mrs Brown*. London: Hogarth.

Woolf, Virginia (1925). "Modern Fiction." ["Modern Novels," 1919]. In *The Common Reader*. London: Hogarth. 184–195.

Woolf, Virginia (1927). "Poetry, Fiction and the Future." *The New York Herald Tribune*, August 14, Section 6, Books: 1, 6–7 and August 21, Section 6, Books: 1, 6.

Woolf, Virginia (1929). *A Room of One's Own*. London: Hogarth.

God, Gods

As the modernist world experienced increased uncertainty about the existence of transcendent spiritual truth, God became a keyword for a broader discussion of the possibilities of belief. The discoveries of biological science, the embedding of Church practices in repressive C19 social and moral prescriptions, increasing materialism, and the brutality of WWI undermined, for many Western people, belief in both traditional religion and cosmic justice. Although some responded to the loss of belief with angst and despair, many continued to affirm traditional beliefs, while others, welcoming a release from seemingly outmoded or even destructive forms, sought ways to translate the function of God into human terms, or to reimagine spiritual engagement through nature, the unconscious, or a collective consciousness. In the process, the meaning of God was expanded and pluralized, not only in a shift from transcendent to immanent spirituality, but also in response to alternative spiritual models, particularly nonwestern and nontraditional religions.

Friedrich Nietzsche's assertion that "god is dead" ([1882]1910) and Sigmund Freud's theory that God is an "illusion" created as wish-fulfillment for an "exalted father" ([1927]1928) articulated the spiritual crisis of the modern age. They were not the first, however, to posit a fundamental change to belief. Among C19 "doubters," Matthew Arnold noted the "uncertainty" around "this important but ambiguous term god," and posed a challenge for his modernist successors: "two

*ABCDEF***G***HIJKLMNOPQRSTUVWXYZ*

Modernism: Keywords, First Edition. Melba Cuddy-Keane, Adam Hammond, and Alexandra Peat.
© 2014 Melba Cuddy-Keane. Published 2014 by John Wiley & Sons, Ltd.

things about the Christian religion must surely be clear. [. . .] One is that men cannot do without it; the other, they cannot do with it as it is" (1875). The need to do "with" led, at one end of the spectrum, to a reaffirmation of God along traditional paths, but with renewed individual commitment to a higher purpose. For C. S. Lewis, religious "doctrines" were a necessary "map" to get people "in touch with God" (1952). Evelyn Waugh emphasized the personal relation to "an all-wise God who has a particular task for each individual soul" (1946), and, in Waugh's *Brideshead Revisited*, Guy asks God for "his chance to do some small service, which only he could perform, for which he had been created" (1945). The necessity of doing "without" led, at the other end of the spectrum, to the idea of God as logically absent from a universe incommensurable with human desire. In Samuel Beckett's *Waiting for Godot* (1954), God is replaced by the diminutive "Godot," a man with a white beard who supposedly promised to come but who does not – and indeed could never – appear in a static world devoid of meaningful action. In Barnes's "The Passion," when an antiquated Princess who has acquired, in her old age, "the power, the authority, and the rot of a high irony" says, "yet if a little, light man with a beard had come to me and said, 'I love you', I should have believed in God," she acerbically implies the self-deceiving romanticism of believing in both God and love (1924).

In addition to implications of God's absence, what God traditionally represented could appear either as distanced or as shrunk. Retaining the attribute of overwhelming power, God could be imagined in vast, impersonal terms: in "The Convergence of the Twain" (1914), Thomas Hardy described the implacable force that destroyed the *Titanic* as the "Immanent Will" and "the Spinner of the Years"; William Faulkner's Mr. Compson names the inscrutable power, "Fate, destiny, retribution, irony – call it what you will" (1936). Alternatively, God could be diminished, envisaged lightly or bitterly as a storybook god, a childish comfort lost in the past. In Rebecca West's "Indissoluble Matrimony," George Silverton yearns for "a child's God, an immense arm coming down from the hills and lifting him to a kindly bosom" (1914), while Wyndham Lewis described "all Gods" as "a repose" and "a refuge," likening them to static comic types as similarly "illusions hugged and lived in" (1917). Deflated to a comical human figure, God is satirized in Woolf's *The Voyage Out* when St John Hirst wonders, "what would happen if God did exist – an old gentlemen in a beard and a long blue dressing gown, extremely testy and disagreeable as he's bound to be" (1915). In *Potterism*, Rose Macaulay similarly mocks simplistic belief when a character who has never "thought [. . .] out" what he meant "by God," vaguely defends going to church because "if they didn't some being called God would be angry" (1920).

The loosening of traditional religious frameworks raised the challenge of how to live without the moral absolutes God's presence implied, prompting some to take up life at a lower, perhaps more human, level of expectation. After the death of his son in WWI, H. G. Wells's Mr. Britling finds himself unable to accept "an omnipotent God who look[s] down on battles and deaths and all the waste and horror of this war" and "lets these things happen," and so conceives a "finite God who struggles in his great and comprehensive way as we struggle in our weak and silly way" (1916). Zora Neale Hurston's Janie in *Their Eyes Were Watching God* reconciles to a god who, while not absent, "would do less than he had in his heart" (1937). In Rose Macaulay's *Told by An Idiot* (1923), Mr. and Mrs. Garden represent two possible reactions to "the absence of God": while Mr. Garden must constantly ask "if there were no God," how could one believe in "absolute standards of righteousness," Mrs. Garden finds that "belief matters very little" and decides "to stay at home" where there is "a good deal to do," and devote herself to "practical things." For Ernest Hemingway's Brett in *The Sun Also Rises* (1926), what "we have instead of God" is the truncated morality of "deciding not to be a bitch"; as for Beckett's Vladimir and Estragon, while the immobility of waiting makes meaningful action impossible, their one possibly positive response is to "go on" together (1954).

Modernists also reflected on the values traditionally signified by God, frequently critiquing the translation of God into secular terms as a perversion of God's original meaning. T. E. Hulme complained of the selfishness and solipsism of ceasing to "believe in a God" and believing "that man is a God" instead ([1911]1924). In T. S. Eliot's *The Rock*, the Chorus chants that "Men have left God" yet continue to "worship gods," naming "Reason," "Money," "Power," "Life," "Race," or "Dialectic" as examples of "gods" in lower case (1934). In F. Scott Fitzgerald's *The Great Gatsby*, George Wilson's naïve hope for justice, exemplified by his belief "you can't fool God! [. . .] God sees everything," is deflated when the object of his gaze is curtly identified as "an advertisement," implying the replacement of God with commercialized values (1925). Yet the alteration of traditional paths could also have a positive side. Fitzgerald's *This Side of Paradise* associates "the much advertised spiritual crisis" with a new freedom: when Amory finds "all Gods dead," he is "not sorry for himself," but feels "safe now, free from all hysteria" to "roam, grow, rebel" (1920). Wells's Mr. Britling labels the theologian's "all powerful" and "omnipotent" God "a Quack God, a Panacea," but nevertheless comes to understand a new God in-dwelling in the spirit of the boys "who laid down their lives" in the war; he thus rephrases God as "the Master," "the King," and "the Captain of the World Republic." Indeed, many sought to translate God into other terms. Considering "the loss of belief in the sort of God in Whom we were all brought up to believe," Wallace Stevens explained that "thinking of some substitute for religion" had become, for him, a "habit of mind" ([1940]1966). Many looked to possibilities of finding god in humanity and community. For Rose Macaulay's Stanley in *Told by an Idiot*, God is a "socialist agitator" who fights "sweated industries" (1923), while, warning that "Nationalism," "a god [that]

101

still lives," asks for sacrifice "at the expense of humanity," Aldous Huxley sought a new "mythology of humanity that will strike the imagination as forcibly as the old mythology of personal gods" and answer the need for "self-sacrifice and corporate activity" in beneficial rather than destructive ways (1931). Some substitutions, however, were fraught with ambiguity. When the fledgling writer Stephen Dedalus in James Joyce's *Portrait of an Artist* struggles to artic- ulate his aesthetic theory, he imagines the artist "like the God of creation" who "remains within or beyond or beyond or above his handiwork, invisible, refined out of existence, indifferent, paring his finger nails"; whether this image elevates art as a secular sacrament or deflates Stephen for the impoverishment of his emo- tional life is for the reader to decide (1916). Ambiguity also troubles secular substitution in Jean Rhys's "Vienne" (1924). The narrator Ella is exposed for critique when she hails the "great god money" for providing "all that's nice in life," including "the luxury of a soul"; her intense "dread" of returning to "poverty" following WWI, however, calls into question the "little middle-class judgement" that would disapprove both of her valuation of money and what she must do to survive when the money is gone.

In contrast, indefinite or abstract substitutions for God could imply an inef- fable and inexpressible spirituality. In "The House-party," Butts's Vincent "resists the easy race-temptation" to use the "old names, religion, God's grace" calling these "counters" for an undefinable "essence that washed his spirit daily" (1930). Dorothy Richardson, gently patronizing man's need to find a linguistic "formula" for god as a "tree" or "a spirit," claimed a deeper spirituality for the "womanly woman" who lives intuitively "in the deep current of eternity" (1924). Evelyn Underhill engaged a long tradition of mysticism, expressing God's unknowability through increasingly indefinite terms: "the God of Christianity, the World-soul of Pantheism, the Absolute of Philosophy" (1911). Virginia Woolf wrote of gazing through other writers' eyes to see how they order "that power which for convenience and brevity we may call God" (1932), and wrote of discovering, through her own writing, "a revelation of some order," "a token of some real thing behind appear- ances" ([1939–1940]1976). Rejecting the idea of an individual creator, however, Woolf located the "real thing," in a collective spirit: "there is no Shakespeare, there is no Beethoven; certainly and emphatically there is no God; we are the words; we are the music; we are the thing itself."

Other gods could be recovered from the past, in the pagan predecessors of Christianity, as exemplified in evocations of Pan varying from W. B. Yeats's early "I sing of Pan" ([1880s]1995) to J. M. Barrie's popular *Peter Pan* (1904), and ranging in effect from horror to positive vitality. Invoking the macabre, in Arthur Machen's "The Great God Pan," Dr. Raymond performs a surgical experiment to unlock "the most awful, most secret forces which lie at the heart of things" and cause his patient to "see the great god Pan," only to discover that "no human eyes can look on such a sight with impunity," for "when the house of life is thus thrown open, there may enter in that for which we have no name" (1894). Invoking a more naturalistic demonic underworld, in Mary Butts's "The House-party," the scorned and abject Paul, whose dissipation seems to the idealist Vincent to be "a rot nibbling at a generation," calls "Pan" "my god," and offers to teach Vincent more about this god, "up the back streets at night" (1930). Positive evocations of pagan gods appear in E. M. Forster's *The Longest Journey*, where Rickie, standing on prehistoric earthworks on the Salisbury plain, nostalgically recalls the "decent people" of the past who "worshipped Mars or Pan – Erda perhaps: not the devil," and dreams of calling his book of short stories "Pan Pipes" (1907). Acknowledging the disruptive effect of Pan on conventional morality, however, Forster distinguished between "the great god Pan, who has been buried these two thousand years" and "the little god Pan, who presides over social contretemps and unsuccessful picnics" (1908). Similarly, imagining "the beginning of the Christian era" resounding with the cry, "Pan is dead! Great Pan is dead!" D. H. Lawrence asserted that while "the old god Pan became the Christian devil," "Pan keeps on being reborn" and is "still alive" among the "aboriginal Indians," who have not yet been lured away, by abstract ideas and the machine, from a "living relation" to the "surrounding universe" (1926).

As alternatives for God proliferated, they expanded into multiple possible gods and alternative belief systems. The growth of comparative religion studies stimulated awareness of expressions for God in varying forms. W. D. Howells observed Case Young Rice's "consoling" faith in "Many Gods" (the title of Rice's volume of poetry), including the "Japanese, Chinese, Hindu, Moslem, Egyptian" (1910). In Willa Cather's *Death Comes for the Archbishop*, the Navajo find "their gods" in the "white cliffs," "just as the Padre's God was in his church" (1927), while D. H. Lawrence described the Pueblo Indians' "cosmic religion" as "vast and pure," and "not broken up into specific gods or saviours or systems" (1931). Gods were also linked to conceptions of the primitive: Wallace Stevens imagined the way "a god might be,/Naked among [men], like a savage source" (1923), and Countee Cullen expressed a longing to return to an Africa that constituted a lost "primal" spiritual homeland of "outlandish heathen gods" (1925). Beliefs and practices outside mainstream Western traditions revealed powerful other ways of relating to God. Nancy Cunard described attending a "negro revivalist" meeting and finding the congregation's Christianity "only accidental, incidental" to a "pure outpouring of themselves, a nature-rite" that is nonetheless "deeply, tenaciously religious" (1934). In *The Sound and the Fury*, William Faulkner located spiritual value in the African American religious community with his depiction of Reverend Shegog who "sees" God, "the resurrection end de light" and brings the congregation together "without words, like bubbles rising in water" (1929). The proliferation of gods raised possibilities as well of communication or communion

103

amongst spiritual systems. In Joyce's *Portrait of the Artist*, the child Stephen tries to imagine a god that comprehends all religions; when he thinks there are "different names for God in all the different languages in the world," he resolves this adult problem in the simple phrasing that "God remained always the same God and God's real name was God" (1916). A more serious and more hopeful treatment of a transcendent, communal god is envisioned in E. M. Forster's *Passage to India*: when Mrs. Moore, a Christian, meets the Muslim Aziz in a Mosque, she articulates God's ubiquity and transcendence of particular religions with the words "God is here" (1924).

New approaches to God could also strengthen belief in the value of uncertainty and doubt. Thinking of soldiers in WWI, John Galsworthy saw "modern man" as taking "what comes without flinching or complaint, as part of the day's work, which an unknowable God, Providence, Creative Principle, or whatever it shall be called, has appointed" (1919b); "the belief of the future," he asserted, "will be belief in the God within; and a frank agnosticism concerning the great 'Why' of things" (1919a). T. S. Eliot argued the need "to face the permanent conditions upon which God allows us to live upon this planet," and "to recover the sense of religious fear, so that it may be overcome by religious hope" (1939). Narrating the story of his conversion to Catholicism, Graham Greene explained, "in January 1926 I became convinced of the probable existence of something we call God, though now I dislike the word with all its anthropomorphic associations and prefer Chardin's 'Omega Point'"; yet the sheer difficulty of belief suggested to him the ultimate testing ground in the "fight for personal survival": "if I were ever to be convinced in even the remote possibility of a supreme, omnipotent and omniscient power I realized that nothing afterwards could seem impossible" (1971). Claiming his "law-givers" to be "Erasmus and Montaigne, not Moses and St Paul," E. M. Forster declared his "motto" to be "'Lord, I disbelieve – help thou my unbelief,'" emphasizing the need to remake the "indwelling spirit" and to formulate one's own faith, albeit faith with a very small "f" ([1938]1939). Sarvepalli Radhakrishna, Professor of Eastern Religion and Ethics at Oxford and later Prime Minister of India, saw religion in both East and West shaken by "the fashionable view that God is but a shadow of the human mind, a dream of the human heart"; yet, he argued, while science "destroys the old dogmatism," it does not "overthrow the old revelation" (1929). In a transformative vision of plurality, Radhakrishna expressed his hope for a new "comprehensive" approach to religion, based on the understanding that religion is "not so much a theory of the supernatural as an attitude of spirit, a temper of mind." Such flexible and pluralist terms encapsulate the way many modernists redefined the spiritual, even while questioning God.

SEE ALSO: *Common Mind, Group Thinking; Hygiene; Personality, Impersonality; Modern, Modernism; Rhythm; Unconscious*

References

Arnold, Matthew (1875). *God and the Bible: A Review of Objections to Literature and Dogma*. London: Macmillan.

Barnes, Djuna (1924). "The Passion." *The Transatlantic Review* (November), 490–496.

Barrie, J. M. (1904). *Peter Pan, or The Boy Who Wouldn't Grow Up*. The Duke of York's Theatre, London. Première, December 27.

Beckett, Samuel (1954). *Waiting for Godot*. New York: Grove.

Butts, Mary (1930). "The House-Party." *Pagany: A Native Quarterly* (January–March), 7–24.

Cather, Willa (1927). *Death Comes for the Archbishop*. New York: A. A. Knopf.

Cullen, Countee (1925). "Heritage." *Survey Graphic*. Harlem: Mecca of the New Negro (March), 674–675.

Cunard, Nancy (1934). "Harlem Reviewed." In *Negro: An Anthology* (ed. Nancy Cunard). London: Lawrence and Wishart. 67–74.

Eliot, T. S. (1934). *The Rock*. London: Faber and Faber.

Eliot, T. S. (1939). *The Idea of a Christian Society*. London: Faber and Faber.

Faulkner, William (1929). *The Sound and the Fury*. New York: Jonathan Cape and Harrison Smith.

Faulkner, William (1936). *Absalom, Absalom!* New York: Random House.

Fitzgerald, F. Scott (1920). *This Side of Paradise*. New York: Charles Scribner's Sons.

Fitzgerald, F. Scott (1925). *The Great Gatsby*. New York: Charles Scribner's Sons.

Forster, E. M. (1907). *The Longest Journey*. Edinburgh: Blackwood.

Forster, E. M. (1908). *A Room with a View*. London: Edward Arnold.

Forster, E. M. (1924). *A Passage to India*. London and New York: Edward Arnold.

Forster, E. M. (1939). *What I Believe*. ["Two Cheers for Democracy," 1938]. London: Hogarth.

Freud, Sigmund (1928). *The Future of an Illusion*. [Die Zukunft einer Illusion, 1927]. Trans. W. D. Robson-Scott. London: Hogarth Press and the Institute of Psycho-Analysis.

Galsworthy, John (1919a). "The Balance Sheet Of The Soldier-Workman." In *Another Sheaf*. London: W. Heinemann. 11–35.

Galsworthy, John (1919b). "Speculations." In *Another Sheaf*. London: W. Heinemann. 110–131.

Greene, Graham (1971). *A Sort of Life*. New York: Simon and Schuster.

Hardy, Thomas (1914). "The Convergence of the Twain." In *Satires of Circumstance: Lyrics, and Reveries, with Miscellaneous Pieces*. London: Macmillan. 9–11.

Hemingway, Ernest (1926). *The Sun Also Rises*. New York: Charles Scribner's Sons.

Howells, W. D. (1910). "Some New Volumes of Verse." *The North American Review* (May), 652–658.

Hulme, T. E. (1924). "Romanticism and Classicism." [1911]. In *Speculations: Essays on Humanism and the Philosophy of Art* (ed. Herbert Read). London: Routledge and Kegan Paul. 113–114, 116–122.

Hurston, Zora Neale (1937). *Their Eyes Were Watching God*. Philadelphia: J. P. Lippincott.

Huxley, Aldous (1931). "In Whose Name?" *Chicago Herald and Examiner* (December 19): 9.

Joyce, James (1916). *Portrait of the Artist as a Young Man*. 1914–1915. New York: B. W. Huebsch.

Lawrence, D. H. (1926). "Pan in America." *Southwest Review* (January), 102–115.

Lawrence, D. H. (1931). "New Mexico." *Survey Graphic* (May 1), 153–155.

God, Gods

Lewis, C. S. (1952). *Mere Christianity*. London: Macmillan.

Lewis, Wyndham (1917). "Inferior Religions." *The Little Review* 4.5 (September): 3–8.

Macaulay, Rose (1920). *Potterism*. London: Collins.

Macaulay, Rose (1923). *Told by an Idiot*. London: Collins.

Machen, Arthur (1894). *The Great God Pan, and The Inmost Light*. Boston: Robert Brothers.

Nietzsche, Friedrich (1910). *The Joyful Wisdom (La gaya scienza)*. With poetry rendered by Paul V. Cohn and Maude D. Petre. [*Die fröhliche Wissenschaft*, 1882]. Trans. Thomas Common. Edinburgh, London: T. N. Foulis.

Radhakrishna, Sarvepalli (1929). *Kalki: Or the Future of Civilization*. To-Day and To-Morrow. London: Kegan Paul, Trench, Trubner.

Rhys, Jean (1924). "Vienne." *The Transatlantic Review* (December), 639–645.

Richardson, Dorothy (1924). "Women and the Future: A Trembling of the Veil before the Eternal Mystery of 'La Giaconda'." *Vanity Fair* (April), 39–40.

Stevens, Wallace (1923). "Sunday Morning." In *Harmonium*. A. A. Knopf. 100–104.

Stevens, Wallace (1966). Letter to Hi Simons, 9 January 1940. [1940]. In *Letters of Wallace Stevens* (ed. Holly Stevens). New York: A. A. Knopf. 346–350.

Underhill, Evelyn (1911). *Mysticism: A Study of the Nature and Development of Man's Spiritual Consciousness*. London: Methuen.

Waugh, Evelyn (1945). *Brideshead Revisited: The Sacred and Profane Memories of Charles Ryder*. London: Chapman and Hall.

Waugh, Evelyn (1946). "Palinurus in Never-Never-Land: or, The 'Horizon' Blue-Print of Chaos." *Tablet* (July 27), 46.

Wells, H. G. (1916). *Mr. Britling Sees It Through*. New York: Macmillan Co.

West, Rebecca (1914). "Indissoluble Matrimony." *Blast* 1 (June): 98–117.

Woolf, Virginia (1915). *The Voyage Out*. London: Duckworth.

Woolf, Virginia (1932). "Robinson Crusoe." In *The Common Reader*, Second Series. London: Hogarth. 51–58.

Woolf, Virginia (1976). "A Sketch of the Past." (1939–1940). In *Moments of Being: Unpublished Autobiographical Writings*. Edited with Introduction and Notes by Jeanne Schulkind. Sussex: The University Press. 61–137.

Yeats, W. B. (1995). "Pan." [1880s]. In *Under the Moon: The Unpublished Early Poetry* (ed. George Bornstein). New York: Scribner.

Hamlet

The modernist period was not unique in its fascination with Shakespeare's *Hamlet*; the period's distinctive obsession was its pervasive reading of the figure of Hamlet as a mirror for the modern self and the modern age. Writing about her friendship with the English poet Edward Thomas, Eleanor Farjeon recollected his saying, "I suppose every man thinks that Hamlet was written for him, but I know he was written for me"; she added, "I found more and more truth in this as I knew him more" (1958). The Canadian novelist Hugh MacLennan wrote that of "the great dramatic characters – Oedipus, Faust, Hamlet, Lear, Othello, Macbeth – only Hamlet is credible today, assuming Hamlet to be a modern man" ([1950]1981). The American writer Upton Sinclair claimed that the three greatest influences on his life were Jesus, Hamlet, and P. B. Shelley; he more generally proposed that "Hamlet is the type of the 'modern man,'" and even speculated that "we can go farther and say that Shakespeare helped to make the modern man what he is; the modern man is more of Hamlet, because he has taken Hamlet to his heart and pondered over Hamlet's problem" (1922). In cinema, no fewer than six silent versions of *Hamlet* were released between 1907 and 1920 (Brode 2001); *Life* magazine, reviewing a production of the play in 1938, described it as "the first piercing analysis of modern man"; and Lawrence Olivier captured the public imagination with his Academy Award-winning performance as Hamlet in 1948. The contemporary relevance of Hamlet surfaced in formal literary analysis as well. In

ABCDEFG**H**IJKLMNOPQRSTUVWXYZ

Modernism: Keywords, First Edition. Melba Cuddy-Keane, Adam Hammond, and Alexandra Peat.

the view of Shakespearean critic Muriel Bradbrook, "Hamlet, the greatest of Shakespeare's characters, is not susceptible of explanation" for "the core of [his] being is a mystery," and yet "in his isolation and self-consciousness he is the prototype of modern man" (1951).

Despite the widespread tendency to read Hamlet as typing the modern, the motivations for doing so could gravitate toward one or the other of two opposing poles. One extreme interpreted Hamlet as representing dysfunctional psychology: some inability, failure, or inadequacy in modern man. The other extreme located the dysfunction in the world itself, in the human condition, and saw Hamlet as representing an extraordinary prescience in grasping this "truth." The polarities are clearly evidenced in two works that could easily serve as period "bookends." In his Preface to *Poems* (1853), Matthew Arnold explained his excision of "Empedocles on Etna" on the grounds that its debilitating "dialogue of the mind with itself" failed to offer the requisite inspiration to an audience suffering themselves a like "state of mental distress": "modern problems have presented themselves; we hear already the doubts, we witness the discouragement, of Hamlet and of Faust." Conversely, in 1952, Yale professor Maynard Mack shifted attention from the play's main character to its "imaginative environment" or, in Mack's term, its "world." Arguing that "the play's very lack of a causal logic seems to be a part of its point," Mack read the play's "interrogative mood" as delineating "a world where uncertainties are of the essence." Unlike the crises of other tragic Shakespearean heroes, he argued, Hamlet's predicament is one he inherits rather than creates, and "its mysteriousness, its baffling appearances, its deep consciousness of infection, frailty, and loss" "appeals to us so powerfully" because it is "an image of our own."

Around the turn of C20, the "two" Hamlets acquired almost mythic status in the opposing theories of Friedrich Nietzsche and Sigmund Freud. In broad terms, Nietzsche, like Mack, read Hamlet as a figure who sees into the "essence of things" and penetrates their "cruel truth." Dismissing equations of Hamlet with "John-a-Dreams," unable to act because he is paralyzed by too much reflection, Nietzsche paired Hamlet instead with passionate "Dionysian man," a figure of strength who, having glimpsed the truth, "sees everywhere only the horror or absurdity of being"; mediated through the dramatic form of tragedy, Hamlet's dilemma combines with the "healing magician, art" to turn such horror "into imaginary constructs which permit living to continue" ([1872]1909). Conversely, Freud, like Arnold, used Hamlet to theorize psychological dysfunction. Although rejecting, like Nietzsche, the notion that Hamlet was "paralyzed by excessive intellectual activity," Freud paired Hamlet with Oedipus as figures depicting the "basic wish-phantasy of the [male] child" – "having sexual intercourse with one's mother." Hamlet then served Freud as the distinctively modern figure in whom the "phantasy" remains repressed and "unconscious," manifesting as "neurosis" in "an hysterical subject" ([1900]1913).

On the dysfunctional side, numerous approaches took Hamlet as typing what modern man should *not* be, perhaps most strikingly in the coinage of the verb, "to Hamletise." Fruitlessly trying to explain (and understand) a totally reconceived relation between the sexes, D. H. Lawrence's Rupert Birkin abandons the attempt, saying, "One shouldn't talk when one is tired and wretched. One Hamletises, and it seems a lie" (1921). But while in *Women in Love*, Hamlet is merely the self-recognized threat of Birkin's becoming an intellectualizing "word-bag," in Lawrence's *Twilight in Italy*, Hamlet more violently represents, like his prototype Orestes, "a mental creature, anti-physical, anti-sensual," portraying "the convulsed reaction of the mind from the flesh, of the spirit from the self, the reaction from the great aristocratic to the great democratic principle" (1916). Finding in Lawrence's response a "free flowing fullness of life," F. R. Leavis staged an ideological battle between T. S. Eliot and Lawrence as "the Opposed Critics on *Hamlet*": the early Eliot prone to Prufrockian weakness and insecurity, unable to grasp the play's significance versus Lawrence's demonstrating "the strength that wasn't Eliot's" in understanding the play as a "great work" but being repelled by it (1969). For Leavis, Lawrence detected in Hamlet "a great change in the European psyche" and heroically rejected it: against Hamlet's implicit decision "*not* to *be*," Lawrence upheld "the will to be King, Father and Supreme I (ego)." A similar condemnation of Hamlet acquired military significance in Fascist culture: Aldous Huxley commented that the Nazis banned productions of Hamlet "for fear that it should cause young Germans to forget the 'heroic' role which they are now supposed to play" (1936).

With diverse inflections, others noted the way reading or identifying with Hamlet could be forms of self-performance. Eliot contrasted his objective identification of the play's problems – the failure of its "objective correlative" – with the putatively subjective readings of Coleridge and Goethe, both of whom, he asserted, substituted "their own Hamlet for Shakespeare's" (1919). As a *dramatis persona* perhaps not to be identified with Eliot, Prufrock self-consciously mocks his own attempt to play Hamlet, demoting himself to the lowly role of Polonius for lacking Hamlet's ability to pose the "overwhelming question" (1915). Christopher Tietjens in Ford Madox Ford's *Parade's End* wonders if he is "a sort of Hamlet of the Trenches," as he obsessively ruminates about codes of morality in the modern age ([1926]1950). In *The Hamlet of A. MacLeish* (1928), Archibald MacLeish calls into question his own identification with Hamlet, proposing that he shares not only the latter's troubled conscience but also his compulsive need to dramatize mental anguish: "Why must I always/Stoop from this decent silence to this phrase/That makes a posture of my hurt?" (1928). Virginia Woolf wrote that "*Hamlet* or a Beethoven quartet is the truth about this vast mass we call the world," but she also foregrounded the audience's role in the performance, adding "we are the words; we are the music; we are the thing itself," ([1939–1940]1976) and commenting elsewhere that "to write down one's impressions of *Hamlet* as one reads it year after year, would be virtually to record one's own autobiography" (1916). Elizabeth Bowen invoked Hamlet's own performative acts in *The Heat of the Day* (1948): Cousin Nettie commits herself to a "home" for "uncertified mental patients" to escape the impossible demands of heterosexual normality, while her nephew Roderick reflects, "Hamlet had got away with it; why should not she?" yet more ambivalently wonders, "But there had been doubts about Hamlet." In this novel about dissembling and masked identities, Hamlet both represents a tactical feigning for survival and functions to question the lines between normal and abnormal, the performance and the real.

Such modernist usages might well recall Hamlet's own words about art's purpose: "to hold, as 'twere, the mirror up to nature, to show [. . .] the very age and body of the time his form and pressure" (III; ii). While modernist scholars continued to analyze and evaluate Shakespeare's play on its own terms, in numerous ways crossing disparate discourses, Hamlet became an image and a testing ground for the modern world.

SEE ALSO: *Atom, Atomic; Einstein; Modern, Modernism; Personality, Impersonality*

References

110

(1938). "'Hamlet': Maurice Evans in Five Hours of Shakespeare." *Life* (November 28), 38–41.

Arnold, Matthew (1853). Preface. In *Poems*. London: Longman, Brown, Green, and Longmans.

Bowen, Elizabeth (1948). *The Heat of the Day*. London: Jonathan Cape.

Bradbrook, Muriel Clara (1951). *Shakespeare and Elizabethan Poetry: A Study of his Earlier Work in Relation to the Poetry of the Time*. London: Chatto & Windus.

Brode, Douglas (2001). *Shakespeare in the Movies: From the Silent Era to Today*. New York: Berkley Boulevard Books.

Eliot, T. S. (1915). "The Love Song of J. Alfred Prufrock." *Poetry* (Chicago) (June), 130–135.

Eliot, T. S. (1919). "Hamlet and His Problems." *The Athenaeum* (September 26).

Farjeon, Eleanor (1958). *Edward Thomas: The Last Four Years*. Oxford: Oxford University Press.

Ford, Ford Madox (1950). *A Man Could Stand Up—*. 1926. Vol. 3 of *Parade's End*. Introduction by Robie Macaulay. 4 vols. New York: A. A. Knopf.

Freud, Sigmund (1913). *The Interpretation of Dreams*. [*Die Traumdeutung*, 1900]. 3rd ed. Translated with an Introduction by A. A. Brill. London: G. Allen and Unwin; New York: Macmillan.

Huxley, Aldous (1936). "Writers and Readers." In *The Olive Tree, and Other Essays*. London: Chatto & Windus. 46–81.

Lawrence, D. H. (1916). *Twilight in Italy*. London: Duckworth.

Lawrence, D. H. (1921). *Women in Love*. London: Martin Secker.

Leavis, F. R. (1969). *English Literature in Our Time and the University*. The Clarke Lectures, 1967. London: Chatto & Windus.

Mack, Maynard (1952). "The World of 'Hamlet.'" *The Yale Review* 41: 502–523.

MacLeish, Archibald (1928). *The Hamlet of A. MacLeish*. Boston: Houghton Mifflin.

MacLennan, Hugh (1981). Letter to John Gray, 7 December 1950. [1950]. In *Hugh MacLennan: A Writer's Life* (ed. Elspeth Cameron). Toronto: University of Toronto Press. 253.

Nietzsche, Friedrich (1909). *The Birth of Tragedy, or Hellenism and Pessimism*. [Die Geburt der Tragödie aus dem Geiste der Musik, 1872.] Trans. William A. Haussmann. Edinburgh and London: T. N. Foulis.

Sinclair, Upton (1922). *The Book of Life: Mind and Body*. Bedford: Applewood.

[Woolf, Virginia] (1916). "Charlotte Bronte." *TLS* (April 13), 169–170.

Woolf, Virginia (1976). "A Sketch of the Past." [1939–1940] In *Moments of Being: Unpublished Autobiographical Writings*. Edited with Introduction and Notes by Jeanne Schulkind. Sussex: The University Press. 61–137.

Highbrow, Middlebrow, Lowbrow

In the modernist period, the brow – literally, the space between eyebrow and hairline and thus, metaphorically, the capacity of one's brain – became both the site of contentious cultural battles and a source of lighthearted fun. In C19, highbrowed appears occasionally to denote a noble appearance combined with superior qualities: George Eliot pays a simple, if gendered, compliment to "gentle maidens and high-browed brave men" ([1848]1954–1978), and somewhat more critically, the editor of the *Canadian Magazine* refers to "high-browed, blue-blooded citizens" whom he wishes would take a more civic role (1897). C20 sees a sudden surge in the use of highbrow(ed), linking intellectual ability to particular attitudes and tastes. In H. G. Wells's *Ann Veronica* (1909), highbrowed signifies the most advanced ideas and fashions, comically typified in the character Mrs. Goopes, who "wrote a weekly column in New Ideas upon vegetarian cookery, vivisection, degeneration, the lacteal secretion, appendicitis, and the Higher Thought generally" and whose "very furniture had mysteriously a high-browed quality." More bitingly, highbrow could connote aloofness and a pretentious, high moral stance: in Sinclair Lewis's *Our Mr. Wrenn* (1914), the eponymous hero declares, "I don't believe much in all them highbrow sermons that don't come down to brass tacks – ain't got nothing to do with real folks." When lowbrow entered the vocabulary, categorization according to brow level began to segregate people into differing, although not necessarily irreconcilable, groups. A 1917 editorial in *The Nation* (NY) proclaimed, "There are regularly recurrent moments in the amusement season when the orbits of the lowbrow and the highbrow touch. The circus is one such instance. The advent of Fred Stone is another." Stone, a circus and variety show performer and the original scarecrow in *The Wizard of Oz*, was admirable proof that different brow levels could intersect. Yet in the period as a whole, with the additional coining of middlebrow, the prevailing tendency was toward cultural divisiveness. The underlying issues escalated from what music you

111

listen to and which books you read to whose culture is more valued, who makes the most money, and who is likely to have the most success. Another trend in the modernist period, however, diffused the high seriousness of the culture wars, treating them more like a game. While possibly trivializing cultural friction, the expansion of brow categories into a dizzying range of lifestyle choices also helped to recast putatively exclusive categories as, in practice, a variable mix.

The rancor surrounding the terms began with the abusive use of highbrow. John Galsworthy argued that if "high-brow" was "complimentary in origin," by the late 1910s, it had "become in some sort a term of contempt" (1919). Frank Swinnerton derided the "neo-Georgian" "caste" of aesthetic "highbrows," arguing that they posed "a small menace to creative writing" (1928), while Arnold Bennett labeled Virginia Woolf's *Orlando* a "high-brow lark," full of "fanciful embroidery, wordy, and naught else!" (1928). E. K. Brown warned that in 1930s Canada, "to prefer Shakespeare to the radio and the movies for the evening's leisure [was] to invite the label 'highbrow,'" which was only slightly removed from "traitor" (1933). George Orwell spoke of a time when it was easily "possible to earn a few guineas by writing an article denouncing 'highbrows,'" although he confessed, "all the same it was the despised highbrows who had captured the young" (1940). Most attacks made the assumption that highbrows harbored an arrogant, anti-democratic dislike for common people and things. In a BBC Radio talk, best-selling writer Gilbert Frankau castigated "Highbrows" as people who "do not believe there is any good in the great heart of the British public" (quoted by Leonard Woolf, 1927); in Australia, Walter Murdoch acknowledged the prevailing view of the highbrow as "the intellectual who wears a perpetual sniff, as if he smelt drains, when in the presence of those whose tastes are different from his own," and the "member of a little clique which has got out of touch with the tastes and ways of the common man" (1937). In the US, Robert Heilman noted "highbrowism ha[d] become almost a standard synonym for un-Americanism," "connot[ing] everything that is unpopular, upperclass, conscious, supercilious, opposed to our tradition of the goodness and wisdom of plain people – in a word undemocratic" (1949). Galsworthy attributed such hostility to resentment of dissident views: "A doubter of [the] general divinity [of Modern Civilization] is labeled 'high-brow' at once," for "any one who questions our triumphant progress is tabooed for a pedant" (1919). Aldous Huxley, himself opposing the "modern industrial state," wryly attributed the dislike to "a society that measures success in economic terms" and considers that "highbrows, being poor consumers, are bad citizens" (1931).

The incendiary nature of highbrow provided the core of a fictional libel case, published in *Punch* (Herbert, 1924). The trial hinges on a review by one Mrs. Tulip of a novel by Miss Celia Trott: "It is no good, Miss Trott. All your murders and detectives, your vamps and mysteries, do not deceive us, charming though they are. The truth is, Miss Trott, *you are a bit of a highbrow.*" Miss Trott bases her defamation claim on the perception that "the word 'highbrow'" has "prejudiced her professionally as a writer of sensational narratives for railway reading, or, as they are sometimes called, it appears, 'best-sellers.'" Following the expert testimony of "nineteen well-known writers and authors, fourteen literary critics, seven editors and two philologists," Justice Wool concludes that highbrow is "the most remarkable word in common use to-day": each expert "came prepared with a full and impressive theory of the origin and significance of the word, but no two of these explanations were in any respect the same"; then, "at the first hint of opposition or disagreement these ladies and gentlemen almost without exception betrayed a degree of passion and obstinacy remarkable in persons devoted to a contemplative way of life." Initially positing that "the word 'highbrow,' having a different meaning in the mouth of every authority, has in fact no meaning whatsoever," Justice Wool ultimately concludes that "the disputed word has two principal meanings which are directly opposed": first, "it is laudatory and signifies intelligence," and second, "it is insulting and signifies intelligence plus arrogance." At the end, the jury – or in this case the judge – is still out.

Though comically portrayed, Justice Wool's predicament exposed a crucial but generally overlooked point: highbrow had different meanings because highbrows were of different kinds. Coming to the defense of the beleaguered animal, Leonard Woolf's *Hunting the Highbrow* (1927) offered one explanation of its different forms. In parodic Latinate manner, Woolf defined two forms of genuine highbrow: (i) *Altifrons altifrontissimus,* "the original, primitive, and real highbrow" who "prefers the appeal to his intellect rather than solely to his senses," and (ii) "*Altifrons aestheticus,* who only likes what is best in literature, art, and music." He then assigned each category its "parasitic" pseudo-species: *Pseudoaltifrons intellectualis,* who "only likes what nobody else can understand," and *Pseudoaltifrons aestheticus,* who "only likes [. . .] the thing which the majority dislikes." For Woolf, the seriousness of "hunting the highbrow," however, was that the genuine could be shot down in pursuit of the pseudo, posing a serious problem for the survival of the small highbrow press.

Woolf was not alone in distinguishing the genuine highbrow from its aping forms. For Maurice Baring, the good highbrow combined accomplishment and humility: "well educated" and "without being ashamed of his knowledge, his intellectual or artistic superiority, or his gifts and aptitudes," the good highbrow "does not think that because he is the fortunate possessor of certain rare gifts or talents, he is therefore a better or more useful man" (1932). Baring located the "worst faults of the bad high-brow" not in "pride, arrogance, and narrow-mindedness" but in "envy," arising either from the fear that real highbrows are intellectually superior or from the suspicion that those who are unconcerned about *not* being highbrows are having a better time. Walter Murdoch judged the popular reaction against the highbrow according to which of its forms was meant: if pseudo-highbrowism was the target, Murdoch stated, he could "understand perfectly why

113

the high-brow has become an object of general dislike"; yet if the genuine highbrow was being attacked – "the intelligent person who is interested in art and poetry and religion and the things of the mind generally" – then he considered "the popular dislike of the high-brow" to be "simply the barbarian's dislike of civilization and the fool's contempt for what he cannot understand" (1937). Speaking to the American Association of University Professors, Robert Heilman differentiated between "good" and "bad highbrowism" in a spirited protest against encroaching "anti-highbrowism" among "teacher[s] of literature" (1949). Heilman "did not deny that the bad sense of the word" – "the sniffy and the snooty" – was "a reality," but he warned against mistaking "changelings for legitimate members of the family." Good highbrowism, he argued, was devoted, first, to "excellence" and the pursuit of "high truth" – "even though the truth be difficult, unpopular, unprofitable, unconsoling, unflattering, and entirely out of accord with dominant prejudices" – and, second, to "an unrelenting standard which does not permit one to be easy upon oneself." Rather than calling to eliminate bad highbrowism, however, Heilman argued it was an unavoidable consequence of having the good. "Artiness is one of the risks of the quest for art," and "lunatic fringes [. . .] are part of the price one must pay in order to have the arts free" for untrammeled exploration. Much more "serious damage" was threatened by well-intentioned "lower middlebrow habits" and "literary lowbrowism" which disparaged "abstract, reflective, speculative thinking" and "plump[ed] for the sentimental, the obvious, the solid, the hearty," calling it "'central' or 'human' or 'whole.'"

114

While a few writers thus argued distinctions between different highbrow forms, most combatants generally confused issues by using one single, undifferentiated term. The introduction of middle and low into discussions muddied the waters even more. Lowbrowism could mean self-conscious posturing as a confrontational stance. Aldous Huxley attacked the complacent anti-intellectualism enshrined in performative lowbrowism: "It is not at all uncommon now," he claimed in "Foreheads Villainous Low," "to find intelligent and cultured people doing their best to feign stupidity and to conceal the fact that they have received an education" (1931). Robert Menner detected a more unconscious oppositional lowbrowism in Australian speech: "The Australian dislike of elegance and affectation leads to a general 'low-browism' of expression and a careless enunciation," evidenced in abbreviations like "mozzie, 'mosquito,' prossie, 'prostitute,'" and "botto, 'bottle'" (1946). Lowbrow also acquired degrees of subtypes, fully independent of middle or high. In Sewell Ford's arguably lowbrow novel *Shorty McCabe* (1906), Shorty, on the trail of an Italian gang, reports in decidedly non-highbrow language, "The spaghetti works was in full blast, with a lot of husky lowbrows goin' in and out, smokin' cheroots half as long as your arm, and acting as if the referee had just declared a draw. The opening for a couple of bare fisted investigators wasn't what you might call promisin'."

The usage of middlebrow was even more mixed. Middle meant between high and low, but it could connote a happy medium as well. An editorial in *London Opinion* asserted that in this "middlebrow country," the "majority of decent men and women" stood for "balance, sanity, substance, humour," combining "the best of both worlds" (1930). The American Donald Rose celebrated the middlebrow in balanced Alexandrine couplets: "The Middlebrow pasture is chiefly found/In the sensible slant and the middle ground" (1927). It might be noted, however, that his own "Magazine for Middlebrows," incorporated after four years as a column in *The North American Review*, belied his praise of "sensible," balanced style. Entitled "Stuff and Nonsense," it excoriated "the national tradition, hoary, venerable and with an ancient and fishlike smell" of belief in the existing two-party system, and it established its own "Book-of-the-Month Club" on the basis of throwing all books "dispassionately at the ceiling" and selecting the one that "falls into the waste basket" (1929). Middlebrow could also be interpreted as box office appeal. In George Kaufman's play *The Butter and Egg Man* (1926), a wily Broadway producer out to woo a potential backer cries, "I got a show that's going to catch everybody, see? It ain't highbrow and yet it ain't lowbrow"; confirming his interlocutor's response, "Sort of – medium brow?" he adds, "it's going to be a knockout." The commercial aspect of middlebrowism figured in an angry (and prudently never submitted) letter from Virginia Woolf to an editor ([1932]1942), in response to a highbrow attack. Defending both highbrows and lowbrows as committed respectively to mental and bodily vitality, Woolf cast middlebrows as anemically driven by profit: "when we [highbrows] have earned enough to live on, then we live. When the middlebrows [. . .] have earned enough to live on, they go on earning enough to buy." For Richard Chase, middlebrow shaded into "mediocre," contaminated by commercialism and conformity (1957). Castigating middlebrowism as immured in "the stagnant waters of conventional success," Chase disputed "this more or less mythic center of taste and opinion," arguing that "this formless middle way of feeling and thought, with its increasing moralism and conventionality," "fundamentally misunderstood and feared the really definitive characteristics of American culture." Margaret Widdemer identified middlebrow with "the majority reader," whom she described as "fairly civilized, fairly literate" but failing to appreciate the "vitality" of good writing and preferring a safe armchair flirtation with contemporary sexual "amoralism" instead: "the middlebrow mind, which was bullied but not quite convinced by the frank lust and plain speaking of the Ulyssean school turns to drawing-room and library amorals with the relief of a tidy lady who must travel the correct road, but would rather emerge with her slippers neat" (1933). In contrast, Widdemer "recommended thinking for one's self." Australian Freda Wedemeyer agreed, arguing that the majority reader "familiarises himself with what is bad and persuades himself that it is good, and then justifies himself by saying he is a plain middlebrow man"; Wedemeyer also stressed the social consequences of bad reading practices, warning, "as he is, so we are, or so we shall become" (1937).

The social consequences of reading underpinned what was possibly the most thorough discussion of brows in the modernist period: Q. D. Leavis's *Fiction and the Reading Public* (1932). Leavis divided "literary periodicals" into three classes, serving three different levels of the reading public which she named "highbrow," "middlebrow," and "lowbrow." But when it came to "bestsellers," Leavis's categories were four: "Highbrow," "'Middlebrow' read as 'literature,'" "'Middlebrow' not read as 'literature' but not writing for the lowbrow market," and "Absolute best-sellers." The lexicographer Eric Partridge, building on Leavis's categories, used the terms highbrows, literary middlebrows, nonliterary middlebrows (presumably Virginia Woolf's middlebrows), and lowbrows instead (1932). The enemy, for both Leavis and Partridge, was not popular novels, but mass-produced formula fiction and passive reading practices. Leavis ambivalently recognized "respected middling novelists of blameless intentions and indubitable skill, 'thoughtful,' 'cultured,' 'impressive,'" who offer "soothing and not disturbing sentiments, yet with sufficient surface stimulus to be pleasing," and reserved her most caustic critique for "the lowbrow, who accepts uncritically the restrictions imposed by the herd." For Partridge, most literary middlebrows "take their work seriously," and both forms of middlebrow, while "somewhat lacking in vitality," "eschew sensationalism and crudity"; he targeted the "lowbrow supersellers" whose "vitality is made to subserve the general morality." Leavis, concerned about the effect of institutionalized reading typified by the Book-of-the-Month Club, protested that "a middlebrow standard of values has been set up" and "middlebrow taste has thus been organized," "preventing the natural progression of taste" that motivated self-improvement in earlier readerships. For Partridge, the "lowbrow bestsellers" "interfere[d] with the reader's free development and his spontaneities," "spoil[ing] the reader for any novel that demands mental readjustment." Walter Murdoch made a similar point on behalf of the majority reader: "We should not allow the common man, the man in the street, to be tyrannised over by the low-brow. We should treat him as the intelligent being which he is, the man who hungers for something better than the fatuous entertainment with which we seek to fill his hours" (1937).

If one trend was thus to taxonomize writers and the reading public, another was to protest the divisiveness such compartmentalism entailed. As early as 1915, Van Wyck Brooks designated Don Quixote the "eternal Highbrow," and Sancho Panza, the "eternal Lowbrow," and while seeing "one so fantastically above, the other so fantastically below the level of right reason," he nevertheless asserted that "to have any kind of relish for muddled humanity is necessarily to feel the charm in both extremes." E. M. Forster said the brows were "responsible for more unkind feelings and more silly thinking than any other pair of words" he knew, introducing "into literature the cleavage which is so lamentable in the world of affairs," "between the brain worker and the manual labourer" (1932). Cyril Connolly held that the "absurd distinction [. . .] between high-brow and low-brow" had "done more harm to both serious and popular art than any other false classification" (1940).

The brows so permeated culture, however, that the concept of taste categorizations moved into the popular realm, providing a source of entertainment and wit. The musical *Here's Howe* (1928) featured Irving Caesar's "Crazy Rhythm," with the lines, "They say that when a highbrow meets a lowbrow/Walking along Broadway,/Soon the highbrow, he has no brow;/Ain't it a shame, and you're to blame!" The Broadway revue *Touch and Go* (1949) similarly included a song entitled "High Brow, Middle Brow, Low Brow" (Kerr and Kerr 1949). Most famously, *Life* magazine published "High-Brow, Low-Brow, Middle-Brow" (1949), summarizing Russell Lynes's somewhat "tongue in cheek" taxonomy of the brows, previously published in *Harper's*: the highbrow is "a shaggy sophisticate found on liberal arts faculties in college towns and often in big cities"; the lowbrow is he whom "culture [. . .] leaves cold" and who "resents the middle-brows" for "try[ing] to sell it to him"; the middlebrow is "hell-bent on improving his mind." Accompanying the article was a full-color two-page chart, designed "To help readers find their places" among characteristic low, lower-middle, upper-middle, and highbrow tastes, in everything from reading, sculpture, and entertainments to salads, furniture, and games. Perhaps the most telling response was offered by *Life*'s readers. In "Letters to the Editor" (1949), Polly MacLeod placed her family and friends in "a niche above the high-brows" since, thriving on "ballet, Brahms or juke boxes," they were "all-around brows." Theodore Lustig noted that a great many "American people" would identify with several items "in each brow-beaten section" of this "arbitrary guidance chart," and he proposed "a fifth classification – the 'zig-zag' or 'wrinkled-brow.'" William S. Power described himself as "an honest, qualified low-brow," but, confronted with the low-brows' supposed preference in food, he declared, "I hate coleslaw." Ultimately, these readers suggested, people are far less categorizable than the goods they choose to consume.

117

SEE ALSO: *Best-seller; Coterie, Bloomsbury; Democracy; Difficulty, Obscurity; Propaganda; Readers, Reading*

References

(1897). "Current Thoughts: Mining and Small Investors." Editorial. *The Canadian Magazine of Politics, Science, Art and Literature* (March), 447.

(1917). "High Comedy and Low Brows." Editorial. *The Nation* (October 25), 444–448.

(1928). *Here's Howe*. A Musical in Two Acts. Music by Roger Wolfe Kahn and Joseph Meyer; Book by Fred Thompson and Paul Gerard Smith; Lyrics by Irving Caesar; Musical Director: Paul Lannin. Broadhurst Theatre. May 1–June 30, 1928.

(1930). "Come In! And Let's Talk About . . ." Editorial. *London Opinion* (August 16), 136.

(1949). "Everyday Tastes from High-Brow to Low-Brow Are Classified on Chart." *Life* (April 11), 100–101.

(1949). "Letters to the Editor." *Life* (May 2), 8–12.

(1949). *Touch and Go*. Musical revue. Music by Jay Gorney. Sketches by Jean Kerr and Walter Kerr. Lyrics by Jean Kerr and Walter Kerr. Music orchestrated by Don Walker. Musical Director: Antonio Morelli. Ballet music by Genevieve Pitot. Vocal arrangements by Antonio Morelli. Choreographed by Helen Tamiris. Directed by Walter Kerr. Broadhurst Theatre. October 13, 1949–March 18, 1950.

Baring, Maurice (1932). "High-Brows and Low-Brows." In *Lost Lectures or The Fruits of Experience*. London: Peter Davies. 159–177.

Bennett, Arnold (1928). "A Woman's High-Brow Lark." *The Evening Standard* (November 8), 7.

Brooks, Van Wyck (1915). "Highbrow and Lowbrow." *The Forum* (April), 481–492.

Brown, E. K. (1933). "The Immediate Present in Canadian Literature." *The Sewanee Review* 41.4 (October–December): 430–442.

Chase, Richard (1957). "The Fate of the Avant-Garde." *The Partisan Review* 24.3 (Summer): 363–375.

Connolly, Cyril (1940). "Comment." *Horizon* (April 1), 234.

Eliot, George (1954–1978). Letter to Sara Sophia Hennell, 23 November 1848. [1848]. In *The George Eliot Letters* (ed. Gordon S. Haight). 9 vols. New Haven: Yale University Press. Vol. 1: 273.

Ford, Sewell (1906). *Shorty McCabe*. New York: Grosset and Dunlap.

Forster, E. M. (1932). "Not New Books." *The Listener* (December 28), 951–952.

Frankau, Gilbert (1927). "An Author's Feelings on Publication Day." BBC Radio Talk. Quoted in Leonard Woolf, *Hunting the Highbrow*. London: Hogarth. 6–7.

Galsworthy, John (1919). "Speculations." In *Another Sheaf*. London: W. Heinemann. 110–131.

Heilman, Robert B. (1949). "An Inquiry into Anti-Highbrowism." *Bulletin of the American Association of University Professors* 35.4 (Winter): 611–627.

Herbert, A. P. (1924). "*Trott* v. *Tulip*: The Highbrow." *Punch* (August 20), 218–220; (August 27), 232–234.

Huxley, Aldous (1931). "Foreheads Villainous Low." In *Music at Night and Other Essays*. London: Chatto & Windus. 201–210.

Kaufman, George Simon (1926). *The Butter and Egg Man: A Play in Three Acts*. New York: Boni and Liveright.

Kerr, Jeane and Walter Kerr (1949). "High Brow, Middle Brow, Low Brow." Jay Gorney, Scores 1916–1975. New York Public Library: Library for the Performing Arts Music Division. T-Mss 1994–002.

Leavis, Q. D. (1932). *Fiction and the Reading Public*. London: Chatto & Windus.

Lewis, Sinclair (1914). *Our Mr. Wrenn*. New York: Grosset and Dunlap.

Menner, Robert J. (1946). "The Australian Language." *American Speech* 21.2 (April): 120–122.

Murdoch, Walter (1937). "The Tyranny of the Low-Brow." *The Australian Quarterly* 9.1 (March): 40–47.

Orwell, George (1940). "Inside the Whale." In *Inside the Whale and Other Essays*. London: Victor Gollancz. 131–188.

Partridge, Eric (1932). "Bestsellers in Fiction." In *Literary Sessions*. London: Scholartis Press. 16–38.

Rose, Donald F. (1927). "Dietary Discriminations." *The Forum* (September), 466.

Rose, Donald (1929). "Stuff and Nonsense." *The North American Review* 5.1 (January): 122–128.

Swinnerton, Frank (as Simon Pure) (1928). "Mrs. Woolf on the Novel." 1924. In *A London Bookman*. London: Martin Secker. 111–118.

Wedemeyer, Freda (1937). "The Corruption of Public Taste." *The Australian Quarterly* 9.4 (December): 70–78.

Wells, H. G. (1909). *Ann Veronica*. London: Harper.

Widdemer, Margaret (1933). "Message and Middlebrow." *The Saturday Review of Literature* (February 18), 433–434.

Woolf, Leonard (1927). *Hunting the Highbrow*. London: Hogarth.

Woolf, Virginia (1942). "Middlebrow" [1932]. In *The Death of the Moth and Other Essays* (ed. Leonard Woolf). London: Hogarth. 113–119.

Hygiene

Hygiene (from Hygeia, the Greek goddess of health) was, by the modernist period, firmly identified with scientific progress and social improvement. As C19 reformers sought to remedy the crowded and disease-ridden factories and cities and to introduce healthier living conditions for the sick and the poor, the usage of the term expanded from personal to public hygiene; however, hygiene also acquired problematic metaphorical implications relating to spiritual and moral health. As these various meanings coalesced in the concept of race hygiene, hygiene's positive significations of physical health and cleaner dwellings became entangled with ominous and threatening ideologies.

119

In eC20, hygiene became a discrete discipline of study, beginning with the founding of the Johns Hopkins School of Hygiene and Public Health in 1916 and the expansion of the London School of Tropical Medicine into the London School of Hygiene and Tropical Medicine in 1929. But to promote hygienic practices more generally, hygiene became a watchword of public education and the focus of massive propaganda campaigns. The first International Hygiene Exhibition in Dresden (1911) attracted worldwide interest and participation; in *Popular Science Monthly* (1912), Henry G. Beyer, the US delegate to the exposition, lauded "the nobility of the undertaking" and expressed the hope that "every living man and woman might receive [its] benefits." The Dresden exhibit defined hygiene broadly as any issue dealing with human health; by the time of the second International Hygiene Exhibition (1930), the categories included physical exercises, food, clothing, and dwellings. In contrast, the American Social Hygiene Association (founded 1913) targeted the specific issue of sex hygiene to combat venereal disease, particularly among soldiers during WWI, and to bring the subject out from the quiet censorship of shame and into the public sphere. The Association's *Journal of Social Hygiene* ran from 1918 to 1954. General health issues became the focus of a yet more extensive campaign. Seeking the widest possible audience, the National Health Council promoted the use of "motion pictures" in health education, while Thomas C. Edwards, Acting Executive Officer, argued that "the instruction of all the people in the principles of hygiene and sanitary science is recognized as essential [. . .] to national vitality" (1926). Noting that, in the 1920s, films such as *Working for Dear Life* (on regular health examinations) and *One Scar or Many* (on the smallpox vaccine) reached audiences in the hundreds of thousands, Edwards went further to propose that illustrations of "public health and hygiene" could be beneficially introduced into "the purely entertainment motion picture" with no detrimental "box office" effect.

In feminist writing, hygiene was invoked to replace the C19 ideal of the delicate, languishing female body with an athletic image of robust health. The popular, if proselytizing, *A Study in Bloomers, or, The Model New Woman: a Novel* (1895) combined the topics of athletics, dietetics, and dress reform, arguing for bloomers as the hygienic choice over long skirts. The heroine, delivering a paper to her women's club, declaims against "unhygienic food" and "lack of exercise" and urges women to wear healthy clothing: "Discard corsets, long skirts, tight garters, cramping shoes, and every other thing that in any way impedes the fullest and freest development of the body." Charlotte Perkins Gilman's *Herland* (1915) – a feminist utopia set in the Amazon jungle – extols the values of "physiology, hygiene, sanitation, physical culture," describing the women as "a clean-bred, vigorous lot, having the best of care, the most perfect living conditions always." The first use of the phrase "feminine hygiene" may have been by Julia Ward Howe, who argued that "the feminine hygiene will be higher and more complete when it is administered by women" (1874); by the 1930s, feminine or "marriage hygiene" was aggressively used in advertisements for Zonite and Lysol, a typical promotion for the latter offering not only a "sense of well being" but the means of transforming "wretched marriages into happy ones" (*McCall's*, 1934), fostering the common notion that such douches provided a means of birth control. Hygiene also promised relief for domestic chores in the home: a pivotal display at the second International Hygiene Exhibition was the Frankfurt Kitchen – the prototype of the modern streamlined working space – designed to enable not only sanitation but ease and efficiency in women's lives. Modern hygiene as an antidote to the oppressive Victorian atmosphere figures comically in Virginia Woolf's *Between the Acts* (1941): Mrs. Lynn Jones admires the fitness of her daughter, who at 40 is still "slim as a wand," and the world in which "each flat has its refrigerator," reflecting that the Victorian home of her parents might have been "not impure, that wasn't the word – but perhaps 'unhygienic'. . . . Like a bit of meat gone sour."

Hygienic efficiency, however, often prompted nostalgic longings for a warmer and cozier past. Mrs. Lynn Jones also remembers the Victorian home as "beautiful," and in Ethel Lina White's *She Faded into Air* (1941), the private detective, Alan Foam, appreciates the "old-fashioned comfort of his drawing room," including the heavy green curtains that his wife, who prefers "a warm atmosphere" to fresh air, describes "guiltily as her 'crime against hygiene.'" Hygienic with reference to clean, unadorned lines could connote the sterility of modern design. Evelyn Waugh, defending Victorian furnishings, attributed the "neurotic boredom" of modern life to the "hygienic blankness" of modern spaces, explaining that the "eye must be caught and held before the brain will work" (1954). John Betjeman humorously protested the invasion of hygienic practice into the English pub, casting the new "air-conditioned bars" as "hygienic and ethe-real" with their meager provision of nothing but "a place to sit and soak in sanit'ry conditions" (1950). Another Betjeman poem, decrying the cultural asepsis of new urban developments, wonders if the modern Garden City resident who "eats her greasy crumpets snugly in the inglenook" can "know the deep depression of this bright, hygienic hell" (1953).

As such examples suggest, connotations of hygiene leapt easily from modern design to modern life and implications of cultural sterility. In Edith Wharton's *Twilight Sleep* (1927), Pauline Manford, given to making speeches to female audi-ences "united by a common faith in the infinite extent of human benevolence and the incalculable resources of American hygiene," thinks her husband should have an office with "concave surbases, as in a hospital ward or a hygienic nursery," with "no corners anywhere to catch the dust." Her belief that "people's lives" also should have "no corners in them" is, in the narrator's words, a desire "to de-microbe life." American novelist Robert Grant expressed ambivalence about the "glorious [democratic] wave of humanitarian and civic impulse which tends to dwarf all ideals other than teaching hygiene to the masses" and protested that "united efforts to ameliorate social conditions" could scarcely be taken "as a syn-onym for culture" (1912). T. S. Eliot similarly warned against a "totalitarian democracy" in which "the Puritanism of a hygienic morality in the interest of efficiency" would threaten the "needs of the individual soul" (1939). Even George Orwell, while supportive of measures to improve standards of living in England's slums, conceded that he wished "the word 'hygiene' could be dropped from the dictionary," for while "bugs are bad, [. . .] a state of affairs in which men will allow themselves to be dipped like sheep is worse" (1937).

Satiric denigrations of hygienic practices generally targeted not healthy sanita-tion, but fanatical enthusiasts who elevated hygiene to a near-righteous cause. In G. K. Chesterton's *The Man Who Was Thursday* (1908), one anarchist dies from drinking "a hygienic mixture of chalk and water as a substitute for milk, which beverage he regarded as barbaric, and as involving cruelty to the cow," while the detective Gabriel Syme's antipathy to anarchism derives from observing the extreme polarizations of his father's dedication to "art and self-realisation" and his mother's obsession with "simplicity and hygiene," to the extent that her enforced vegetarianism drives the father near to the point of "defending canni-

121

balism." In Edgar Wallace's African adventure novel *Bones of the River* (1923), Mr. Commissioner Sanders appreciates his well-intentioned but bumbling assistant's "efforts on behalf of hygiene" (here, guarding against "microbes" by keeping windows closed) but claims he would nonetheless "rather die of disease than endure this stink." Overly earnest instruction in hygiene came in for satirical treatment as well. In Nathanael West's *Day of the Locust* (1939), Tod Hackett's bumbling attempts to convince Faye Greener to give up prostitution leave him shouting ridiculously "like a YMCA lecturer on sex hygiene." In W. F. Harvey's *The Beast with Five Fingers* (1928), when a character begs his companion to open a window, the other retorts, "we're not a couple of boarding-school misses fresh from a course of hygiene lectures."

The gap between proselytizers and critics widened as hygiene was co-opted into increasingly metaphorical use, with moral, spiritual, or aesthetic implications. Addressing the teaching of democratic manners in the schools, former Harvard President Charles W. Eliot argued the need "to go beyond the motive of personal hygiene to the altruistic motive of caring for the health and comfort of others" (1911). Aldous Huxley argued that "'spiritual' or transcendental values" ought to be reconceived in "terms of hygiene"; "vice," he asserted, is "hygienically unsound" since it prevents a man from realizing his potential, whereas "a great deal of morality and religion" could be usefully reinterpreted "as rules of health for the attainment and keeping up of an ideal efficiency" (1932b). In *The Road I Know* (1942), a record of his late wife's experiences as a psychic, Stewart Edward White quoted her notes: "What we vaguely, mistily call spiritual" is "as real, natural and joyous as the flesh and blood"; since "we have proved the wisdom and comfort of physical hygiene, why not teach the next generation a little spiritual hygiene?" Art, too, could be reconceived in terms of hygiene. As the ultimate aesthetic application, F. T. Marinetti lauded Futurism for replacing the old "ideologies" with "formulas for spiritual hygiene" that were "creative and revolutionary" (1920); more ambivalently, Dylan Thomas cast W. H. Auden's poetry as "a hygiene [. . .] based on a brilliantly prejudiced analysis of contemporary disorders" and thus both "a sanitary science and a flusher of melancholies" (1937).

The most sinister connotations of hygiene arose from its association with eugenics and racial cleansing. *Rassenhygiene* [race hygiene] was coined in 1895 by the physician Alfred Ploetz, who argued that protecting the weak threatened the strength of the German people. Although less militant in its implications, the English term quickly spread. While Beyer's review of the first Hygiene Exhibition welcomed information concerning "the customs and habits of the different races peopling our globe and their common desire for a [. . .] healthy life," he approved the introduction of race hygiene to educate the public in "the transmission through heredity of acquired characters and of diseases" and the consequent need to exercise "care in the selection of a life partner." Feminists more commonly used social hygiene to refer to sex education, but their arguments for controlled pregnancies and protection from venereal disease were often bolstered by arguments for improving the race. As Margaret Sanger, the founder of Planned Parenthood, wrote, "Birth control places in our hands the key to that greatest of human problems – how to reconcile individual freedom with the necessities of race hygiene" (1925). Although by race, Sanger meant the human species, and by American race, she meant "the best of all racial elements" "fused into an amalgam" (1920), feminist arguments for eugenicist improvement became entangled with ideas of racial purity. While the improved race in Perkins Gilman's *Herland* (1915) refers to a new sexual race of parthenogenic women, the women are notably all of "Aryan" descent and defend the preservation of "pure stock" as preventative of such problems, in the old "bisexual race," as contagious diseases. The popular Canadian writer Emily Murphy ("Janey Canuck") – also the first female police magistrate in the British Empire – served as well on the Canadian Committees of both social hygiene and mental hygiene; arguing that "70% of Alberta's insane [. . .] come from countries outside of Canada" and that "90 per cent" of these cases "may be traced to heredity," she was typical of efforts to relieve overcrowding in the mental institutions in her support for "the sterilization of the unfit" (1932). In the annals of C20, the application of race hygiene exposed the inherent violence of eugenicist dreams, and Marinetti's slogan, "War, the world's only hygiene" (1909), proved devastatingly true. Reflecting Hitler's obsession with racial cleansing, the Nazi press officer Paul Schmidt declared, "the Jewish question is not a question of humanity and it is not a question of religion, it is rather a question of political hygiene" (1943). The horrors of totalitarian eugenics were indeed chillingly forecast in Aldous Huxley's *Brave New World* (1932a). When the World State convert Lenina Crowne intones the maxim that "cleanliness is next to fordliness," the protagonist Bernard ironically recites "the second hypnopaedic lesson in elementary hygiene": "civilization is sterilization." In a terrible reversal, literal hygiene, with its promise of healthier living conditions, especially for the disadvantaged, accrued metaphorical applications that lent support to oppression and death.

SEE ALSO: *God, Gods; Fascism; Race; Woman, New Woman*

References

(1930). "International Hygiene Exhibition." *The British Journal of Nursing* 78 (February): 50.

(1934). Advertisement for Lysol disinfectant. *McCall's Magazine* (June), 120.

(1937). "Sixteen Comments on Auden." *New Verse* (November), 23–30.

Betjeman, John (1950). "The Village Inn." *Harper's Bazaar* (May), 61.

Betjeman, John (1953). "Huxley Hall." *Punch* (July), 115.

Beyer, Dr. Henry G. (1912). "The International Hygiene Exhibition at Dresden." *Popular Science Monthly* (February), 105–128.

Chesterton, G. K. (1908). *The Man Who Was Thursday*. London: J. W. Arrowsmith.

Edwards, Thomas C. (1926). "Health Pictures and Their Value." *Annals of the American Academy of Political and Social Science* 128.217 (November): 133–138.

Eliot, Charles W. (1911). "Democracy and Manners Apropos of an Inquiry into the Teaching of Manners in the Public Schools." *The Century Magazine* 83 (December): 173–178.

Eliot, T. S. (1939). *The Idea of a Christian Society*. London: Faber and Faber.

Gilman, Charlotte Perkins (1915). *Herland*. Auckland: Floating Press.

Grant, Robert (1912). *The Convictions of a Grandfather*. New York: Charles Scribner's Sons.

Hall, George (1895). *A Study in Bloomers, or, The Model New Woman: A Novel*. Chicago: American Bible House.

Harvey, W. F. (1928). "The Beast with Five Fingers." In *The Beast with Five Fingers and Other Tales*. London: J. M. Dent.

Howe, Julia Ward (1874). Chapter 1. In *Sex and Education: A Reply to Dr. E. H. Clarke's "Sex in Education"* (ed. Julia Ward Howe). Boston: Roberts Brothers. 13–31.

Huxley, Aldous (1932a). *Brave New World*. London: Chatto & Windus.

Huxley, Aldous (1932b). *Jesting Pilate*. London: Chatto & Windus.

Marinetti, F. T. (1909). "Le Futurisme." *Le Figaro* (February 20), 1.

Marinetti, F. T. (1920). *Al di la del Comunismo* [Beyond Communism]. Milan: La Testa di Ferro.

Murphy, Emily (1932). "Sterilization of the Insane." *Vancouver Sun* (September 24), n.p.

Orwell, George (1937). *The Road to Wigan Pier*. London: V. Gollancz.

Sanger, Margaret (1920). *Woman and the New Race*. New York: Brentano's.

Sanger, Margaret (1925). "The Need of Birth Control in America." In *Birth Control: Facts and Responsibilities* (ed. Adolph Meyer). Baltimore: Williams and Wilkins. 11–49.

Schmidt, Paul (1943). Qtd. in "Gefallene Bollwerke: Die einstige Macht des Judentums in den Staaten und Städten des Südostens und ihre fortschreitende Liquidierung." *Donauzeitung* (Belgrade) (July 3), 3.

Wallace, Edgar (1923). *Bones of the River*. London: G. Newnes.

Waugh, Evelyn (1954). "Those Happy Homes." Rev. of *The Victorian Home* by Ralph Dutton. *Sunday Times* (November 28), 5.

West, Nathanael (1939). *Day of the Locust*. New York: Random House.

Wharton, Edith (1927). *Twilight Sleep*. New York: D. Appleton.

White, Ethel Lina (1941). *She Faded into Air*. New York: Harper. White, Stewart Edward (1942). *The Road I Know*. New York: E. P. Dutton.

Woolf, Virginia (1941). *Between the Acts*. London: Hogarth.

Impression, Impressionism

The root of impress, in the sense of physical stamp or imprint, lent an objective and physiological meaning to mental and sense impressions from at least C17. But impression took a decidedly different turn when it became newly associated with aesthetic style in lC19. The labeling of some artists as impressionists derives from *Impression, soleil levant*, a painting by Claude Monet displayed in an 1874 exhibition in Paris that showcased works by a revolutionary group of painters calling themselves the *Société anonyme des artistes peintres, sculpteurs, graveurs, etc.* Impressionism was soon coined in a humorous review by Louis Leroy in *Le Charivari* – the French equivalent of *Punch*. Leroy's satirical spoof proclaimed the death of realist painting: a visitor to the exhibit, first confounded by what he takes to be mere scratches on canvas, becomes so converted to the new style that, in a fit of mad ecstasy, he mistakes the museum guard for a painting and in a frenzied outburst condemns the guard's facial features as unnecessary detail on which the "painter" had wasted his time (1874). In a more serious vein, art critic Jules Castagnary associated impressionists with "idealism" (in the sense of mind-dependent), explaining that "they do not render a landscape, but the sensa-tion produced by the landscape" (1874). Anti-realism was thus the first critical verdict of Impressionist painting, a judgment perpetuated in current literary glos-saries that define impressionism as a personal, subjective manner of writing which aims not to describe the material world but to register its effect.

ABCDEFGH*I*JKLMNOPQRSTUVWXYZ

Modernism: Keywords, First Edition. Melba Cuddy-Keane, Adam Hammond, and Alexandra Peat.
© 2014 Melba Cuddy-Keane. Published 2014 by John Wiley & Sons, Ltd.

Impression, Impressionism

For many Anglo-American literary modernists, however, painterly impressionism bore the opposite connotation of being merely an automatic recording of external reality. Henry James castigated the same French painters as "partisans of unadorned reality and absolute foes to arrangement, embellishment, selection" ([1876]1956). Ezra Pound decried Impressionism and Futurism as alike the "CORPSES of VORTICES" because both, being obsessed with reproduction rather than pattern, dispersed rather than released energy (1914b). Early discussions of *literary* impressionism similarly associated it with external realism. H. G. Wells responded positively to the "impressionism" of Frank Swinnerton's novel *Nocturne* (1917), praising Swinnerton's "clear, detached objectivity" and his rendering of "life as it is" but "more intensely." Impressionism, however, was a style for which Wells could find "personally [. . .] no use at all" since it "does not want you or any one to do anything." He judged that Dorothy Richardson had "probably carried impressionism in fiction to its furthest limit." Citing the first two volumes of Richardson's *Pilgrimage*, Wells disparaged not only the passivity of the heroine's mind, which he described as "not a mentality but a mirror," but also the triviality of content: "a series of dabs of intense superficial impression" that avoided "the depths for the sake of the surface." Ezra Pound later distinguished two streams of literary impressionism: one, following Flaubert, was "intent on exact presentation"; the other, imitative of Monet's "softness," was nothing but a "rosy, floribunda bore" (1914b). To the extent that Pound was an "imagist," however, he would have found his own writing implicated in later criticisms of the triviality of impressionism, negatively associated with "the minute and the fragmentary" and given a gendered slant: for critic William C. Frierson, "both imagism and impressionism were presided over by women," whose "feminine" qualities included the limiting absence of "a cosmic, philosophical view" (1942).

As opposed to the negative critics, the writer who most embraced impressionism and attempted to formulate a set of literary doctrines about it was Ford Madox Ford, although he used the word somewhat reluctantly, submitting to the "persistence" of "one person and another" who labeled him in this way (1914). The aim of "literary Impressionism," Ford explained, was "to produce an illusion of reality in the mind of one's readers," to make them feel they were "present at an affair in real life." The impressionist method was to "record the observations of one moment," eliminating the "correlated chronicle" and anything else extraneous to the experienced moment that would destroy the illusion's effect. While emphasizing concentration of feeling, however, Ford noted that an impression can sustain the "superimposed emotions" of past and present, "like so many views seen through bright glass," in which we see both what is ahead of us and what is reflected from behind. While fragmentary and complex, the impression for Ford was nonetheless not vague, but "as hard and definite as a tin-tack."

These general principles developed out of Ford's collaboration with Joseph Conrad. According to Ford, both writers accepted the "stigma" of Impressionism, because they "saw that Life did not narrate, but made impressions on our brains," and they knew that, to produce "an effect of life," they too "must not narrate but render impressions" (1924). Conrad, however, never described himself as an impressionist writer, although he once wrote that he was "an impressionist by instinct" when explaining his reading of a poem and urging a more exact word to "convey the notion" of the "voice of the sea" ([1897]1983–1988). The term he favored was impression, with a signification that strongly combined inner "notion" and outer "voice." Defining art "as a single-minded attempt to render the highest kind of justice to the visible universe," he simultaneously explained that, through art, the writer appeals to the reader and that the "appeal, to be effective, must be an impression conveyed through the senses." The aim in conveying an impression was to "make you see" ([1897]1914). Conrad's impression thus implies both a subject–object relation (between the author and "the visible universe") and a subject–subject relation (between minds of author and reader).

In discussions of literary work, impression indeed occurs much more frequently than impressionism and with connotations that clearly counter the stasis, passivity, and triviality that hostile responses associated with the latter term. Henry James described the novel as "a personal, a direct impression of life," but he also emphasized the nature of impressions as an ongoing flow: equating "experience" and "impressions," he noted that "experience is never limited, and it is never complete" (1884). Virginia Woolf associated impressions with multiplicity when she described "an ordinary mind on an ordinary day" as receiving "a myriad impressions – trivial, fantastic, evanescent, or engraved with the sharpness of steel" (1925). But multiplicity could mean disparity, and Woolf also noted the increased challenges for modern writers, who find it harder "to believe that [their own] impressions hold good for others" ([1923]1925). The gap in transmitting impressions contributed, however, to Woolf's positive sense of the reader's active role. Reading, she wrote, involves a first stage of "opening the mind wide to the fast flocking of innumerable impressions," followed by a second stage in which "we must make of these fleeting shapes one that is hard and lasting" (1916), gathering "the multiplicity of incidents together" into "a single impression of an overwhelming kind" (1920), a feeling that "remains in our minds as the book itself" (1922).

127

Impressions were thus valued as sensuous and emotional response, but – retaining the root sense of impress or stamp – impression also implied the source of impressions outside the individual mind, in the "visible universe" (Conrad [1897]1983–1988). On the one hand, Walter Pater upheld the subjective nature of impressions, claiming that art gives "the highest quality" to "[our] moments" of intense experience, and that "education grows in proportion as one's susceptibility to these impressions increases in depth and variety"; on the other hand, Pater sought an understanding of beauty, not through "abstract" and putatively "universal formula," but through an apprehension of works of art as "receptacles of so many powers or forces," each with the "property [. . .] of affecting one with a special, a unique, impression of pleasure" (1873). Blending subject and object, the role of aesthetic criticism, for Pater, was to use subjective experience to understand external reality: to analyze the way the artwork "produces this special impression of beauty or pleasure, to indicate what the source of the impression is, and under what conditions it is experienced." Marcel Proust similarly conceived impression as involving subject–object mediation: "all impression is two-fold, half-sheathed in the object, prolonged in ourselves by another half which we alone can know" ([1927] 1931). The latter, too often neglected, demands that we employ "intuition" and expend "personal effort" in order to perceive the "true impression" by overcoming the distorting and falsifying influences of unthinking habit and the conscious will. But Proust was equally clear that the intuitive process is not to "create," not to "invent," but to "discover" and "interpret." The "book" we "decipher" has been "printed within us by reality itself": "Whatever idea life has left in us, its material shape, mark of the impression it has made on us, is still the necessary pledge of its truth." For Ford as well, impression implied an imbrication of within and without; also, like Pater and Proust, Ford attributed a spiritual dimension to impressions, describing the experience as "a bathing in the visible world" akin to the "Brahmin" state of "contemplation" (1905).

Impression's reliance on sensation, perception, and intuition, its power of fusing multiple times and associations, and its effect of disrupting logical order all placed emphasis on the moment as a spontaneous eruption in what Proust called "cinematographic procession" ([1927] 1931). Ford similarly described the impression as a necessary pause in logical and chronological progression, allowing a deeper perception of reality: "in the breaks, in the marking time [. . .] the course of a life becomes visible and sensible." Significantly, too, Ford cast these moments of heightened perception as accessible to all: positing their occurrence in "a third state between work and amusement," Ford argued, "whether we are of the leisured class, whether we are laundry-women, agricultural labourers, dock labourers, or bank clerks, it is that third state that makes us live" (1905). Distinguishing, however, between "the Leisured Class" with its "life of display" and "the pause in the beat of the clock that comes now and then to make life seem worth going on with," Ford named the latter "perhaps the real Leisure." For that pause offers the nonmaterial wealth of "little personal impressions, of small, futile things that, seen in moments of stress and anguish, have significances so tremendous and meanings so poignant." As a modernist literary term, impression thus mediated not only subject and object but also the big and the small.

SEE ALSO: *Bigness, Smallness; Form, Formalism; Readers, Reading; Reality, Realism; Unconscious*

References

Castagnary, Jules (1874). "L'Exposition du boulevard des Capucines, les impressionnistes." *Le Siècle* (April 29), 3.

Conrad, Joseph (1914). Preface. ["Author's Note," 1897]. In *The Nigger of the "Narcissus"*. Garden City, NY: Doubleday, Page. 11–16.

Conrad, Joseph (1983–1988). Letter to E. L. Sanderson, 17 October 1897. [1897]. In *The Collected Letters of Joseph Conrad* (eds. Frederick R. Karl and Laurence Davies). 4 vols. Cambridge: Cambridge University Press. Vol. 1: 1861–1897: 398–399.

[Ford] Hueffer, Ford Madox (1905). *The Soul of London: A Survey of a Modern City*. London: Alston Rivers.

Ford, Ford Madox (1914). "On Impressionism." *Poetry and Drama* 2 (June): 167–175; (December): 323–334.

Ford, Ford Madox (1924). *Joseph Conrad: A Personal Remembrance*. London: Duckworth.

Frierson, William Coleman (1942). *The English Novel in Transition, 1885–1940*. Norman: University of Oklahoma Press.

James, Henry (1956). "The Impressionists." ["Parisian Festivity," 1876]. In *The Painter's Eye: Notes and Essays on the Pictorial Arts* (ed. John L. Sweeney). Madison: University of Wisconsin Press. 114–115.

James, Henry (1884). "The Art of Fiction." *Longman's Magazine* 4 (September): 180–186.

Leroy, Louis (1874). "Exposition des Impressionnistes." *Le Charivari* (April), 79–80.

Pater, Walter H. (1873). *Studies in the History of the Renaissance*. London: Macmillan.

Pound, Ezra (1914a). "Dubliners and Mr James Joyce." *The Egoist* 1 (July 15): 267.

Pound, Ezra (1914b). "VORTEX." *Blast* 1: 153–154.

Proust, Marcel (1931). *Time Regained*. [*Le temps retrouvé*, 1927]. Trans. Stephen Hudson. Vol. 8 of *Remembrance of Things Past* [*À la recherche du temps perdu*]. 8 vols. London: Chatto & Windus.

Wells, H. G. (1917). Introduction. In Frank Swinnerton's *Nocturne*. New York: George H. Doran. vii–xiv.

[Woolf, Virginia] (1916). "Charlotte Bronte." *TLS* (April 13), 169–170.

Woolf, Virginia (1920). "The Cherry Orchard." *The New Statesman* (July 24), 446–447.

[Woolf, Virginia] (1922). "On Re-Reading Novels." *TLS* (July 20), 465–466.

Woolf, Virginia (1925). "How It Strikes a Contemporary." [1923]. In *The Common Reader*. London: Hogarth. 292–305.

Woolf, Virginia (1925). "Modern Fiction." ["Modern Novels," 1919]. In *The Common Reader*. London: Hogarth. 184–195.

129

International, Internationalism

In 1789, Jeremy Bentham welcomed the emergence of international as a new English word, specifically of use in the law; by eC20, international had become part of the general vocabulary, applied to all walks of life. A prominent and increasing use was in the titles of organizations formed to standardize global practice, such as the International Committees created by the Metre Convention (1875), the International Meridian Conference (1884), the International Phonetic Association (1888), and the International Federation for Human Rights (1922).

International, Internationalism

A slightly different purpose animated associations intended to link peoples with shared interests and concerns, including the International Olympic Committee (1894), the International Save the Children Union (1920), the Boy Scouts International Bureau (1920), the International Association of Department Stores (1928), and the International Youth Hostel Association (1932). Indeed, the period saw such an upsurge in international organizations that it coined a new phrase: the international community, used, for example, by A. T. Mahan in "those general rights which all possess as members of the international community" (1900). Yet these usages pull in opposing directions: establishing common standards, with the goal of regulation, versus coordinating peoples, with the aim of ongoing conversation. The tension inheres in the different semantic possibilities in the term itself: the double roots of "inter-national" signifying relations between nations and the composite word "international" suggesting a transcendence of national borders in light of a common world.

Stimulated by the catastrophes of WWI, the political realm focused on conflicts between nations, pressured by the difficulties of negotiating differences in peaceful ways. The academic discipline of International Relations has its origins in this time, beginning with Leonard Woolf's *International Government* (1916). Written shortly after the outbreak of war at the request of the socialist Fabian Society, this pioneering work launched the task of transforming vague hopes of international cooperation into more definite political terms. Following the war, the League of Nations (1920) – founded, in the words of its Covenant, "to promote international co-operation and to achieve international peace and security" – generated hopes for ameliorating world conflict not only through governmental bodies but through "lay" organizations as well. A subsidiary organization, the International Institute of Intellectual Cooperation (founded 1926), undertook, for example, to promote education about League goals in the schools.

With a somewhat different focus, the umbrella concept of international functioned, from the mC19, as a socialist rallying cry, connoting solidarity amongst segments of different nations united in common cause. The International Workingmen's Association (IWA) (1864–1876), also known as the First International, founded by Karl Marx to promote joint political action of working classes in all countries, was revived in the Second International (1889–1916); the "Internationale" (French lyrics 1871; music 1888) was virtually adopted as a socialist and communist anthem. Other socialist-inspired usages include the inauguration of International Women's Day (March 11, 1911) and the *International Handbook of Adult Education* (1929) produced for the first World Conference on Adult Education for the working class. Other bonds of international solidarity united victims of oppression. Alain Locke claimed that "as with the Jew, persecution is making the Negro international," explaining that for "the American Negro" internationalism is "primarily an effort to recapture contact with the scattered peoples of African derivation" (1925). International solidarity also mobilized into defense of others, witnessed in the many volunteers, both communist and non-communist, who fought either with or alongside the International Brigades against Fascism in the Spanish Civil War (1936–1939), including numerous artists and writers, such as Julian Bell, John Dos Passos, Ernest Hemingway, and George Orwell.

Controversies arose, however, concerning relations between internationalism and nation. In its most optimistic usages, internationalism was conceived as overcoming the narrowness of national affiliations with broader views of the common destiny of the human race. An article in *The New Age* on the Federal Conference on Education (1907) argued vociferously against using the Oxford–Cambridge model for the design of colonial universities: "We can only suggest a vigorous propaganda of internationalism and even of cosmopolitanism. After all we are citizens of the world, or ought to be; and the future of the human race is vastly more important than the future of the Anglo-Saxon section." An article by R. M. on socialism and nationalism in the same journal defined communal loyalty in an ascending scale: "first, the will to do one's best for people of one's own race; secondly, to do one's best for the people of every race; thirdly, to abolish in one's mind the last traces of nationalism and to do one's best for man as a single species" (1907). The author further declared, "Every genuinely international society is in its way a human institution; while every nationalist society is in its way an obstacle on the path of humanity." A similar approach from a Hindu perspective is implied in E. M. Forster's *A Passage to India* (1924). When the Muslim doctor Aziz retires to a Hindu state and devotes much of his time to writing poetry, the Brahmin Godbole likes only the poem in which Aziz "had skipped over the motherland (whom he did not truly love) and gone straight to internationality." Envisioning India in advance of western nations, Godbole remarks, "Ah, India, who seems not to move, will go straight there while the other nations waste their time." Internationalism, however, could also be seen as a threat to those whose loyalty was to national identity first. Joseph Conrad's character Razumov in *Under Western Eyes* (1911) jots down the notes, "Patriotism not Internationalism" and "Unity not Disruption." An article by Saint Fiacre in *The Egoist* celebrated a royal visit in 1914, on the grounds that such "collective [national] manifestations awaken the individual to himself," whereas "Internationalism [. . .] annihilates the individual." As WWI proceeded, nationalism threatened internationalism's demise: In "Notes of a Cosmopolite," Alexander Kaun despaired that "the International has fallen in ruins," conquered "by the underestimated imponderabilia, that of primitive patriotism" (1915).

In its most complex construction, international comprised both one world and multiple nations, in a paradoxical mix. An editorial in *The New Age* on "What is Internationalism?" argued that "Internationalism does not, as we understand it, involve any repudiation of patriotism; indeed, the very word 'international' implies the continued existence of nations," adding that a Socialist can "regard Socialists of other countries as his comrades and fellow workers" without any implication of being "anti-patriotic" (1907). Another Socialist, John Bruce Glasier, declared, "Internationalism does not mean the extinction of nationhood. It means the bringing of nations together in the bonds of friendship and brotherhood" (1920). Although focusing only on "the civilized world" and its responsibilities, Nicholas Butler defined the international mind as a habit of thought and action that conceives other nations "as cooperating equals," "in sharp antagonism to that internationalism which would break down the boundaries of nations and merge all mankind" (1925). The same article framed the challenge more bluntly: "We are truly standing at a crossroads in the history of the world. [. . .] The problem of the One and the Many lies at the bottom [. . .] of the problem of nationalism and internationalism."

This fundamental tension similarly infects two terms of particular relevance to literary modernism: International Style and the international novel. In the US, International Style referred to the building design inspired by architects such as Le Corbusier in France and Walter Gropius and members of the Bauhaus school in Germany. The term originated in Henry-Russell Hitchcock and Philip Johnson's *International Style* (1932), written to accompany the International Exhibition of Modern Architecture at the Museum of Modern Art in New York. Hitchcock and Johnson named the style international to defend "the art of architecture" against the mere "science of building," whose proponents, the American functionalists, putatively denied the importance of the aesthetic element in design. Gropius himself, however, had used the word international but with a more socially inflected intent; as he explained, "Architecture is always national, also always individual, but of the three concentric circles – individual – people – humanity – the last and greatest encompasses the other two. Therefore the title: *Internationale Architektur*" (1925). While MOMA's nomenclature gave rise to the identification of modernism with a noninstrumental aesthetics, designating art or architecture as international style had a definite political edge in the context of totalitarian Germany. By the 1930s, international modernism's implied opposition to Nazi doctrine triggered Hitler's war against "un-German" degenerate art (*Entartete Kunst*): in 1933, the Bauhaus was forced to close, and soon afterward Hitler proclaimed, "all those mutually supporting and thereby sustaining cliques of chatterers, dilettantes, and art forgers will be picked up and liquidated," or else "those prehistoric Stone-Age culture-barbarians and art-stutterers can return to the caves of their ancestors and there can apply their primitive international scratchings" ([1937]1954). International style was thus both aesthetic *and* political in its aims.

Literary applications continue the complex dynamics of the term. When Oscar Cargill named Henry James's *The American* "the first international novel" (1958), he had in mind a narrative that transplants a character into a foreign environment where the mores differ from those at home: the subject is the tension between national cultures rather than a united world view. James himself testified that "the 'international' light lay thick" on his "observation"; he described his continuing theme, however, as the failure of Americans to *be* international: they arrived in Europe "destitute of elements of preparedness" and thus deficient as well in apprehensions of "responsibility" and "reciprocity" (1908a). James further explained that "behind all [his] small comedies and tragedies of the international" lurked "the idea of some eventual sublime consensus" – "a common intelligence and a social fusion" to ameliorate the "old rigours of separation" (1908b). Admitting nonetheless that "half our instincts work for the maintained differences," he feared the increasing "mixture of manners" was "fusion" becoming too "thick": in what he referred to as "the *great* international cases," so many social references abound that "social incoherence [. . .] has at last got itself accepted, right and left, as normal."

James's *novelistic* internationalism thus focuses on cultural difference, while his *critical* internationalism considers both the desirability and the dangers of cultural fusion. Another approach to the international novel, however, more closely echoed the universalism of International Style. Ford Madox Ford also placed James in "the main stream of the international novel" (1930), but Ford had in mind a trans-historical and trans-geographical tradition. As opposed to the "nuvvle," which *relates* its subject often with moralizing intent, Ford's international novel – which includes, as exemplars, Samuel Richardson, Gustave Flaubert, and Ivan Turgenev – realistically *renders* its matter in form. Ford's international is a transnational style, as opposed to James's articulation of an international theme. The belief that an international sensibility is not incompatible with national literatures was eloquently expressed by Sir Alfred Zimmern – the first professor of International Politics both in Wales and in the world; citing "Shakespeare, Molière and Goethe," he wrote: "It is the most characteristic figures of a national literature who are also the most international, and it is through them that understanding must come" (1923). Turning to the word "nationality" rather than "nationalism," Zimmern supported the need for a "group-consciousness" derived from a sense of "home"; however, he believed as well that when a national culture came "of age," it would incorporate both appreciation of and bonding with others, so that "an enduring network of internationalism will some day be knit and a harmony of understanding established in a world of unassailable diversity."

Zimmern and others like him who believed in the power of ideas, concepts of justice and morality, and a cooperatively established framework of international law, came to be labeled "idealist" as the aftermath of WWII saw the rise of the "realist" school of international relations with its emphasis on *machtpolitik* (power politics) and the rule of force. Internationalism also came under siege from the American far right, who viewed it as a conspiracy against the sovereign power of the US. In a public opinion survey of seven periodical publications from "the extreme Right," sociologist Stanley Bigman documented the recurrent theme of a "plot to abolish the United States," attributed to the (vaguely defined) machinations of Communists and/or Jews (who were frequently condemned in language similar to Hitler's denunciation of "the Jewish international attempt to destroy European civilization" and his paradoxical labeling of Jews as both "Communists" and "financiers") (1950). Noting the lack of substance in the allegations, however, Bigman concluded that the language of conspiracy was mere rhetoric employed in support of policies "called 'isolationist' by their opponents and 'nationalist' by their adherents."

Like its putative other "nationalism," internationalism in the modernist period was thus a plurally charged word. Yet its conflicting usages signal not error or confusion, but the diverse interpretations of the tensions, or the indeed the synergies, between individual and communal life. At the end of WWII, Frank Walters, writing to *The Spectator*, prophetically warned, "the whole future of the human race depends on the outcome of the struggle between nationalism and internationalism" (1945). For the supporters of internationalism, Walters left this sobering note: "The pattern is familiar: internationalism is overwhelmingly victorious in theory, nationalism continues to control the means of action."

SEE ALSO: *Atom, Atomic; Common Mind, Group Thinking; Democracy; Race; Universal; Words, Language*

References

(1907). "Imperial Education." *The New Age* 1.6 (June 6): 84.

(1907). "What is Internationalism?" *The New Age* 1.17 (August 28): 1.

Bentham, Jeremy (1789). *An Introduction to the Principles of Morals and Legislation.* Printed in the year 1780, and now first published. London: T. Payne.

Bigman, Stanley K. (1950). "The 'New Internationalism' Under Attack." *Public Opinion Quarterly* 14 (2): 235–261.

Butler, Nicholas Murray (1925). "Internationalism and Public Opinion." *The Rotarian* (January), 6–7, 56–57.

Cargill, Oscar (1958). "The First International Novel." *PMLA* 74 (September): 418–425.

Conrad, Joseph (1911). *Under Western Eyes.* London: Methuen.

Ford, Ford Madox (1930). *The English Novel from the Earliest Days to the Death of Joseph Conrad.* London: Constable.

Forster, E. M. (1924). *A Passage to India.* London and New York: Edward Arnold.

Glasier, John Bruce (1920). *The Meaning of Socialism.* New York: T. Seltzer.

Gropius, Walter (1925). *Internationale Architektur.* München: Albert Langen Verlag. Translated by Kenneth H. Kaiser with the assistance of Professor Stanford Anderson.

In *Walter Gropius and the Ideas of Modern German Architecture 1910–1925*, by Kenneth H. Kaiser. BSc Dissertation: MIT, 1964. 30–34.

Hitchcock, Henry Russell and Philip Johnson (1932). *The International Style: Architecture since 1922*. New York: W. W. Norton.

Hitler, Adolf (1954). Speech at the opening of the Haus der Deutschen Kunst (House of German Art), Munich, July 18, 1937. [1937]. Excerpted and translated by Hellmut Lehmann-Haupt. In *Art under a Dictatorship*, by Hellmut Lehmann-Haupt. New York: Octagon Books.

James, Henry (1908a). Preface to *The Reverberator*. In *The Novels and Tales of Henry James*. New York Edition. 26 vols. New York: Charles Scribner's Sons. Vol. 13: v–xxi.

James, Henry (1908b). Preface to "Lady Barbarina." In *The Novels and Tales of Henry James*. The New York Edition. 26 vols. New York: Charles Scribner's Sons. Vol. 14: v–xxii.

Kaun, Alexander S. (1915). "Notes of a Cosmopolite." *The Little Review* 2.4: 9–17.

Locke, Alain (1925). "The New Negro." In *The New Negro: An Interpretation* (ed. Alain Locke). New York: Albert and Charles Boni. 3–16.

Mahan, A. T. (1900). "The Merits of the Transvaal Dispute." *The North American Review* (March), 312–326.

R. M. (1907). "Socialism and Nationalism." *The New Age* 1.5 (May 30): 74.

Saint Fiacre (1914). "Passing Paris." *The Egoist* 1.9 (1 May): 169.

Walters, Frank (1945). "The Conference Deadlock." Letters to the Editor. *The Spectator* (October 19), 360.

Woolf, Leonard (1916). *International Government*. Westminster: Fabian Society.

Zimmern, Alfred E. (1923). "Nationalism and Internationalism." *Foreign Affairs* 1.4 (June 15): 115–126.

135

Manifesto

The manifesto entered the modernist period with strong military associations. It derived its connotations from France, where in C16 a manifesto was a public announcement by a powerful group or an edict by a sovereign, such as a declaration of war. During the French Revolution, the term underwent an important semantic shift. Gracchus Babeuf's "Manifeste des plébéiens" (1795) and Sylvain Maréchal's "Manifeste des égaux" (1796) articulated the demands of disenfranchised rather than powerful groups, declaring war not on a rival state but on the state itself. Following the French Revolution, the manifesto became increasingly associated with revolutionary groups demanding social change from below, as most famously in Marx and Engels's (1848).

Artistic manifestos came to maturity in the modernist period and inherited the genre's radical and violent associations. The purest example is F. T. Marinetti's "Manifeste du Futurisme," included in his "Le Futurisme" (1909), which describes poetry as "a violent assault against unknown forces" and sets out "to glorify war – the only hygiene of the world – militarism, patriotism, the destructive gesture of anarchists, beautiful Ideas that kill, and contempt for woman." Many continental artistic movements produced manifestos in this bombastic tradition. Though it begins by declaring itself "against manifestos," Tristan Tzara's *Dada Manifesto* (1918) deploys the genre's characteristically violent rhetoric, picturing

ABCDEFGHIJKL**M**NOPQRSTUVWXYZ

Modernism: Keywords, First Edition. Melba Cuddy-Keane, Adam Hammond, and Alexandra Peat.
© 2014 Melba Cuddy-Keane. Published 2014 by John Wiley & Sons, Ltd.

fellow Dadaists as "a furious wind [. . .] preparing the great spectacle of disaster, fire, decomposition." André Breton's *Manifesto of Surrealism* (1924) is milder in tone, yet nonetheless calls on the manifesto's heritage to attack the "realistic attitude": "I loathe it," Breton says, "for it is made up of mediocrity, hate, and dull conceit."

Some artistic manifestos in this tradition exist in English. The "Manifesto of the Indian Progressive Writers' Association, London" (1935), for example, expresses the radical demands of a disenfranchised group, promising to "fight cultural reaction" and "further the cause of Indian freedom and social regeneration." The manifestos of Wyndham Lewis's *Blast* (1914), uttering attacks like "CURSE WITH EXPLETIVE OF WHIRLWIND THE BRITANNIC ÆSTHETE," would seem to employ the genre's inherent violence as well. But their deliberate self-contradiction – their avowed policy to "discharge ourselves on both sides" of binaries, to both "blast" and "bless" England – serves to undermine the clear-cut distinction between ally and enemy upon which the Marinettian manifesto depends. Similarly, Mina Loy's "Feminist Manifesto" ([1914]1996) both embraces and rejects the manifesto's military associations. She adopts its rhetoric, advocating "Absolute Demolition" of "the rubbish heap of tradition," but undercuts Marinetti's specific manifestos by seeking to "demolish" the binary logic of his "division of women into two classes the mistress, & the mother." Eugene Jolas's "Revolution of the Word" (1929) – which a promotional flyer inserted in his journal *transition* described as "A Paris Group Manifesto" – employed the violent rhetoric characteristic of the genre but disclaimed any political or military ambitions: "WE ARE NOT CONCERNED WITH THE PROPAGATION OF SOCIOLOGICAL IDEAS, EXCEPT TO EMANCIPATE THE CREATIVE ELEMENTS FROM THE PRESENT IDEOLOGY" (Jolas and signateurs, 1929).

137

Although in late C20, critics began to refer to many modernist essays as manifestos, most modernist writing in English did not label their own work in this way or truly adopt the form. Although Ezra Pound favored "a clear announcement of a program," he scrupulously avoided the connotations of a manifesto, expounding the central tenets of Imagism in an article, "Imagisme" (Flint [Pound], 1913), and publishing it under the name of his less illustrious colleague F. S. Flint (Pound, 1930). "Imagisme," moreover, stated specifically that the movement "had not published a manifesto." If Pound's motivations for avoiding the manifesto are a matter of speculation, others clearly rejected the form for its associations with group thinking and conformity. In his inaugural editorial note in *The Calendar of Modern Letters*, introduced by the words "Instead of a Manifesto," Edgell Rickword explained that the journal did not seek readers who share "any particular set of admirations and beliefs,"

Manifesto

since "for the modern mind the age of herds is past" (1925). In "Views and Opinions" (1913), *The New Freewoman* employed the style of the manifesto but did so with an interesting twist: "The nearest approach to a Cause it desires to attain, is to destroy Causes." This periodical likewise positioned itself against any associations with group action: "The NEW FREEWOMAN is not for the advancement of Woman, but for the empowerment of individuals – men and women." In *Three Guineas* (1938), Virginia Woolf mocked the manifesto that a "gentleman" had purportedly asked her to sign, pointing out that its "rather abstract terms" were both divorced from the real need to put its "promise into practice" and preposterously out of touch with the disadvantaged life situations of the women who were being asked to sign: "To ask them to sign your manifesto would be to ask a publican to sign a manifesto in favour of temperance." The first issue of John Lehmann's *New Writing* (1936) subverted the military connotations of the genre by ignoring them. Exhibiting neither the aggressive style nor the violent intentions of Marinetti's founding document, Lehmann's "Manifesto" humbly promised that "NEW WRITING will appear twice yearly, and will be devoted to imaginative writing, mainly of young authors."

SEE ALSO: *Avant-Garde; Modern, Modernism*

References

(1913). "Views and Opinions." *The New Freewoman* 1.2 (July 1): 25.

(1935). "All-India Progressive Writers' Manifesto." *The Left Review* II.V (February 1936): 248.

Breton, André (1924). *Manifeste du surréalisme*. Paris: Éditions du Sagittaire.

Flint, F. S. [and Ezra Pound] (1913). "Imagisme." *Poetry: A Magazine of Verse* 1.6 (March): 198–200.

Jolas, Eugene and signateurs (1929). "Revolution of the Word." *transition: An International Quarterly for Creative Experiment* 16–17 (June): 11–14.

Lehmann, John (1936). "Manifesto." *New Writing* 1 (Spring): 9.

[Lewis, Wyndham] (1914). "Manifesto [1]." *Blast* 1 (June 20): 9–28.

Loy, Mina (1996). "Feminist Manifesto." [1914]. In *The Lost Lunar Baedeker* (ed. Roger L. Conover). New York: Noonday. 153–154.

Marinetti, F. T. (1909). "Le Futurisme." *Le Figaro* (February 20), 1.

Pound, Ezra (1930). "Small Magazines." *The English Journal* 19.9 (November): 703.

[Promotional flyer] (1929). *transition: An International Quarterly for Creative Experiment* 16–17 (June): Insert.

[Rickword, Edgell] (1925). "Comments and Reviews." *The Calendar of Modern Letters* 1 (March): 70–71.

Tzara, Tristan (1918). "Dada Manifesto." *Dada* 3 (December).

Woolf, Virginia (1938). *Three Guineas*. London: Hogarth.

Modern, Modernism

"Modern/Modernity/Modernism . . ." – all three words appear together, likely for the first time, in the poem "As He Sees It" by Emanuel Carnevali, published in 1918. Beginning as conventional romanticism ("A wondrous voice is urging me within/And thrills me with a pain, alas!"), the poem "descends" into Imagism ("My throat sings/Like a stiff red silk ribbon"), then to bare style ("The throat shivers/Pain"), before collapsing into incoherence ("I am above my throat,/I have a right to forget"), as the uncertainty about the self translates into uncertainty about writing poetry ("Nobody home/The poet has left for the asylum"). Bad Keats ends in a foretaste of bad Beckett. As either humorous or dyspeptic self-satire, the poem mocks the modernist revolution in language, as well as modernism's dismantling of the unified self and questioning of the relation between perception and reality. Suggesting a modernist ability to laugh at oneself (Carnevali prefaces his poem by stating, "Here is what I feel sometimes about our own stuff"), the poem also reveals that this particular version of modernism had taken sufficient shape, by 1918, to be the subject of parodic critique.

In the period as a whole, however, literary and cultural modernism took many forms. The first use of modernism to designate a historical cultural phenomenon occurs in two places, at approximately the same time, on opposite sides of the Atlantic, and – strikingly – in the works of two diametrically opposed writers on the pessimism–optimism scale. In *Wessex Tales* (1888), Thomas Hardy had used "modernism" merely to refer to the new style of housing, in which modern efficiency was replacing "old-fashioned" dignity and charm; but in Hardy's *Tess of the D'Urbervilles* (1891), Angel Clare thinks of Tess as suffering from "feelings which might almost have been called those of the age – the ache of modernism," suggesting a questioning of the meaning of existence for which no answers can be found. Angel immediately reflects that such "advanced ideas" are "but the latest fashion in definition" for "sensations which men and women have vaguely grasped for centuries," making modernism both historical and timeless; nonetheless, the passage implies that the intensification of such feelings specifically characterized the "modern age." In the same year, however, Walt Whitman published an article on the future of American literature – a future he posited as blending respect for (yet also critique of) the old with the driving force of the new. Imagining the future of spiritual belief, Whitman envisioned the replacement of the "old" "conception of Deity" with "a Deific identity and scope superior to all limitations," befitting "the scientific and democratic and truly philosophic and poetic quality of modernism" (1891). Yet finding that current "modern verse generally lacks quite altogether the modern," Whitman called for "superior, more heroic, more spiritual, more emotional, personalities and songs," celebrating human capacities "as they are and are to be." These two opposing conceptions

139

capture the ambiguity of modernism at its core: a doubleness of anxiety combined with immense hope.

Modern, rather than modernism, was the term most generally employed, although the two words became generally interchangeable as C20 progressed. The meanings of modern were divided, however, between the straightforward sense of "current, present" (since C15) and more nuanced understandings, suggesting something distinctively different and new. The word meant simply "of the day" when the *Literary Digest* described the decidedly medieval linguist and philosopher Thomas Davidson as "A Modern Wandering Scholar" (1901) or when Franz Boas wrote about "Ten Folktales in Modern Nahuatl" (1924). Yet most uses of modern suggested something advanced and, especially in popular culture, usually fresh, exciting, and appealing. An ad in *Cosmopolitan*, headed "A Practical Present," touted "Rubdry towels" as "a sign of modernism and true refinement" (1911). In a discussion of how "modern dressmakers" served "modern women," Marie Beynon Ray noted that "the mode that is called Modernist" included "Modernist Art, Modernist Decoration and now Modernist Dress," all "peculiarly expressive of our times" (1929). An item entitled "The Lady," in the *New Age*, on the anonymously authored *Mind and Manners*, commended the book as "'up to the minute' in its modernism," presenting "life as we live it now" (1918). The popularity of being "modern" was expressed in a proliferation of titles: from W. D. Howell's novel *A Modern Instance* (1909); to handbooks on *Modern Marriage* (1925); to the journals *Modern Quarterly: A Journal in Radical Opinion* (1925–1929), *Modern Music: A Quarterly Review* (1924–1946), and *The Modern Scot* (1930–1936); to such films as Charlie Chaplin's *Modern Times* (1936) and John Dillon's *We Moderns* (1925). There was even a short-lived journal entitled *The Modernist* (surviving for one issue) advertised in *The Little Review* as "Radical in policy; international in scope," "Devoted to the common cause of toiling peoples," and "A forum for active minds and vital art" (1919). Yet an unsigned article in *The Saturday Review of Literature*, entitled "Modernism," expressed skepticism about this term "which is talked about which such a knowing air," concluding that the word was "convenient because meaningless" since "modernism means what we are doing today, no more and no less" (1932).

Modernism, however, began to be specifically associated with the rejection of authority, interpreted as either welcome freedom or moral collapse. The most prevalent use of modernism referred to movements within the Anglican and Roman Catholic Churches that advocated a rationalist, historical interpretation of the Bible and the reconciliation of religion and science, notably evolutionary biology. Declared a heresy in 1907 by Pope Pius X, theological modernism came more broadly to denote liberalism and individualism. When T. S. Eliot denounced "modernism" as a "mental blight which can affect the whole intelligence of the time," criticizing it for "muddy thinking" halfway between Christianity and atheism, it was indeed religious, not literary, modernism that he had in mind (1928). Guy B. Johnson analyzed the rise of the white supremacist Ku Klux Klan as "A Reaction to Modernism," by which he meant "all those forces which have been pulling away at the foundations of the established order of American society," from disinclination to "religious conformity" to such features of "modern life" as the "movie," "the automobile," "modern dance," "the economic and political independence" of women, "freedom" and "frankness" "between the sexes," and "socialistic and communistic doctrines" – "modernistic tendencies" that were causing "conservative people to hold grave doubts and fears" (1923). In Henry James, *linguistic* modernism was the source of conservative fear. Using modernism in its older sense (from C18), referring to what we might call "popular lingo," James condemned it as "uncontrolled assault" on the "native atmosphere" of American speech (1905). Concerned about the loss of a "common language," James denounced "the high modernism" of "the common schools" and the "newspapers" as "excellent for diffusion, for vulgarization, for simplification," but "below the mark for discrimination and selection."

Yet the tie between modernism and a break with authority also figured positively as an empowering but demanding freedom. Defending "New Humanism," Irving Babbitt defined "to be modern" as "to refuse to receive anything as an authority 'anterior, exterior and superior' to the individual"; yet he posited a more vibrant authority in "the wisdom of the ages, a central core of normal human experience," arguing that "the individual who submits himself to such a wisdom does 'inner obeisance to something higher than his ordinary self, whether he calls this something God, or, like the man of the Far East, calls it his higher Self, or simply the Law'" (1924). John Middleton Murry placed the beginnings of "modern consciousness" "historically with the repudiation of established Christianity," since "the vital motion of religion becomes petrified into dogmas and ceremonies" (1924). In contrast, for Murry, "modern consciousness" was "a movement of the soul which begins with the assertion of the I AM against all external spiritual authority" but "proceeds from this condition of rebellion and isolation to a new life-adjustment" and "the ultimate recognition of a new principle of authority in and through the deeper knowledge of the self."

Modernism began gradually to acquire a more specialized meaning, denoting works of art of a particular innovative kind. Among writers, the term was used mainly by poets and about poetry, but there was no firm agreement about definition, nor even about the desirability of definition being sought. There was more consensus about what modernism is not: *not* pious and sentimental conventionality and – despite sharing with theological modernism the rejection of traditional authority – *not* a predominantly rational mode. Middleton Murry linked modernism to *Rhythm*, the name of his quarterly journal. Stating that "the artist must return to the moment of pure perception to see the essential forms," Murry

141

continued, "Modernism [. . .] penetrates beneath the outward surface of the world, and disengages the rhythms that lie at the heart of things, rhythms strange to the eye, unaccustomed to the ear, primitive harmonies of the world that is and lives" (1911). In its subscription notice, Harriet Monroe's *Poetry: A Magazine of Verse* announced its "special interest" in poems of "modern significance" (1913), but Monroe defined modernism only indirectly: complaining about poetry that falsely "asserted its modernism by rhyming of slums and strikes" or by "moralizing in choppy odes, or in choppier prose [. . .] upon some social or political problem of the day," she rejected identifications of modernism with social realism or discordant sound, advocating instead "the keenest vision of the new beauty, and the richest modern message in the poetry" of Rabindranath Tagore (1913). John Crowe Ransom exposed the ambiguity of the term by using it in opposite ways: positively, he associated modernism with the Imagist goals of "honesty of theme and accuracy of expression," "spontaneity of the Word," and a more "elastic" use of meter; negatively, he lamented "the fatal irritant of Modernism," meaning that "the ecstasy which is the total effect of poetry" was being destroyed by the "*enfant terrible* of logic" – a usage that invoked theological modernism's rationalist sense (1924). In contrast, Virginia Woolf explained that her critical "prejudice" as a "modernist" meant abandoning "the old angle; the old reticences" and probing more deeply *beyond* the rational limits of the mind: "the moderns make us aware of what we feel subconsciously; they are truer to our own experience; they even anticipate it, and this gives us a particular excitement" (1927).

142

In criticism, the first detailed attempt to define literary modernism was R. Scott-James's *Modernism and Romance* (1908), a work written well before the establishment of any modernist "canon." With such subjects as Galsworthy, Kipling, Hardy, James, and Conrad, the "psychological" novelists Mrs. Humphry Ward and Robert Hichens, the "popular" authors Marie Corelli and Katherine Cecil Hurston, the letters of Lafcadio Hearn, and the poetry of John Davidson, Scott-James adopted a broad, inclusive approach to modernism as an eclectic mix. Yet while acknowledging diversity and separate groups (decadents, rebels, fugitives, mystics), Scott-James placed modernism as a whole as antithetical to romance. With his own allegiances clearly on the side of romance, Scott-James isolated as modernist characteristics "the scientific habit of analysis," "rebellion against authority," and the attributes of being "individualistic," "prone to self-analysis and self criticism" and without "a great fund of emotion." Yet he acknowledged exceptions and blendings as well, defining Romance with reference to Joseph Conrad and praising "a few authors" who make "a direct, conscious appeal to the inexhaustible stock of emotions which lie beneath the border" and "a few men" who give us "the old thrill of romance without seeking to wean us from the modern habit of mind." Modernism remained without clear definition; as Scott-James ambivalently declared, "The air resounds with a magnificent roar of clamorous opinions, which testify to the chaotic freedom of authorship, the democracy of letters."

The narrowing of modernism to designate one selective group of writers was a move taken largely with reference to poetry and in two collaborative pairings of poet–critics: Laura Riding and Robert Graves's *A Survey of Modernist Poetry* (1927) and Lucia Trent and Ralph Cheyney's essay "What is This Modernism?" (1934). The former focuses on understanding modernist poetry and the latter on promoting it, and the two works differ in tone as well, echoing the difference between Hardy and Whitman. *A Survey* is a troubled, worried book, concerned to justify modernist poetry "against criticism not proper to it" – criticism, that is, based on the expectations of the previous age – and often inadvertently giving strong voice to the critical views. In contrast, "What is This Modernism?" is boisterous and joyous. While *A Survey* concludes that the modernist poetry that has been its focus, from roughly 1918 to 1927, is passing into history, leaving the next generation to learn from its weaknesses and strengths, Trent and Cheyney's essay, part of their volume *More Power to Poets*, radiates optimism and belief in modernist poetry's "new life."

Rehearsing the complaints about modernist poetry's difference from traditional poetry – its perceived "difficulty," its typographical "freakishness," its failure to offer "Spiritual Elevation," its "chaotic" originality, and its "gloom" – *A Survey* alternately explains and rebuts. Distinguishing modernist poetry's "common-sense" "cynicism" from "sentimental" "pessimism," Riding and Graves offer an understanding of this modern spirit as originating in the heightened "scale of emotional excitement and depression," resulting from WWI and the new "knowledge experiences" of modern times. But they also reverse the criticism of modernist poetry to judge the limitations of the "plain reader" too: a reluctance to "think harder or work harder" and a desire for poetic meaning amenable to "prose summary." *A Survey* also deflects criticism by distinguishing "false" from "genuine modernism": the first aims self-consciously to be advanced in a mistaken evolutionary view of poetry's historical progress; the second seeks merely what all "fresh" poetry attempts – "to remind people what the universe really looks like and feels like, that is, what language means." Trent and Cheyney agree that traditional expectations pose problems, with readers desiring "pleasant subjects" and "uplifting truths." Their definition of modernism, however, is powerful and energetic: modernist poets are "kicking over old walls," defying the "Do nots" of traditional prohibitions. For the modernists, "Any subject can be made poetic"; no word is too "frank," "earthy," "strong," or "slangy"; grammar is not "a fossilized skeleton" but a "living," "changing" force. Modernist poetry finds inspiration for economy in the "tanka and hokkum," and for myth, in "American Indian legends and native ballads." Modernist poetry is "not for timid souls," being neither a "sugared sedative" nor "a tonic." It expands "consciousness" and expresses "new valuations": it is like "sap, blood."

Modern, Modernism

Whatever the attitudes toward modernism, its characteristics were widely seen as inseparable from the nature of the modern age. Despite his predilections for traditional writing, R. Scott-James accepted modernism as a necessary expression of its time: "the life about [the writer] has changed and he has changed with it." The Australian critic Ethel Anderson wrote of "Modernism" as a "newer intimacy" between reader and art, an attempt "to reconstruct our Universe in terms of to-day," and a technique "in harmony with value-symbols that are not incongruous to life" (1929). In *The Modern Temper*, Joseph Krutch expressed a more ambivalent view, simultaneously decrying the "modern world" for offering no "aid to the robust and serious mind which is searching for some terms upon which it may live" and asserting "we have discovered the trick that has been played on us" so that "we are no longer dupes" (1929). The academic and writer Addison Hibbard affirmed more positively that the modernist writer was "saying things in a different way because of a new mood," and argued that "what has happened to writing may be what has happened to life itself": "Life *has* become more complex; science *has* broadened our knowledge and taught us a scattered interest; unity *has* departed from a civilization wracked with the warring attitudes of fascism, communism, and democracy; psychology *has* diverted our attention from externals to internals" (1939).

If modernism was "of its time," however, it could also travel broadly in geographical place. Suggesting both national difference and continuity, the Canadian poet Charles G. D. Roberts proposed that "modernism has come softly into the poetry of Canada by peaceful penetration rather than by rude assault" (1931). The implications of using a British art term in the settler colonies, however, generated conflicting response. The Australian nationalist P. R. Stephensen denigrated modernism as a passing phase: "Each decade of history is 'modern' to itself, and every modernism passes with the inexorable march of time," he argued; only a national culture could "transcend modernism and ephemerality" and survive the vicissitudes of change (1936). M. Barnard Eldershaw (pseudonym of Australian literary collaborators Marjorie Barnard and Flora Eldershaw) took a more open, international approach, arguing that *The Fortunes of Richard Mahony* by female author Henry Handel Richardson "benefits at once by what is virtually a Victorian revival and by the modernist attitude of mind" (1938), while poet Max Harris subdivided Australian poetry into "the Nationalist poets, the 'Reportage' poets, and the 'Angry Penguins' or modernist school," to which he devoted staunch "partisan" support (1944).

Underlying many "current-time" definitions, however, was a sense of modernism as something fundamental and persistent in human response. Riding and Graves suggested that "modernist" "should describe a quality that should be in all excellent poetry" inspired by "sincerity or truthfulness," and that "true modernist poetry can appear at all stages of historical development from Wordsworth to

Miss Moore." Trent and Cheyney quoted Edith Sitwell to suggest a blend of the universal and the new: "Modern poets are building among the common movements of life, just as Wordsworth built, only the modern poet has a different stylisation, that is all." Middleton Murry considered the attempt to reconcile external and internal modes of knowledge "the great paradox of the modern consciousness," yet described the paradox as "much older than the Renaissance," "universal in the world, and eternal in the human mind"; it was "the awareness of the paradox" that had "become most acute" (1924). Returning to modernism as used by "modernists" thus releases the term from narrow use: in the modernist period, modernism represents something distinctive yet heterogeneous about this particular age and, at the same time, something ubiquitous and permanent in human life.

References

(1901). "A Modern Wandering Scholar." *The Literary Digest* (January 5), 10.

(1911). "A Practical Present." Advertisement for Rubdry Towels. *Cosmopolitan* (June), 105.

(1913). "Subscription Notice." *Poetry: A Magazine of Verse* 1.5 (February).

(1918). "The Lady." *The New Age* 33.11 (July 11): 176.

(1919). Advertisement for *The Modernist: A Monthly Magazine of Modern Art and Letters* (ed. James Waldo Fawcett). *The Little Review* 6.5 (September): Front pages.

(1932). "Modernism." *The Saturday Review of Literature* (November 12), 233.

Anderson, Ethel (1929). "Modernism and the Naturalists." *The Australian Quarterly* 1.1 (March): 102–112.

Babbitt, Irving (1924). *Democracy and Leadership*. Boston: Houghton Mifflin.

Beynon Ray, Marie (1929). "Sheer Modernism." *Collier's: The National Weekly* (August 17), 19.

Boas, Franz and Herman K. Haeberlin (1924). "Ten Folktales in Modern Nahuatl." *The Journal of American Folklore* 37.145/146 (July–December): 345–370.

Carnevali, Emanuel (1918). "As He Sees It." *Poetry: A Magazine of Verse* 12.2 (May): 113–114.

Eldershaw, M. Barnard [Marjorie Barnard and Flora Eldershaw] (1938). "Two Women Novelists: Henry Handel Richardson and Katharine Susannah Prichard." In *Essays in Australian Fiction*. Melbourne: Melbourne University Press. 1–40

Eliot, T. S. (1928). "A Commentary: Modernism in England." *The Criterion* 8.31 (December): 185–190.

Hardy, Thomas (1888). *Wessex Tales: Strange, Lively and Commonplace*. London: Macmillan.

Hardy, Thomas (1891). *Tess of the D'Urbervilles*. London: J. R. Osgood, McIlvaine.

Harris, Max (1944). "Commentary on Australian Poetry." *Voices: A Quarterly of Poetry*. Australian Issue, edited by Harry Roskolinko and Elizabeth Lambert. 118 (Summer): 44–46.

Hibbard, Addison (1939). "The Road to Modernism." *The Saturday Review of Literature* (January 21), 3–4, 16.

James, Henry (1905). *The Question of Our Speech; The Lesson of Balzac. Two Lectures*. Boston and New York: Houghton Mifflin.

Johnson, Guy B. (1923). "A Social Interpretation of the New KKK Movement." *The Journal of Social Forces* 1 (May): 440–445.

145

Krutch, Joseph Wood (1929). *The Modern Temper: A Study and a Confession*. New York: Harcourt, Brace.

Monroe, Harriet (1913). "The New Beauty." *Poetry: A Magazine of Verse* 2.1 (April): 22–25.

Murry, John Middleton (1911). "Art and Philosophy." *Rhythm* 1.1 (Summer): 9–12.

Murry, John Middleton (1924). "Literature and Religion." In *The Necessity of Art*, by A. Clutton Brock, Percy Dearmer, A. S. Duncan-Jones, John Middleton Murry, Alfred W. Pollard, and Malcolm Spencer. London: Student Christian Movement. 137–165.

Popenoe, Paul (1925). *Modern Marriage: A Handbook*. New York: Macmillan.

Ransom, John Crowe (1924). "The Future of Poetry." *The Fugitive* 3.2 (February): 2–4.

Riding, Laura and Robert Graves (1927). *A Survey of Modernist Poetry*. London: W. Heinemann.

Roberts, Charles G. D. (1931). "A Note on Modernism." In *Open House* (eds. William Arthur Deacon and Wilfred Reeves). Ottawa: Graphic.

Scott-James, R. A. (1908). *Modernism and Romance*. London: John Lane.

Stephensen, Percy Reginald (1936). *The Foundations of Culture in Australia: An Essay Towards National Self-Respect*. Gordon: W. J. Miles.

Trent, Lucia and Ralph Cheyney (1934). "What is This Modernism?" In *More Power to Poets*. New York: Henry Harrison. 106–110.

Whitman, Walt (1891). "Have We a National Literature?" *The North American Review* (March), 332–338.

Woolf, Virginia (1927). "An Essay in Criticism." *The New York Herald Tribune* (October 9), Section 7, Books: 8.

Negro, New Negro

In July and August 1937, *The Afro-American* newspaper polled its readers in five eastern cities about their preferred racial designation (1937a–d). In the final totals, 893 people preferred "Negro" and 1590 chose "Colored," while numerous others rejected both designations, often indicating a preference for African, Ethiopian, Afro-American, or "just plain American" instead. Respondents cited various reasons for their choice: Harold Whitley of New York preferred Negro "because colored is mixed with all races," and John F. Speller of Philadelphia preferred Negro since it "represents a definite anthropological type" bestowing "a heritage of tradition and of ancient culture of which [the American Negro] should be duly proud" (July 31). Miss Louise Williams of Philadelphia rejected Negro "because it is so often associated with the word 'n----,'" while Miss Julia Gamby of Baltimore proposed "colored Americans" since "we range in color from black to white" (July 14). Clarence Hoyt of New York preferred colored "because it is time that we changed" (July 24), while Samuel Hearns of New York opined, "It doesn't make much difference what we are called" (August 7). Such discussions of self-designation pervaded the modernist period, prompting gradual shifts in the most commonly used terms: blacks, colored, and Afro-American predominated at the turn of C20, succeeded by the increasing legitimation of Negro, only to see the return of black and African American at the period's end. Together with woman and queer (see entries), these words offer some of the clearest indications

ABCDEFGHIJKLM**N**OPQRSTUVWXYZ

Modernism: Keywords, First Edition. Melba Cuddy-Keane, Adam Hammond, and Alexandra Peat.
© 2014 Melba Cuddy-Keane. Published 2014 by John Wiley & Sons, Ltd.

of the difficulty of attaching words to intrinsic meanings, revealing the greater importance of how words are being used and by whom. The newspaper cited above recorded a vibrant chorus of voices, as African Americans expressed their views in a public sphere and took their destiny into their own hands. Words became an exciting site of engagement and dialogue, and that activity itself became instrumental in prompting change. Changing the words, as well as the way the words acquired their meanings, was crucial both to dispel the prejudicial stereo-types accrued from the days of slavery and to foster a new sense of solidarity, confidence, and self-esteem.

One of the strongest markers of both attitudinal and social change, given the negative connotations of Negro, was the linguistic companioning of Negro and New. At the turn of C20, newspapers reported a host of developments such as new Negro colleges and hospitals, new Negro homes, new Negro dailies, and new Negro voters. But "new" quickly evolved from a simple descriptor to form a revolutionary compound term. A chorus of anthologies, edited collections, and essays featured the "New Negro," including *A New Negro for a New Century* (1900); *The New Negro* (1916); "The New Negro – What is he?" (1920); and "Harlem: Mecca of The New Negro" (1925c). Parallels were drawn to the New Woman: a column by "B. Square" in *The Freeman* (1895) admitted, "the 'New Negro,' like the 'New Woman' is in his infancy," while *The New York Herald*, reporting on "Negro Progress" as a "Big Feature" of the 1895 Atlanta Exposition, quoted I. Garland Penn's words: "'We hear a good deal,' said he, 'about the new woman at present, but when the exposition opens we will show to the rest of the world a new negro'" (*The New York Herald*, 1895).

But the meaning of New Negro was not consistently the same. For the most part, emphasis fell on New, signaling advance and progress. Penn extolled the way the exhibition would portray "the negro as a merchant, as a banker, [. . .] as a conductor of big enterprises" and the producer of art, books, newspapers, paint-ings, and sculpture, thus demonstrating a clear break with the past. The "new negro," in his words, represented the "frugal, thrifty, and intelligent class of my race" and the "types of the best civilization," utterly unlike "the indolent, indif-ferent class who give us such a bad name." The Reverend J. W. E. Bowen, who delivered the address on Negro Day at the exposition, agreed, saying that "a new Negro has come upon the stage of action," and explaining, "What is he doing? He is thinking! And by the power of thought, he will think off those chains and have both hands free to help you build this country and make a grand destiny of him-self" (1895). Yet Bowen also invoked the legacy of the past, combining heritage and modernity: possessing the spirit "of his fathers made over," his "new Negro" would doubly display "the consciousness of a racial personality under the blaze of a new civilization." On the side of radical change, a column of "Pointers" in the *Times-Observer* (Topeka, Kansas) announced, "The new Negro has appeared on the stage," and quoted from a commentary on "Afro-American voters": "There is a change in the race kaleidoscope caused by the shaking of the hand of education and progress," with the consequence that "new and brighter figures" "have shook off the temerity born and nurtured, in slavery's existence" (1891). On the side of continuity, William Pickens asserted, "The new Negro is not really new; he is the same Negro under new conditions and subjected to new demands" (1916). Insisting that "there is no sharp line of demarcation between the old and the new in any living organism," he judged that "the present generation of Negroes have received their chief heritage from the former and, in that, they are neither better nor worse, higher nor lower than the previous generation."

As C20 progressed, definitions of the New Negro increasingly diverged, especially along political and cultural lines. Declaring the need for "a definite and clear portrayal of The New Negro," the editors of the socialist journal *The Messenger*, A. Philip Randolph and Chandler Owen, defined the New Negro's "interests [as] all tied up with workers" and asserted that he "should support a working class political party" and "join labour unions" (1920). Radical and oppositional, they argued, "the New Negro is a product of the same world wide forces that have brought into being the great liberal and radical movements that are now seizing the reins of political, economic and social power in all the civilized countries of the world." A different conception, of particular relevance for the arts, was proposed by Alain Locke. In the journal *Survey Graphic*'s special number, "Harlem: Mecca of the New Negro" (1925c), and then in his influential anthology, *The Negro* (1925b), Locke heralded a social and cultural "Negro Renaissance" (1925b), alternatively called the New Negro Movement and the Harlem Renaissance, as it is most frequently termed today. In positing his New Negro, Locke shared the common aim of ridding American culture of the old stereotypes, describing the "Old Negro" as a "more of a formula than a human being," derived from "the day of 'aunties,' 'uncles' and 'mammies' [. . .] Uncle Tom and Sambo" (1925a). But he also sought to transform the reigning conception of the Negro – which he attributed to "both races" – as "a social problem," exchanging "the status of a beneficiary and ward for that of a collaborator and participant in American civilization." Rather than oppositional to mainstream culture, Locke's approach emphasized the need for "collective efforts in race cooperation" to open the path to "the fullest sharing of American culture and institutions." The validity of Locke's belief that "cultural recognition" would "prove the key to that revaluation of the Negro" can be judged by subsequent history: his anthology included such writers as Countee Cullen, Jessie Fauset, Langston Hughes, Zora Neale Hurston, Claude McKay, and Jean Toomer.

The literary and intellectual nature of Locke's New Negro, however, limited it as a common term. Locke focused on "the thinking Negro" who had migrated "city-ward and to the great centers of industry," and his cooperative model

149

depended on "the enlightened minorities of both race groups." Langston Hughes subsequently critiqued the "Nordicized Negro intelligentsia" as unable to break free from "the mountain standing in the way of any true Negro art in America": the debilitating internalization of the "old subconscious 'white is best'" (1926). Arguing that the self-styled "'high-class' Negro" was more prone to the "aping of things white than in a less cultured or less wealthy home," Hughes upheld the "majority," "the so-called common element" who "still hold their own individuality in the face of American standardizations." The idealism of the New Negro artists was targeted in Wallace Thurman's satirical novel *Infants of the Spring* (1932), in which the autobiographical character Raymond Taylor loses hope that anything permanent will be achieved: "This, he kept repeating to himself, is the Negro renaissance, and this is about all the whole damn thing is going to amount to." Mocking their pretensions to being *literati*, Taylor facetiously names the building where they live "Niggeratti Manor."

While New Negro was thus subject to controversy, Negro itself was gradually garnering respect and emerging as the recognized public and official term. The 1916 *Negro Year Book* observed, "The word Negro has a permanent place as a race designation in both ethnology and anthropology and is used to designate the black race; [. . .] There is an increasing use of the word 'Negro' and a decreasing use of the words 'colored' and 'Afro-American' to designate us as a people. The result is that the word 'Negro' is, more and more, acquiring a dignity that it did not have in the past." The American Negro Academy was established in 1897; the National Negro Business League, in 1900. The *Journal of Negro History* began in 1916; the *Journal of Negro Education*, in 1932. In 1930, detailing the great accomplishments of the "two hundred thousand Negroes" who were now "an integral part of the New York citizenry," James Weldon Johnson extolled those "forces" that were "helping to bring about an entirely new national conception of the Negro," changing "many of the connotations of the very word 'Negro'" as well. In 1937, Dr. Kelly Miller mounted a spirited defense of the word, noting that "the term Negro is far superior to the term colored in grammatical inflection, for [the former] may be used either as a noun or as an adjective," and adding that "any race or group, in the long run, will derive its reputation from its character and worth, and not from the appellation by which it is known." Miller was also highly supportive of the long-standing campaign to end what he considered "typological discrimination." Noting the inconsistency of upper and lower case initial letters in a printed list "consisting of Englishmen, Germans, Italians, Jews, and *negroes*," and arguing for standardization, he countered the possible objection that "Negro is not derived from a country or geographical division" with the response, "neither is Jew." In "Designations for Colored Folk" (1944), H. L. Mencken paid tribute to the long campaign culminating in 1930 when *The New York Times* announced that it would "capitalize the word Negro thereafter," followed by a similar announcement three years later by *The Style Manual of the Government Printing Office*. Mencken credited the efforts of journalist Lester Aglar Watson, who began the capitalization movement as early as 1913, and had by 1930 already a sizeable number of newspapers, national magazines, and government agencies on side. Not everyone, however, agreed: Mencken also reported the response of George S. Schuyler – to Mencken, "the best Negro journalist, and by a long shot, ever heard of." Schuyler argued that "it doesn't matter a tinker's damn whether Negro is spelled with a small or large N," since it "does not in the least elevate him socially." For Schuyler, Negro in either form simply bolstered the status quo, with its "socio-chromatic caste system." But Schuyler also went further to object to all racial designations, on the grounds that they "strengthened the superstition that 'all coons are alike,'" and invited "all the 'racial' nonsense of Hitler, Bilbo, and all the myriads who believe as they do." By the end of the modernist period, Negro was thus still a controversial term. The 1931 *Negro Year Book* juxtaposed a quotation from *The Messenger* that Negro was a term of "opprobrium," being "founded on slavery and forced degradation" with one from *The Amsterdam News* (NY): "The term 'Negro' is no longer 'Negro,' meaning black, but is now a proper noun designating a group of people, a race."

A greater consensus formed around the use of nigger, yet that word was controversial too. Originating as a Southern pronunciation of Negro, nigger quickly accrued the pejorative connotations of white racist usage, in both the South and the North. African American newspapers of eC20 generally put the word in quotation marks and not without complaint – Sylvester Russell, for example, commented that "Billy Caldwell [African American Vaudevillian] has written a new coon song with the word 'nigger' in it, in spite of disapproval" (1903). In 1931, the *Negro Year Book* quoted much stronger "advice to white speakers addressing audiences of colored people": "nigger" was included in a list of words they should never use, since "nothing arouses a stronger feeling of resentment in the hearts of colored people than to hear expressions of this sort from one of another race." Extreme controversy surrounded Carl Van Vechten's novel *Nigger Heaven* (1926). In the novel itself, the phrase, which referred to the topmost and cheapest seats in the theatre, appears in a protest against racism and discrimination: "Nigger Heaven!" one character exclaims; "That's what Harlem is. We sit in our places in the gallery of this New York theatre and watch the white world sitting down below in the good seats in the orchestra." Yet Van Vechten's title, which by itself provided no such context, received strong critique. Those against banning the term, however, argued the need to capture and preserve black vernacular speech. According to H. L. Mencken, when Elmer A. Carter, editor of the magazine *Opportunity*, was asked by the first assistant superintendent of schools of Washington to "discontinue the policy of using any opprobrious term or terms in referring to the Negro," Carter refused, defending the magazine's policy of using nigger only in "quotations from other writers" or in "the reproduction in poem or story of the speech and conversation of characters who commonly use this term." Preserving the black vernacular helped to preserve black vernacular narrative too: *Nigger to Nigger* (1928) by white physician Edward C. L. Adams presented tales recording "the humor, the philosophy of the Negro who is close to the soil," while "Niggers," a short story by Julian Elihu Bagley published in *The Crisis* (1923), foregrounds the word as a source of profound reflection for the young black protagonist. "Little Cless Jerihdo," accepting his grandmother's definition of nigger as "low-down, mean, good-for-nothing folks" whose "faces can be as white as snow," sees the term tragically envelop all the players in his world. Gradually, nonetheless, lexicographers drew the wider public's attention to the need to avoid the term. Discussing a variety of "powder-keg" words, a 1949 article in *American Speech* by Rossell Hope Robbins summed up the "change in dictionary definitions": whereas 1930s dictionaries typically glossed the term as "colloquial, usually derogatory," the *American College Dictionary* (1947) "omits the 'usually' and says, outrightly, 'offensive.'" Robbins berated H. W. Fowler's *Modern English Usage* (1926) for its "curiously equivocal and paltering entry": "nigger, applied to others than full or partial negroes, is felt as an insult by the person described, and betrays in the speaker, if not deliberate insolence, at least a very arrogant inhumanity." Fowler's second edition (1965) employed much stronger and more accurate wording: "N. has been described as 'the term that carries with it all the obloquy and contempt and rejection which whites have inflicted on blacks'"; as a dictionary of usage, it foregrounded the issue of utterance as well: "To be called a n. is now regarded as an insult by an American negro, unless the word is used affectionately by one negro of another."

The complexities of language, including the wide range of its speaking voices, are fully reflected in the African American fiction, poetry, and drama of the time. The literature collectively employs the full range of self-designating terms, while the meaning and connotations of the words vary depending on whether the character is Southern or Northern, urban or rural, white or black, racist or not, or degrees in between. Thus, Langston Hughes writes "The Negro Speaks of Rivers" (1921), and the urbanized narrator of Zora Neale Hurston's *Their Eyes Were Watching God* (1937) uses Negro respectfully, while the rural characters vernacularly use colored, black, nigger, and darky, with differing inflections and connotations. In Nella Larsen's *Passing* (1929), Negro is double voiced in the character Irene's consciousness, where it signifies both what it means to her as positive self-designation and what it would mean to the others in the white-only restaurant if they knew her race. Nigger is both an affectionate and an evil word in Jean Toomer's *Cane* (1923); and in Ralph Ellison's *Invisible Man* (1947), the complicated position of the protagonist within a maze of racial and political exploitation is articulated through the varying employments of Negro, colored, black, and nigger. In Claude McKay's *Home to Harlem* (1928), transatlantic difference is marked in different inflections of the words. Jake hears an "Englishman say 'darky' without being offended," whereas "back home he would have been spoiling for a fight. There he would rather hear 'nigger' than 'darky' for he knew that when a Yankee said 'nigger' he meant hatred for Negroes, whereas when he said 'darky' he meant friendly contempt," encoding a more insidious and therefore more difficult racism to combat. Other terms were used as well: W. E. B. Du Bois wrote *The Souls of Black Folks* (1903), and George Schuyler, *Black No More* (1931); McKay used Aframerican in his novella, *Harlem Glory: A Fragment of Aframerican Life* ([1940s] 1990). Negro words, their variations, and their reiterations both attack racism and convey affection; both connect to heritage and traditional community and carve out a new and hopeful future. The history of such usage presents the challenge of ridding the language of hate words without losing the voices of those who used the words without hate; but perhaps above all, it captures a vibrant mix of voices offering thoughtful, self-conscious, and transformative considerations of our speech.

SEE ALSO: *Primitive; Race; Words, Language*

References

(1891). "Pointers." *The Times-Observer* (Topeka) (September 4), 2.

(1895). "B Square's Bluster." *The Freeman: An Illustrated Colored Newspaper* (August 3), 3.

(1895). "Negro Progress on Big Feature. In Atlanta's K Exposition the Race Will Show Its Advance in Art and Science." *The New York Herald* (September 9), 8.

(1937a). "How to Begin an Argument: Afro Asks Readers to Vote on Racial Designation They Prefer." *Afro-American* (Washington, DC) (July 24), 9.

(1937b). "How to End an Argument: Final Installment of Answers to the Query, Do You Prefer Colored or Negro?" *Afro-American* (Washington, DC) (August 21), 4.

(1937c). "How to Extend an Argument: Afro Asks Readers to Vote on Racial Designation They Prefer." *Afro-American* (Washington, DC) (August 7), 22.

(1937d). "How to Extend an Argument: Afro Asks Readers to Vote on Racial Designation They Prefer." *Afro-American* (Washington, DC) (July 31), 11.

Adams, Edward C. L. (1928). *Nigger to Nigger*. New York and London: Charles Scribner's Sons.

Bagley, Julian Elihu (1923). "Niggers." *The Crisis: A Record of the Darker Races* (November), 21–23; (December), 68–69.

Bowen, J. W. E. (1895). *An Appeal to the King: The Address Delivered on Negro Day in the Atlanta Exposition, October 21, 1895*. Atlanta: [s.n.].

Du Bois, W. E. B. (1903). *The Souls of Black Folk*. Chicago: McClurg.

Ellison, Ralph (1947). *Invisible Man*. New York: Random House.

Fowler, H. W. (1926). *A Dictionary of Modern English Usage*. Oxford: Oxford University Press.

Fowler, H. W. (1965). *A Dictionary of Modern English Usage*, 2nd ed. Oxford: Oxford University Press.

153

Hughes, Langston (1921). "The Negro Speaks of Rivers." *The Crisis: A Record of the Darker Races* (June), 71.

Hughes, Langston (1926)."The Negro Artist and the Racial Mountain." *The Nation* (June 23), 692–694.

Hurston, Zora Neale (1937). *Their Eyes Were Watching God*. Philadelphia: J. P. Lippincott.

Johnson, James Weldon (1930). *Black Manhattan*. New York: A. A. Knopf.

Larsen, Nella (1929). *Passing*. New York: A. A. Knopf.

Locke, Alain (1925a). "Enter the New Negro." *Survey Graphic*. Harlem: Mecca of the New Negro (March), 631–639.

Locke, Alain (ed.) (1925b). "Foreword." In *The New Negro: An Interpretation*. New York: Albert and Charles Boni. ix–xi.

Locke, Alain (ed.) (1925c). *Survey Graphic*. Harlem: Mecca of the New Negro, 6.6 (March).

McKay, Claude (1928). *Home to Harlem*. New York: Harper and Brothers.

McKay, Claude (1990). *Harlem Glory: A Fragment of Aframerican Life*. [1940s]. Preface by Carl Cowl. Chicago: Charles H. Kerr.

Mencken, H. L. (1944)."Designations for Colored Folk." *American Speech* 19.3 (October): 161–174.

Pickens, William (1916). *The New Negro: His Political, Civil and Mental Status and Related Essays*. New York: Neale.

[Randolph, A. Philip and Chandler Owen] (1920). "The New Negro—What is He?" Editorial. *The Messenger* (August), 73–74.

Robbins, Rossell Hope (1949). "Social Awareness and Semantic Change." *American Speech* 24.2 (April): 156–158.

Russell, Sylvester (1903). "A Little of Everything." *The Freeman: An Illustrated Colored Newspaper* (March 7), 5.

Schuyler, George S. (1931). *Black No More, Being an Account of the Wonderful Workings of Science in the Land of the Free, A.D. 1933–1940*. New York: Macaulay.

Thurman, Wallace (1932). *Infants of the Spring*. New York: Macaulay.

Toomer, Jean (1923). *Cane*. Foreword by Waldo Frank. New York: Boni and Liveright.

Van Vechten, Carl (1926). *Nigger Heaven*. New York: A. A. Knopf.

Washington, Booker T., Fannie Barrier Williams and Noeman Barton Wood (eds.) (1900). *A New Negro for a New Century*. Chicago: American Publishing House.

Work, Monroe N. (ed.) (1916). *Negro Year Book: An Annual Encyclopedia of the Negro, 1916–1917*. Tuskegee Institute: Negro Year Book Publishing Co.

Work, Monroe N. (ed.) (1931). *Negro Year Book: An Annual Encyclopedia of the Negro, 1931–32*. Tuskegee Institute: Negro Year Book Publishing Co.

Personality, Impersonality

In Henry James's *The Portrait of a Lady* ([1880–1881]1908), Ralph Touchett thinks of his cousin Isabel, "A character like that, [. . .] a real little passionate force to see at play is the finest thing in nature." Approximately 80 years later, Saul Bellow, reflecting upon the recent course of the novel, commented that "instead of a unitary character and his unitary personality," "modern literature" has given us a "cubistic, Bergsonian, uncertain, eternal mortal," "impossible to circumscribe in any scheme of time" (1962). The difference between these two statements signals the way human character, over the modernist period, shifted from being a complex center of attention to signifying a chimera that might not exist. The fluidity of character had long been noted; as Mr. Farebrother remarks in George Eliot's *Middlemarch* (1872), "character is not cut in marble – it is not something solid and unalterable." Nonetheless, thinking about the self became so revolutionary that Virginia Woolf was led hyperbolically to remark, "in or about December 1910 human character changed" (1924). Changing views of the self were reflected both in new modes of fictional representation and in a developing vocabulary, yet the pattern of change was no simple transition from A to B. What distinguishes the modernist period may lie most in a new spirit of questioning: the diverse and disparate usages of character, personality, and self point to a fundamental reexamination of what it is to "be."

ABCDEFGHIJKLMNO**P**QRSTUVWXYZ

Modernism: Keywords, First Edition. Melba Cuddy-Keane, Adam Hammond, and Alexandra Peat.
© 2014 Melba Cuddy-Keane. Published 2014 by John Wiley & Sons, Ltd.

Personality, Impersonality

The new complexity of character was expressed, by some writers, in a distinction between inner self and surface personality. D. H. Lawrence used personality to designate "the self that is begotten and born from the idea," "created from the mind, downwards," and formed according to the "handed-down ideals" of the previous generation; castigating this "millstone" as "a spurious, detestable product," he contrasted the stultifying "*ideal* self" of personality with the "living self" of "creative life," characterized by "spontaneous mutability" (1919;1936). Virginia Woolf similarly used personality to suggest an outer, social role. In *To the Lighthouse* (1927), Mrs. Ramsay finds positive release in "losing personality," referring to the constructed self presented to the world, "our apparitions, the things you know us by"; in private moments, apart from "the fret, the hurry, the stir," Mrs. Ramsay experiences an inner world of freedom, where her "self having shed its attachments [is] free for the strangest adventures." In Mulk Raj Anand's *Untouchable* (1935), personality signifies the social conditioning that Bakha has internalized as an outcaste and "the shackles of slavery" that keep him tied to "the dreary routine of one occupational environment": separating outer from inner self, the narrator explains, "He could not reach out from the narrow and limited personality he had inherited to his larger yearning." In a radically different social context, F. Scott Fitzgerald similarly implied a gap between surface identity and inner intensity when Jay Gatsby dismisses the love that Daisy might have felt for her husband Tom with the words, "it was just personal" (1925). E. M. Forster also distinguished between limited and expansive versions of self; he did so, however, by dividing personality into two forms: "each human mind has two personalities, one on the surface, one deeper down" (1925). "The upper personality," Forster asserted, "has a name," "is conscious and alert," and "differs vividly and amusingly from other personalities." The less conscious "lower personality" was harder to define, but Forster associated it with a positive "anonymity," believing it to be "general" and "common" to everyone and adding that unless a literary writer "dips a bucket down into it occasionally he cannot produce first-class work." The "upper personality" is called "the old conception of personality" by Aldous Huxley's character Anthony Beavis, who notes that "Fascists and Communists," who depend on "strong and sharply defined personalities" to provide a "single 'right' ideal," now "have to go out of their way to manufacture them" (1936). In contrast, Beavis notes that "Hamlet didn't have a personality – knew altogether too much to have one. He was conscious of his total experience, atom by atom and instant by instant, and accepted no guiding principle which would make him choose one set of patterned atoms to represent his personality rather than another." If these usages all demoted personality in favor of something more complex and less definable, T. E. Hulme took the opposite approach of contrasting "that bastard thing Personality" with the "stability and permanence" of the "religious attitude" (1924). Personality, he argued, was the creation of a debilitating subjective and relativist romanticism, which he pitted against "the *objective* character of ethical values" and "an order or *hierarchy* among such values," understood to be "absolute and objective."

While, according to Bellow, "the old unitary personality" still flourished "in popular magazine stories, in conventional best-sellers, in newspaper cartoons, and in the movies," yet another complicating discourse about personality infiltrated into the public sphere. Despite the way personality continued to be celebrated – particularly in biography – to mark the heroic achievements of prominent individuals, from the turn of C20, phrases such as "Dual Personality," "Multiple Personality," "Divided Personality," and "Split Personality" began increasingly to appear. While, for the most part, such compartmentalizations were looked on as personality disorders, both psychology and sociology posited models involving multiple facets of the normal self. Samuel C. Kohs, for example, writing in *The American Journal of Psychology*, explained, "We are all," in various degrees, "examples of split-off personal[i]ties"; "All of us are a bundle of characters, of selves, each very different from the other, and each in varying stages of development" (1914). While he considered such "diverse personalities" to be "normal manifestations," he noted the way "psychopathologic conditions" result from selves being "repressed," "split off," or "dissociated." "Synthesis," he argued, "is the keynote of mental hygiene." Kohs's basic description characterizes the dynamics in numerous theories of the time: Sigmund Freud's tripartite model of the id, ego, and superego, almost as warring partners; Carl Jung's division of the self into consciousness, personal unconscious, and collective unconscious, and his theory of personae as our socially adaptive masks; George Herbert Mead's model of the "me," an accumulation of socially constructed selves which the individual learns from experiencing himself as an object of in the consciousness of the "generalized other," and the "I," his active response. Despite their diversity, these theories all viewed the self as an ongoing process of negotiating multiplicities – with the goal being, if not synthesis, at least balance.

157

Self, in the modernist period, thus both underwent fragmentation and acquired a new dynamic density, and the degree of optimism or pessimism accompanying this change may have depended on which of these elements most influenced the view. Unlike the use of personality to designate definable, unified character, however, the multiple self was rarely described with consistent terms. Indeed, like the unconscious realm that contributed so much of its multiplicity, the new, complex self was more often expressed in images. *The Education of Henry Adams* ([1907]1918) registered the shock of the transformation from stability to uncertainty with both fearful wonder and comic, self-deprecating effect. Noting that "the psychologists" had "distinguished several personalities in the same mind," Adams envisioned the new self through an image of modern communication, conceiving "personality" as "split [. . .] into complex groups, like telephonic centres and systems." Pondering the possible lack of any "central control," Adams further imagined the self as "a bicycle-rider, mechanically balancing himself by inhibiting all his inferior personalities, and sure to fall into the sub-conscious chaos below, if one of his inferior personalities got on top," and as "an acrobat, with a dwarf on his back, crossing a chasm on a slack-rope, and commonly breaking his neck." Redefining the self as a conflux of forces, Adams cast the mind as a "magnet" engaged in rhythmic oppositions: "mechanically dispersing its lines of force when it went to sleep, and mechanically orienting them when it woke up," with no indication which was the "normal" state. Writing in her journal in the 1920s, Katherine Mansfield expressed a similar view with a remarkably similar image: "For what with complexes and repressions and reactions and vibrations and reflections, there are moments when I feel I am nothing but the small clerk of some hotel without a proprietor, who has all his work cut out to enter the names and hand the keys to the wilful guests" ([1920]1939). Also like Adams, Mansfield worried about the absence of a "central control" or "proprietor" to coordinate these "hundreds of selves," noting "our persistent yet mysterious belief in a self which is continuous and permanent." Her way of imagining continuity, however, was still unlike the old unified personality, for her relief lay paradoxically in "the moment of direct feeling when we are most ourselves and least personal." Zora Neale Hurston offered yet another striking image in "How It Feels to be Colored Me" (1928), writing, "I feel like a brown bag of miscellany propped against a wall," along "with other bags, white, red and yellow." While simultaneously celebrating her "Negro" ancestry, Hurston used the random plurality of the self as something common to all. Imagining that the contents of these bags, "a jumble of small, things priceless and worthless," might all be "dumped in a single heap and the bags refilled without altering the content of any greatly," Hurston humorously contemplated a world so designed by "the Great Stuffer of Bags." Aldous Huxley, like Mansfield desiring more coordination, redefined personality as musical composition; stating that "temporal gaps separate the elements of a personality from one another," he argued that "each individual has to build up his personality – to compose it," "so that the discontinuous states may reveal themselves as part of a whole, developing in time" and "the natural discords are harmonized by some principle of unity," some "framework of purposive ideals strong enough to bridge the gaps between them" (1927). For E. M. Forster, the new complexity of self could be managed by separating what we know and how we behave: acknowledging that "Psychology has split and shattered the idea of a 'Person'" and that "something incalculable in each of us" might "at any moment rise to the surface and destroy our normal balance," Forster declared a working compromise: "For the purpose of living one has to assume that the personality is solid, and the 'self' is an entity, and to ignore all contrary evidence" ([1938]1939).

In a positive way, however, the new diffusive self could offer greater continuity and connection between the self and the world. Henry James's Madame Merle asks, "What shall we call our 'self'? Where does it begin? Where does it end? It overflows into everything that belongs to us – and then it flows back again" ([1880–1881]1908). D. H. Lawrence and Virginia Woolf both released the self from confining categorical definition, Lawrence writing, "If I say of myself, I am this, I am that! [. . .] I turn into a stupid fixed thing like a lamp-post," "trying to cut myself out to pattern" ([1920s]1936), while Woolf gave Clarissa Dalloway the similar thought, "she would not say of Peter, she would not say of herself, I am this, I am that" (1925). And both Lawrence and Woolf used images to suggest the self's permeable borders and a positive diffusion into a larger life. Writing to Katherine Mansfield that he was "weary to death of these dead, dry leaves of personalities which flap in every wind," Lawrence indicated that he sought "some new non-personal activity," "a new common life, a new complete tree of life," which would grow "from our deepest underground roots, out of the *unconsciousness*," yielding "a harmony of *purpose*, rather than of personality" ([1915]1932). Woolf's Clarissa thinks of her social self as a multifaceted yet nonetheless clear-cut "diamond shape," but imagines her deeper self more continuously and ubiquitously as "laid out like a mist between the people she knew best, who lifted her on their branches as she had seen the trees lift the mist, but it spread ever so far, her life, herself," so that "to know her, to know any one, one must seek out the people who completed them, even the places." Mergings of consciousness were also expressed through metaphors of ghosts and haunting: Clarissa wonders if this "unseen part of us [. . .] might survive, be recovered somehow attached to this person or that, or even haunting certain places, after death"; William Faulkner's Quentin Compson thinks of himself, "he was not a being, an entity, he was a commonwealth," indeed "a barracks filled with stubborn back-looking ghosts" (1936). Bernard, in Virginia Woolf's *The Waves* (1931), similarly thinks, "I am not one person; I am many people; I do not altogether know who I am" "or how to distinguish my life from theirs." The idea of a collective mind often showed the influence of Eastern sources. In Huxley's *Eyeless in Gaza*, Doctor Miller, whom Anthony Beavis consults, warns that "if you're not careful, prayer just confirms you in the bad habit of being personal," making you "more yourself, more separate"; in contrast he recommends the Buddhists, who "don't exalt personality; they try to transcend it." Conceiving God as "an impersonal mind of the universal," "they meditate – or, in other words, try to merge their own minds in the universal mind."

The shifting and sometimes elusive meanings of personal and impersonal come further into play in theories concerning the presence or absence of the writer's self in the text. Ford Madox Ford confronted his readers with a seeming paradox, stating first that "the Impressionist author is sedulous to avoid letting his personality appear in the course of his book," then adding, "his whole book, his whole poem is merely an expression of his personality." But if "letting his personality appear" means the intrusion of personal details and attributes, while "expression of his personality" involves offering "the fruits of his own observations" and conveying a particular "frame of mind" through technique, the apparent contradiction resolves (1914). Sherwood Anderson similarly warned of the dangers, to the writer, of the personal self while yet arguing the need for the writer to "give out of himself": "The thing we call self," he wrote, "is often very like a disease. It seems to sap you, take something from you, destroy your relationship with others," whereas "losing sense of self" can be "los[ing] yourself in others," causing "a new world," through "imagined figures," to "open out" ([1939]1947). The idea of going beyond personal self-expression underwrites the meaning T. S. Eliot gave to impersonality. Urging that the poet must perform "a continual surrender of himself" and a "continual extinction of personality" in order to access "something which is more valuable," Eliot contrasted "the expression of personality" as "a turning loose of emotion" with "an expression of significant emotion," "which has its life in the poem and not in the history of the poet" (1919). Eliot's statement, "the emotion of art is impersonal," meant not that art is transcendent and autonomous but that its emotion arises from numerous voices and expresses a collective, not personal, self. The impersonality of Tiresias in *The Waste Land* (1922) – whom Eliot described as "a mere spectator and not indeed a 'character'" – derives from the way, like the poet who becomes a "medium" (1919), Tiresias is a collective voice "uniting all the rest" (1922).

  Impersonal could thus signify communal rather than personal, but it could also mean either impartial, fair, and objective or distant, machinelike, and lacking emotion. Anaïs Nin had in mind some combination of the latter two meanings when she claimed her diary writing as a distinctive "feminine activity," "a personal and personified creation," in contrast to the masculine fictions of Henry Miller and Lawrence Durrell, who, refusing to admit the "personal source" of their art, were "pretending to be impersonal" ([1937]1966–1980). Nin further contrasted the impersonality of masculine "objectivity," "abstractions," "depersonalization," "separateness," and "proud consciousness" to the personal feminine mode of "empathy," "feeling," "immersion," "connection," and "consciousness of the *other*," frequently explaining, "the personal life, lived deeply, takes you beyond the personal," since "if you go deeply enough, the personal life really goes beyond that and reaches universality" (1975). The numerous inflections of both personal and impersonal become dizzyingly apparent in the writings of Virginia Woolf. Woolf could ask, "has any writer, who is not a typewriter, succeeded in being wholly impersonal?" (1937), while stating, "it may be that the greatest passages in literature have about them something of the impersonality which belongs to our own emotions at their strongest" ([n.d.] 1947). She could castigate Charlotte Brontë for leaving "her story [. . .] to attend to some personal grievance" (1929b) but praise Dorothy

Wordsworth because "by being herself without effort or emphasis, she envelops all these odds and ends in the flow of her own personality" (1929a). Woolf could urge women writers to direct attention away "from the personal centre" toward "the impersonal," focusing less on "individual lives" and more on "social evils and remedies" (1929c), yet admit that readers want from an author "the character, the personality, 'which is at the very root of like and dislike'" ([n.d.] 1947).

What these variances signify, however, is not confusion, but a mobile vocabulary in which personal and impersonal could be cast in opposition, as gradations along a spectrum, or closely related, like two sides of a coin. Personality can refer to distinct unified character in contrast to the impersonality of detached spectatorship, or it can be the self's distinct social formation as opposed to a freer, more anonymous, inner core. When personality is conceived as plural and diffuse, however, it can blend into forms of impersonality that imply a heterogeneous collective mind. The fertile and indeterminate nature of this subject is vibrantly reflected in the diversification of the language emerging to describe its multiple forms.

SEE ALSO: *Atom, Atomic; Biography, New Biography; Common Mind Group Thinking; Form Formalism; Reality, Realism; Universal; Unconscious; Woman, New Woman*

References

Adams, Henry (1918). *The Education of Henry Adams*. Boston and New York: Houghton Mifflin. Privately printed, Washington, 1907.

Anand, Mulk Raj (1935). *Untouchable*. London: Wishart Books.

Anderson, Sherwood (1947). "A Writer's Conception of Realism." Limited Publication, 1939. In *The Sherwood Anderson Reader* (ed. Paul Rosenfeld). Boston: Houghton Mifflin. 337–347.

Bellow, Saul (1962). "Where Do We Go From Here: The Future of Fiction." *Michigan Quarterly Review* (Winter): 27–33.

Eliot, George (1871–1872). *Middlemarch: A Story of Provincial Life*. 4 vols. Edinburgh: W. Blackwood.

Eliot, T. S. (1919). "Tradition and the Individual Talent." *The Egoist* 6.5 (November/December): 72–73.

Eliot, T. S. (1922). *The Waste Land*. New York: Boni and Liveright.

Faulkner, William (1936). *Absalom, Absalom!* New York: Random House.

Fitzgerald, F. Scott (1925). *The Great Gatsby*. New York: Charles Scribner's Sons.

Ford, Ford Madox (1914). "On Impressionism." *Poetry and Drama* 2 (June): 167–175; (December): 323–334.

Forster, E. M. (1925). "Anonymity: An Inquiry." *The Atlantic Monthly (November)*, 588, 592–593.

Forster, E. M. (1939). *What I Believe*. ["Two Cheers for Democracy," 1938]. London: Hogarth.

Hulme, T. E. (1924). "Humanism and the Religious Attitude." In *Speculations: Essays on Humanism and the Philosophy of Art* (ed. Herbert Read). London: Routledge and Kegan Paul. 1–71.

Hurston, Zora Neale (1928). "How it Feels to be Colored Me." *The World Tomorrow* (May 11), 214–216.

Huxley, Aldous (1927). "Personality and the Discontinuity of the Mind." In *Proper Studies*. London: Chatto & Windus. 260–271.

Huxley, Aldous (1936). *Eyeless in Gaza*. London: Chatto & Windus.

James, Henry (1908). *The Portrait of a Lady*. [1880–1881]. *The Novels and Tales of Henry James*. New York Edition. New York: Charles Scribner's Sons. Vol. 3–4.

Kohs, Samuel C. (1914). "The Association Method in Its Relation to the Complex and Complex Indicators." *The American Journal of Psychology* 25.4 (October): 544–594.

Lawrence, D. H. (1932). Letter to Katherine Mansfield, 12 December 1915. [1915]. In *The Letters of D. H. Lawrence* (ed. Aldous Huxley). London: W. Heinemann. 288–290.

Lawrence, D. H. (1936). "Democracy III: Personality." 1919. In *Phoenix: The Posthumous Papers of D. H. Lawrence*. Edited with an Introduction by Edward D. McDonald. London. W. Heinemann: 709–713.

Lawrence, D. H. (1936). "Why the Novel Matters." [1920s]. In *Phoenix: The Posthumous Papers of D. H. Lawrence*. Edited with an Introduction by Edward D. McDonald. London: W. Heinemann. 533–538.

Mansfield, Katherine (1939). "The Flowering of the Self." Journal entry [July 1920]. In *The Scrapbook of Katherine* Mansfield (ed. John Middleton Murry). London: Constable. 136–137.

Nin, Anaïs (1966–1980). "Diary entries, February, August, October, 1937." [1937]. In *The Diary Of Anaïs Nin* (ed. Gunther Stuhlmann), 7 vols. New York: Harcourt, Brace and World. Vol. 2: 1934–1939: 165–177, 223–241, 257–266.

Nin, Anaïs (1975). "The Personal Life Lived Deeply." In *A Woman Speaks: The Lectures, Seminars and Interviews of Anais Nin* (ed. Evelyn J. Hinz). Chicago: Swallow. 148–180.

Woolf, Virginia (1924). *Mr Bennett and Mrs Brown*. London: Hogarth.

Woolf, Virginia (1925). *Mrs. Dalloway*. London: Hogarth.

Woolf, Virginia (1927). *To the Lighthouse*. London: Hogarth.

Woolf, Virginia (1929a). "Dorothy Wordsworth." *The Nation and Athenaeum* (October 12), 46–48.

Woolf, Virginia (1929b). *A Room of One's Own*. London: Hogarth.

Woolf, Virginia (1929c). "Women and Fiction." *The Forum* (New York) (March), 179–183.

Woolf, Virginia (1931). *The Waves*. London: Hogarth.

Woolf, Virginia (1937). "Craftsmanship." *The Listener* (May 5), 868–869.

Woolf, Virginia (1947). "Personalities." In *The Moment and Other Essays*. London: Hogarth. 135–139.

Primitive

Primitive signifies, in its most basic sense, a prime or first state. In C15, the word carried the neutral meaning of "original" or "beginning," as in primitive church or primitive cause; by the modernist period, however, subsequent usages had introduced significant confusions. The C18 sense of original inhabitants of a land became increasingly identified with native inhabitants before the invasion of

European explorers; this use then collided and often fused with the C19 sense of early stages of physiological or psychological human development. In the specialized vocabulary of the arts, primitive signified natural, simple, and often untutored, and was most commonly applied to Western art before the Renaissance's rules for perspective and three-dimensional form, or to self-taught American painters (Janis, 1942). More loosely, however, primitive was used variously to describe the art of the earliest peoples, contemporary nonindustrialized societies, children, or the modernist avant-garde. The term thus incorporated differing assumptions concerning *where* the primitive is located and *when*. Primitive also became an evaluative, though highly conflicted term, signifying either pure and unsullied or backward and nonprogressive.

Such ambiguities stemmed from changes in the Western world. Modernization heightened the contrast between societies with a low level of technology and the highly developed technologies associated with civilization. The rise of anthropology, sociology, psychoanalysis, and linguistics focused attention on origins and evolutionary development. The accessibility of world travel and the popularity of documentary film and world exhibitions promoted Western exposure to nonindustrialized cultures. The resulting constructions inevitably reveal less about putatively primitive peoples than about what Western writers thought of themselves, as they struggled to fit themselves into their widening historical and geographical world.

One ambiguity in the meaning of primitive pertained to its placement in three different times: (i) as a previous phase of present civilization, (ii) as a contemporary cultural form, and (iii) as a universal, timeless state. Implying sense (i), Sigmund Freud linked "primaeval times" to "primitive races" and considered primitive "a necessary stage of development through which every race has passed" ([1913]1918). Invoking sense (ii), however, Freud complicated the implied identification of primitive with a static, anterior place, arguing that "primitive races are not young races but are in fact as old as civilized races"; more explicitly, Franz Boas considered "primitive culture" to be the "product of historical development no less than modern civilization," noting that the "mode of life, customs, and beliefs of primitive tribes are not stable," although the "rate of change" "is slower than among ourselves" (1927). Sense (i) predominates in popular evolutionary histories, such as H. G. Wells's *The Outline of History* (1920), although an element of sense (iii) appears in Sir James Frazer's assertion that "the primitive tendency to personify nature survives in poets," who are "representatives of a earlier mode of thought" and "who perceive by intuition what most of us have to learn by laborious collection of facts" (1918). More firmly adopting sense (iii), Bronislaw Malinowski argued that the "primitive mind" "is the human mind as we find it universally" (1928); similarly addressing elements inherent in human nature, Bertrand Russell used "primitive desire" to denote desires of which we are not consciously aware (not necessarily because they have been repressed), and to

163

indicate "the form in which man shows his affinity to his animal ancestors" (1922). Regarding language, Russell also commented that "the meaning of images seems more primitive than the meaning of words," adding that "our more elementary beliefs, notably those that are added to sensation to make perception, often remain at the level of images."

Another ambiguity stemmed from a difference in what primitive was thought to define: modes and habits of mind or forms of social organization. Levy-Bruhl introduced the phrase "primitive mentality" [*La mentalité primitive*] to describe distinctive patterns of thought, which he characterized as mystical, prelogical, collectivist, and "blended" in subject–object relations, in contrast to the abstract, differentiating, logical, and individualistic reasoning predominant in civilized societies ([1922]1923). Aldous Huxley advanced a similar distinction, stating that primitive minds focus on "particulars" and civilized minds, on "the general and abstract" (1933a). In contrast, Sir James Frazer's highly influential work on comparative religion, *The Golden Bough*, looked for common narrative elements in early myths, rituals, and folklore, exposing the continuities with Christian beliefs ([1890]1906–1915). While resembling Levy-Bruhl in isolating mysticism and totemism as aspects of "primitive man," Frazer also complicated his comparisons by suggesting that primitive people were more logical than civilized Europeans in the way they viewed animals, while Christianity relied more on superstition than was commonly perceived. Other approaches attempted definition based on societies. For Huxley, primitive societies tend to be "more stable" and "more content," qualities ideally to be combined with the complementary "good features of civilization – knowledge, elasticity of mind, health of body and power over the natural environment" (1933b). T. S. Eliot, rejecting claims that "the savage" possessed unique "gifts of mystical insight or artistic feeling," argued instead that "primitive art and poetry help our understanding of civilized art and poetry" (1919); however, he differentiated between primitive and civilized *societies*, arguing that the former's "social-religious-artistic complex" organically integrated poetry and ritual, giving communal expression to crucial emotional values that his own society had abandoned and lost (1939).

In both approaches, primitive generally derived its meaning through a contrast, or at least comparison, to civilization. Yet, while seeming to assert categorical binary definition, many writers recognized the provisionality of such pioneering work. Levy-Bruhl noted that his study dealt only with the mentality of primitive peoples, omitting their "often complex institutions," and his Preface concluded by challenging the difference that his title implied: he aimed, he explained, to promote understanding of "those whom we, very improperly, term 'primitives' – beings who are both so far removed from, and so near to, ourselves." Frazer offered his study as a contribution to a "still youthful science," asserting that it "will have to be done over again and done better, with fuller knowledge and deeper insight, by those who come after us" (1900). Yet despite such qualifiers, the identification of primitive with instinct, sense perception, and emotion, versus civilization's rationality became widely entrenched.

Allied with instinct, primitive accrued negative connotations associated with a lower level of mental development and tendencies to savage behavior (an equally fraught word). For William Sumner, the "lowest groups of men" found "in the slums of the great cities" contained "horrible shadows of all the old primitive barbarism" (1883). In D. H. Lawrence's *Women in Love*, Hermione praises Gudrun's carvings as "perfectly beautiful – full of primitive passion," but when Ursula asks if "playing at killing" reveals "some primitive desire for killing," she associates primitive with violence (1921), as does the cynic Lord Henry Wotton in Oscar Wilde's *The Picture of Dorian Gray* (1891), who facetiously remarks, "women appreciate cruelty [. . .]. They have wonderfully primitive instincts." Cesare Lombroso – an Italian doctor whose theories of phrenology variously fascinated writers ranging through Joseph Conrad, H. G. Wells, Jack London, Theodore Dreiser, Stephen Crane, and Frank Norris – interpreted criminality as "a return to the characteristics peculiar to primitive savages" ([1899]1911). In popular fiction, primitive could substitute for sensually degenerate: in the detective novel *Thank You, Mr. Moto* (1937), a character describes the "tribal rhythms" of dancing at a party in contemporary "Peiping" as having descended "to a primitive sort of plane, that had to do with biology and taboos and natural selection." Yet some popular usages reflected a growing sensitivity to the prejudicial implications of the term. In a special issue on the Empire Exhibition at Wembley, *The Illustrated London News* reserved "primitive" to describe locomotives at an Australian bush mill and the earliest forms of Malayan Art, while showcasing modern-day ethnic dress throughout the Empire under the headline "Picturesque Types" (1924). A 1932 MOMA exhibition chose to designate American Primitive Painting as "American Folk Art" instead (Nathan, 1942).

In other uses, primitive could signify in positive, even idealistic, ways, implying natural simplicity or closeness to nature. Joseph Conrad described storms at sea as reawakening, "in the breast of one civilized beyond that stage," "the instinct of primitive man" who understands his "close dependence" on elemental forces (1906). W. H. Hudson's novel *The Purple Land* – while mocked in *The Sun Also Rises* for inspiring romanticism in Robert Cohn – presents a narrator who learns to respect the people of C19 Uruguay, "so primitive in their ways" and with their "primitive simplicity of mind," not as inhabitants of a "Utopia" without "folly, crime, or sorrow," but as superior, with their freedom and absence of "class or caste difference," to his own British "ultra-civilised condition" (1885). Popular fiction (and film) often treated primitive in heroic but gendered and chauvinist ways. In Jack London's *Sea-Wolf*, the "primitive man" is associated with "magnificent atavism" and "strength," while the effete Humphrey Van Weyden must tap into the "primitive deeps" of his "nature" in order to become "the fighting male" (1904). Edgar Rice Burroughs enticed readers (and filmgoers) with Tarzan of the Apes as the ultimate "primitive man, the hunter, the warrior," yet also – supporting the civilized narrative of progress – as "an allegorical figure of the primordial groping through the black night of ignorance toward the light of learning" (1914).

In the US, primitive was associated with African Americans, exposing polarizations of race. The white supremacist Lothrop Stoddard used primitive as a label to castigate darker skinned people as a threat to the white race, believing that "the more primitive a type is," "the more prepotent it is" (1920). Conversely, although the novel *Porgy* (1925) – adapted for theatre by Dorothy Heyward and later the basis for the popular Gershwin musical *Porgy and Bess* (1935) – is vulnerable to charges of stereotypical characterization, author Edwin DuBose Heyward explained his positive intent: "I saw the primitive Negro as the inheritor of a source of delight that I would give much to possess" (1928). While radically differing in evaluative judgments, Stoddard and Heyward both applied primitive to others; the implications inevitably differ from the perspectives of those self-identifying in the "primitive" group. Reversing the denigration writers like Stoddard implied, some African Americans claimed the term to express racial pride. Zora Neale Hurston used "primitive" to characterize "Negro expression," referring to a rich pictorial use of language, full of metaphor and "action words" (1934). J. A. Rogers wrote of jazz as a "rejuvenation, a recharging of the batteries of civilization with primitive new vigor (1925)." Even such positive usages, however, were attacked as reproducing stereotypes, and primitive became laced with double meanings and ironies. Claude McKay's *Banjo* (1929) exposed the way that the new stature being accorded to African culture also signaled appropriation, dispossession, and co-opted use. McKay's protagonist marks his double-sided position as both inspiration and specimen: noting that the artists who paint him in Paris "talked a lot about primitive simplicity and color and 'significant form' from Cezanne to Picasso," he dryly observes, "their naked savage was quickly getting on to civilized things." Yet elsewhere McKay used primitive to highlight complexities of relations *within* the African American community: jazz, he reflected, was both disturbing and releasing for a mixed black, yellow, and brown populace, stirring up "that primitive, ancient, eternal, inexplicable antagonism in the color taboo of sex and society" (1928). Differences within the African American community could be erased, however, when primitive was used as a stereotyping, homogenizing term. Langston Hughes suffered the devastating loss of his patron Charlotte Mason because she wanted him to be "primitive in the simple, intuitive and noble sense of the word," failing to grasp that he was "not African," but "an American Negro," who had "grown up in Kansas City, Chicago and Cleveland" (1940).

The use of primitive by literary writers was also profoundly influenced by the use of the term in the other arts, though again the meanings were varied and complex. In England, Roger Fry worked tirelessly to convert a shocked public to the acceptance of Post-Impressionist painting by upholding its rejection of reigning prescriptions for "photographic vision" in favor of "the principles of primitive design" and art's original roots: "its power to express emotional ideas" "in response to human passion and human need" (1910). However, offering as examples the medieval painters Giotto and Cimabue, as well as Byzantine art, Fry clearly used primitive in the established aesthetic sense of pre-Renaissance art. As he learned more about the arts of Africa and the Incas, Fry found in them a perfection of three-dimensional "plastic form" much superior to the lesser art of primitive European races, which he considered too regulated by mental conceptions (1910, 1918). The problematic reverse side of Fry's binary, however, was his corresponding assumption that primitive societies lacked the "conscious" intellectual tradition of aesthetic criticism that civilized cultures possessed (1920). The association of primitive with a more vibrant creative tradition was equally prevalent in modern music and dance. Isadora Duncan found inspiration in the "unrestricted, natural and beautiful" "movements of the savage, who lived in freedom in constant touch with Nature" and in the "Greek gods" who were "representatives of natural forces" ([1909]1928). Duncan also argued, however, that "the dance of the future" would not be "a revival of the antique dances or even of those of the primitive tribes"; she heralded "a new movement, a consequence of the entire evolution which mankind has passed through," belonging not "to a nation but to all humanity." Elizabeth Selden described Martha Graham's *Primitive Mysteries* (1931) as effectively employing the "primitive type of action-modes" to suggest "Christian symbols translated into Indian ideology"; like Fry, however, Selden defined "the primitive" – "(in the *true* sense of the word)" – through medieval painting, referring to Giotto to explain Graham's "simultaneous presentation in space of action which in reality appears successively in time: another characteristic of primitive painting of all ages" (1935). In music, pianist Alfred Cortot alluded to "that sensation of elementary and primitive force which is one of the most recent, if not the most characteristic acquisitions of music" (1922); Cecil Gray wrote, rather disparagingly, of Igor Stravinsky's "primitive and barbaric rhythmical sense" (1926); and Adrian Pelham described Stravinsky's *Le Sacre du Printemps* (*The Rite of Spring*) as an "apotheosis of primitive man" (1924). T. S. Eliot fused ancient and modern in his praise of Stravinsky's music for possessing both the spirit of "primitive ceremony" and "a quality of modernity" (1921). As in the general cultural discourse, primitive in the arts was variously located in the past, in the modern world, or in the timeless human realm.

The semantic history of primitive is thus fraught with ambiguities, uneasy fusions, and conflicting perspectives. While inaccurate in labeling others, many

167

uses of primitive usefully challenged attitudes about the supremacy of white Anglo-European culture, helping to undermine ideological justifications for imperialism and colonization. When Henry Adams's faith in C18 rational discourse was shaken by the raw electrical energy of the dynamo, he was prompted to question inherited assumptions of hierarchical rank: "All the so-called primitive races [. . .] raised doubts which persisted against the most obstinate convictions of evolution" (1918). Conrad blamed a loss of primitive sensibility on a competitive age that "hardens its heart in the progress of its own perfectability" (1906); Aldous Huxley, treating the difference between primitive and civilized minds as a matter of "training," cleverly drew out a self-humbling implication for the latter: whereas "primitive" minds tend "to accept the existing order as right" (1933a), "civilized" minds "have been made to believe in Progress – which means that they believe that they are not in possession of the absolute truth and the perfect ethic" (1933b). At the period's end, Laurens Van der Post signaled an impending breakdown in the categories themselves. Prompted by a new consciousness of his words being read by the people assumed to be primitive, he wrote, in his Preface to *The Dark Eye in Africa* (1955): "To my black and coloured countrymen who may read this book I would like to explain my use of the words 'primitive' and 'civilised' man. I use these words only because I know no others [. . .]. I am, however, fully conscious of their limitations and relativity." Acknowledging a "general difference between indigenous and European men in Africa," Van der Post affirmed that his words were "not intended to convey a feeling of superiority," but rather a relation of mutual need and respect: "two halves designed by life to make a whole."

SEE ALSO: *Form, Formalism; Empire, Imperialism; Race; Universal; Woman, New Woman*

References

(1924). "Subjects of the King from Many Climes at Wembley: Picturesque Types at the British Empire Exhibition." *Illustrated London News*. Wembley Empire Exhibition Number, Saturday, May 24: 934–935.

Adams, Henry (1918). *The Education of Henry Adams*. Boston and New York: Houghton Mifflin. Privately printed, Washington, 1907.

Boas, Franz (1927). *Primitive Art*. Cambridge: Harvard University Press.

Burroughs, Edgar Rice (1914). *Tarzan of the Apes*. New York: Grosset and Dunlap.

Conrad, Joseph (1906). "The Character of the Foe." In *The Mirror of the Sea*. New York: Harper and Brothers. 117–131.

Cortot, Alfred (1922). *The Piano Music of Claude Debussy*. London: J. and W. Chester.

Duncan, Isadora (1928). "The Dance of the Future." [1909]. In *The Art of The Dance* (ed. Seldon Cheney). New York: Theatre Arts, Inc. 54–63.

Eliot, T. S. (1919). "War-Paint and Feathers." *The Athenaeum* (October 17), 1036.

Eliot, T. S. (1921). "London Letter." *The Dial* 71.10 (October): 452–455.

Eliot, T. S. (1939). *The Idea of a Christian Society*. London: Faber and Faber.

Frazer, J. G. (1900). "Preface to the Second Edition." In *The Golden Bough: A Study in Magic and Religion*, 2nd ed. 3 vols. London, New York: Macmillan Co. Vol. 1: xiii–xxiii.

Frazer, James George (1906–1915). *The Golden Bough: A Study in Magic and Religion*. 1890. 3rd ed. 15 vols. London: Macmillan.

Frazer, James George (1918). *Folklore in the Old Testament*. Studies in Comparative Religion, Legend, and Law. 3 vols. London: Macmillan.

Freud, Sigmund (1918). *Totem and Taboo: Resemblances Between the Psychic Lives of Savages and Neurotics*. [*Totem und Tabu* 1913]. Trans. A. A. Brill. New York: Moffat, Yard and Co.

Fry, Roger (1910). "Bushman Paintings." *Burlington Magazine for Coinnoisseurs* (March), 334–338.

Fry, Roger (1910). "The Grafton Gallery – I." *The Nation* (November 19), 331–332.

Fry, Roger (1918). "American Archaeology." *Burlington Magazine for Coinnoisseurs* (November), 154–157.

Fry, Roger (1920). "Negro Sculpture at the Chelsea Book Club." *The Athenaeum* (April 16), 516.

Gray, Cecil (1926). "Russia and 'Les Noces.'" Letter to the Editor. *The Nation and Athenaeum* 34 (August 7): 525–526.

Heyward, DuBose (1925). *Porgy*. New York: G. H. Doran.

Heyward, DuBose (1928). Introduction. In *Porgy: A Play in Four Acts*, by Dorothy and DuBose Heyward. Garden City: Doubleday, Doran. ix–xxi.

Hudson, W. H. (1885). *The Purple Land that England Lost: Travels and Adventures in the Banda Oriental, South America*. 2 vols. London: Sampson Low, Marston, Serle, and Rivington.

Hughes, Langston (1940). *The Big Sea: An Autobiography*. New York: A. A. Knopf.

Hurston, Zora Neale (1934). "Characteristics of Negro Expression." In *Negro: An Anthology* (ed. Nancy Cunard). London: Lawrence and Wishart. 39–46.

Huxley, Aldous (1933a). "Names and Things." *Chicago Herald and Examiner* (January 7), 7.

Huxley, Aldous (1933b). "Primitive and Civilized." *Chicago Herald and Examiner* (May 20), 6.

Janis, Sydney (1942). *They Taught Themselves: American Primitive Painters of the 20th Century*. New York: Dial Press.

Lawrence, D. H. (1921). *Women in Love*. London: Martin Secker.

Lévy-Bruhl, Lucien (1923). *Primitive Mentality*. [*La mentalité primitive*, 1922]. Trans. Lilian A. Clare. London: George Allen and Unwin; New York: Macmillan Co.

Lombroso, Cesare (1911). *Crime: Its Causes and Remedies*. [*Le crime: causes et remédes*, 1899]. Translated by Henry P. Horton. Introduction by Maurice Parmelee. London: W. Heinemann; Boston: Little, Brown and Co.

London, Jack (1904). *The Sea Wolf*. London: W. Heinemann; New York: Grosset and Dunlop.

Malinowski, Bronislaw (1928). Rev. of *The Mothers: A Study of the Origins of Sentiments and Insitutions* by Robert Briffault and *The Mystic Rose: A Study of Primitive Marriage and of Primitive Thought in its Bearing on Marriage* by Ernest Crawley. *Nature* 121.1039 (January 28): 126–130.

Marquand, John P. (1937). *Thank You, Mr. Moto*. London: H. Jenkins.

McKay, Claude (1928). *Home to Harlem*. New York: Harper and Brothers.

McKay, Claude (1929). *Banjo: A Story without a Plot*. New York, London: Harper and Brothers.

169

Primitive

Nathan, Walter L. (1942). Rev. of *American Primitive Painting* by Jean Lipman. *The New England Quarterly* 15.2 (June): 368–373.

Pelham, Adrian (1924). "Music: Stravinsky and Cowell Break the Ice of Tradition – Carnegie Hall Hears a New Masterpiece." *Theatre Magazine* (April), 34, 54.

Rogers, J. A. (1925). "Jazz at Home." *Survey Graphic*. Harlem: Mecca of the New Negro (ed. Alain Locke). 6.6 (March 1): 665.

Russell, Bertrand (1922). *The Analysis of Mind*. London: G. Allen and Unwin; New York: Macmillan.

Selden, Elizabeth (1935). *The Dancer's Quest: Essays on the Aesthetic of Contemporary Dance*. Berkeley: University of California Press.

Stoddard, Lothrop (1920). *The Rising Tide of Color Against White World-Supremacy*. New York: Charles Scribner's Son.

Sumner, William Graham (1883). *What the Social Classes Owe to Each Other*. New York: Harper and Brothers.

Van der Post, Lauren (1955). *The Dark Eye in Africa*. London: Hogarth.

Wells, H. G. (1920). *The Outline of History, Being a Plain History of Life and Mankind*. New York: Macmillan; London: Cassell.

Wilde, Oscar (1891). *The Picture of Dorian Gray*. 1890. London; New York: Ward, Lock.

Propaganda

Propaganda experienced three major developments in the modernist period: a marked increase in frequency of employment; a tremendous broadening of reference, from religion to war, politics, mass media, and culture; and a hardening of negative connotations, as the dominant associations shifted from information, to persuasion, to brainwashing. The evolution of the term is strikingly visible in successive issues of the *Encyclopedia Britannica*. The entry on propaganda in the ninth edition (1875–1889) used the term unapologetically in the neutral sense of disseminating ideas, referring to Pope Gregory XV's establishment in C17 of the Sacred Congregation for the Propagation of the Faith (*Sacra Congregatio de Propaganda Fide*) and the "splendid" results of missionary work in North America. The eleventh edition (1910–1911) had no entry on propaganda, mentioning the term only in passing in an article on biological propagation. A long entry in the fourteenth edition (1929), ignoring the religious context but covering advertising, political propaganda, and especially WWI propaganda, defined "a propaganda" negatively as a campaign "to promote the interests of those who contrive it, rather than to benefit those to whom it is addressed." The entry in the post-WWII revised fourteenth edition (1951) focused on propaganda by fascists and communists, emphasizing the destructive effects of limiting the individual's capacity for independent choice, weakening democracy as a result.

WWI was the pivotal event in the history of the word propaganda, as modernists themselves were aware. In "A Good Word Gone Wrong," Agnes Repplier blamed the war for "investing this honorable word with a sinister significance, making it at once a term of reproach and the plague and torment of our lives" (1921). Will Irwin similarly argued that before WWI, propaganda "meant simply the means which the adherent of a political or religious faith employed to convince the unconverted," whereas after the war, "it meant the next thing to a damned lie" (1936). Sensitivity to the increasingly negative connotations of propaganda appears in the renaming of the British War Propaganda Bureau (est. 1914) as Wellington House in 1915 and its 1917 absorption into the neutrally named Department of Information; nonetheless, as late as 1918, Britain established a Department of Enemy Propaganda, while the US created an American Propaganda Department. Indeed, the shift in connotations occurred gradually and unevenly. Negative usages predated WWI: contrasting Catholic usage, a C19 dictionary noted that American Protestants used propaganda as a "term of reproach" applied to "secret associations for the spread of opinions" (Brande, 1843), and in a scene in Joseph Conrad's *Under Western Eyes* (1911), Razumov describes a fellow student as an "imbecile victim of revolutionary propaganda." Conversely, neutral usages survived into the interwar period, as in a League of Nations report describing the instruction of youth as "one of the most effective means of propaganda" (1926) and in H. G. Wells's commendation of the "extraordinary value" of "League of Nations propaganda" (1921).

Increasingly negative perceptions of propaganda, however, emerged in critiques of the domestic politics of communist, fascist, and even capitalist countries for using propaganda as a means of control by manipulating emotions rather than appealing to reason. Amber Blanco White described propaganda as "the chief internal weapon of governments," charging that its aim was "to keep whole populations in a complete, and [. . .] perpetual emotional subjection" (1935). Alexander Johnston Mackenzie argued that propaganda was employed as a "systematic political weapon" in totalitarian states, where "subjects by the hundred million have forfeited the right to think for themselves" (1938). Lawrence Childs held that widespread popular debates about propaganda had produced a situation in which "the world is both propaganda-conscious and dictator-conscious," adding that "propaganda has been propagandized with quite as much zeal and effectiveness as the tenets of fascism and communism" (1938).

Such negative critiques, however, were sooner to appear in the US than in Europe. Leonard Doob argued that while in America "the word 'propaganda'" had acquired "a bad odor" through its association with "the war and with other evil practices," it possessed "other connotations" in Germany, where Goebbels – "a realistic demagogue" – "[did] not hesitate to have himself called 'Minister of Public Enlightenment and Propaganda'" (1935). George Seldes noted, "The term propaganda [had] not the sinister meaning in Europe which it has acquired in America"; whereas in the US, it was used in "conjunction with the adjective

'German'" and associated with WWI, "in European business offices," it possessed a neutral association with "advertising or boosting generally" (1929).

Whatever its connotations, examples of propaganda expanded, throughout the interwar period, to numerous areas of culture and everyday life. Targeting a phenomenon he named *The Propaganda Boom*, Alexander Johnston Mackenzie identified "the press, the films, and broadcasting" as the "three main agencies" of propaganda, concluding, "never before has there been such widespread activity on the mental front" (1938). F. C. Bartlett similarly found the "insistent voice" of propaganda to be inescapably "in the air and on it," arguing that propaganda "fashion[s] the education of the child, the ambitions of youth, the activities of the prime of life, and it pursues the aged to the grave" (1940). Stating that "we may legitimately suspect propaganda in all social activity," Richard S. Lambert asked, "Is the Aldershot Tattoo [a performance highlighting military skills and music] propaganda for recruiting and for armaments, or is it merely entertainment for charitable purposes, or is it both?" Noting that "our huge cosmetics industry owes ninety per cent of its modern growth to a fashion set by films," he asked, "Are the facial attractions of Hollywood stars on the films propaganda for the use of cosmetics?" (1938). No aspect of life seemed immune from propaganda's reach.

In connection with literary practice, attitudes to propaganda exposed fundamentally different conceptions of art. Propaganda appeared negatively as a derogatory synonym of "bad art" overly subservient to an ideology or, conversely, was opposed to "art for art's sake" and associated positively with social engagement. Many pre-WWI uses suggested the positive sense of providing instruction, as in George Bernard Shaw's description of art as "the most effective instrument of moral propaganda in the world" (1902) or Marinetti's proclaimed belief "in the usefulness of a literary propaganda" (1911). Ford Madox Ford, however, argued that the artist "must not write propaganda," out of respect for a reader "who has too clear an intelligence to let his attention be captured or his mind deceived by special pleadings in favour of any given dogma" (1914). (Ford was himself employed in 1914 as a writer of anti-German propaganda for the War Propaganda Bureau.) In *Three Guineas* (1938), Virginia Woolf cautioned, "if we use art to propagate political opinions, we must force the artist to clip and cabin his gift to do us a passing service." In *The Principles of Art* (1938), R. G. Collingwood derided propagandistic works as "pseudo-art" forced to serve some "utilitarian end"; the creation of "propaganda" by an artist, he said, was "a degradation far more frightful than the prostitution or enslavement of the mere body."

Many positive uses of propaganda, however, upheld precisely such utilitarian ends. W. E. B. Du Bois asserted "all art is propaganda and ever must be, despite the wailing of the purists," and he defended propagandistic art on the grounds that it intervened positively in social struggle: "whatever art I have for writing has been used always for propaganda for gaining the right of black folk to love and enjoy" (1926). Eric Gill, complaining that "art and propaganda are held to be mutually exclusive terms," claimed that "all art is propaganda," given the impossibility of "mak[ing] anything which is not expressive of 'value'" (1935). George Orwell, summarizing the literature of the 1930s, described it as "swamped by propaganda," but was careful to note that this did not make it "bad" art; indeed, Orwell's ambivalence captured the complexity of the art-propaganda debate (1941). While welcoming the infusion of "pamphleteering" for "debunk[ing] art for art's sake" and reminding readers "that propaganda in some form lurks in every book," Orwell nevertheless warned, "you cannot sacrifice your intellectual integrity for the sake of a political creed." For him, "the frontiers of art and propaganda" constituted a meeting place where a precarious balance should be maintained.

The literary associations of propaganda were thus complicated by ongoing controversy over the value of the approach. In his introduction to *New Signatures* (1932), Michael Roberts expressed doubt whether the propagandistic poetry of the Auden group was a sign of "emancipation" or "enslavement," writing somewhat ambivalently that Stephen Spender's "The Funeral" was poetry "turned to propaganda" but nonetheless "propaganda for a theory of life which may release the poet's energies for the writing of pure poetry." By the time of the next year's *New Country* (1933), Roberts was calling on left-wing "intellectuals" to use their "lingering prestige" and "technical ability as organizers and propagandists" for the revolutionary cause, while at the same time disclaiming "the cruder Marxian evaluation that equates a work of art to its social purpose or propaganda value." Even within the pages of a single publication, the word could thus reverberate in numerous ways. While Geoffrey Grigson, in his journal *New Verse*, dismissed Michael Roberts as "a cardinal presiding over a Propaganda" (1933), Dylan Thomas [D. M. T.], writing in the same journal, complained that Spender's *Vienna* lacked "any real intensity of propagandistic mission" (1934).

173

Yet another use of propaganda suggested that whatever the problems of any single propaganda, a free competition of discordant propagandas could serve a positive, democratic end. Multiple propagandas would encourage readers to engage actively, provided that all sides were given the right to be heard. W. E. B. Du Bois qualified his remark, "I do not care a damn for any art that is not used for propaganda," by adding, "but I do care when propaganda is confined to one side while the other is stripped and silent" (1926). Dorothy Richardson described the "talkie" as "a medium of propaganda," fearing its ability to "sway an audience in whatever direction a filmateur desires"; but, she continued, where filmmakers were free to propagandize any position they wished, film could "assist Radio in turning the world into a vast council-chamber" (1926). The positive valuation of competing propagandas extended from art into education and politics. H. G. Wells lamented the "general tendency in universities on both sides of the

Propaganda

Atlantic to treat propaganda as infection": as a Protestant, he nonetheless regretted that "there is no good Roman Catholic propaganda available for my sons in college life," and he complained of the "ridiculous attempt to suppress Bolshevik propaganda" (1921). Julius Yourman attacked the Nazis not because they produced one-sided propaganda, but because they prevented dissenting voices from doing the same: he complained that their "methods made difficult and dangerous the promulgation of competing propagandas" (1939).

The reaction against propaganda begun in WWI, however, was cemented in WWII, as the ideal of competing propagandas turned into the reality of propaganda wars. Analyzing German radio broadcasts to the US, Harold N. Graves cast their propaganda as "psychological warfare" (1940). Yet anti-Nazi – soon joined by anti-Soviet – protests were not immune from using propaganda themselves. A publication of the Council for Democracy resorted to shock in its title, *Nazi Poison: How We Can Destroy Hitler's Propaganda Against the Jews* (1941), as did Serge Chakotin's *The Rape of the Masses: The Psychology of Totalitarian Political Propaganda* (1940), which accused Nazi and Soviet propaganda of "psychic violence." Edward Hunter bolstered his attacks on communist propaganda with charges of "brainwashing," a word he claimed was derived from the Chinese for "wash brain" and used by refugees from Red China to describe the cleansing of the middle-class mind under Mao (1951). While stating that "the world paid a stupendous price for failure to detect Hitler's insanity," Hunter equally accused communist countries of "Government by the Insane" (1953). Propaganda became, at the end of the modernist period, the language of the Cold War (roughly 1945–1989), and the establishment of organizations dedicated to anti-Communist propaganda – such as the Voice of America (1942) and the CIA (1947) – paved the way to McCarthyism and the anti-communist purges of the 1950s.

Propaganda once meant neutral information; by the end of the modernist period, information was thoroughly entangled in invested propagandas. In 1942, George Orwell (while writing propaganda for the BBC) wrote in his diary, "All propaganda is lies, even when one is telling the truth." However, his ambivalence again intervened: writing that "our radio strategy is even more hopeless than our military strategy" and yet that "one rapidly becomes propaganda-minded and develops a cunning one did not previously have," he somewhat quixotically added, "I don't think this matters so long as one knows what one is doing, and why" ([1942] 1968). Other views, however, claimed that the difference absolutely matters for readers. Marshall McLuhan voiced concerns about "people who can't read well" being "completely victimized by propaganda of any type," because they lacked "the tools of discrimination"; the study of English, he argued, must focus on "habits of careful reading" (1948). Northrop Frye placed both advertising and propaganda among the "anti-arts of persuasion and exhortation" designed "to stun and demoralize the critical consciousness"; modern art, he concluded, is "born on a battlefield" and demands "an active response with an intensity that hardly existed before," since "the whole structure of society" is an "anti-art [. . .] that needs to be created anew" (1967).

SEE ALSO: *Advertising; Common Man; Common Mind, Group Thinking; Fascism; Form, Formalism; Hygiene; Manifesto; Race*

References

(1929). "Propaganda." *Encyclopedia Britannica*, 14th ed. 176–185.
(1941). *Nazi Poison: How We Can Destroy Hitler's Propaganda Against the Jews*. New York: Council for Democracy.
Bartlett, F. C. (1940). *Political Propaganda*. Cambridge: Cambridge University Press.
Bianco White, Amber (1939). *The New Propaganda*. Left Book Club. London: Victor Gollancz.
Brande, W. T. (1843). *A Dictionary of Science, Literature, and Art*. New York: Longmans.
Chakotin, Serge (1940). *The Rape of the Masses: The Psychology of Totalitarian Political Propaganda*. New York: Fortean Society.
Childs, Harwood Lawrence (1936). "Introduction." In *Propaganda and Dictatorship: A Collection of Papers* (ed. Harwood Lawrence Childs). Princeton, NJ: Princeton University Press. 3–7.
Collingwood, R. G. (1938). *Principles of Art*. Oxford: Clarendon.
Conrad, Joseph (1911). *Under Western Eyes* London: Methuen.
D.M.T. [Dylan Thomas] (1934). "Fey, Dollfuss, Vienna." Rev. of *Vienna* by Stephen Spender. *New Verse* 12 (December): 19–20.
Doob, Leonard (1935). *Propaganda: Its Psychology and Technique*. New York: H. Holt.
Du Bois, W. E. B. (1926). "Criteria for Negro Art." *The Crisis: A Record of the Darker Races* 32 (October): 290–297.
Ford, Ford Madox (1914). *Henry James: A Critical Study*. London: Martin Secker.
Frye, Northrop (1967). *The Modern Century*. Toronto: Oxford University Press.
Gill, Eric (1935). "All Art is Propaganda." In *5 on Revolutionary Art*. Foreword Betty Rea. London: Wishart. 45–49.
Graves, Harold N., Jr. (1940). "Propaganda by Short Wave: Berlin Calling America." *The Public Opinion Quarterly* 4.4 (December): 601–619.
Grigson, Geoffrey (1933). "Faith or Feeling?" *New Verse* 1.2 (March): 15–17.
Hunter, Edward (1951). *Brain-Washing in Red China: The Calculated Destruction of Men's Minds*. New York: Vanguard.
Hunter, Edward (1953). "Government by the Insane." *The Freeman: An Illustrated Colored Newspaper* (March 23), 443–446.
International Committee on Intellectual Co-Operation (1926). *Sub-Committee of Experts for the Instruction of Children and Youth in the Existence and Aims of the League of Nations. Recommendations*. Geneva: League of Nations.
Irwin, Will (1936). *Propaganda and the News or, What Makes You Think So?* New York and London: Whittlesley House (division of McGraw Hill).
Lambert, Richard S. (1938). *Propaganda*. London: Thomas Nelson.
Mackenzie, Alexander Johnston (1938). *The Propaganda Boom*. London: J. Gifford.

Marinetti, F. T. (1911). *Le Futurisme*. Paris: Éditions Sansot.

McLuhan, Marshall, William Eliot, Dr. J.F. MacDonald and Jack Smith (1948). *Poor Grammar Among 1940s Youth*, The Varsity Story, CBC Radio Broadcast, November 25. CBC Digital Archives. Web.

Orwell, George (1941). "The Frontiers of Art and Propaganda." *The Listener*, Broadcast BBC Overseas Service, Empire Service, Indian Service, April 30, 1941 (May 29), 768–769.

Orwell, George (1968). "War-time Diary": Diary entry, 14 March 1942. [1942]. In *The Collected Essays, Journalism and Letters of George Orwell* (eds. Sonia Orwell and Ian Angus). 4 vols. London: Secker and Warburg. Vol. 2: My Country Right or Left: 1940–1943: 410–412.

Repplier, Agnes (1921). "A Good Word Gone Wrong." *Independent and the Weekly Review* (October 1), 5.

Richardson, Dorothy (1932). "Continuous Performance: The Film Gone Male." *Close Up* 9.1 (March): 36–38.

Roberts, Michael (1932). "Introduction." In *New Signatures* (ed. Michael Roberts). London: Hogarth. 7–20.

Roberts, Michael (1933). "Preface." In *New Country: Prose and Poetry by the Authors of New Signatures*. London: Hogarth. 9–21.

Seldes, George (1929). *You Can't Print That!: The Truth Behind the News, 1918–1928*. New York: Payson and Clark.

Shaw, Bernard (1902). "The Author's Apology." In *Mrs. Warren's Profession: A Play in Four Acts*. London: G. Richards. vii–xxxvi.

Wells, H. G. (1921). *The Salvaging of Civilization*. London, Toronto: Cassell.

Woolf, Virginia (1938). *Three Guineas*. London: Hogarth.

Yourman, Julius (1939). "Propaganda Techniques Within Nazi Germany." Special Issue: Education Under Nazism. *The Journal of Educational Sociology* 13.3 (November): 148–163.

Queer, Gay

Queer in this entry stands both for a cluster of words and for a word that, for a variety of reasons, is unspoken. When Lord Alfred Douglas wrote in his poem "Two Loves" of "the love that dare not speak its name" (1894), he alluded to the disapproval or even punishment that naming homosexuality would bring (homosexuality was illegal in Britain until 1967, while criminalization of homosexuality was not ruled unconstitutional in the US until 2003). "Not naming" in this poem furthermore resists the pejorative naming imposed by the speaker's antagonist, who alleges, "his name is Shame." In the modernist context of censorship and prosecution, silence or circumlocution could be a strategy of self-preservation, but it could also be a means for subverting limited and categorical labels imposed from outside. Queer emerged as a word for homosexual possibly just because its meaning is elusive and vague. Since C16, queer generally signified strange, curious, out of bounds, or suspiciously disreputable, making it an appropriate word for both coded communication outside conventional mores and vocabulary, and forms of sexuality that cannot be reduced to or contained in one word.

As a word for alternative sexualities, queer developed in speech rather than writing, making its emergence impossible to locate exactly in time or place. In 1914, however, readers outside the homosexual/bisexual community would have encountered its sexualized usage when the *Los Angeles Times* reported on the arrest of 31 men for "social vagrancy" ("Long Beach"). Although the reporter

ABCDEFGHIJKLMNOP**Q**RSTUVWXYZ

Modernism: Keywords, First Edition. Melba Cuddy-Keane, Adam Hammond, and Alexandra Peat.
© 2014 Melba Cuddy-Keane. Published 2014 by John Wiley & Sons, Ltd.

expressed repugnance at "a certain class of vice" practiced by "male degenerates," the reported testimony of one officer, detailing what one of the arrested
men had said to him, provided an inadvertent opportunity for the queer community
to speak from its own point of view and in its own voice: "He said that the Ninety-
six Club was the best; that it was composed of the 'queer' people," and "He said
that at these 'drags' the 'queer' people have a good time." Another instance of the
word's appearance in a court room is documented in a 1922 government report
on juvenile delinquents; a judge commented that a young man, "probably 'queer' in
sex tendency," was "unusually fine in other characteristics," but "we can't have
him going around snipping girls' hair." The author of the report, psychiatrist
William Healy, argued the futility of four months' incarceration as the court's
response. An article in *American Speech* (1935), defining underworld "argot" in
use 30 years or so earlier, listed three meanings for "queer": an unprofitable job,
"counterfeit money," and "a male homosexual." Although the writer David
Maurer offered no commentary on the usages, "on the outside" and "in disguise"
are continuities that may be implied. What Maurer did remark is the significance
of private vocabulary for marginalized groups: "As soon as argot words become
popular with respectable people, they gradually cease to function in the underworld; and by the time an underworld phrase has established itself firmly in print,
it is practically dead in the argot, and a new word has taken its place."

178   The literary uses of queer show a wide range of private to public vocabulary and
the fragile borders between. In Radclyffe Hall's autobiographical lesbian novel,
The Well of Loneliness (1928) – the focus of a widely publicized obscenity trial,
which resulted in the novel being banned in the UK until 1949 – queer signifies as
a sexual reference only obliquely. Only the striking repetitions indicate that there
is something particularly significant about the word: Hall's protagonist Stephen
is "a queer kid" who writes "queer compositions" and is regarded by her compan-
ions as "queer and absurd." If Hall's usage implies private undercover communication within a knowing community, however, the short story "Miss Knight" in
Robert McAlmon's *Distinguished Air* (1925) outs the word for all to hear. Miss
Knight, an extrovert drag queen based on the same real-life diva as Djuna Barnes's
garrulous Doctor Matthew O'Connor (1936), proclaims her queerness in colorful
words: "I was talkin' to a guy – one of these here highbrows, you get me, just
scientifically interested and all that, you know – and he sez to me, 'did you get
queer in the army?' and I sez to him, 'my god Mary, I've been queer since
before you wore diddies.'" McAlmon's book, however, circulated mainly in a
private community; only 150 copies were printed, through his own private press,
notable for previously publishing Ernest Hemingway, William Carlos Williams and
concurrently publishing Gertrude Stein. It would not have been judged, as Hall's book
was, as likely to be read by young girls. By 1936, however, even a conservative
mainstream audience could be expected to understand the implications of queer.

In James Gould Cozzens's, *Men and Brethren* (1936), when one man hears of another's "unfortunate secret," he asks, "He's not queer, or something, is he?" only to be told, "Lord, no! Worse than that. He's a convert." (The novel, however, indeed portrays an Episcopalian minister who tries to help another priest, who has been defrocked due to his relations with young boys.) Christopher Isherwood's *Goodbye to Berlin* (1939) enacts yet another twist in usage, where in the hallucinatory days of Berlin during the Nazi's rise to power, queerness moves from the margins into the center. At the entrance to a cabaret, a young American asks in disbelief, "Men dressed as *women*? [. . .] So you mean they're *queer*?" to which he receives the dry response, "Eventually we're all queer," suggesting a world in which normal no longer obtains.

Two different vocabularies were circulating, however, separating medical psychological discourse from usages, primarily coded, in vernacular speech. Titles themselves indicate the emergence of specialist terminology, as in Edward Carpenter's *Homogenic Love* (1894) and *The Intermediate Sex* (1908) and Havelock Ellis and John Addington Symonds's *Sexual Inversion* ([1896]1897). *Sexual Inversion* used "homosexual" in combination with "passion," "inclinations," "instincts," and "attraction," while in *Psychopathia Sexualis* ([1886] 1892), Richard von Krafft-Ebing referred to "the homo-sexual instinct" and "Lesbian love," and advocated the medical use of "hypnotic suggestion" to repress "homo-sexual feelings and impulses" and encourage "hetero-sexual desires." An article in *American Medicine* entitled "Masked Homosexuality" (1914), translated from Wilhelm Stekel, not only explained Sigmund Freud's three classes of inverts (absolutely inverted, amphigenously inverted, and occasionally inverted) but used bisexual in a striking way: *"What civilized humanity is least willing to acknowledge is its bisexual constitution."* The third edition of Ellis's *Sexual Inversion* cited Sándor Ferenczi's term "ambisexuality." Such publications did not mean, however, that medical awareness of sexual diversity was widespread. In his Preface to the first edition, Krafft-Ebing explained his choice of a scientific title and technical terminology that only "the learned" would understand, "in order that unqualified persons should not become readers," while justifying on the same grounds his use of Latin "for the most revolting passages." Such obscurity seems to have created a barrier for the learned as well: Stekel's translator expressed astonishment that "there are physicians even in New York City who have never heard of homosexuality and who do not know that such a condition exists." Symonds's name was dropped from the second edition of *Sexual Inversion* to protect his family, with apparent justification: its bookseller was indicted for "obscene libel," and the book was subsequently suppressed. Naming and speaking were difficult even within the professional realm.

In such a repressive environment for public speech, private words circulated in alternative communities for self-identification, bonding, and disguise. Sapphic had for centuries been used in connection with the Greek poet Sappho (C1 BC), referring to Sapphic Odes and Sapphic Verses; however, when Virginia Woolf said of Vita Sackville-West, "she is a pronounced Sapphist, & may have an eye on me" ([1923] 1977–1984), the word conveys the allure of a flamboyant, wealthy, somewhat camp, and heterogeneously cosmopolitan lesbian/bisexual community. Gay was another widely circulating term, jostling with such inherited meanings as lively person, flashy dresser, or female prostitute. Its first nonambiguous use in print to mean homosexual was likely in Lew Levenson's *Butterfly Man* (1934), in which a young man in theatrical New York announces to another cast member, "I'm going gay"; an older homosexual also refers to their circle as "the third sex." Marcel Proust used invert (*L'investi*) in his novel *Within a Budding Grove* ([1918] 1924), but the coded terms used in the French title of the later novel *Sodome et Gomorrhe* were hidden in the English translation, *Cities of the Plain* ([1922] 1927). W. H. Auden referred more elliptically, in "The Climbers" (1936), to the "left-handed."

The positive use of coded words in self-naming, however, confronted the negative formation of slur words labeling homosexual groups from outside. Maurer includes "nancy" along with queer in his dictionary of underworld argot, and Lee Duncan's *Over the Wall, The Autobiography of an Ex-convict* (1936) refers to a place "where the 'fairies', 'pansies', and 'queers' conducted their lewd practices." Slur words entered the work of homophobic modernist writers as well, with Wyndham Lewis blasting the "'Nancyism' of the joy-boy or joy-man" (1926) and entitling a chapter of his savagely satiric *The Apes of God* (1930), "Lesbian-Apes." From the opposite perspective, poet Robert Duncan protested what he found to be a "cult of homosexual superiority" and "a secret language, the *camp* [. . .] loaded with contempt for the human," in which "the word 'jam' remains, designating all who are not homosexual," "with an unwavering hostility and fear" (1944).

In the context of mutual hostility and censorship, slippery speech was a crucial strategy when speaking to the outside world. When asked, at his trial for gross indecencies, to explain "the love that dare not speak its name," Oscar Wilde employed a kind of doublespeak in response. Defending such love as "deep spiritual affection," Wilde proclaimed, "there is nothing unnatural about it," but his words could be read in two ways: it was not unnatural because it was platonic, or homosexual love is not unnatural at all. The court's inability to comprehend and accept the second meaning, however, meant that it could not be directly expressed: "It is in this century misunderstood," Wilde commented, "the world does not understand." Gertrude Stein similarly wrote a double discourse operating on two levels, playing on both gay and regular as having different meanings for different groups. In "Miss Furr and Miss Skeene" (1922), she wrote, "They were regular in being gay [. . .] they were gay every day, they were regular, they were gay, they were gay the same length of time every day, they were gay, they were quite regularly gay." The linguistic turns suggest that the meanings of gay and regular, like Wilde's unnatural, depend upon point of view, but the playfulness also subtly undermines any one specific meaning and indeed the desire to make any word a label meaning one thing. Similarly, in his poem "Café 3 A.M." (1951), Langston Hughes subverts the "vice squad" labels "fairies" and "degenerates" with the destabilizing view that "Police lady or Lesbian," if it is a difference, is indistinguishable to the eye.

While public censorship and misunderstanding could thus be privately reversed, public silencing was also perceived as exacting a cost. As Virginia Woolf wrote to Roger Fry, Goldie Lowes Dickinson had written a "dialogue upon homosexuality which he won't publish, for fear of the effect upon parents who might send their sons to Kings: and he is writing his autobiography which he won't publish for the same reason. So you see what dominates English literature is the parents of the young men who might be sent to Kings" ([1921]1975–1980). Enabled by the relative freedom of writing in the journal she founded, *The Little Review*, Margaret Anderson strongly protested the avoidance of homosexuality in a lecture by Mrs. Havelock Ellis, writing, "It is not a question of what could or could not be said on a public platform; it is a question of what *should* be said"; Anderson herself referred explicitly to homosexuality, intermediate types, sexual inverts, homosexualist, and heterosexualist, pointedly noting the difference between inversion and perversion and quoting a manifesto from a homosexual group in Germany who expressed gratitude "for every single voice that speaks in our favor in the forum of mankind" (1915). The frustration of silencing was poignantly captured in W. H. Auden's "Two Worlds" (1936), where freedom is sought "underground": "And since our desire cannot take that route which is straightest,/Let us choose the crooked," so that "on the new façade of a bank/Employed, or conferring at health resort,/[we] May, by circumstance linked,/More clearly act our thought."

The problem of the coded text for the non-comprehending reader, however, is exposed in F. R. Leavis's disparagement of Auden's poetry for obscurity and immaturity; Leavis quoted these lines as overly obsessed with "private neuroses and memories" and "the nameless terrors of childhood or their neurotic equivalent" (1936). Conversely, readers who comprehended the nature of the content could be profoundly moved: one reviewer described Proust's portrait of Monsieur de Charlus as "the most complete and faithful analysis" of "sexual inversion" "ever attempted in fiction" (Flores, 1928), and John Cowper Powys wrote, "Proust has depicted in this man's proud perversity the most touching, pitiful, tragic-comic embodiment of sexual inversion to be found in all literature; a picture so penetrating and withal so sympathetic that the mere contemplation of it has a sensitizing and enlarging effect upon our moral imagination" (1924). Yet another view, however, was urged by the poet Robert Duncan. Writing as a homosexual, Duncan read Charlus as portraying not uniquely "a homosexual" but more universally "a human being" in whom "the forces of pride, self humiliation in love, jealousy, are not special forces but common to all men and women" (1944). Describing himself as one of those who "must face in their own lives both the hostility of society in that they are 'queer' and the hostility of the homosexual cult of superiority in that they are human," Duncan nonetheless asserted that the true liberation for gay writers, like Melville, Proust, and Hart Crane, would be recognition not for "one's special nature and value," but for "a devotion to human freedom, toward the liberation of human love, human conflicts, human aspirations."

SEE ALSO: *Negro, New Negro; Race; Words, Language*

References

(1914). "Long Beach Recital of Shameless Men." *Los Angeles Times* (November 19), II: 1.

Anderson, Margaret C. (1915). "Mrs. Ellis's Failure." *Little Review* 2.1 (March): 16–19.

Auden, W. H. (1936). *Look, Stranger!: Poems*. London: Faber and Faber.

Barnes, Djuna (1936). *Nightwood*. London: Faber and Faber.

Carpenter, Edward (1894). *Homogenic Love and its Place in a Free Society*. Printed for private circulation only. Manchester: Labour Press Society.

Carpenter, Edward (1908). *The Intermediate Sex: A Study of Some Transitional Types of Men and Women*. London: G. Allen and Unwin.

Cozzens, James Gould (1936). *Men and Brethren*. New York: Harcourt, Brace and Co.

Douglas, Lord Alfred (1894). "Two Loves." *The Chameleon* 1.1: 26–28.

Duncan, Lee (1936). *Over the Wall, the Autobiography of an Ex-convict*. New York: E. P. Dutton.

Duncan, Robert (1944). "The Homosexual in Society." *Politics* (March), 209–211.

Ellis, Havelock and John Addington Symonds (1897). *Sexual Inversion*. 1st Engl. ed. [*Das konträre Geschlechtsgefühl* 1896]. London: Wilson and Macmillan.

Flores, Angel (1928). "Marcel Proust in Review." *The Bookman* (US) (May), 272–276.

Hall, Radclyffe (1928). *The Well of Loneliness*. London: Jonathan Cape; Garden City: Sun Dial.

Healy, William (1922). *The Practical Value of Scientific Study of Juvenile Delinquents*. Monograph prepared for the Children's Bureau. U.S. Department of Labor. Washington, DC: Government Printing Office.

Hughes, Langston (1951). "Café 3 A.M." In *Montage of a Dream Deferred*. New York: Henry Holt. 32.

Isherwood, Christopher (1939). *Goodbye to Berlin*. London: Hogarth.

Krafft-Ebing, R. von (1892). *Psychopathia Sexualis*. With Special Reference to Contrary Sexual Instinct: A Medico-Legal Study. [*Psychopathia Sexualis: eine Klinisch-Forensische Studie*, 1st ed. 1886]. Trans. of 7th enl. and rev. German ed. Trans. Charles Gilbert Chaddock. Philadelphia and London: F. A. Davis.

Leavis, F. R. (1936). "Mr. Auden's Talent." Rev. of *Look, Stranger! Poems* by W. H. Auden and *The Ascent of F.6* by W. H. Auden and Christopher Isherwood. *Scrutiny* 5 (December): 323–327.

Levenson, Lew [pseudonym] (1934). *Butterfly Man*. New York: Macaulay.

Lewis, Wyndham (1926). *The Art of Being Ruled*. London: Chatto & Windus.

Lewis, Wyndham (1930). *The Apes of God*. London: Arthur.

Maurer, David W. (1935). "The Lingo of the Good-People." *American Speech* 10.1 (February): 10–23.

McAlmon, Robert (1925). *Distinguished Air* (Grim Fairy Tales). Paris: Printed for Contact editions at the Three Mountains Press.

Powys, John Cowper (1924). "Marcel Proust." *The North American Review* (March), 408–412.

Proust, Marcel (1924). *Within a Budding Grove* [*À l'ombre des jeunes filles en fleurs*, 1918]. Trans. C. K. Scott-Moncrieff. Vol. 2 of *Remembrance of Things Past* [*À la recherche du temps perdu*]. 8 vols. New York: T. Seltzer; Modern Library.

Proust, Marcel (1927). *Cities of the Plain* [*Sodome et Gomorrhe*, 1922]. Trans. C. K. Scott-Moncrieff. Vol. 4 of *Remembrance of Things Past* [*À la recherche du temps perdu*]. 8 vols. New York: A. and C. Boni.

Stein, Gertrude (1922). "Miss Furr and Miss Skeene." In *Geography and Plays*. Boston: Four Seas Co.

Stekel, Dr. Wilhelm (1914). "Masked Homosexuality." Translated and annotated by S. A. Tannenbaum M. D. *American Medicine* 20 (August): 530–537.

Woolf, Virginia (1975–1980). Letter to Roger Fry, 17 October 1921. [1921]. In *The Letters of Virginia Woolf* (eds. Nigel Nicolson and Joanne Trautmann). 6 vols. London: Chatto & Windus. Vol. 2: 484–485.

Woolf, Virginia (1977–1984). "Diary entry, February 19, 1923." [1923]. In *The Diary of Virginia Woolf* (ed. Anne Olivier Bell). 5 vols. London: Hogarth. Vol. 2: 235.

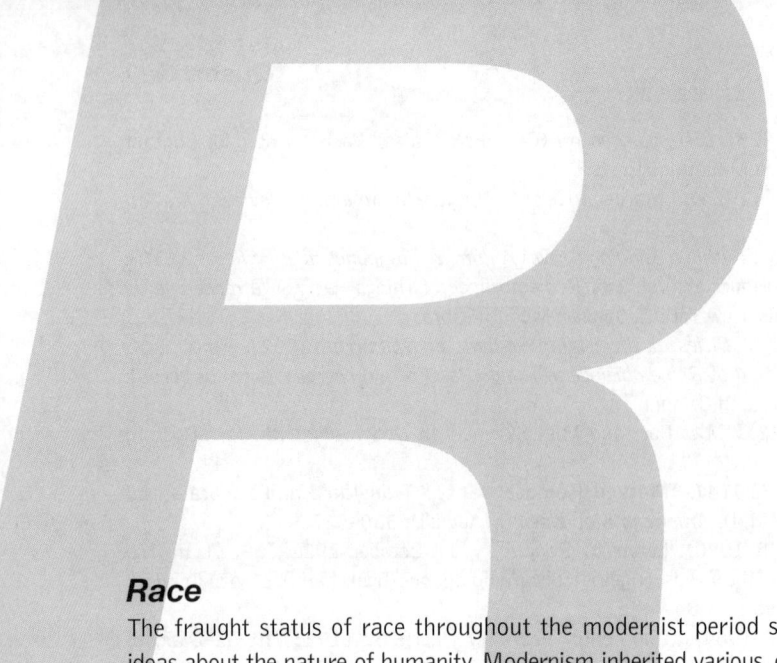

Race

The fraught status of race throughout the modernist period speaks to changing ideas about the nature of humanity. Modernism inherited various, often contradictory, meanings for race, while adding numerous new formulations of its own. The use of race to denote human race or "people" was still prominent in C20, but was accompanied by a confusing and proliferating array of applications to genetic or cultural groups. Concepts of distinct racial identity were employed for group solidarity or for critical self-examination but could also embody destructive assumptions concerning the superiority or inferiority of specific racial groups. The entrance of racist (1925) and racism (1932) into public discourse indicated growing concerns about "racial prejudice" (1859). The increasing appearance of alternative nomenclatures, such as "minority peoples" (1932) and "ethnic groups" (1935), reflects the search for a new vocabulary adequate to the increasing complexity of social, economic, political, and cultural relations. With the growing understanding that, as Jean Toomer put it, "words were the original germ carriers of the majority of our prejudices" ([1935]1993), race was examined, qualified, placed in quotation marks, and disclaimed.

The generalized use of race for humanity encountered new challenges for conceiving universals in light of human difference. As an inclusive term, human race appears in contexts concerning the life and survival of the human species. In celebrating poetry's "Promethean" power, Edith Sitwell wrote that "the human

ABCDEFGHIJKLMNOPQ**R**STUVWXYZ

Modernism: Keywords, First Edition. Melba Cuddy-Keane, Adam Hammond, and Alexandra Peat.
© 2014 Melba Cuddy-Keane. Published 2014 by John Wiley & Sons, Ltd.

race began/with but a single word" (1948), while W. H. Auden recalled how his boyhood self despairingly threw his poems into the school pond, on the grounds that "the human race would be saved by science" (Pudney, 1960). Inherited notions of the human race as a universal category, however, acquired conflicted associations as modernists debated whether one's primary allegiance should be globally to the human race or locally to one's own community. An editorial in the *New Age*, urging "a vigorous propaganda of internationalism and even of cosmo-politanism," declared, "we are citizens of the world, or ought to be; and the future of the human race is vastly more important than the future of the Anglo-Saxon section" ("Imperial," 1907). Conversely, a subsequent letter to the editor argued that "human race" is a meaningless "abstraction" and that Socialism must turn to the local community or the State for "economic salvation" (C. Chesterton, 1907). Other usages conceived human race as newly defined by pervasive intermixing. W. E. B. Du Bois wrote that a modern world that was "shrinking together" spelled an "increased and increasing contact of groups and nations and races" that made "race or group separation" "not only impracticable" but "against the whole trend of the age" (1908). Ford Madox Ford found that the "vastness" of London as a "world town" "destroyed all race characteristics," and he declared "the almost obsolete word 'race'" to be an inaccurate definition for "a people so mixed already" (1905).

When used to denote distinct identity, racial categories were eclectically derived from ancestry, biology, cultural history, or geographical region, as in generalized references to the African, Celtic, Anglo-Saxon, or Oriental races. Reflecting a heightened interest in self-ethnography, James Joyce's Stephen Dedalus proclaims of his Irish heritage, "this race and this country and this life produced me," and announces his goal to "forge in the smithy of my soul the uncreated conscience of my race" (1916); one of John Galsworthy's characters describes the English as "one of the plainest and most distorted races of the world," adding, however, a slight commendation for their "good temper" and "guts" (1924). In other, still looser, usages, race identified linguistic community: English- and French-speaking populations were identified as "two races" whose political struggles represented the "racial trouble in Canada" ("The Canadian Elections," 1900). In South Africa, indigenous peoples were described as "native races," but discussion of "reconciliation" and "union" more likely referred to tensions between "the two white races" (Harmsworth, 1908). When Leonard Barnes writes of "racialistic emotion," "racial hostility," and "racial feeling" in South Africa, he refers to rela-tions between "the Briton and the Dutchman" (1930). Race could also refer to class. Henry James's Valentin de Bellegarde calls the French aristocracy his race ([1877]1907), while in James Oppenheim's "Bread and Roses" – the poem that gave a slogan to the American labor movement – the line "the rising of the women means the rising of the race" implies the improvement of the human race through the efforts of the working class, especially the activist women in the trade union movement (1911). When Henry James writes of George Sand's "duty of avenging on the unscrupulous race of men their immemorial selfish success with the plastic race of women" (1897), or William Faulkner's Amstrid compares the "woman race" and "man race" (1932), race becomes a synonym for gender. A 1903 essay on romanticism – invoking a need for "comparative raciology" – even uses race as a literary category, arguing that the ancient folk consciousness of "a single racial mind" became channeled, through "spiritual and physical miscegenation," into the various "race streams" of modern literature (Swiggett 1903).

As race became increasingly used to designate hereditary, ethnic, or national groups, it accrued evaluative elevations and denigrations. D. H. Lawrence singled out the Italians for praise as "almost the only race with the souls of artists" (1916), but Yoshio Markino, arriving in America, was horrified by the way the "savage people" in San Francisco treated the Japanese "as an inferior race," a situation happily contrasted with the "cosmopolitan ideas" he later encountered in London (1910). At an official level, the notion of "the governing races" as the "guardians and trustees of the subject races" had provided the ideological foundation for British Imperialism and, despite increasing recognition of the abuses and fundamental wrongs of the system, arguments were still being made urging "responsibilities" to "peoples who are passing through the difficult transition period between barbarism and civilization" (Harmsworth, 1908). Concepts of a "superior" race were bolstered by the influence of eugenics, a school of thought whose founder, Sir Francis Galton, endorsed practices of "judicious mating [. . .] to give the more suitable races or strains of blood a better chance of prevailing speedily over the less suitable" (1883). While Galton was concerned primarily with improving the human race by weeding out those deemed to be intellectually and physically feeble, his comparative assessments of different races provided a foundation for Hitler's declaration of the superiority of the Nordic race and his identification of the "international" "Jewish race" as "a parasite living on the body and the productive work of other nations," liable to incur its own "annihilation" in Europe ([1939]1942). From the 1920s on, anti-Semitism became the main target of protests against race prejudice in the UK. As reported in the *TLS*, a 1926 socialist book *Are the Jews a Race?* answered its rhetorical question with a "no," arguing that Jews were a group of people characterized by the effects of forced urbanization, while *The Jew and His Neighbour* explained the causes of anti-Semitism as first economic, then racial, and, in contemporary Germany, a blend of the two, supported by the Hegelian ideal of a homogeneous nation-state (1931). In 1939, Wyndham Lewis provocatively entitled his protest against anti-Semitism *The Jews: Are they Human?* while numerous Jewish voices protested categorizations of Jews as a race. Max Margolis declared it "self-evident" that "we Jews are not a race in the sense of a black or yellow race" (1910), and Rabbi

186

Milton Steinberg asserted that the term "race" was "altogether inapplicable to Jewry," recommending the term "people" instead (1945). The first appearances of racist and racism were indictments of national ideologies in Europe based on belief in racial superiority. The OED records the combined use, in the *Manchester Guardian* (1926), of "the German Nationals and the Racists" and, in the *Christian Science Monitor* (1932), of "Fascism or Racism."

The turn of C20 saw a resurgence of nativist movements in the US based on notions of the racial purity (and superiority) of the original settlers, mixing a reaction against US imperialist expansionism with resistance to foreign immigration at home. Bolstered by eugenicist theory, Madison Grant's *The Passing of a Great Race* (1916) argued that "the intrusion of hordes of immigrants of inferior racial value" was threatening to destroy the Nordic-based "American aristocracy" who alone could offer government by the "wisest and best." At the same time, fears of declining birth rates among the native-born American population spawned the hyperbolic term "race suicide." On the opposite side, arguments arose for racial intermixing. Gustave Michaud's "What Shall We Be? The Coming Race in America" (1903), while delineating specific characteristics for what he considered distinct racial groups, argued for the inclusion in America of the Baltic and the Alpine/Mediterranean, for "we need every one of the qualities of the two alien races." A character in Israel Zangwill's *The Melting Pot* (1909) speaks of America as the "crucible" in which "all the races of Europe are melting and reforming." Nativist arguments were also countered with protests that it was not the Nordic race that was threatened. In *Our America* (1919), Waldo Frank described America as "a turmoiled giant" whose "feet are sunk in the quicksands of racial and material passion," deploring the "march of the white man across the continent" as "the flowing of a Stream" that "overwhelmed the life that stood in its way." Zane Grey's *Vanishing American* (1925) was the native "Indian" threatened by "the incredible brutality and ruthlessness of white men toward his race."

187

Increasingly, racial categorization hardened along the lines of skin color. The first novel in Thomas Dixon's Klan trilogy, *The Leopard's Spots* (1902), describes the South in terms of "two hostile armies [. . .] with race marks as uniforms – the Black against the White." F. Scott Fitzgerald's Tom Buchanan, reading a book on "The Rise of the Colored Empires" by "this man Goddard" – a possible conflation of Madison Grant and Lothrop Stoddard – epitomizes the nativist fear that "if we don't look out the white race will be [. . .] utterly submerged" (*Gatsby*, 1925); on the other side, Marcus Garvey asserted the right to believe in "a pure black race just as how all self-respecting whites believe in a pure white race" ([1923]1986). The "dawning consciousness of race" (Stone, 1908) forced discussion of what was increasingly identified as the "race problem" (Fleming, 1906). In 1903, W. E. B. Du Bois described "the problem of the twentieth century" as the "relation of the darker to the lighter races" – a verdict that seemed tragically born out in the 1919 "Race Riots" (most drastic in Chicago but extending as far as Cardiff, Wales). While the acknowledgement that whites were the greater perpetrators in the violence prompted efforts to combat racial prejudice, as the very *naming* of the riots indicates, the conflict was attributed more to skin color than to the labor unrest that erupted following the return of soldiers after WWI. While the riots thus further ensconced ideas of racial division, the black newspaper the *Chicago Whip* responded by calling for "men in public office who are class and color blind" (Editorial, 1919), and research from the emerging discipline of sociology often promoted integration rather than segregation: from the Chicago school, Robert E. Park's influential theory of "race relations" that posited a social progression through competition, conflict, accommodation, and assimilation (1921); and from North Carolina, the inauguration, in 1922, of *The Journal of Social Forces*, featuring a regular section on "inter-racial co-operation."

At the same time, the New Negro Movement, later known as the Harlem Renaissance, treated race as a source of pride. Black artists and activists strove not only to combat racism through the arts but also to educate and inspire African Americans by celebrating their distinct identity. *The Brownies Book*, a periodical aimed at African American children, for which Jessie Fauset was literary editor, was established after calls for a children's magazine to "help us reach the goal of race unity" and "awaken in the consciousness of children race consciousness and race pride" (Clifford, 1917). Lamenting the lack of stories of "great Negroes," Fauset believed it "urgent that ambitious Negro youth be able to read of the achievements of their race" and advocated "a sort of 'Plutarch's Lives' for the Negro race" to disprove the idea that there were "only great white people" (1932). African American culture also received support from outside: Nancy Cunard devoted significant attention to the "strength" and "beauty" of the "Negro race," railing against "color prejudice" and "race barriers" on "all sides" (1934). D. D. T. Jabavu described a "general world movement of awakening race-consciousness that is stirring all coloured peoples in Japan, China, Egypt, the United States and the British West Indies" as well as South Africa (1922).

Despite such persistent tendencies to think in terms of racial characteristics, race was increasingly questioned as a meaningful category. Numerous writers rejected the belief in fixed inherited traits, the attribution of sharp divisions between peoples, and the presumed homogeneity of particular groups. As early as 1901, H. G. Wells condemned those "unobservant, scholarly people" who "talk or write in the profoundest manner about a Teutonic race or a Celtic race." Aldous Huxley similarly dismissed the word race as a "conductor of nonsense," adding, "there are no snakes in Ireland and no races in Europe" (1933). E. M. Forster believed it "extraordinary [. . .] that governments which claim to be realistic should try to base themselves on anything so shadowy and romantic as race" (1951). "We must ask ourselves," Margery Perham posed in *The Times*, "whether we can continue to indulge ourselves any longer in an attitude of mind which, at its worst, regards other races of men almost as if they were another species" (1942). Du Bois declared, "race is psychology; not biology" (1933); Julian Huxley and A. C. Haddon criticized Hitler's *Mein Kampf* as falsely constructing "'racial' characterizations" based on "physical descent" rather than "social and cultural elements" (1935). Huxley and Haddon indeed proposed that "race" be "dropped from the vocabulary of science," preferring "ethnic" as a term that would acknowledge "language, religion, culture or tradition" as "at least as important" as "kinship" in producing cohesion in groups. In light of the difficulties inherent in concepts of racial difference, "human race" came back into use but in tentative, less uniform, and more complex ways. Jean Toomer, explaining his reluctance to be defined as a black artist, wrote, "I am at once no one of the races and I am all of them. [. . .] It may be the turning point for the return of mankind, now divided into hostile races, to one unified race, namely the human race" ([1928]1996). While William Carlos Williams, skeptical about the way unification could mean sameness and the death of the individual imagination, wrote parodically of "the human race, yellow, black, brown, red and white, agglutinated into one enormous soul" (1923), in Virginia Woolf's *The Years* – a novel that probes the desire, as articulated by one character, to be both the "bubble" (individual) and "the stream" (the collective) – the homosexual, Russian, and probably Jewish Nicholas Pomjalovsky raises his glass to "the human race," adding, "which is now in its infancy, may it grow to maturity!" (1937). How to combine unity and difference is a problem foregrounded in modernist language once again.

SEE ALSO: *Common Mind, Group Thinking; Democracy; Empire, Imperialism; Fascism; Hygiene; International; Negro, New Negro; Primitive; Universal*

References

(1900). "The Canadian Elections." *The Literary Digest* (November 24), 626–627.
(1907). "Imperial Education." *The New Age* 1.6 (June 6): 84.
(1919). "A Dangerous Experiment." Editorial. *The Chicago Whip* (August 9): 7.
(1922). "Inter-Racial Co-operation." *The Journal of Social Forces* 1.1 (November): 40–42.
(1926). "racist, n. and adj." *Manchester Guardian* (September 5). OED Online. Oxford University Press.
(1932). "racism, n." *Christian Science Monitor* (October 8). OED Online. Oxford University Press.
Barnes, Leonard (1930). *Caliban in Africa: An Impression of Colour Madness.* London: V. Gollancz.
Chesterton, Cecil (1907). "Correspondence." *The New Age* (June 13): 111.
Clifford, Carrie (1917). "Our Children." *The Crisis: A Record of the Darker Races* (October), 306–307.

189

Race

Cunard, Nancy (1934). "Harlem Reviewed." In *Negro: An Anthology*. Ed. Nancy Cunard. London: Lawrence and Wishart. 67–74.

Dixon, Thomas (1902). *The Leopard's Spots: A Romance of the White Man's Burden – 1865–1900*. New York: Doubleday, Page.

Du Bois, W. E. B. (1903). *The Souls of Black Folk*. Chicago: McClurg.

Du Bois, W. E. B. (1908). "A Reply to Stone." *American Journal of Sociology* 13: 834–838.

Du Bois, W. E. B. (1933). "The Negro College." *The Crisis: A Record of the Darker Races* (August): 175–177.

Faulkner, William (1932). *Light in August*. New York: Smith and Hass.

Fitzgerald, F. Scott (1925). *The Great Gatsby*. New York: Charles Scribner's Sons.

Fleming, William H. (1906). *Slavery and the Race Problem in the South: With Special Reference to the State of Georgia*. Address of the Hon. Wm. H. Fleming, before the Alumni society of the State University, Athens, June 19, 1906. Boston: D. Estes.

[Ford] Hueffer, Ford Madox (1905). *The Soul of London: A Survey of a Modern City*. London: Alston Rivers.

Forster, E. M. (1951). "Racial Exercise." 1939. In *Two Cheers for Democracy*. London: Edward Arnold. 29–32.

Frank, Waldo David (1919). *Our America*. New York: Boni and Liveright.

Galsworthy, John (1924). *The White Monkey*. New York: Charles Scribner's Sons.

Galton, Sir Francis (1883). *Inquiries into Human Faculty and Its Development*. London: Macmillan.

Garvey, Marcus (1986). "A Letter from Garvey to the White Press of the World: An Explanation of the Aims and Objectives of the UNIA, January 1923." [1923]. In *The Marcus Garvey and Universal Negro Improvement Association Papers* (ed. R. A. Hill). Berkeley: University of California Press. 5.

Grant, Madison (1916). *The Passing of a Great Race; or, the Racial Basis of European History*. New York: Scribner.

Grey, Zane (1925). *The Vanishing American*. New York: Harper and Brothers.

Harmsworth, Cecil Bisshopp (1908). *Pleasure and Problem in South Africa*. London: John Lane, The Bodley Head; New York: John Lane.

Hitler, Adolf (1942). Speech delivered in the Reichstag on 30 January 1939 (extracts). [1939]. An English translation of representative passages arranged under subjects and edited by Norman H. Baynes. In *The Speeches of Adolf Hitler, April 1922–August 1939*. Edited and translated by Norman H. Baynes. 2 vols. London: Oxford University Press. Vol. 1: 735–743.

Huxley, Aldous (1933). "The Race Racket." *Chicago Herald and Examiner* (November 3), 9.

Huxley, Julian and Alfred C. Haddon (1935). *We Europeans: A Survey of "Racial" Problems*. With a chapter on Europe over-seas by A. M. Carr-Saunders. London: Jonathan Cape.

Jabavu, D. D. T. (1922). "Native Unrest in South Africa." *The International Review of Missions* 11.42 (April): 249–259.

James, Henry (1897). "She and He: Recent Documents." *The Yellow Book* 12 (January): 15–38.

James, Henry (1907). *The American*. [1877]. *The Novels and Tales of Henry James*. The New York Edition. 26 vols. New York: Charles Scribner's Sons. Vol. 2.

Joyce, James (1916). *Portrait of the Artist as a Young Man*. 1914–1915. New York: B. W. Huebsch.

Lawrence, D. H. (1916). *Twilight in Italy*. London: Duckworth.

Lewis, Wyndham (1939). *The Jews: Are they Human?* London: G. Allen & Unwin

Margolis, Max (1910). "What Are We?" *B'nai B'rith News* (March–April), 3.

Markino, Yoshio (1910). *A Japanese Artist in London*. London: Chatto & Windus.

Michaud, Gustave (1903). "What Shall We Be? 1. The Coming Race in America." *The Century Magazine* (March), 683–689.

Oppenheim, James (1911). "Bread and Roses." *American Magazine* (December), 214.

Park, Robert Ezra and Ernest W. Burgess (eds.) (1921). *Introduction to the Science of Sociology*. Chicago: University of Chicago Press.

Perham, Margery (1942). "The Colonial Empire II: Capital, Labour, and the Colour-Bar." *The Times* (London) (March 14), 5.

Pudney, John (1960). *Home and Away: An Autobiographical Gambit*. London: Michael Joseph.

[Stannard, H. M.] (1926). "Socialism and Judaism." Rev. of *Are the Jews a Race?* by Karl Kautsky. *TLS* (September 23), 622.

[Stannard, H. M.] (1931). "Anti-Semitism." Rev. of *The Jew and His Neighbour: A Study of the Causes of Anti-Semitism* by James Parkes. *TLS* (March 5), 166.

Starkey, Marion L. (1932). "Jessie Fauset." *Southern Workman* 61 (May): 217–20.

Sitwell, Edith (1948). "For T. S. Eliot." In *T. S. Eliot: A Symposium*. Compiled by Richard March and Tambimuttu. London: Editions Poetry. 33–34.

Steinberg, Milton (1945). *A Partisan Guide to the Jewish Problem*. Indianapolis: Bobbs-Merrill.

Stone, Alfred Holt (1908). "Is Race Friction Between Blacks and Whites in the United States Growing and Inevitable?" *American Journal of Sociology* 13.5 (March): 676–697.

Swiggett, Glen Levin (1903). "What is Romanticism?" *The Sewanee Review* 11.2: 144–160.

Toomer, Jean (1993). "Germ Carriers." An excerpt from p. 13 of Toomer's second draft of "Preface #3" for "BOOK X." [March 13, 1935]. In *A Jean Toomer Reader: Selected Unpublished Writings* (ed. Frederik L. Rusch). New York: Oxford University Press. 82.

Toomer, Jean (1996). "The Crock of Problems" [1928]. In *Jean Toomer: Selected Essays and Literary Criticism* (ed. Robert B. Jones). Knoxville: University of Tennessee Press. 55–59.

Wells, H. G. (1901). "Anticipations: An Experiment in Prophecy V." *The North American Review* (October), 554–566.

Williams, William Carlos (1923). *Spring and All*. Paris: Contact.

Woolf, Virginia (1937). *The Years*. London: Hogarth.

Zangwill, Israel (1909). *The Melting Pot: Drama in Four Acts*. New York: Macmillan.

191

Readers, Reading

Modernism was the first literary period to experience near-universal literacy in English-speaking countries, a development of which modernist writers were intensely aware. Henry Seidel Canby noted, "Substantially all can read now" (1926), while Virginia Woolf observed, "For the first time in history there are readers – a large body of people, occupied in business, in sport, in nursing their grandfathers, in tying up parcels behind counters – they all read now" (1932b).

Readers, Reading

The widespread significance of this enlarged readership was registered in the proliferation of descriptive terms for it. When addressed individually, the reader could be the "ordinary reader" (Joseph Conrad), the "plain reader" (Laura Riding and Robert Graves), the "common reader" (Virginia Woolf, quoting Samuel Johnson), the "average reader" (Arnold Bennett), the "general reader" (Wyndham Lewis), and the "low-brow reader" (Ezra Pound). When addressed as a group, readers could be the "generality of readers" (D. H. Lawrence), the "greater public" (Rupert Brooke), the "general public" (Galsworthy), or even the "Dummy Public" (Mina Loy). The new expanded readership attracted strongly divided opinions, in response to its vast size and diversification. In one view, the reading public could be classified according to class, education, taste, and native abilities; in another approach, audiences were segregated by different reading practices, in which the gap between amateur and specialist reading played a large role. Readers and reading thus posed challenging questions for writers and critics. Who was the modernist reader, or was it possible to know? What were the tastes and abilities of the ordinary reader, and could these be improved? Was it better to write for all readers or for the sympathetic few? Was the reader merely the recipient of the text or a kind of cocreator of the work? The plurality of answers to these questions – both in different writers and within the divided consciousnesses of some individuals – reveals the question of audience to be a primary modernist concern.

192

Regarding the audience for literature, the general reader most commonly signified the newly literate and/or less culturally privileged reader, and therefore the dominant group in terms of size. The vastness of the composite readership and its potential influence in the marketplace fostered oppositional constructions of putatively competing readerships, as vividly portrayed in Arnold Bennett's "The 'Average Reader' and the Recipe for Popularity" (1901). Claiming that "everyone is an artist, more or less," Bennett objected to "the division of the world into two classes" – the "minority" and the "majority" – and the former's claim to "a monopoly" on "'artistic feeling.'" Yet Bennett devoted much of his essay to characterizing the "average reader" in strikingly ambivalent terms. While "an intelligent and reasonable being," and "neither an idiot nor perverse," this reader, Bennett stated, differed from "many members of the minority who have a passion and a true though limited taste for books." The average reader, Bennett claimed, even possessed "some of the instincts of the untutored savage," preferring "crudity" to "fine shades": "Unless he is knocked down, or blinded, or deafened, he does not consider that he has been impressed." Moreover, Bennett contended, "the average reader does not care to have the basic ideas of his existence disturbed," and can harbor a "personal animus" against authors who attempt to "readjust his scheme of things." Such a limiting assessment of the average reader was shared by at least two of Bennett's contemporaries – somewhat oddly, since both, like Bennett, were best sellers and popularly well received. Advising a young writer to bring an essay to a clear conclusion, Joseph Conrad warned of the "inconceivable stupidity of the common reader – the man who forks out the half-crown," explaining that the "ordinary reader [. . .] wants the nail hit on the head before his eyes simply in order that he should see the nail" ([1908]1990a) – an advice, however, he clearly did not take himself, confessing later that year that he had just written an "obscure beginning and an unfathomable *denoûment*" ([1908]1990b). John Galsworthy held it "unfortunately true" that "the greater public will by preference take the lowest article in art offered to it" (1919). Q. D. Leavis blamed the publishing industry for this state of affairs: by offering merely "What the Public Wants," publishers produced an environment in which "poetry and criticism is not read by the common reader," nor even "modern literature," so that the "critical minority to whose sole charge modern literature [had] fallen" was left "isolated, disowned by the general public and threatened with extinction" (1932).

Such dim views of the fate of readership were balanced, however, with belief in readers' potentials. Galsworthy qualified his pessimism by arguing that taste would improve if reading matter of better quality were marketed to the greater public: "if a better article be substituted, the greater public very soon enjoys it every bit as much as the article replaced" (1919). Broadcasting with her husband Leonard, Virginia Woolf voiced her faith in readers' natural development: although they "rush for the sweets and cakes first – for the easy books and the flashy books and the books that ask no trouble in reading" yet, as "they grow to maturity as readers, they will tire of the sweets and pastries, and will demand good beef and mutton – that is to say, interesting books, difficult books, histories, biographies, poetry" ([1927]2006). Like Q. D. Leavis, Henry Seidel Canby tied the nature of the reader to the nature of the proffered reading. In "High-Brow Editorial" (1926), he deplored the "barren triviality" of most printed material, arguing that "excessive reading" of "flat and flatulent" newspapers and magazines meant the "print-fed modern" with his "type-crammed brain" could "connect his mind, like a telephone, to anything, anywhere" but was no longer capable of original thought. Six years later, however, Canby adopted a different perspective, stating that "not half enough has been said for the reader" and arguing that "only the defeatist and the intellectual snob will believe that the masses with new reading time are incapable of better reading than the slush now offered them" – referring again to "pulp magazines and tabloid newspapers" (1932). Turning his attention to "Proletariat Literature," Canby further judged the current literature being written "about the proletariat," with its "record of injustice and thwarting," to be inappropriate for the coming "emancipated workers" with "new hours of freedom"; instead, he called for a "new proletariat literature" (written presumably *by* the proletariat) depicting "the kind of life that a steel worker on a five-day week will find that he can read about with profit and pleasure."

193

While arguments thus proliferated for better writing for the general public, the increasing diversity and complexity of modern readership added significantly to the challenges of the writer's task. In Harold Nicolson's view, "the spread of education, the popular press, the wireless and the cinema" had "increased the reading public until it ha[d] become immeasurable, impersonal and vast" (1931). Reflecting on the difficulty of communicating personal memories, Virginia Woolf lamented, "one may well despair of rendering a clear account to a third person, let alone to a multiple of many people such as the general public" (1918). The goal of inclusive readership was also a bone of contention: was it more democratic to write for all or to have the freedom to write for a sympathetic and comprehending few? Bennett's essay, although written expressly to explain the "majority" to the "minority," nonetheless advocated their combination: "I believe that a novel could be written which would unite in a mild ecstasy of praise the two extremes – the most inclusive majority and the most exclusive minority" (1901). In contrast, D. H. Lawrence defended his right to write in his own way and the right of readers either to read him or not, as they chose. Explaining that he didn't "intend [his] books for the generality of readers" or the "generality of critics," and holding it "a mistake of our mistaken democracy, that every man who can read print" should "believe that he can read all that is printed," Lawrence left it to the reader to decide: "if anybody wants to read it, let him. But why anybody should read one single word if he doesn't want to, I don't see" (1922). Ezra Pound's *How to Read*, however, identified its intended readership as broad and mixed, stating that it was written for instructors, students, "men who haven't had time for systemized college courses," and for "health of thought outside literary circles and in non-literary existence, in general and communal life" (1931). In her two volumes addressed to *The Common Reader*, Woolf went further to align herself with the amateur reader, valuing "the opinion of people reading for the love of reading, slowly and unprofessionally" (1932a), and placing herself not against the cultured minority, but against the narrow specialist practices she identified with the study of English within the universities of her time. Despite attracting just such a specialized readership, T. S. Eliot held that "the poet naturally prefers to write for as large and miscellaneous an audience and possible" and "would like to be something of a popular entertainer"; he extolled the theatre for appealing to a diverse audience simultaneously on different levels and to "larger groups of people collectively" (1933).

The most positive and hopeful modernist approaches saw the reader as collaborator and cocreator in the production of the literary work. The same Joseph Conrad who warned about the "inconceivable stupidity of the common reader" wrote to his friend and supporter R. Cunninghame Graham, "To know that *You* could read me is good news indeed – for one writes only half the book: the other half is with the reader" ([1897]1983–1988). Conrad similarly praised Arthur

Symonds for what his responses had "given": "A reader like you puts so much of his own high quality into a work he is reading directly the writer has been lucky enough to awaken his sympathy!" ([1908]1990b). Ernest Hemingway's famous image of the iceberg expressed a sense of unspoken intimacy between author and reader: "If a writer of prose knows enough about what he is writing about," Hemingway wrote, "he may omit things that he knows and the reader, if the writer is writing truly enough, will have a feeling of these things as strongly as though the writer had stated them"; just as "the dignity of movement of an ice-berg is due to only one-eighth of it being above water," so too the movement of good prose, Hemingway suggested, is due to the writer's willingness to trust the reader to intuit seven eighths of his story (1932). Woolf held that "the art of writing consists in laying an egg in the reader's mind from which springs the thing itself" (1947), and she urged the reader to be the writer's "fellow worker and accomplice" (1932a). Louise Rosenblatt, a pioneer of what would later be called reader-response criticism, argued in *Literature as Exploration* (1938) that "literature [could] only result from creative activity on the part of the reader himself." Reading for her was a "synthesizing process" in which "the reader performs the poem or the novel, much as the violinist performs the sonata": "under the guidance of the text, out of his own thoughts and feelings and sensibilities, the reader makes a new ordering, the formed substance that is for him the literary work of art." In *The Craft of Fiction* (1921), Percy Lubbock had argued much earlier, "the reader of a novel [. . .] is himself a novelist" since "he is the maker of the book which may or may not please his taste when it is finished, but a book for which he must take his own share of responsibility." "The reader," he claimed, must "never [permit] himself to suppose that the creation of the book is solely the affair of the author": "both of them make the novel."

195

SEE ALSO: *Advertising; Best Seller; Coterie, Bloomsbury; Democracy; Difficulty, Obscurity; Form, Formalism; Highbrow, Hiddlebrow, Lowbrow; Propaganda*

References

Bennett, E. A. [Enoch Arnold] (1901). "The 'Average Reader' and the Recipe for Popularity." In *Fame and Fiction: An Enquiry into Certain Popularities*. London: Grant Richards. 3–20.

Canby, Henry Seidel (1926). "A High-Brow Editorial." *The Saturday Review of Literature* (October 9), 165.

Canby, Henry Seidel (1932). "Proletariat Literature." *The Saturday Review of Literature* (November 19), 249–250.

Conrad, Joseph (1983–1988). Letter to R. B. Cunninghame Graham, 5 August 1897. [1897]. In *The Collected Letters of Joseph Conrad* (eds. Frederick R. Karl and Laurence Davies). 4 vols. Cambridge: Cambridge University Press. Vol. 1: 1861–1897: 370.

Conrad, Joseph (1990a). Letter to Arthur Symonds, 29 August 1908. [1908]. In *The Collected Letters of Joseph Conrad. Vol. 4: 1908–1911* (eds. Frederick R. Karl and Laurence Davies). Cambridge: Cambridge University Press. 113.

Conrad, Joseph (1990b). Letter to Norman Douglas, 29 February 1908. [1908]. In *The Collected Letters of Joseph Conrad. Vol. 4: 1908–1911* (eds. Frederick R. Karl and Laurence Davies). Cambridge: Cambridge University Press. 51–55.

Eliot, T. S. (1933). "Conclusion." In *The Use of Poetry and the Use of Criticism*. London: Faber and Faber. 143–156.

Galsworthy, John (1919). "The Drama in England and America." In *Another Sheaf*. London: W. Heinemann. 88–109.

Hemingway, Ernest (1932). *Death in the Afternoon*. New York: Charles Scribner's Sons.

Lawrence, D. H. (1922). *Fantasia of the Unconscious*. New York: Thomas Seltzer.

Leavis, Q. D. (1932). *Fiction and the Reading Public*. London: Chatto & Windus.

Lubbock, Percy (1921). *The Craft of Fiction*. London: Jonathan Cape.

Nicolson, Harold (1931). "Are Modern Writers Selfish?" *The Listener* 6.145 (October 21): 684–686.

Pound, Ezra (1931). *How to Read*. London: D. Harmsworth.

Rosenblatt, Louise M. (1938). *Literature as Exploration*. New York and London: D. Appleton-Century.

Woolf, Leonard and Woolf, Virginia (2006). "Are Too Many Books Written and Published?" [1927]. Ed. Melba Cuddy-Keane. *PMLA* 121: 235–244.

Woolf, Virginia (1932a). "How Should One Read a Book?" In *The Common Reader: Second Series*. London: Hogarth. 258–270.

Woolf, Virginia (1932b). "A Letter to a Young Poet." In *The Hogarth Letters*. London: Hogarth. 5–28.

Woolf, Virginia (1947). "Fishing." In *The Moment and Other Essays*. London: Hogarth. 176–179.

Reality, Realism

Modernist debate surrounding the terms reality and realism was intense and wide-ranging, taking in every stage of the artistic process. Which literary method is truest to reality? What aspect of reality is most important to represent? Who is served by realistic writing? What social aims can realism achieve? What is reality? Disagreement abounded on each of these fundamental questions. Underlying wide-ranging opinions, however, was a broadly shared assumption: with very few exceptions – for example, Oscar Wilde, who declared, "as a method realism is a complete failure," and proposed, "truth is entirely and absolutely a matter of style" (1889) – modernist artists of opposing camps shared the aim of expressing reality and defended their own method on the ground that it came closest to doing so. Virginia Woolf's response to Arnold Bennett's claim, "it is only if characters are real that the novel has any chance of surviving" (1923), was characteristically not to reject the project of realistic representation, but to question the right of traditional authorities to dictate what reality is: "what is reality?," she asked, "and who are the judges of reality?" (1924). Bertolt Brecht argued, "the concept of realism [. . .] must first be cleansed before use, for it is an old concept, much used by many people and for many ends" ([1938]1974). The continual process of "cleansing" conventional literary methods of depicting reality, of seeking out new ways to capture an ever-evolving reality, is characteristic of most schools of literary modernism – as is the recognition that a constantly shifting reality will elude final representation.

Before C20, "reality" was already a disputed term, defined in various binaries with contradictory results: as the imaginative or spiritual truth underlying material appearance, as the concrete opposed to abstract, or as the (practical) actuality contrasted to the (unrealistic) ideal (Williams, 1976). What is perhaps most characteristic in the modernist literary response to the problem of "reality," however, is the embrace of reality in all its contradictions. Rather than insisting upon a particular vision of reality, many modernists believed there were many realities, that these overlapped and were irresolvable to any single essence, and thus that the whole question was difficult – if not impossible – to judge. Henry James described as "commendable" Maupassant's claim, "it is [. . .] absurd to say that there is, for the novelist's use, only one reality of things" (1888), and in "The Art of Fiction" (1884), James himself argued, "the measure of reality is very difficult to fix." F. T. Marinetti declared, "nothing is as paradoxical [. . .] or fantastic as reality" (1911), and Eugene Jolas described the interwar generation as dominated by "the tendency [. . .] to deny the absoluteness of reality" (1928). H. D.'s *The Walls Do Not Fall* suggested almost infinite overlapping subjective realities, each offering a different approach to realities that were shared: "But my mind (yours)/ has its peculiar ego-centric/personal approach/to the eternal realities/and differs from every other/in minute particulars" (1944). Wallace Stevens argued, "The poet has his own meaning for reality, and the painter has, and the musician has; and besides what it means to the intelligence and to the senses, it means something to everyone." "Reality is things as they are," Stevens asserted; "The general sense of the word proliferates its special senses. It is a jungle in itself" (1942).

197

The modernist recognition of the multiplicity of reality underlay an effort to develop forms that would express many-sidedness and avoid the trap of presenting one reality as universally valid. In the heat of public debate, however, arguments about the best form for representing reality tended to become polarized into two opposing camps: those arguing for an external, objective approach to reality and those arguing for an internal, subjective approach. Debate about the external school – called "realism" and "naturalism," among other names – centered on the theory and practice of Émile Zola, whose *Le Roman experimental* ([1880]1893), widely disseminated in English, presented an artistic method modeled on scientific experiment and premised on the belief that "it is necessary to descend into the objective reality of things." Writers influenced by Zola tended to highlight the gritty, sordid aspects of reality conventionally deemed nonliterary; Frank Norris's *McTeague* (1889) is typical in its focus on the "horrible reality" of "grimy rags and rust-corroded iron." The social argument of the external school was that objective presentation of conventionally neglected aspects of reality could prompt social change. Zola wrote of "the spirit of truth transforming society" ([1879]1893); in Theodore Dreiser's *The Genius* (1915), the paintings exhibited by the character Eugene "[stand] forth in all their rawness and reality" and shock into heightened awareness those "people [. . .] who do not see life clearly and directly, but only through other people's eyes."

Contemporaries of Zola, however, charged that his approach ignored beauty: Arthur Tilley argued that "true realism" discovered "a halo of romance and interest" in the "apparently commonplace" and held that the "sin of Zola" was being "merely a faithful transcriber" (1883); W. S. Lilly similarly argued that external realism failed the role of art, which should be to "extract from human life, even [. . .] in its most vulgar realities, what it contains of secret beauty" (1885). The most serious critique was that external realism failed to capture reality. Ambrose Bierce, who defined "realism" in *The Devil's Dictionary* (1911) as "the art of depicting nature as it is seen by toads," argued that it missed what was characteristically human. Among modernist writers, the external approach was repeatedly denounced as superficial and incapable of expressing underlying truths. Arnold Bennett anticipated this criticism in an article on the 1910 Post-Impressionist Exhibit; acknowledging the widespread interpretation of his work as "photographic," Bennett wondered if writers like himself were "concerning [them]selves unduly with inessentials" and "worrying [them]selves to achieve infantile realisms" (1910). Samuel Beckett agreed with Proust's "contempt for the literature that 'describes,' for the realists and naturalists worshipping the offal of experience, [. . .] and content to transcribe the surface, the façade, behind which the Idea is prisoner" (1931). Wyndham Lewis contrasted a naturalist painting – presenting the world "as seen by the Camera" – with a Vorticist abstraction which, he argued, captured "REALITY, the essential truth" (1915). In "Notes on Reality" (1929), Eugene Jolas concluded, "Zola's method is not for us. He expressed a milieu and described a segment of his time and world by copying it." Marxist critics in Europe also described external realism as superficial, criticizing it for failing to perceive the social forces at work behind observable reality. Georg Lukács argued, "great realism" looked past "an immediately obvious aspect of reality" to depict "one which is permanent and objectively more significant, namely man in the whole range of his relations to the real world" ([1938]1977). Brecht wrote, "We shall not speak of a realistic manner of writing only when [. . .] we can smell, taste, and feel everything"; rather, "realistic" means "discovering the causal complexes of

198

society" and "unmasking the prevailing view of things as the view of those who are in power" ([1938]1974).

For many modernists, the positive solution to the superficiality of external realism was to develop forms focusing on the interior, the subjective, and the non-scientific. In 1916, Arthur Waugh described "a New Realism of the emotions," which rejected the "conventional realism of conditions and environment" and focused on "the spiritual achievement of man." Virginia Woolf argued that "Modern Fiction" ([1919]1925) should focus on "life or spirit, truth or reality" – "the essential thing" which "refuse[d] to be contained" in the "ill-fitting vestments" of external realism. Rebecca West praised Woolf's *Orlando* for achieving "the profoundest reality" through "the frankest contempt for realism"; though it was "no photograph" and "as inexact a copy of appearances as tapestry," it nonetheless left "in the mind" a subjectively true "picture" "which once apprehended will be incorporated in one like one's own experience" (1928). In responding to the excesses and omissions of the traditional external method, many writers recorded not only subjective experience but also the everyday, focusing on the small, seemingly insignificant detail to suggest the quality of a life. Though Virginia Woolf acknowledged that Defoe approached experience "the opposite way from the psychologist," she praised his "sense of reality" and "genius for fact," noting the way his simple description of "a plain earthenware pot" conjures up "remote islands and the solitudes of the human soul" (1932). In *Mimesis: The Representation of Reality in Western Literature* ([1946]1953), Erich Auerbach in turn praised Woolf's *To the Lighthouse* for the "realistic depth" of everyday scenes such as "the measuring of [a] stocking." Whether employing interior monologues or the simple detail, the aims of these writers were broadly similar: to apprehend reality directly, to represent it truly, and to impart to the reader a new – often unsettling or shocking – way of seeing. William Carlos Williams argued that new forms "must be real, not 'realism' but reality itself": "It is not a matter of 'representation' – which may be represented actually, but of separate existence./enlargement – revivification of values" (1923). For Gertrude Stein, the strangeness of modern reality called for new ways of seeing: "there is no point in being realistic about here and now," she wrote, since "there is no realism now, life is not real it is not earnest, it is strange which is an entirely different matter" (1945). Mina Loy argued that what appeared mere "technical eccentrics" in "Modern Poetry" (1925) were crucial to "the poem's reality": "seeming strangeness is inevitable when any writer has come into an independent contact with nature" and is perceiving it "in a new manner." For many women writers, cleansing perceptions of reality entailed casting off the gendered assumptions of the past. In her foreword to *Pilgrimage* (1938), Dorothy Richardson called her own method – which gave "contemplated reality [. . .] its own say" – "a feminine equivalent of the current masculine realism."

199

Reality, Realism

Such criticism of external realism begat its own responses, particularly from socialist writers who felt that the emphasis on the personal came at the expense of the public. Lukács criticized subjective realism as he did the external variety: through its "fragmentation of objective reality," its "arbitrariness," and its "lack of hierarchic structure," it remained on the surface of experience, failing to penetrate to underlying social causes ([1958]1963). Storm Jameson complained of the "desperate stylists" who "distort reality to verbal ends" and lamented "the paradox of a work drilling deeper and deeper into reality, in order to petrify it" (1950). The form preferred by many socialist writers, particularly in the 1930s, was an external realism based not upon Zola's naturalism – which Sean O'Faoláin rejected for its "bitterness," "aimless objectivity," and "distaste for what it handles" (1937) – but on the documentary film. Storm Jameson argued that the writer, like the photographer, must "keep himself out of the picture while working ceaselessly to present the fact"; while the work must stir the emotions of the reader, "the emotion should spring directly from the fact," and the writer's "job is not to tell us what he felt, but to be coldly and industriously presenting, arranging, selecting, discarding from the mass of his material to get the significant detail" (1937). The narrator of Christopher Isherwood's *Goodbye to Berlin* represents himself not as a photographer but as the camera itself, his passivity, however, suggesting a possible failure of ethical responsibility in such a stance: "I am a camera with its shutter open, quite passive, recording, not thinking" (1939). Walter Benjamin emphasized positively the socialist value of film realism, arguing that "for contemporary man the representation of reality by the film is incomparably more significant than that of the painter" because it presents "an aspect of reality which is free of all equipment" ([1936]1968).

While public debates tended to become polarized along antithetical lines of external versus internal realism, modernist writers from various schools recognized the need to mix representational modes and to combine internal and external approaches. Frank Norris, associated with the Zola school of external realism, argued that if "Accuracy is realism and Truth romanticism," his own version of "Naturalism" represented a middle way, "striv[ing] hard for accuracy and truth" (1901). Virginia Woolf, planning what would become *The Years*, described her desire to capture "both of the realities": to "give the whole of present society – [. . .] facts as well as the vision" ([1933]1977–1984). Sherwood Anderson distinguished "two kinds of realism, the realism to actual life that is the challenge to the journalist and the realism to the book or the story-life"; the latter, while remaining true to the purposive world of the artist's imagination, "must constantly feed on [the former] reality or starve" ([1939]1947). For Ernest Hemingway, the task of the writer was to approach the subjective by means of the objective: to "state [. . .] purely" "the real thing, the sequence of motion and fact which made the emotion" (1932). The ability to combine methods was for many critics a distinguishing feature of modernist art. Erich Auerbach regarded a hybrid "approach to objective reality by means of numerous subjective impressions received by various individuals" as central to "the modern technique" ([1946]1953). Stephen Spender praised W. H. Auden's and Christopher Isherwood's *The Ascent of F6* for maintaining "a rhythmic contrast [. . .] between two entirely different methods of presentation": "realistic scenes of political reportage" and "fantasy or allegory" (1936). Observing the mingling of techniques in "The Novels of Dorothy Richardson," May Sinclair summed up modernism's blended, comprehensive approach to the real: Richardson's style "defies you to distinguish between what is objective and what is subjective either in the reality presented or the art that presents" and demonstrates that "it is absurd to go on talking about realism and idealism, or objective and subjective art" (1918). In a postdualistic age, Sinclair suggested, the most "realistic" forms were those in which disparate realisms overlapped.

SEE ALSO: *Atom, Atomic; Einstein; Form Formalism; Impression, Impressionism; Modern, Modernism; Words, Language*

References

Anderson, Sherwood (1947). "A Writer's Conception of Realism." Limited Publication, 1939. In *The Sherwood Anderson Reader* (ed. Paul Rosenfeld). Boston: Houghton Mifflin. 337–347.

Auerbach, Erich (1953). *Mimesis: The Representation of Reality in Western Literature.* [*Mimesis: Dargestellte Wirklichkeit in der abendländischen Literatur*, 1946]. Trans. Willard R. Trask. Princeton: Princeton University Press.

Beckett, Samuel (1931). *Proust.* London: Chatto & Windus.

Benjamin, Walter (1968). "The Work of Art in the Age of Mechanical Reproduction." ["L'œuvre d'art à l'époque de sa reproduction mécanisée," [1936]; "Das Kunstwerk im Zeitalter seiner technischen Reproduzierbarkeit," [1955]]. Trans. Harry Zorn. In *Illuminations.* Edited with an Introduction by Hannah Arendt. New York: Harcourt, Brace and World.

Bennett, Arnold (as Jacob Tonson) (1910). "Books and Persons." *The New Age* 8.6 (December 8): 135–136.

Bennett, Arnold (1923). "Is the Novel Decaying?" *Cassell's Weekly* (March 28), 47.

Bierce, Ambrose (1911). *The Devil's Dictionary.* Cleveland: World Publishing.

Brecht, Bertolt (1974). "Against Georg Lukács: IV." ["Volkstümlichkeit und Realismus," 1938, 1967]. Trans. Stuart Hood. *The New Left Review* 1.84 (March–April): 48–53.

Dreiser, Theodore (1915). *The Genius.* New York, London and Toronto: John Lane, Bodley Head, S. B. Gundy.

H.D. (1944). *The Walls Do Not Fall.* Oxford: Oxford University Press.

Hemingway, Ernest (1932). *Death in the Afternoon.* New York: Charles Scribner's Sons.

Isherwood, Christopher (1939). *Goodbye to Berlin.* London: Hogarth.

James, Henry (1884). "The Art of Fiction." *Longman's Magazine* 4 (September): 180–186.

James, Henry (1888). "Guy De Maupassant." *The Fortnightly Review* 49 (March): 364–386.

Jameson, Storm (1937). "Documents." *Fact* (July), 9–18.

Jameson, Storm (1950). "The Form of the Novel." In *The Writer's Situation and Other Essays*. London: Macmillan. 37–61.

Jolas, Eugene (1928). "Notes." *transition: An International Quarterly for Creative Experiment* 14 (Fall): 180–185.

Jolas, Eugene (1929). "Notes on Reality." *transition: An International Quarterly for Creative Experiment* 18 (November): 13–20.

Lewis, Wyndham (1915). "The London Group." *Blast* 2 (July): 77–79.

Lilly, W. S. (1885). "The New Naturalism." *The Fortnightly Review* (August), 240–256.

Loy, Mina (1925). "Modern Poetry." *Charm* 3.3 (April): 16–17.

Lukács, Georg (1963). "The Ideology of Modernism." [Gegenwartsbedeutung des kritischen Realismus, 1958]. Trans. John and Necke Mander. In *The Meaning of Contemporary Realism*. Preface George Steiner. London: Merlin Press. 17–46.

Lukács, Georg (1977). "Realism in the Balance." ["Es geht um den Realismus," 1938]. Trans. Rodney Livingstone. In *Aesthetics and Politics*, by Theodor Adorno, Walter Benjamin, Ernst Bloch, Bertolt Brecht and Georg Lukács. Afterword Fredric Jameson. Translated and edited by Ronald Taylor. London: New Left Books. 28–59.

Marinetti, F. T. (1911). "Le mépris de la femme." [Contempt for Woman]. In *Le Futurisme*. Paris: Éditions Sansot.

Norris, Frank (1889). *McTeague: A Story of San Francisco*. New York: Doubleday and McClure.

Norris, Frank (1901). "Frank Norris' 'Weekly Letter'." *Chicago American Literary Review* (August 3): 5.

O'Faoláin, Sean (1937). "The Proletarian Novel." *The London Mercury* 35 (April): 583–589.

Richardson, Dorothy (1938). Foreword. In *Pilgrimage*. 4 vols. New York: A. A. Knopf. Vol. 1: 9–10.

Sinclair, May (1918). "The Novels of Dorothy Richardson." Rev. of *Pointed Roofs, Backwater, and Honeycomb. The Egoist* 5.4 (April): 57–59.

Spender, Stephen (1936). "Fable and Reportage." *The Left Review* 2.14 (November): 779–782.

Stein, Gertrude (1945). *Wars I Have Seen*. New York: Random House.

Stevens, Wallace (1942). "The Noble Rider and the Sound of Words." In *The Language of Poetry*, by Philip Wheelwright, Cleanth Brooks, I. A. Richards, and Wallace Stevens (ed. Alan Tate). Princeton: Princeton University Press. 91–105.

Tilley, Arthur (1883). "The New School of Fiction." *The National Review* (April), 257–268.

Waugh, Arthur (1916). "The New Realism." *The Fortnightly Review* (May), 849–858.

West, Rebecca (1928). "High Fountain of Genius." *The New York Herald Tribune* (October 21), 1, 6.

Wilde, Oscar (1889). "The Decay of Lying: a Dialogue." *The Nineteenth Century: A Monthly Review* 25 (January): 35–56.

Williams, William Carlos (1923). *Spring and All*. Paris: Contact.

Williams, Raymond (1976). *Keywords: A Vocabulary of Culture and Society*. London: Fontana/Croom Helm.

Woolf, Virginia (1924). *Mr Bennett and Mrs Brown*. London: Hogarth.

Woolf, Virginia (1925). "Modern Fiction." ["Modern Novels," 1919]. In *The Common Reader*. London: Hogarth. 184–195.

Woolf, Virginia (1932). "Robinson Crusoe." In *The Common Reader*, Second Series. London: Hogarth. 51–58.

Woolf, Virginia (1977–1984). "Diary entry, April 25, 1933." [1933]. In *The Diary of Virginia Woolf* (ed. Anne Olivier Bell). 5 vols. London: Hogarth. Vol. 4: 151–152.

Zola, Émile (1893). "The Experimental Novel." [*Le Roman experimental*, 1880]. Trans. Belle M. Sherman. In *The Experimental Novel and Other Essays*. New York: Cassell. 1–56.

Zola, Émile (1893). "A Letter To The Young People of France." ["Pis'mo k molodeži," 1879; "Lettre à la jeunesse," 1879]. Trans. Belle M. Sherman. In *The Experimental Novel and Other Essays*. New York: Cassell. 57–108.

Rhythm

The curious centrality of rhythm in early discussions of modernist art is both explained, and yet intriguingly not explained, in John Middleton Murry's autobiography *Between Two Worlds* (1935). For Murry and his associates in the first decade of C20, rhythm was "the distinctive element in all the arts," and "the real purpose of 'this modern movement,'" as they saw it, "was to reassert the pre-eminence of rhythm." Yet they possessed only a vague sense of what this "potent word" meant. "We never made any attempt to define it," Murry wrote: "All that mattered was that it had some meaning for each of us." Murry called his first magazine *Rhythm* and advertised it in *The Poetry Review* as "the UNIQUE MAGAZINE OF MODERNIST ART" (1912). Yet its first issues made no attempt to define its title, and the teasingly entitled article "The Meaning of Rhythm," in *Rhythm*'s fifth issue, mentioned the term only once, in passing (1912). Such was the role of the word rhythm in the modernist period: it was widely employed with a wide variety of associations, it was widely acknowledged as central to discussions of modernist art, and yet few could pinpoint its meaning. The term's very elusiveness, however, was central to its appeal to modernist writers looking for a way of capturing that which escaped final description, representation, or categorization.

203

Most modernist writers agreed, nevertheless, on one important point: that rhythm was fundamentally different from poetic meter. Two writers for Murry's journal specifically contrasted the regularity and uniformity of meter with the looser patterns of rhythm. C. J. Holmes argued for a "definition of rhythm" premised on "inequality rather than equality," condemning "all methods of work which incline to mechanical repetition." Rhythm was not, for Holmes, the absence of metrical pattern, however, but rather a looser and more complex pattern: "regularity, indeed, some repetition, our touch must have, or the result will be chaos and ineptitude, but the repetition must vary with the subject matter" (1911). Laurence Binyon, holding that "rhythm is subtle and natural, unendingly various, like the waves of wind in the corn," similarly argued that "rhythm imposed is no rhythm; it is like the scansion-tortured words of the incompetent versifier" (1912). Outside the pages of *Rhythm*, rhythm was widely seen as a more organic, more naturally various form of repetition. In the quasimanifesto "Imagisme" (1913), Ezra Pound and F. S. Flint wrote, "As regarding rhythm," one ought to "compose in sequence of the musical phrase, not in sequence of a metronome." Clive Bell observed that the influence of Jazz "syncopation" had produced a "rag literature" which "flout[ed] traditional rhythms and sequences and grammar and logic" (1921). In *Principles of Literary Criticism* (1924), I. A. Richards approached rhythm from the reader's perspective, defining it as "texture of expectations, satisfactions, disappointments, surprisals, which the sequence of syllables brings about," arguing that this conception of rhythm permitted a broader application to nonlinguistic art – in which "rhythmic elements [. . .] may not be successive but simultaneous" – rendering "obsolete" the old conception of meter as fixed regularity.

In its modernist usage, rhythm was also applied to an ever-broadening range of phenomena. For many, like Richards, rhythm was a defining quality not just of poetry but of art generally – serving indeed to distinguish art from life. Richards argued that artistic rhythm produced a "'frame' effect," "isolating" the artistic sphere from "the accidents and irrelevancies of everyday experience" (1924). In James Joyce's *Portrait of the Artist as a Young Man* (1916), Stephen Dedalus produces a similar formulation, arguing that to "feel the rhythm of [an artwork's] structure" is to "apprehend it as complex, multiple, divisible, separable, made up of its parts, the result of its parts and their sum, harmonious" and thus to reach a crucial stage in the "aesthetical apprehension" of an object – even an ordinary object like a butcher boy's basket – in its own terms. In *Aspects of the Novel* (1927), E. M. Forster distinguished between "pattern" and "rhythm," the former eliminating the "accidents and irrelevancies" of life from art and the latter expressing them artistically. A novel written with "pattern" – Forster gives the example of Henry James's *The Ambassadors* – sacrifices the "messiness" of "life" to a preconceived plan in order to achieve beauty, regularity, and order. A "rhythmic" novel preserves the messiness of life through a looser structure. Proust's *À la recherche du temps perdu*, Forster wrote, is "chaotic, ill-constructed" and has "no external shape," yet "hangs together because it is stitched internally, because it contains rhythms."

For other writers, rhythm was connected with the notion of individuality, serving as a kind of stylistic fingerprint denoting distinctive patterns of thinking or being. Ezra Pound wrote, "A man's rhythm must be [. . .] his own, uncounterfeiting, uncounterfeitable" (1918). T. S. Eliot described rhythm as "a highly personal matter" – "not a verse-form" but rather "the scheme of organization of thought, feeling, and vocabulary, the way in which everything comes together" (1923), and John Middleton Murry wrote of his "vague" but "real" sense that the life of a friend "had rhythm," alluding further to rhythm as "that essential living positive thing" (1935). Yet if rhythm was the property of an individual, the rhythms of others could interfere with one's own. F. Scott

Fitzgerald told Ernest Hemingway that he had to stop rereading him because, as he said, "I was afraid that your particular rhythms were going to creep in on mine by process of infiltration" ([1934]1963). Listening to Wagner on the radio, Virginia Woolf noted, "His rhythm destroys my rhythm" ([1931]1975–1980). Jazz improvisation, however, involved a different relation between individual rhythms. Langston Hughes explained, "I listen to what they say in their playing, and that affects my own rhythms when I read. We listen to each other" (Hentoff, 1958).

While often thus signifying an individual quality, rhythm at other times bore a nearly opposite sense, associated with the unconscious and collective identity. W. B. Yeats connected "what is most subtle and living in poetry – its pulse and breath, its rhythm" – with "that element in every race which is most strong" but worried that "every generation has more and more loosened [. . .] those great rhythms" of "the old story-tellers" and so lost "their rhythmical wills" (1906). More optimistically, Huntly Carter, reviewing the first issue of *Rhythm*, argued that "the revolutionary movement" in the arts was "designed to promote the expression of the rhythmical life of mankind": it "demand[ed] a unity where hitherto there [had] been nothing but separation" and sought to "destroy the convention of setting a man in a forest and giving each a separate atmosphere" (1911). The association of rhythm with group consciousness, however, could also be strongly negative. For Wyndham Lewis, rhythm provided a metaphor for the mass control on which modern states – both democratic and communist – depended, and he deplored "the emotionally-excited, closely-packed, heavily-standardized mass-units acting in a blind ecstatic union, as though in response to the throbbing of some unseen music." Arguing against any regulation in political life, Lewis wrote, "there should be no adventitiously imposed rhythm for life in the rough," which must exist in its "natural grace, chaos and beauty" and not be "cut down and arranged into a machine-made system" (1927). In a related sense, Miss La Trobe in Virginia Woolf's *Between the Acts* (1941) associates rhythm negatively with another form of group thinking, social convention, when she writes, "Let's break the rhythm and forget the rhyme."

205

The association of rhythm with group consciousness prompted, as with Yeats, the further idea that each race possessed its own unique rhythm. Discussing the "foreign influences" that had served to "enrich the range and variety of English verse," T. S. Eliot described English poetry as "an amalgam like the amalgam of races," combining the "rhythms of Anglo-Saxon, Celtic, Norman French, of Middle English and Scots [. . .] together with the rhythms of Latin, and [. . .] of French, Italian and Spanish" (1942). The assumption could then be made, however, that some races were more "rhythmic" than others. Thaddeus Bolton held that "a highly civilized people is not easily affected by mere rhythms," noting that "negro[es]" and "the lower classes of people" were especially prone to "recitative speaking" (1894). Unfamiliar cultural rhythms could also be met with disparagement or trepidation. Clive Bell grudgingly admitted the "nourish[ing]" influence of jazz "nigger rhythms" on Stravinsky and T. S. Eliot but castigated Virginia Woolf for her "syncopation," writing disapprovingly that "she 'leaves out' with the boldest of them" (1921). Mary Austin celebrated "the rhythmic modes of the aboriginal American" as expressive of "rhythmic form in nature" but warned that "Afro-American rhythms that go by the name of jazz" could dangerously "unharness the body from its civilized inhibitions"; yet while she described the "bond-loosening, soul-disintegrating, jazz-born movements" of Carl Sandburg as tending "toward spiritual disintegration," she nonetheless argued that jazz rhythms had "immensely stimulated" the "subjective appreciation of rhythmic form" among "Europeanly derived American[s]" (1930). The association of jazz and blues rhythms with African Americans could also produce racial stereotyping. Helga Crane, the mixed-raced protagonist of Nella Larsen's *Quicksand* (1928), internalizes the pejorative association of jazz with uncivilized: having been transported by "a sudden streaming rhythm," she experiences "a shameful certainty that not only had she been in the jungle, but that she had enjoyed it." Even when positive, associations of African Americans with jazz could be limiting and demeaning: Langston Hughes recounted the way his high school classmates "unanimously" elected him "class poet," because "most white people think, of course, that *all* Negroes can sing and dance, and have a sense of rhythm" (1940). Repossessing rhythm in his own terms, however, in "The Negro Artist and the Racial Mountain" (1926a), Hughes wrote of the "rhythm and warmth" that characterized African American "racial individuality," and in poems like "Weary Blues" and "Jazzonia" (1926b), he infused poetry with jazz and blues rhythms, empowering the African American voice. Claude McKay's *Banjo* (1929) brought these rhythms into prose: "Rough rhythm of darkly-carnal life. Strong surging flux of profound currents forced into shallow channels. Play that thing!" John R. Chamberlain ecstatically described McKay's *Home to Harlem* as "a book that is beaten through with the rhythm of life that is a jazz rhythm," embodying a "dramatic depiction of rude, boisterous and Nietzschean lives" (1928). Rhythm could also cross cultures. Ralph Ellison recalled finding the "rhythms [of *The Waste Land*] were often closer to those of jazz than were those of the Negro poets" (1964), and Mina Loy considered the English language to be "enriched and variegated" by the rhythmic combinations resultant from racial mixing in America. But race, she argued further, was only one determiner of rhythm: on the streets of Manhattan, "every voice swings to the triple rhythm of its race, its citizenship and its personality" (1925).

In its most general and wide-ranging modernist usage, rhythm stood for harmony not only between sounds in a line of verse, or formal elements in a poem, or individuals in a group but between the human body and the natural

206

world. This sense was already present in the first issue of *Rhythm*, where Murry argued that the role of "Modernism" was to "penetrat[e] beneath the outward surface of the world, and disengag[e] the rhythms that lie at the heart of things, rhythms strange to the eye, unaccustomed to the ear, primitive harmonies of the world that is and lives" (1911). Later, while editing *The Adelphi*, Murry continued to argue that the role of literature was to promote harmony of mind and body, individual and nature: "the more harmony and rhythm" a person "achieves within himself," he wrote, "the more harmony and rhythm he discovers in the world of his experience" (1926). Music educator Émile Jaques-Dalcroze developed "Eurhythmics" as "a psycho-physical training based on the cult of natural rhythms," both "to harmonize body and mind" and to promote "the future art of expressing emotion through a crowd" (1921a); rather than being uniform and regular, however, such rhythms would echo "the mighty rhythm of the universe," "a compound of myriads of synchronizing rhythms of infinite diversity, each possessing individual life" and together yielding "a whole polyrhythm of incomparable richness" ([1915]1921b). In D. H. Lawrence's *Women in Love* (1921), Gudrun – a character loosely modeled on Katherine Mansfield, Middleton Murry's wife – performs Dalcroze movements "in a strange impulsive rhapsody," her body "clutched in pure, mindless, tossing rhythm." In "Street Music" (1905), one of her earliest essays, Virginia Woolf similarly emphasized the corporeality of rhythm: "The beat of rhythm in the mind is akin to the beat of the pulse in the body," she noted, going on to argue that rhythm unites not only the human mind and body but links the human and the nonhuman as well – "In forests and solitary places an attentive ear can detect something very like a vast pulsation." For Woolf – as for T. S. Eliot, who argued "a poem, or a passage of a poem may tend to realize itself first as a particular rhythm before it reaches expression in words" (1942) – art originates from a prelinguistic bodily sensation she called "rhythm" or "a wave in the mind" which "in writing one has to recapture" ([1926]1975–1980). In "A Letter to a Young Poet" (1932), Woolf counseled the younger generation of writers "to stand at the window and let [their] rhythmical sense open and shut" until the human and nonhuman were set in harmony – "until one thing melts into another, until the taxis are dancing with the daffodils, until a whole has been made from all these separate fragments."

The promise of rhythm, for so many modernists, lay in its ability to create patterns and wholes by a process that was loose, natural, and inclusive – to bring together that which was fragmented without resorting to mechanical or tyrannical methods. The concept remained vague, possibly because it resists explicit definition in words. The power of rhythm as a force of life was captured, however, in the mobile prose of Claude McKay's *Banjo*: "the grand rhythm of life rolled on everlastingly without beginning or end in human comprehension, but the patterns were ever changing, the figures moving on and passing, to be replaced by new ones" (1929). And the starting place of perception was evocatively offered in Hughes's *The First Book of Rhythm* (1954), written for children. Hughes encouraged his readers to listen to "the heard and unheard rhythms of our world," many of which "men do not yet understand," assuring them that "all men's lives, and every living thing, are related to those vaster rhythms of time and space and wonder beyond the reach of eye or mind." "Rhythm," he continued, "is something we share in common, you and I, with all the plants and animals and people in the world, and with the stars and moon and sun, and all the whole vast wonderful universe beyond this wonderful earth which is our home."

SEE ALSO: *Common Mind, Group Thinking; God, Gods; Form, Formalism; Unconscious; Universal*

References

(1912). *The Poetry Review* 1 (January): back pages.

Austin, Mary (1930). *The American Rhythm*. Boston: Houghton Mifflin.

Bell, Clive (1921). "Plus de Jazz." *The New Republic* (September 21), 92–96.

Binyon, Laurence (1912). "The Return to Poetry." *Rhythm* 1.4 (Spring): 1–2.

Bolton, Thaddeus (1894). "Rhythm." *The American Journal of Psychology* 6.2: 145–238.

Carter, Huntly (1911). "Letters from Abroad: The New Idea of Dramatic Action IV: The Static Theatre." *The New Age* 9.15 (August 10): 345–347.

Chamberlain, John R. (1928). "Jazz Days." Rev. of *Home to Harlem* by Claude McKay. *The New York Times* (March 11): BR32.

Eliot, T. S. (1923). "Marianne Moore." *The Dial* 75 (December): 594–597.

Eliot, T. S. (1942). *The Music of Poetry:* The third W. P. Ker Memorial Lecture delivered in the University of Glasgow 24 February 1942). Glasgow: Jackson.

Ellison, Ralph (1964). "Hidden Name and Complex Fate: A Writer's Experience in the United States." In *Shadow and Act*. New York: Random House. 144–166.

Fitzgerald, F. Scott (1963). Letter to Ernest Hemingway, 1 June 1934. [1934]. In *The Letters of F. Scott Fitzgerald* (ed. Andrew Turnball). New York: Scribner. 334–337.

Flint, F. S. [and Ezra Pound] (1913). "Imagisme." *Poetry: A Magazine of Verse* 1.6 (March): 198–200.

Forster, E. M. (1927). *Aspects of the Novel*. London: Edward Arnold.

Hentoff, Nat (1958). "Langston Hughes: He Found Poetry in the Blues." *Mayfair* (August): 26–27, 43–49.

Holmes, C. J. (1911). "Stray Thoughts on Rhythm in Painting." *Rhythm* 1.3 (Winter): 1–3.

Hughes, Langston (1926). "The Negro Artist and the Racial Mountain." *The Nation* (June 23), 692–694.

Hughes, Langston (1926b). *Weary Blues*. New York: A. A. Knopf.

Hughes, Langston (1940). *The Big Sea: An Autobiography*. New York: A. A. Knopf.

Hughes, Langston (1954). *The First Book of Rhythm*. New York: Franklin Watts.

Jaques-Dalcroze, Émile (1921). "Eurhythmics and Musical Composition 1915." [1915]. Trans. Harold F. Rubinstein. In *Rhythm, Music, and Education*. New York: G. P. Putnam's Sons. 145–161.

Jaques-Dalcroze, Émile (1921). "Foreword." Trans. Harold F. Rubinstein. In *Rhythm, Music, and Education*. New York: G. P. Putnam's Sons. v–xi.

Joyce, James (1916). *Portrait of the Artist as a Young Man*. 1914–1915. New York: B. W. Huebsch.

Larsen, Nella (1928). *Quicksand*. New York: A. A. Knopf.

Lawrence, D. H. (1921). *Women in Love*. London: Martin Secker.

Lewis, Wyndham (1927). *Time and Western Man*. London: Chatto & Windus.

Loy, Mina (1925). "Modern Poetry." *Charm* 3.3 (April): 16–17.

McKay, Claude (1929). *Banjo: A Story Without a Plot*. New York and London: Harper and Brothers.

Murry, John Middleton (1911). "Art and Philosophy." *Rhythm* 1.1 (Summer): 9–12.

Murry, John Middleton (1926). "The Fourth Year." *The Adelphi* 4.1 (July): 1–10.

Murry, John Middleton (1935). *Between Two Worlds*. London: Jonathan Cape.

Murry, John Middleton and Katherine Mansfield (1912). "The Meaning of Rhythm." *Rhythm* 2.5 (June): 18–20.

Pound, Ezra (1918). "A Retrospect." In *Pavannes and Divisions*. New York: A. A. Knopf. 95–111.

Richards, I. A. (1924). *Principles of Literary Criticism*. London: Kegan Paul, Trench, Trubner.

[Woolf, Virginia] Stephen, Virginia (1905). "Street Music." *The National Review* (March), 144–148.

Woolf, Virginia (1932). "A Letter to a Young Poet." In *The Hogarth Letters*. London: Hogarth. 5–28.

Woolf, Virginia (1941). *Between the Acts*. London: Hogarth.

Woolf, Virginia (1975–1980). Letter to Ethel Smyth, 7 April 1931. [1931]. In *The Letters of Virginia Woolf* (eds. Nigel Nicolson and Joanne Trautmann). 6 vols. London: Chatto & Windus. Vol. 4: 303.

Woolf, Virginia (1975–1980). Letter to Vita Sackville-West, 16 March 1926. [1926]. In *The Letters of Virginia Woolf* (eds. Nigel Nicolson and Joanne Trautmann). 6 vols. London: Chatto & Windus. Vol. 3: 247.

Yeats, W. B. (1906). "Introduction." In *Poems of Spenser*. Edinburgh: T.C. & E.C. Jack. xlii–xliii.

Sentimental, Sentimentality

Contrasting Victorian and modern responses to Laurence Sterne's *The Sentimental Journey* (1768), Virginia Woolf asserted, "it is Sterne's sentimentality that offends us and not his immorality" (1928). Arnold Bennett, so often placed oppositionally to Woolf, held in this respect very similar views, attacking the Municipal Free Library for its endless supply of "outmoded, viciously respectable, viciously sentimental fiction" (1909), condemning the plays of Eugène Brieux for their "wish-wash of sentimentalism" (1910a), and damning "all mid-Victorian novels" as "incurably ugly and sentimental"(1910b). Whereas in C18, Sterne could use "sentimental" positively to designate "refined feeling," in the modernist period, "sentimentality" had come to signify a false and/or excessive indulgence in emotion. Writers agreed almost universally that sentimentality was a sin to avoid.

In common usage, sentimentality could denote a host of improprieties: intellectual softening, nostalgic lassitude, effeminacy, or romanticism. Geoffrey Grigson, editor of *New Verse*, accused poet Michael Roberts of "feeling without thought," arguing that such "passive [. . .] sentimentality" could not be considered art (1933). American man of letters Fred Lewis Pattee boasted that *The Atlantic Monthly* "kept its pages free from the sentimental and the conventional" (1923). Art critic Anthony Bertram derided the taste for period styles in design as "irrelevant sentimentality," connoting romantic nostalgia (1938). The Harlem Renaissance writer Alain Locke welcomed the loss of "sentimental interest" in the Negro as a

ABCDEFGHIJKLMNOPQR**S**TUVWXYZ

Modernism: Keywords, First Edition. Melba Cuddy-Keane, Adam Hammond, and Alexandra Peat.
© 2014 Melba Cuddy-Keane. Published 2014 by John Wiley & Sons, Ltd.

sign of "deliver[ance] both from self-pity and condescension" (1925). The reaction against sentimentality pervaded popular culture as well: when *The Sentimental Bloke* (1919), a wildly successful Australian silent film, was reissued in the US, the promoters decided that the film would have a wider appeal with American audiences if subtitled *The Story of a Tough Guy* (1920).

The negative gendering of sentimentality was reinforced by its associations with both femininity and a putatively effeminate literary bent. Such pejorative attitudes are clearly reflected in modernist fiction, though generally from a character's, not an author's, point of view. D. H. Lawrence's Birkin in *Women in Love* (1921) dismisses Ursula's view of love as "sentimental cant"; E. M. Forster's Ronnie in *A Passage to India* (1924), upholding British imperialism, asserts that his mission in India is "to hold this wretched country by force" and that he is "not a missionary or a Labour Member or a vague sentimental sympathetic literary man"; in Woolf's *Mrs Dalloway* (1925), both Clarissa and Sally worry that Peter will consider them "sentimental." In Winifred Holtby's fiction, female characters themselves worry about their vulnerability to sentimentality. Mary Robson in *Anderby Wold* (1923) accuses herself of being a "sentimental neurotic fool. Cheap, vulgar, sentimental," while Penelope Bentley-Sturge in Holtby's "You Know What Russians Are!" (1934) admonishes herself (wrongly as it turns out), "sentimental music, rich food, shaded lights and wine [. . .]. What an old, old trap for the emotions."

Virginia Woolf summed up the male critic's response to the woman writer as first genuine bafflement at her "attempt to alter the current scale of values," then disparagement of what he regarded as "not merely a difference of view, but a view that is weak, or trivial, or sentimental, because it differs from his own" (1929). But women could attack women for sentimentalism as well. Critic Beatrice Hastings (1911) condemned Katherine Mansfield's "lachrymose sentimentality," and while Louise Bogan (1973) argued that women's emotional aptitude made them especially effective as writers, she nonetheless wrote about May Sarton, "If she would only stop writing sentimental poems! I had her take out two mentions of 'kittens,' from one poem. 'Cats,' yes, 'kittens,' no." The stereotype of the unduly emotional female voice had political as well as aesthetic implications; the American Floyd Dell bristled at the "corruption" of the women's movement by "rampant" and "abhorrent" sentimentality, suggesting, in *Women as World Builders* (1913), that feminists ought to fight sentimentality as one "would fight prostitution, or any other social disease."

Conversely, if male writers were accused of being sentimental, it could denote a fear of expressing real feeling or confronting deep problems. Reviewing Ezra Pound's *Pavannes et divisions* (1918), Emanuel Carnevali deemed the book to be "the throttled cry of the non-confessed inhibitionists" and declared Pound's evasion of emotion "most absurdly sentimental" (1920). Similarly, Baker Brownell argued in "The Code of Minority" (1922) that such "hard, cool" poets as Wallace Stevens or Yvor Winters

211

are "protectively sentimental" in their refusal to delve beneath concrete "certainties."
Or a male writer might turn the charge of feminine sensibility against himself: in a
1904 letter to the poet AE [George Russell], W. B. Yeats wrote: "In my *Land of the
Heart's Desire*, and in some of my lyric verse of that time, there is an exaggeration of
sentiment & sentimental beauty which I have come to think unmanly. [. . .] it is sentiment & sentimental sadness, a womanish introspection" ([1904]1954).

The reaction against sentimentality cast an extremely wide net, leading I. A.
Richards to observe that "among the politer terms of abuse there are few so effective as 'sentimental'," which he judged "one of the most overworked words in the whole
vocabulary of literary criticism" (1929). Such scattershot use is well evidenced in *The
New Age*, where sentimental is used to modify claptrap, pieties, hypocrisy, slush, bleat-
ings, slobber, flapdoodle, lunacy, twaddle, nonsense, trappings, platitude, raving,
drivel, cant, mediocrity, stuff, idealism, bathos, humor, optimism, slop, virtues, tosh,
belief, delusions, and escapes. Summarizing his survey of student responses to
poetry, Richards concluded that although sentimental "often *may* mean something
precise and capable of definition," it is "sometimes not so much the instrument of
a statement as an expression of contempt." Nonetheless, Richards analyzed three
ways in which sentimental could usefully signify something "wrong" with "feelings": they might be "too great for the occasion," or "crude" and "violent," or
determined by selective memories of past experience, and hence "inappropriate"
to the immediate situation. Richards doubted that antisentimentalism was merely
a reaction to the "excesses of the Victorians," noting a possible cause in the
breakdown of firm beliefs and the consequent fear of "free expansive emotion." In
his own articulation of aesthetic principles, Richards eschewed the words sentiment and feeling, employing emotive and emotion instead (1924).

A challenge for modernists was thus to discriminate between spurious sentiment
and genuine feeling. In Ford Madox Ford's *The Good Soldier* (1915), for example,
the narrator John Dowell both expresses his contempt for Edward Ashburnham's
"sentimental gurglings" and yet aligns with Ashburnham against a world of coolly
pragmatic self-interests, bitterly noting that "society does not need too many sen-
timentalists." In Virginia Woolf's *The Years* (1937), Peggy Pargiter stumbles
more positively toward a balance of sentiment and feeling: "'Sentimental' was it?
Or, on the contrary, was it good to feel like that . . . natural . . . right?" In "The
Patron and the Crocus" (1924), Woolf suggested that readers should help writers
to avoid sentimentality on the one hand and the "craven fear" of emotional expression on the other, and in "A Letter to a Young Poet" (1932), she urged beginning
writers to "be silly, be sentimental, imitate Shelley, imitate Samuel Smiles; give
the rein to every impulse; [. . .] loose anger, love, satire." Knowing your own
sentimentality, she implied, is the way to "learn to write."

SEE ALSO: *Conventional, Conventionality; Form, Formalism; Woman,
New Woman*

References

(1919). *The Sentimental Bloke*. Silent film, black and white. Dir. Raymond Longford. Australia, Southern Cross Feature Film Co. Release date October 4; Reissued with edits and new subtitles as *The Sentimental Bloke: The Story of a Tough Guy* (U.S. 1920).

Bennett, Arnold (as Jacob Tonson) (1909). "Books and Persons." *The New Age* (February 18): 347–348

Bennett, Arnold (as Jacob Tonson) (1910a). "Books and Persons." *The New Age* (February 17): 376.

Bennett, Arnold (as Jacob Tonson) (1910b). "Books and Persons." *The New Age* (September 22): 495–496.

Bertram, Anthony (1938). *Design*. Harmondsworth: Penguin.

Bogan, Louise (1973). *What the Woman Lived: Selected Letters of Louise Bogan 1920–1970*. Edited with an Introduction by Ruth Limmer. New York: Harcourt Brace Jovanovich.

Brownell, Baker (1922). "The Code of Minority." *Poetry: A Magazine of Verse* 19.6 (March): 347–350.

Carnevali, Emanuel (1920). "Irritation." Rev. of *Pavannes et divisions*, by Ezra Pound. *Poetry: A Magazine of Verse* 20.4 (January): 211–220.

Dell, Floyd (1913). *Women as World Builders: Studies in Modern Feminism*. Chicago: Forbes.

Ford, Ford Madox (1915). *The Good Soldier*. London: John Lane.

Forster, E. M. (1924). *A Passage to India*. London and New York: Edward Arnold.

Grigson, Geoffrey (1933). "Faith or Feeling?" *New Verse* 1.2 (March): 15–17.

[Hastings, Beatrice] (1911). Rev. of *In a German Pension* by Katherine Mansfield. *The New Age* 10.8: 188.

Holtby, Winifred (1923). *Anderby Wold*. London: John Lane, The Bodley Head.

Holtby, Winifred (1934). "You Know What Russians Are!" In *Truth is Not Sober and Other Stories*. London: Collins. 119–132.

Lawrence, D. H. (1921). *Women in Love*. London: Martin Secker.

Locke, Alain (1925). "Enter the New Negro." *Survey Graphic*. Harlem: Mecca of the New Negro (March). 631–639.

Pattee, Fred Lewis (1923). *The Development of the American Short Story*. New York: Biblo and Tannen.

Richards, I. A. (1924). *Principles of Literary Criticism*. London: Kegan Paul, Trench, Trubner.

Richards, I. A. (1929). *Practical Criticism*. London: Kegan Paul, Trench, Trubner.

Woolf, Virginia (1924). "The Patron and the Crocus." *The Nation and Athenaeum* (April 12): 46–47.

Woolf, Virginia (1925). *Mrs. Dalloway*. London: Hogarth.

Woolf, Virginia (1928). "The 'Sentimental Journey.'" *The New York Herald Tribune* (September 23), Section 12, Books: 1, 6.

Woolf, Virginia (1929). "Women and Fiction." *The Forum* (New York) (March), 179–183.

Woolf, Virginia (1932). "A Letter to a Young Poet." In *The Hogarth Letters*. London: Hogarth. 5–28.

Woolf, Virginia (1937). *The Years*. London: Hogarth.

Yeats, W. B. (1954). Letter to George Russell (AE), ?April 1904. [1904]. In *The Letters of W. B. Yeats* (ed. Allan Wade). London: Rupert Hart-Davis. 433–435.

Shock, Shell Shock

Shock was a byword of the modernist period; its range of meaning, however, varied from up-to-date fashion to devastating trauma. First adopted to describe a military encounter in C16, the word was, by C18, used to define the effects of over-stimulation or violent emotion. Shock retained a military meaning throughout C20, in such usages as shock troops and shell shock, but the latter sense expanded into a broad medical exploration of hysteria and neurosis. The rise of psychoanalysis and psychiatry generated new approaches to the treatment of shock as psychological injury yet also led, in the 1930s, to the use of electroconvulsive or shock therapy to treat schizophrenia, bipolar disorder, and severe depression (notably among writers, Robert Lowell, Ernest Hemingway, and Sylvia Plath were subjected to electric shock). Yet in everyday usage, shock referred more generally to the cataclysmic innovations of technological and philosophical modernity, either of which could prompt feelings of liberating freedom or fear of the new.

In popular culture, shock implied the overthrow of convention by the provocative, exciting, and modern. In a daring coinage, Italian designer Elsa Schiaparelli launched her perfume "Shocking" in 1937 and introduced the shade "shocking pink" in her fashion collection that same year. Explaining her label, Schiaparelli wrote that while "find[ing] the name of a perfume is a very difficult problem because every word in the dictionary seems to be registered," she was inspired by a color "flash[ing] in front of [her] eyes": "Bright, impossible, impudent, becoming, life-giving, like all the light and the birds and the fish in the world put together, a color of China and Peru but not of the West – a shocking colour, pure and undiluted" (1954). Surrealist artist Salvador Dali quickly adopted the color, using Schiaparelli's Peruvian-inspired shocking pink chullo to adorn a mannequin at the 1938 *Exposition internationale du surréalisme*. As Betina Wilson recounted in *Vogue*, Dali's mannequin sported "Schiaparelli's shocking pink knitted helmet on her head, a penguin on top, a broken egg on her chest, and tiny coffee spoons all over"; the Parisian audience, however, well acquainted with Dadaist art born "about twenty years before," was reportedly bored: "It doesn't even shock you any more!" (1938). Nonetheless, in America, fashion designer Esther Dorothy created a monogrammed fur bath rug dyed "shocking pink, blue, and white" (Lewis, 1946), and by 1949, *Newsweek* reported that "shocking pink had gone into standard color charts" and "hundreds of thousands of women" were "dousing themselves with 'Shocking'" (1949). As Schiaparelli claimed, "the colour 'shocking' established itself for ever as a classic," signifying the fashionable and fabulous. Shocking pink could also signify the aesthetically or intellectually avant-garde: the editor of *Poetry*, George Dillon, described the audience for a T. S. Eliot lecture in Paris as including "famous French writers, society people, students, combat soldiers, artists looking like *maquisards*, esthetic-looking officers," setting "the shirt of 'shocking' pink next to the priest's cassock" (1945).

To shock, however, could be a sign not of fashion, but of moral, particularly sexual, depravity. Shocking pink signified tawdriness when Marion Bradley disparaged "sex-fiction" with "shocking-pink negligees on the cover" (1953), and the color carried the taint of crime in Frances Crane's mystery, *The Shocking Pink Hat*, when Nancy Landon's pink hat is found in a car with the dead body of her estranged husband (1946). In H. G. Wells's *Tono-Bungay*, Mrs. Grundy – long a synonym for conventional respectability – is somewhat excitedly "shocked – pink and breathless" when her morally upright but prurient husband "tells her things are shocking" (1908). Shock was particularly associated with the subversion of conventional female codes of behavior, such that Roscoe Pound declared, if the canon of Victorian literature was "Thou shalt not shock a young lady," the slogan of C20 seemed to be, "Thou canst not shock a young lady" (1928). In Katherine Mansfield's "Bains Turcs" [Turkish Baths], a conventional German Hausfrau shares in the general "shocked prudery" at the behavior of two modern and fashionable women she assumes are "hussies," betting that "those filthy women had a good look at each other. Pooh! women like that. You can't shock them" (1913). The conventional habit of being shocked by sex, however, was also seen as covert censorship. Reviewing a talk by Mrs. Havelock Ellis, Margaret Anderson complained about "something altogether too suggestive of 'Did my lecture shock you?' in Mrs. Ellis's attitude"; matters of sexuality, including homosexuality, Anderson protested, are "not shocking," adding, "so long as the truth about them is faced squarely they should carry no hint of shock" (1915).

Shock was frequently attributed to provocation in art, where it could be judged as either a powerful strategy or a cheap trick. In Europe, Walter Benjamin designated the way that the "work of art of the Dadaists" hit "the spectator like a bullet" as "the shock effect" ([1936]1968), while John Cowper Powys disparagingly noted that, if readers desired "the excitement of the unusual, the shock of the abnormal," there were "plenty of European writers" ready to oblige (1915). For Powys, a "work of art" is neither "good because it speaks daringly and openly about things that shock certain minds" nor "bad because it avoids all mention of such things"; the "question" is whether the artist has "made out of it an imaginative, suggestive, and convincing work of art." Frank Stuhlman, a reader of *The Little Review*, complained that depending "upon shock to taste and convention" for "success" was the way "freak" magazines attempted to "hold an audience" (1918), while Arthur Walkley protested that the "fun of theatrical experiment" was discovering "what shocks the public will stand and what it can't," nonetheless adding that what the public wants is not a "shocking incident" but a "rare experience" (1921). Shock was also considered subjective and relative: Gladys Jones, in defense of "The Futurists," described "shocks" as depending "on the breadth of the gulf between respective minds" and as emanating from "moral rather than intellectual" difference (1912). For "jh" [Jane Heap] of *The Little Review*, the real problem with "shocking people" was that it was impossible to "shock them to the foundations" (1917). Evelyn Waugh's antihero Basil Seal expresses agreement when he tells Ambrose Silk, an aspiring editor of a literary magazine, that "you can't shock people nowadays with sex" and advises instead "a little poem in praise of Himmler – something like that?" (1942).

Recognized as an inescapable component of modern life, shock could signal either destructive disorder or possibilities for productive change. As early as 1895, American educator and writer Vida Dutton Scudder considered that English poets had passed "into the clash and shock of thought which belongs to the modern world," while W. T. Stead's *Review of Reviews* quoted Viscount Georges D'Avenel's words that "the more complex the conditions of modern life the greater the shock consequent upon the abrupt interruption of its accustomed course" (1915). In the fictionalized autobiography of Henry Adams, shock(s) or shocked occurs 31 times, becoming a leitmotif of Adams's journey into the modern age ([1907]1918). Pervasive shock fostered desires for shock immunization: arguing that "the corporate life of a great business" was "not secure against shock," Equitable Life offered insurance for "the big men" in order to "guard 'gainst the blow'" "when an able leader dies" (1910), while Ford Madox Ford's John Dowell naively evolves plans for a "shock-proof world" (1915). Yet shock could also connote potentially positive effects. An item in *The Literary Digest* entitled "The Benefits of Shock" offered that "human nature needs a sudden shock to jar it out of its rut" and quoted from *The American Machinist*, "Barren earth is made prolific by dynamite" (1916); Hugh Walpole argued that the "idea" of someone being "plunged [. . .] suddenly, into experience and beaten to the ground with the shock of it" was "packed with possibilities" (1913); and Virginia Woolf considered "the shock-receiving capacity" to be what made her "a writer," explaining how "a shock" for her was "followed by a desire to explain it," so that "it is or will become a revelation of some order," "the token of some real thing behind appearances" ([1939–1940]1976).

Shock's most significant modernist variant was shell shock, a word that first underwent concerted attempts to establish precise medical definition and then bifurcated in opposite directions: at once banned by the military as an inadequate diagnosis but embraced in the popular imagination as a ubiquitous response to modern life. Coined in the early years of WWI, shell shock initially described the epidemic proliferation of a new war malady, attributed to the advent of high explosives: psychologist Charles Myers, after studying three soldiers affected by their physical proximity to exploding shells, argued for "a definite class" of war injury "arising from the effects of shell-shock" (1915). The question arose, however, of whether the condition was physical or psychological, especially when symptoms appeared in soldiers who had not been in close proximity to a blast. Opening a discussion on "Shell Shock without Visible Signs of Injury" (1916), President of the Royal Society of Medicine Fred Mott distinguished between "cerebral commotion" – later termed "commotional shock" (1919) – and "emotional shock caused by terror." *The British Medical Journal* posited a combination of "Mental and Nervous Shock" arising from "the severe strain and tension of the fighting line" and "the horrible sights and sounds of modern battlefields" (1914), while some doctors, like Harold Wiltshire, went further to argue that "the vast majority of cases, if not all, were due to psychic shock, and not to physical shock" (1916).

Determining causes, however, proved difficult. Wiltshire observed that generally "two or three [. . .] factors are combined in the production of psychic shock, making it difficult to apportion the measure of blame due to each." Myers came to see "shell shock" as "singularly ill-chosen" and "singularly harmful," noting that "a shell may play no part whatever in the causation" which could be "any 'psychical trauma' or 'inadjustable experience'" (1940). Substituting the terms "shell concussion" and "nervous shock," Myers hoped to expand genuine casualties to "cover cases of shock not due to shelling" but also to reduce "the number of cases" since, given the opprobrium surrounding "nervous," "fewer would be disposed to boast of suffering from this disorder." Separating the genuine from the fabricated proved problematic as well. According to Mott, "The detection of conscious fraud is not easy in many cases of shell shock [. . .], for it is difficult in many cases to differentiate malingering from a functional neurosis due to a fixed idea" (1916). Although Myers admitted that many soldiers would "glibly" say they were "suffering from 'shell shock'" when there was nothing wrong "save 'funk'," he was dismayed when, seeking clearer distinctions, the Director-General of Medical Services authorized the designations shell shock W ("wound class") and shell shock S ("sick class") (1940). As Myers noted, those who succumbed immediately after a blast could be given a respectable "wound stripe," whereas a man who tried to hold out would more likely be "stigmatized as 'nervous.'"

Regarding the treatment of psychic shock, psychological approaches divided between avoidance and recall of the traumatic events. In one view, the antidote was rest to restore the damaged system. An item in *The British Medical Journal* hoped that the public would support £10,000 for "a large quiet house in London and a convalescent home in the country" ("Mental," 1914), while Mott advised doctors to "tak[e] the man's mind off himself with amusements, games, and occupation, if possible in the open air. Look cheerful and be cheerful should ever be the mode of greeting these patients" (1916). In contrast, W. H. R. Rivers argued for selective acceptance of "the distinctive feature of Freud's system," noting that "many of the symptoms which follow the shocks and strains of warfare depend on the repression of painful experience," and he recommended guided remembering of the "emotional experience," so that it could become "integrated with the normal personality of the sufferer" (1917). But from both therapeutic viewpoints, shell shock was increasingly seen as an unsatisfactory term. For those believing the sufferer should forget, shell shock counterproductively implanted the idea of a permanent wound and nonrecovery. On the other side, it was feared that a diagnosis of shell shock "hindered the acceptance of a purely psychological explanation" and therapeutic measures based on the premise that "the recall of buried memories results in a cure" ("Treatment," 1918). *The Report of the War Office Committee of Enquiry into "Shell-Shock"* concluded that "'shell-shock' has been a gross and costly misnomer," since its symptoms were "practicably indistinguishable from the forms of neurosis known to every doctor under the ordinary conditions of life" (1922). Breaking associations with the front line of battle, the medical profession sought terminology applicable to trauma outside war as well. Gibbons's Soldier and Sailor Words and Phrases (1925) noted that while shell shock was "officially adopted in 1916," it had subsequently been "abolished, in favour of the technical term 'Psycho-neurosis'." Other emerging terms, such as "post-traumatic concussion state" and "post-traumatic psychoneurotic state" (Schaller, 1939), foreshadowed the present usage of PTSD.

Abandoned in professional vocabulary, shell shock was absorbed into literary discourse and popular speech. The combatant's viewpoint was compassionately presented by Siegfried Sassoon in his poem "Survivors," which describes "the shock and strain" and "stammering, disconnected talk" of shell-shock victims (1918), and in his later recollection of the "unspeakable tragedy of shell-shock" which befell "the finer types of men" (1936). Dorothy L. Sayers created a new kind of hero out of the shell-shock victim with the debonair detective Sir Peter Wimsey, who suffers from "a little remains of shell-shock" like "so many good, brave, young men" (1923). The discrepancy between combatant and civilian views figured as well. In Winifred Holtby's ironically titled story "Such a Wonderful Evening!" (1934), Jack, who has been "in and out of the hospital" with "shell shock," panics at the sight of a staged military display, his agony starkly contrasting with the simplistic advice, "Pull yourself together, lad," and the oblivious laughing crowd. WWI poet Gunner Macphail captured such lack of comprehension in the bitter cliché of his title "Just Shell Shock" (1916), countering with "what a wreck it leaves a chap." But shell shock could also be understood as a general human vulnerability. Airman Norman Archibald remembered the "story" of a pilot "suffering from shell-shock" being taken "with a grain of salt" and "ridiculed" until being told that the man was "quite ill." Archibald later revised his view of his own resistance to shell shock as courage, deciding that he was merely one of the "lucky" as opposed to "unlucky" (1935). During WWII, Lord Moran – by then Winston Churchill's physician – gave more credit to "commotional" over "emotional shock," writing that "when a man is hit he deserves more consideration than when he is frightened," yet he expended more sympathy for the latter, whose experiences in WWI resonated with his own (1945). Movingly writing about the universal susceptibility to fear, he offered that "no man has an unlimited stock of courage and that when this is done he is finished."

It was, then, an easy segue to connect shell shock to shock in ordinary life. Combatant and civilian experiences collapse in Rebecca West's *The Return of the Soldier* (1918) when the cousin of a shell-shocked soldier's wife warns of the need to prepare her for the "shock" of her husband's condition. Both this novel and Ford Madox Ford's *Parade's End* (1950) connect shock in the war, the shock *of* the war, and the larger shock of changing cultural values, expressing some ambivalence about the value of amnesia in a shock-torn world. Similarly, in Virginia Woolf's *Mrs Dalloway* (1925), in which Septimus Smith is reductively advised "Try to think about yourself as little as possible" by a doctor who acknowledges "the deferred effects of shell shock" only after Septimus's suicide, the shell-shocked condition goes beyond war injury to signify a feeling response to the cruelties of conventionally normalized "human nature," suffered by soldiers and civilians alike. The parameters of shell shock expand even further in the WWII "Entertainment," *The Ministry of Fear* (1943) by Graham Greene. When Arthur Rowe loses his memory due to a blast from a bomb-triggered suitcase, he wakes up to find himself in "the fin[est] shell-shock clinic in the country"; the clinic, however, turns out to be a front for covert operations by enemy infiltrators and, more broadly, a metaphor for a world dominated by a Ministry of Fear, where "you feel you can't depend on a soul," "a Ministry as large as life to which all who loved belonged."

Shell shock became indeed a catchall for any violent event. Explaining the roots of anti-Semitism, Horace Kallen stated that "dynamic fear" in wartime went by the "generic name *shell-shock*" but that "the peace was a more radical case of community 'shell-shock'" in which "the same fear" of the enemy "incarnated itself in a new symbol": the Jews (1932). Harry Overstreet described the "occupational shell-shock" caused by "protracted unemployment" (1934); Australian historian A. G. Butler linked shell shock with symptoms manifested in the financial depression of the 1930s: "a flight from reality into neurotic illness" (1943); and Max Lerner wrote of those "who have suffered intellectual shell-shock at the triumphant march of fascism in Europe" and "the tendencies toward a socialist totalitarianism" in Russia (1938). Shell shock was also loosely applied to daily life. In Henry Kitchell Webster's *Mary Wollaston*, Rush, just back from the war and out of touch with the challenges confronting a modern woman, dismisses his sister's stress as "hypersensitiveness due to the strain of war work," jokingly calling it "a case of shell-shock" (1920). Poignantly illustrating how the once powerful term shell shock came to mean everything and nothing, a popular children's story by Percy Keese Fitzhugh depicts some camping children joking that a character who has "tripped over the apron while he was trying to flop an omelet" so "the omelet came down on his head" is suffering from "shell shock" or "omelet shock" (1920). The move from shocking pink to shell shock to "omelet shock" reveals the incredible slipperiness of this modernist term. Shock ranged over emotions from playfulness to horror; it celebrated breaking convention and recorded the imprint of catastrophic change; it signified both overwhelmingly disruptive and unbearable experience and exciting new possibilities. In its very inconsistency, shock epitomizes the extremes of the modern age.

SEE ALSO: *Hygiene; Modern, Modernism; Unconscious*

References

(1910). "Business Insurance: An Advertisement by Elbert Hubbard, The Equitable Life Assurance Society." *American Magazine* (October 6), ADV 124.

(1914). "Nervous and Mental Shock Among the Wounded." *The British Medical Journal* 2.2810 (November 7): 802–803.

(1915). "Who Will Profit by The War?" Editorial. Stead's *Review of Reviews* (Melbourne) (May–June), 410–411.

(1916). "The Benefits of Shock." *The Literary Digest* (December 16), 1597.

(1918). "The Treatment of War Psycho-neuroses." *The British Medical Journal* 2.3032 (December 7): 634.

(1949). "Schiaparelli the Shocker." *Newsweek* (September 26), 51–53.

Adams, Henry (1918). *The Education of Henry Adams*. Privately printed, Washington, 1907. Boston and New York: Houghton Mifflin.

Anderson, Margaret C. (1915). "Mrs. Ellis's Failure." *The Little Review* 2.1 (March): 16–19.

Archibald, Norman (1935). *Heaven High, Hell Deep: 1917–1918*. New York: Albert and Charles Boni.

Army (1922). *Report of the War Office Committee of Enquiry into "Shell-Shock"* Presented to Parliament by Command of His Majesty. London: HMSO. Cmd. 17344.

Benjamin, Walter (1968). "The Work of Art in the Age of Mechanical Reproduction." ["L'œuvre d'art à l'époque de sa reproduction mécanisée," [1936]; "Das Kunstwerk im Zeitalter seiner technischen Reproduzierbarkeit," [1955]]. Trans. Harry Zorn. In *Illuminations*. Edited with an Introduction by Hannah Arendt. New York: Harcourt, Brace and World.

Bradley, Marion S. (1953). Letter. In "The Reader Speaks." *Thrilling Wonder Stories* (June), 123–153.

Butler, A. G. (1943). "Moral and Mental Disorders in the War of 1914–1918." In *The Australian Army Medical Services in the War of 1914–1918* (ed. A. G. Butler). 3 vols. Canberra and Melbourne: Australian War Memorial. Vol. 3: 56–147.

Crane, Frances [Kirkwood] (1946). *The Shocking Pink Hat*. New York: Grosset and Dunlop; Random House.

Dillon, George (1945). "Correspondence." *Poetry: A Magazine of Verse* 67.1 (October): 49–54.

Fitzhugh, Percy Keese (1920). *Roy Blakeley's Camp on Wheels*. New York: Grosset and Dunlop.

Ford, Ford Madox (1915). *The Good Soldier*. London: John Lane.

Ford, Ford Madox (1950). *Parade's End.* [*Some Do Not ... 1924; No More Parades* 1925; *A Man Could Stand Up*—1926; *The Last Post* 1928]. Introduction by Robie Macaulay. New York: A. A. Knopf.

Fraser, Edward and John Gibbons (1925). *Soldier and Sailor Words and Phrases; Including Slang of the Trenches and the Air Force; British and American War-words and Service Terms and Expressions in Every-day Use; Nicknames, Sobriquets, and Titles of Regiments, with their Origins; the Battle-Honours of the Great War Awarded to the British Army.* London: G. Routledge and Sons.

Greene, Graham (1943). *The Ministry of Fear: An Entertainment.* London: W. Heinemann; New York: Viking.

Holtby, Winifred (1934). "Such a Wonderful Evening!" In *Truth is Not Sober and Other Stories.* London: W. Collins. 268–272.

j. h. [Jane Heap] (1917). "The Little Review." Reply to Anonymous Letter in "The Reader Critic." *The Little Review* 4.4 (August): 24–25.

Jones, Gladys (1912). "The Futurists." Letter to the Editor. *The Freewoman* (May 9), 498.

Kallen, Horace Meyer (1932). *Judaism at Bay; Essays Toward the Adjustment of Judaism to Modernity.* New York: Bloch.

Lerner, Max (1938). *It is Later Than You Think: The Need for a Militant Democracy.* New York: Viking.

Lewis, Dorothy Roe (1946). "Fun with Furs." *Collier's* (December 21), 86–88.

Macphail, Gunner (1916). "Just Shell Shock." *Springfield War Hospital Gazette* (September), 8.

Mansfield, Katherine (1913). Epilogue III. "Bains Turcs." *The Blue Review* 1.3 (July): 181–185.

Moran, Lord (1945). *The Anatomy of Courage.* London: Constable.

Mott, Fred W. *et al.* (1916). "Special Discussion on Shell Shock without Visible Signs of Injury." *Proceedings of the Royal Society of Medicine* 9 (Sections of Psychiatry and Neurology): i–xliv.

Mott, Fredk. W. *et al.* (1919). *War Neurosis and Shell Shock.* London: Henry Frowde with Hodder and Stoughton.

Myers, Charles S. (1915). "A Contribution to the Study of Shell Shock: Being an Account of Three Cases of Loss of Memory, Vision, Smell, and Taste, admitted into The Duchess of Westminster's War Hospital, Le Touquet." *The Lancet* (February 13), 316–320.

Myers, Charles Samuel (1940). *Shell Shock in France 1914–18: Based on a War Diary Kept by Charles S. Myers.* Cambridge: The University Press.

Overstreet, H. A. (1934). *A Guide to Civilized Leisure.* New York: W. W. Norton & Co.

Pound, Roscoe (1928). "The Social Order and Modern Life." In *The Creative Intelligence and Modern Life* (eds. Francis John McConnell *et al.*). Boulder: University of Colorado Press.

Powys, John Cowper (1915). "Theodore Dreiser." *The Little Review* 2.8 (November): 7–13.

Rivers, W. H. R. (1917). "Freud's Psychology of the Unconscious." *The Lancet* (June 16), 912–914.

Sassoon, Siegfried (1918). "Survivors." Craiglockhart [October 1917]. In *Counter-Attack, and Other Poems.* London: W. Heinemann; New York: E. P. Dutton. 55.

Sassoon, Siegfried (1936). *Sherston's Progress.* London: Faber and Faber; Garden City: Doubleday, Doran.

Sayers, Dorothy L. (1923). *Whose Body?* New York: Harper and Row.

Schaller, Walter F. (1939). "After-Effects of Head Injury: The Post-Traumatic Concussion State (Concussion, Traumatic Encephalopathy) and the Post-Traumatic Psychoneurotic State (Psychoneurosis, Hysteria): A Study in Differential Diagnosis." *JAMA: The Journal of the American Medical Association* 113.20 (November 11): 1179–1785.

Schiaparelli, Elsa (1954). *Shocking Life*. London: J. M. Dent and Sons.

Scudder, Vida Dutton (1895). *The Life of the Spirit in the Modern English Poets*. New York: Houghton, Mifflin and Co.; E. P. Dutton.

Stuhlman, Frank (Vernon, N. Y.) (1918). "The Reader Critic: I have not read much in this number—." Letter to the Editor. *The Little Review* 5.3 (July): 64.

Walkley, A. B. (1921). "Grand Guignolism." In *Pastiche and Prejudice*. London: W. Heinemann. 133–137.

Walpole, Hugh (1913). "The Novel: Imagination." *The Blue Review* 1.2 (May 17): 123–127.

Waugh, Evelyn (1942). *Put Out More Flags*. London: Chapman and Hall; Boston: Little, Brown.

Webster, Henry Kitchell (1920). *Mary Wollaston*. Indianapolis: Bobbs-Merrill.

Wells, H. G. (1908). *Tono-Bungay*. New York: Duffield; London: Odhams.

West, Rebecca (1918). *The Return of the Soldier*. New York: Century.

Wilson, Betina (1938). "Surrealism in Paris." *Vogue* (New York) (March 1), 106–107, 144.

Wiltshire, Harold (1916). "A Contribution to the Etiology of Shell Shock." *The Lancet* 187.4842 (June 17): 1207–1212.

Woolf, Virginia (1925). *Mrs. Dalloway*. London: Hogarth.

Woolf, Virginia (1976). "A Sketch of the Past." [1939–1940]. In *Moments of Being: Unpublished Autobiographical Writings*. Edited with Introduction and Notes by Jeanne Schulkind. Sussex: The University Press. 61–137.

Unconscious

Unconscious entered the English language in C18; during the modernist period, it became a locus of public controversy and personal conviction and a magnet for scientific speculation and research. Much of the vigorous new interest in the unconscious derived from the emerging field of psychoanalysis, but there was little consensus over whether the unconscious could be studied scientifically and what unconscious processes actually entailed. And while the unconscious increasingly figured in broad, generalized discussions of selfhood, a key debate was whether it was a source of creativity and interpersonal connection or the repository of uncontrollable, antisocial impulses. Despite emerging professional terminology, most popular usage continued to employ unconscious in its older sense of not knowing or lacking awareness, whether as a result of inattention, insensitivity, injury, or oncoming death. To express the newer substantive idea of active unconscious forces, literary writers frequently resorted to imagery – especially images of darkness, descent, and watery immersion – and personal vocabulary, such as Lawrence's "blood consciousness" or Virginia Woolf's "under mind." The plurality of these approaches demonstrates not only the complexity and diversity of interest in unconscious mental processes but also the inherent difficulty that mapping such elusive processes entails.

The romantic period initiated the shift in unconscious from absence (lack of awareness) to presence (cognitive activity of which we are unaware), opening up

ABCDEFGHIJKLMNOPQRST*U*VWXYZ

Modernism: Keywords, First Edition. Melba Cuddy-Keane, Adam Hammond, and Alexandra Peat.
© 2014 Melba Cuddy-Keane. Published 2014 by John Wiley & Sons, Ltd.

a field of investigation into an obscure but productive part of the human mind. In *The Prelude*, William Wordsworth described spiritual connection with nature as "unconscious intercourse with Beauty" ([1805]1926); Samuel Taylor Coleridge attributed "the genius" in a work of art to "unconscious activity," referring as well to "unconscious thoughts" (1836–1839). As the century progressed, the concept of an active unconscious became a meeting ground between spiritualism and science. F. W. H. Myers, cofounder of the Society for Psychical Research (SPR, 1882), desiring to "break down that artificial wall" between scientific "experiment" and the question of "a life beyond the life we know," conducted investigations into what he termed the "*subliminal* or *ultra-marginal consciousness*" (1903). Although declaring his work "an exposition rather than a proof," Myers presented exhaustive comparative analysis of such "ghostly phenomena" as dreams, hallucinations, hypnotic trances, automatic writing, telepathy, and "the subliminal uprushes of genius" as evidence for the existence of a spiritual world. A more physiological understanding was sought by William Carpenter, who coined "Unconscious Cerebration" to designate "automatic Mental activity"; believing such activity to be influenced by "the whole previous training and discipline of our Minds," Carpenter posited the importance of "the Moral Atmosphere" in early life for "shaping" the "unconscious thinking" affecting "our Common Sense judgments" (1874). Charles M. Child undertook to produce a "Statistics of 'Unconscious Cerebration'," seeking "experimental verification" by analyzing answers to a questionnaire distributed to 200 subjects; the study tabulated differences according to age and gender based on remembered instances when facts or solutions to problems or creative work popped into consciousness after periods of distraction or sleep (1892). While refraining from expressing an opinion himself and stopping "on the threshold of the mystery," Henri Bergson nonetheless acknowledged the importance of findings produced by the "rigorous" method and "indefatigable zeal" of the SPR, affirming that "to explore the most secret depths of the unconscious, to labor in what I have called the subsoil of consciousness, that will be the principal task of psychology in the century which is opening" (1914).

Unconscious acquired a radically different meaning through the works of Sigmund Freud, which were rapidly translated into English, beginning with *The Interpretation of Dreams* (3rd ed. [1900]1913). Breaking the psyche into different components, Freud distinguished between the unconscious and the preconscious, the latter functioning, he argued, "like a screen between the unconscious and consciousness." The revolutionary Freudian approach was to posit that screen as censor, either preventing the unconscious from reaching consciousness through the mechanism of repression or altering its contents through projection and sublimation. The application of Freud's unconscious not just to neurosis but to everyday life led to its widespread popularization. E. S. Grew, writing in the *Pall Mall Magazine* (1913), explained to a lay public that "everybody dreams," that "every dream is a wish," that these wishes express the "infantile mind" focused on the "gratification of appetites," and that, according to Freud, every dream reveals "an infantile memory." While expanding repressed appetites considerably beyond Freud's focus on sexuality, Grew claimed the new "science" revealed the "unconscious mind" to be "governed by laws quite as surely as the actions of the body are governed by laws." But numerous modifications were posed to Freud's theory. W. H. R. Rivers expressed concern that negative reaction to some of Freud's specific ideas threatened to obscure Freud's foundational influence; however, in *Instinct and the Unconscious*, Rivers – noted for his treatment of shell shock during WWI – chose the term "suppression" over "repression"; the instinctual unconscious, Rivers asserted, plays a positive role as a protective mechanism, which, like the immobility of an animal in danger, protects the system from threatening intrusion (1920). Jared Moore, while similarly adopting Freud's "general theory," went further to cast the unconscious as "potential psychic energy" (1921) and to place foreconscious (the later translation of Freud's preconscious) and unconscious together as subconscious mental phenomena potentially capable of "unconscious thinking" (1928). The main rival to the Freudian unconscious, however, was posed by Carl Jung. Jung's early work on word association gave him insights into unconscious "thinking by analogy," evidenced in dreams as well as fairy tales (1910), and led to his theory that the "personal unconscious" "rests upon a deeper layer" of the "collective unconscious," which is "universal" and "inborn." Biologically, he argued, humans have inherited the propensity for certain psychic experiences, such as the "experience of the Divine," which become translated into the universal images he named "archetypes" ([1934]1959). Although Jung's delineation of specific archetypes would not see sustained attention until the end of the modernist period – undergoing, by Northrop Frye, an extension into "an archetype of genres as well as images" (1951) – modernists credited Jung with bringing a creative dimension to the unconscious and a global attention to myth. A reviewer in *Scrutiny* wryly commented that "the collective unconscious" restores "the balance against conscious Americanization by fishing up the East that lies hidden in us all" (Harding, 1934). The modernist jury, however, was still out. While Vanderbilt professor Eugene Bugg wrote, "whereas Freud made the unconscious something to abhor, Jung actually raises it to the status of the World-Ground" (1934), Bernard DeVoto judged that Freud's theory "constantly referred to things, to observed and recorded phenomena," while Jung's theory "leads to a morass of uncontrolled mysticism" (1939).

Writing about "Freud's Influence on Literature," DeVoto also distinguished between Freud's pervasive and positive influence on "unconscious symbolism" and the more problematic application of Freud's theories "at second hand." Virginia Woolf's essay "Freudian Fiction" (1920) similarly disputed the simplistic use of psychoanalytic theory as a "key" to fictional character, while Eugene Jolas (1929)

225

complained about "the childish applications of Freudian theories," citing *Strange Interlude* (1928) by Eugene O'Neill. Modernist fiction, however, abounds in attempts to capture unconscious or half-conscious "thought," although it most often avoids the word unconscious or uses it in its older sense. In Dorothy Richardson's *The Tunnel*, Miriam Henderson employs the sense of unconscious as absence: she describes a man as "unconscious of his surroundings," thinks of a group of scientifically minded people as "unconscious" with "a kind of deadness," and is told in a hospital of someone being "unconscious" and unlikely to "last through the night" (1919). Yet May Sinclair (1918), importing a phrase from William James, characterized Miriam's thoughts as "stream of consciousness going on and on" and quoted passages from Richardson's *Honeycomb* with images and syntax invoking an unconscious realm: "Something that was not touched, that sang far away down inside the gloom [. . .] Deeper down was something cool and fresh endless an endless garden." Henry James similarly employed unconscious to mean simply nonsentient, as in "the bristling line of hard unconscious heads" (1908); yet when James recounted the genesis of *The American*, he fused a sub-terranean image and William Carpenter's term: after encountering the original germ for the plot, James explained, he "dropped [the idea] for the time into the deep well of unconscious cerebration," waiting for the propitious time for the "buried treasure to come to light" (1907). James's image was in turn seized by the critic James Livingston Lowes, who used "The Deep Well" as the title for a chapter in his study of Coleridge's poetry (1927). While admitting that, in using "unconscious," he was "playing with fire" – he refuted Robert Graves's Freudian biographical reading of Coleridge – Lowes traced the way "the streamy nature of association" in the unconscious is shaped by "creative Vision" into "unique and lovely Form" (1927).

226

Unconscious could also mean, however, automatic conditioned response. Ezra Pound called on his reader to "speak against unconscious oppression" and "the tyranny of the unimaginative" (1913). T. S. Eliot expressed concerns about Christians becoming "de-Christianized by all sorts of unconscious pressure," when "paganism holds all the most valuable advertising space" (1939), and decried the human tendency "to exert an unconscious pressure on [another] person to turn him into something that we can understand" ([1946]1948). Dorothy Richardson described the way women in the arts confront a world infused with "masculine traditions" "based on assumptions that are largely unconscious" (1925), while W. E. B. Du Bois wrote to African Americans of the need to overcome the way "black is caricature in our half conscious thought," causing the response of being "instinctively and almost unconsciously ashamed" (1920). I. A. Richards warned of the way "conscious or unconscious" preconceptions about the nature of poetry distorted interpretation, along with the similar unjustified reaction he named the "stock response" (1924). The "new" unconscious could also be a target of disparagement or jest: the narrator in Mary Roberts Rinehart's *Sight Unseen*, a popular thriller about psychical research, scoffs at the psychoanalysts' "patter," casting their unconscious as "a sort of bonded warehouse from which we clandestinely withdraw our stored thoughts and impressions" and as woefully inadequate for understanding "that still uncharted territory, the human mind" (1921).

Many literary writers, however, developed their own understandings of the unconscious as a creative force. For D. H. Lawrence, arguably the writer who most developed his own theory, the unconscious was an alternate epistemology, which "overwhelms, obliterates, and annuls mind-consciousness" (1923). Describing the indescribable with such phrases as "blood-consciousness" (1921b, 1923), "blood prescience," a "rich positivity" (1920), and "our most elemental consciousness" (1922), Lawrence rejected the "Freudian unconscious" as "the cellar in which the mind keeps its own bastard spawn" and proposed instead a "true unconscious" as "the well-head, the fountain of the real motivity" (1921a). Lawrence further connected his ideas to "the sexual consciousness," positing that "the blood is divided in a dual polarity between the sexes," causing "a tremendous magnetic urge [of the male] towards the magnetic blood of the female." Stating that "we know no word, so say 'electricity,' by analogy," he believed that in coitus, a "deep circuit" can form "the profound basis" of "deep blood renewal." While in some ways resembling the Victorian ideal of the union of souls, Lawrence's "polarized magnetic field" preserves difference and even opposition between the sexes, and his unconscious, as an anarchic force, involves violence and destruction as well as creative drive.

227

While idiosyncratic, Lawrence's unconscious participates in a modernist search for some deeper nonanalytic connection between the self and what lies outside it. Discussing Gertrude Stein's "Handing a lizard," Mina Loy explained that Stein assumes "the consciousness or rather the unconsciousness of the lizard"; "so intimate is the liaison of her observation with the sheer existence of her objective" that "to interpret her description of the lizard you have to place yourself in the position of both Gertrude Stein and the lizard at once" (1924). Hart Crane wrote of the possible integration of machinery and the mind, arguing that "the power and beauty of machinery" "can not act creatively in our lives until, like the unconscious nervous responses of our bodies, its connotations emanate from within" (1930). Eugene Jolas found connection between writer and reader at the unconscious level, extolling the way dislocated language in the prose poems of Léon-Paul Fargue gives us "quick flashes into his subconscious mind, and lets us participate in the dynamic evocations of his word" (1928).

The conception of the unconscious as fluid, porous, and heterogeneous led many writers, like Henry James, to connect it with the creative process. Jolas, echoing James, described "the subconscious as a new well of inspiration" and "a subterranean stream," manifesting itself diversely in "the dream," "neuropathic conditions," and "poetic inspiration" (1929). Uniting the general theories of Freud and Jung, Jolas conceived the subconscious as both personal and collective: an "immense basin into which flow [not only] all the inhibited components of our being" but also "the collective mythos thus establishing connection with the social organism and even the cosmic forces." Such "flow" did not mean simply chaotic welter: Herbert Read argued that "there is no real contradiction between art, conceived as design, and the unconscious" and that "even in its plastic manifestations the unconscious possesses a principle of organization" and "design" (1952). Jolas, however, charted a middle approach, believing, "The subconscious is not enough. We must organize." Illuminating the name of his journal *transition*, he emphasized the necessary "transition between the active tendencies and those of the interior impulses" and "from life as biological existence into the formed existence of creation," to achieve an ultimate "synthesis of *all* the forces of life." Conrad Aiken supported a similar interaction between the unconscious and consciousness; finding Freud's explanation of poetic inspiration as "due entirely to 'hidden complexes, largely erotic' to be insufficient," Aiken hypothesized "that words, like other sensory impressions derived from contact with reality, are stored in the mind, not discretely, but in chains of association, where they become unconscious, and appear to be forgotten; but that upon a given stimulus these chains of associated words begin automatically unravelling, become again conscious" (1917). Virginia Woolf similarly suggested the unconscious as a rich fertile reservoir, using the recurrent image of "the dark pool of the mind" (1928); but she too pursued a synthetic view, asking, "Who was it who said, through the unconscious one comes to the conscious, & then again to the unconscious?" ([1935]1977–1984). Explaining that "the writer needs to become unconscious before he can create," she described "unconsciousness" as a state where "the undermind works at top speed while the upper-mind drowses" (1940), and in Dostoevsky she found "the whole train of thought in all its speed," both "the vivid streak of achieved thought" and "the dim and populous underworld of the mind's consciousness where desires and impulses are moving blindly beneath the sod" (1917).

As a whole, modernist usages of unconscious depict its gradual evolution from an adjective signifying passivity (to be unconscious) to an active, substantive noun (the unconscious). They also reveal the close ties of literature and psychology. DeVoto proposed that the "motive of individual behavior" was "the foremost consideration of both psychoanalysis and fiction," and Woolf declared that "the point of interest" for "the moderns" lay "very likely in the dark places of psychology" ([1919]1925). While the philosopher C. D. Broad remarked in 1923 that "the looseness with which the word 'unconscious' is at present used is a psychological scandal of the first magnitude," such multiplicity itself illuminates two significant modernist perceptions: the difficulty in finding a language adequate for expressing what exceeds the linguistic and the crucial significance of what exceeds the conscious mind (1922–1923).

SEE ALSO: *Common Mind, Group Thinking; Personality, Impersonality; Rhythm; Shock, Shell Shock; Universal; Words, Language.*

References

Aiken, Conrad (1917). "The Mechanism of Poetic Inspiration." *The North American Review* (December), 917–924.

Bergson, Henri (1914). *Dreams.* Translated with an Introduction by Edwin E. Slosson. New York: Huebsch.

Broad, C. D. (1922–1923). "Various Meanings of the Term 'Unconscious'." *Proceedings of the Aristotelian Society,* New Series, 23: 173–198.

Bugg, Eugene G. (1934). Rev. of *Modern Man in Search of a Soul* by C. G. Jung. Trans. W. S. Dell and C. F. Baynes. *The American Journal of Psychology* 46.3 (July): 536.

Carpenter, William B. (1874). *Principles of Mental Physiology with their Applications to the Training and Discipline of the Mind and the Study of its Morbid Conditions.* New York: D. Appleton.

Child, Charles M. (1892). "Statistics of Unconscious Cerebration." *The American Journal of Psychology* 5.2 (November): 249–259.

Coleridge, Samuel Taylor (1836–1839). Lecture XIII: "On Poesy or Art"; Fragment of an Essay on Beauty 1818. In *The Literary Remains of Samuel Taylor Coleridge* (ed. Henry Nelson Coleridge). 4 vols. London: William Pickering. Vol. 1: 216–230, 270–273.

Crane, Hart (1930). "Modern Poetry." In *Revolt in the Arts: A Survey of the Creation, Distribution and Appreciation of Art in America* (ed. Olive M. Saylor). New York: Brentano's. 294–298.

DeVoto, Bernard (1939). "Freud's Influence on Literature." *The Saturday Review of Literature* (October 7), 10–11.

Du Bois, W. E. B. (1920). "Opinion of W E B Du Bois." *The Crisis: A Record of the Darker Races* (October), 261–263, 266.

Eliot, T. S. (1939). *The Idea of a Christian Society.* London: Faber and Faber.

Eliot, T. S. (1948). "Appendix: Broadcasts 1946." [1946]. In *Notes Towards the Definition of Culture.* London: Faber and Faber. 110–124.

Freud, Sigmund (1913). *The Interpretation of Dreams.* [*Die Traumdeutung,* 1900]. 3rd ed. Translated with an Introduction by A. A. Brill. London: G. Allen and Unwin; New York: Macmillan.

Frye, Northrop (1951). "The Archetypes of Literature." *The Kenyon Review* 13.1 (Winter): 92–110.

Grew, E. S. (1913). "The Factory of Dreams: How and Why We Have Them." *Nash's Pall Mall Magazine* (September), 358–365.

Harding, D. W. (1934). Rev. of *Modern Man in Search of a Soul* by C. G. Jung. *Scrutiny* (June): 109–110.

James, Henry (1907). "Preface to *The American.*" In *The Novels and Tales of Henry James.* New York Edition. 26 vols. New York: Charles Scribner's Sons. Vol. 2: v–xxiii.

James, Henry (1908). "The Jolly Corner." *The English Review* 1.1 (December): 5–35.

Jolas, Eugene (1928). "Notes." *transition: An International Quarterly for Creative Experiment* 14 (Fall): 180–185.

Jolas, Eugene (1929). "Notes on Reality." *transition: An International Quarterly for Creative Experiment* 18 (November): 13–20.

229

Jung, C. G. (1959). "The Archetypes and the Collective Unconscious." ["Über die Archetypen des kollektiven Unbewussen," 1934]. Trans. R. F. C. Hull. In *Collected Works of C. G. Jung* (eds. Sir Herbert Read, Michael Fordham and Gerhard Adler). London: Routledge and Kegan Paul; Princeton: Princeton University Press. Vol. 9, Part 1: 3–41.

Jung, Carl G. (1910). "The Association Method." Trans. A. A. Brill. *The American Journal of Psychology* 21.2 (April): 219–269.

Lawrence, D. H. (1920). "The Blind Man." *The English Review* 31 (July): 22–41.

Lawrence, D. H. (1921a). *Psychoanalysis and the Unconscious*. New York: Thomas Seltzer.

Lawrence, D. H. L. (1921b). *Women in Love*. London: Martin Secker.

Lawrence, D. H. (1922). *Fantasia of the Unconscious*. New York: Thomas Seltzer.

Lawrence, D. H. (1923). "Nathaniel Hawthorne and *The Scarlet Letter*." In *Studies in Classic American Literature*. New York: Thomas Seltzer.

Livingston Lowes, James (1927). *The Road to Xanadu: A Study in the Ways of the Imagination*. Boston and New York: Houghton Mifflin.

Loy, Mina (1924). "Gertrude Stein." *The Transatlantic Review* 2.3 (September): 305–309; "Gertrude Stein." Continued. 302.304 (October): 427–430.

Moore, Jared Sparks (1921). *The Foundations of Psychology*. Princeton: Princeton University Press.

Moore, Jared S. and Knight Dunlap (1928). "Consciousness, the Unconscious, and Mysticism." *The Philosophical Review* 37.1 (January): 72–74.

Myers, Frederic W. H. (1903). *Human Personality and its Survival of Bodily Death*. 2 vols. New York and Bombay: Longmans, Green, and Co.

Pound, Ezra (1913). "Commission." *Poetry: A Magazine of Verse* 2.1 (April): 10–11.

Read, Herbert (1952). "Paul Nash." In *The Philosophy of Modern Art: Collected Essays*. London: Faber and Faber. 174–194.

Richards, I. A. (1924). *Principles of Literary Criticism*. London: Kegan Paul, Trench, Trubner.

Richardson, Dorothy (1919). *The Tunnel*. London: Duckworth.

Richardson, Dorothy (1925). "Women in the Arts: Some Notes on the Eternally Conflicting Demands of Humanity and Art." *Vanity Fair* (May), 47, 100.

Rinehart, Mary Roberts (1921). *Sight Unseen and The Confession*. New York: George H. Doran.

Rivers, William H. R. (1920). *Instinct and the Unconscious: A Contribution to a Biological Theory of the Psycho-Neuroses*. Cambridge Medical Series. (eds. Sir Clifford Albutt and Sir Walter Fletcher). Cambridge: Cambridge University Press.

Sinclair, May (1918). "The Novels of Dorothy Richardson." Rev. of *Pointed Roofs, Backwater, and Honeycomb. The Egoist* 5.4 (April): 57–59.

[Woolf, Virginia] (1917). "More Dostoevsky." *TLS* (February 22), 91.

[Woolf, Virginia] (1920). "Freudian Fiction." Rev. of *An Imperfect Mother* by J. D. Beresford. *TLS* (March 25), 199.

Woolf, Virginia (1925). "Modern Fiction." ["Modern Novels," 1919]. In *The Common Reader*. London: Hogarth. 184–195.

Woolf, Virginia (1928). *Orlando*. London: Hogarth.

Woolf, Virginia (1940). "The Leaning Tower." *Folios of New Writing* 2 (Autumn): 11–33.

Woolf, Virginia (1977–1984). "Diary entry, February 27, 1935." [1935]. In *The Diary of Virginia Woolf* (ed. Anne Olivier Bell). 5 vols. London: Hogarth. Vol. 4: 282–283.

Wordsworth, William (1926). *The Prelude: or, Growth of a Poet's Mind*. [1805]. Edited with Introduction from the Manuscripts, Textual and Critical Notes by Ernest de Selincourt. Oxford: Clarendon Press.

Universal

When Jane Austen opened *Pride and Prejudice* with the gently ironic words, "It is a truth universally acknowledged," she plucked a string that has vibrated down to the present time: as knowledge of the universe grows increasingly vast and complex and as its interacting peoples differ increasingly in perspectives and values, what possibilities remain for belief in shared truths? The modernist period was obsessed with universals, but in diametrically opposite trends. While empirical science promised objective and demonstrable truths about the physical universe, both quantum physics and increasing awareness of world cultures argued the plurality and relativity of views. Universal could accordingly be synonymous with absolutes, yet it could also be provisional and flexible, referencing a range of practices and values that could be willingly shared. The meanings of universal thus ranged between something agreed upon by a large group of people and something inherent and essential in human nature or in the universe itself.

Modernism was notably a time of big universal projects. Universal suffrage, universal education, universal religion — established usages before the modernist period — were continuing concerns; universal time, universal language, and universal human rights were initiated in the modernist period. In addition, the modernist period saw the establishment of the universal decimal system devised by John Dewey for the cataloguing of books; the classification of universal donors and universal recipients for the donation and transfusion of blood (identifying a blood type transferable among all blood groups); and even the formation of an agency titled Universal Aunts which provided childcare, house-sitting, dog walking, and other domestic services, largely for travelers to London or those traveling away from their London homes. The examples show universal signifying in three different ways: (i) something asserted as rightfully pertaining to everyone (suffrage, education, human rights), (ii) an agreed-upon convenience to facilitate communication (time, language, library classifications), and (iii) comprehensive scope (hirable "Aunts," like the C19 nomenclature Universal Provider for the general store). The people encompassed in such universality range from everyone (sense i) to a self-selected group (sense iii).

These senses were not always distinct, as evidenced in coinages such as Universal History, Universal Knowledge, or Universal Literature. Here universal functions as a substitute for world, with comprehensive scope as the primary meaning, but the first two terms in particular also imply uniform principles applicable to all. Universal clearly implies categorical truth in Phillips's *The Universal Plot Catalog* (1916), a handbook for writers that, in simplified terms, listed all forms of the plot, long before Westerners had access to Vladimir Propp's typology of actions (functions) and characters (actants) in the Russian folktale ([1928]1958). But universal means worldwide rather than absolute in the

Universal Anthology (1899), a vast compilation of world literature in 33 volumes, in which volume 1, for example, includes selections from ancient Rome, Greece, India, Egypt, China, Ireland, Finland, Estonia, Russia, as well as from the Bible. Although the anthology aimed to collect the "Best Literature" in the world, senior editor Richard Garnett explained that the selection was based on those works that had best survived, noting "the want of any standard of excellence universally agreed upon" and proclaiming that "the age of literary canons [. . .] is gone by." Universal in scope did not necessarily imply universality of values.

Universal in sense (ii), an agreed-upon convention, informs another prolific use: the numerous proposals for universal language. Esperanto, first proposed by Ludovic Lazarus Zamenhof in 1887, is the best known of these languages today (1889), but other roughly contemporaneous contenders included Volapük (The World's Speech), invented by a German priest, Johann Martin Schleyer (1885); Alwato, the "Universal Language" of Universology, Stephen Pearl Andrews's scheme for the unification and communication of all scientific knowledge (1871); and Universal Language (Die Weltsprache Universal), devised by Heinrich Molenaar (1906). Later proposals included C. K. Ogden's Basic English (1929, 1930) and Lancelot Hogben's Interglossa (1943). Other related projects included Pasigraphy, for universal writing, and Euphonetics, for standardization of the spoken word.

232

While possibilities for universal language had been mooted since at least C17, the upsurge in internationalism in the early modernist period brought the idea to the fore. As a reviewer of Volapük commented, "The want of a World's Speech became [. . .] more and more urgent, as telegraphs, railways and steamers seemed to annihilate distances, and to bring the nations of the earth nearer and nearer to each other" (Schele de Vere, 1887). As a speaker for the Australasian Esperanto Association reportedly said, "There is nothing in the world to-day so important as international friendship, and there is nothing which can inculcate that like a common language" ("Universal Language," 1922). Euphonetics envisioned a "World-Standard" in pronunciation to move people beyond the narrow outlooks of regionalism and provincialism toward the larger "unselfish cooperation" of international goals (De Witt, 1925); Sylvia Pankhurst defended "Interlanguage" by noting that "the desire for world-friendship" had been "quickened to an ardent flame by the agonies of World-war," and she anticipated a time when "the peoples of the world shall be one people: a people cultured and kind [. . .] speaking a common language, bound by common interests, when the wars of class and of nations shall be no more" (1927). Universal in these instances was less about regulation than about cooperation and peace (Esperanto means "one who hopes"). There was also no intent to displace native languages with a single form. As W. J. Clark explained, "One bogy which has caused much misdirected criticism is raised by misunderstanding of the word 'universal'": "in the phrase '*universal language*'," he insisted, "'universal' means universally adopted and everywhere current *as an auxiliary* to the mother-tongue for purposes of international communication. It does not mean a universal language for home consumption as a substitute for national language" (1907). Pankhurst agreed, stating that "the world-auxiliary, used by everyone as a second language, will obviate the general need for any other language save the native one" and "enable small nations to meet the Great Powers on equal linguistic terms."

A perceived complication, nonetheless, was how to achieve such universality without unequal relations of power, fueling debates about whether universal language should be natural or artificial, or in linguists' terms, "a posteriori" (created out of an existing language) or "a priori" (created from scratch). Arguments for both sides were feelingly articulated by W. T. Stead. Initially, he expressed hesitation about artificial languages, arguing "though we may be educated up to the artificial as the universal supplement to the mother tongue, yet a man instinctively prefers a language which embodies the heart of a people" (1902b). After listening to arguments that choosing "a living tongue" would necessarily disadvantage native speakers of other tongues, he gave his support to Esperanto: "A true international language cannot be the product of one mind; if all are to accept all must be consulted about its formation" (1902a). Yet the key determinant was, as Stead stated, "if all are to accept." Even artificial languages bore the imprint of native grammars and roots (often Latinate), and even a neutral language would still require effort to learn. Defenders of natural language therefore urged its practicality. Ogden's Basic English rested on an easily acquired core vocabulary of 850 words, with supplemental terms for specialist use; furthermore, it was based on a language already spoken around the world. English, Ogden argued, was "increasing as the second language of all South American countries," was already "the second language of the East," and had been adopted and developed "in the United States, Canada, and Australasia" (1930). Envisioning, too, that "Standard English" might be "enriched and cosmopolitanized" and that "Basic" would "meet the universal demand for a compact and efficient technological medium," Ogden speculated that "English will become not only the International Auxiliary language, but the Universal language of the world." To demonstrate the commensurability of the simple and the complex, Ogden translated part of Joyce's *Finnegans Wake* into Basic English, perhaps surprisingly with not ridiculous result (1932). Ernest Fenollosa and Ezra Pound, in contrast, championed Chinese as the basis for a universal language, believing that the ideogram gave direct expression to the realm of objects and things, and thus to the "universal form of action in nature" (1920). "Such a pictorial method," they stated, "whether the Chinese exemplified it or not, would be the ideal language of the world."

233

Universal

In the Fenollosa–Pound construction, a universally adopted convention of language merges with a concept of fundamental universal nature, going beyond global communication to posit global unity. For many writers, universal in this sense was associated with a generalized apprehension of the spiritual and often associated with poetry. In offering the Chinese-written character as "the medium for poetry," Fenollosa–Pound sought the "universal elements of form which constitute poetics"; they furthermore argued that "the best poetry deals not only with natural images" but also with "natural truth," "hidden in processes too minute for vision and in harmonies too large, in vibrations, cohesions and in affinities," adding that "the Chinese compass these also, and with great power and beauty." For T. S. Eliot, the French poet Baudelaire introduced "something new and something universal in modern life": "the voice of his time" – the superficial and fashionable decadence of his period – was "redeemed by *meaning something else*," a perception of the fundamental and "real problem of good and evil" (1930). By elevating the "imagery of common life," even "the sordid life of a great metropolis" "to the first intensity," Eliot claimed, Baudelaire made it "represent something much more than itself" and so "created a mode of release and expression for other men." Canadian poet Annie Charlotte Dalton contrasted universalism not with period fashion but with "Nationalism, implying war – the only kind of Nationalism that the world so far has known"; she envisioned "future poets" as "much more concerned with the Universal than with National or even International themes," expressing her faith in Canada as "the finest jumping-off place for the Spirit" (1931). Dorothy Richardson found such spiritual form in the silent film which, contrary to "masculine," "characteristically occidental thinkers" devoted to evolutionary becoming, captured in its silence a form of memory that "pile[s] up its wealth only round universals, unchanging, unevolving verities that move neither backwards nor forwards and have neither speech nor language" (1932). Concerned that in becoming "audible," film was acceding to "a masculine destiny" vulnerable to "propaganda," Richardson still hoped for the retention of that silent movement, whose "power to evoke, suggest, reflect, express [. . .] something of the changeless being at the heart of all becoming" she perceived as "essentially feminine." Replacing masculine–feminine with English–Hindu, E. M. Forster warned that different communicative forms can mask the sharing of such universal perception. In *A Passage to India* (1924), when Adela, speaking with English logical rationality, urges, "There will have to be something universal in this country – I don't say religion, for I'm not religious, but something, or how else are barriers to be broken down?" Aziz's poetic mind instinctively withdraws: "She was only recommending the universal brotherhood he sometimes dreamed of, but as soon as it was put into prose it became untrue." Universality of both essence and expression is captured; however, in the Hindu festival, where, dancing and singing, the participants "loved all men, the whole universe, and scraps of their past, tiny splinters of detail, emerged for a moment to melt into the universal warmth." In such examples, feeling, indirectness, and suggestivity prevail over logic and rationality, to make universality not prescribed, but sensed.

Universals could also be critiqued, however, as too prescriptive or too vague. Clement Greenberg deplored the way kitsch, a "mass product of Western industrialism," was becoming "a universal culture, the first universal culture ever beheld"; without "any regard for geographical and national cultural boundaries," kitsch was "crowding out and defacing native cultures in one colonial country after another": "Today the native of China, no less than the South American Indian, the Hindu, no less than the Polynesian, have come to prefer to the products of their native art, magazine covers, rotogravure sections and calendar girls" (1939). If the universal prominence of kitsch was too strong for Greenberg, for Bipin Chandra Pal, Rabindranath Tagore's "abstract universalism" was too weak (1918). Pal, a rational thinker, disagreed with Tagore's mystical "cosmopolitanism," arguing instead that "the way to the universal is through the particular": "The universal is not something which exists by destroying the particularities of the particulars but which rather completes and fulfils them." "Universal Humanity," he argued, just like national society, depends on "the perfection of the lives of the individuals composing it."

Numerous modernists thus sought to unite universal with local and particular. Admitting that "it is only through personality that the artist can make his appeal," critic Arthur Waugh nonetheless countered that "the individual personality acquires acceptance precisely as it relates itself to the universal heart of the world" (1916). Reflecting back on the "horrible events" of 1933–1945, Leonard Woolf coined the somewhat paradoxical term "universal individuality," signifying "the right of everyone to be treated as an individual, a free fellow human being"; for Woolf, a true hatred of human cruelty depends on the recognition that "all other human beings," "even the chicken, the pig, and the dew bedabbled hare," have an "I" like yourself with "the same fearful consciousness of death" (1969). Some formulations more surprisingly fused the national and the universal. Claiming that "the English Character is based on the Sea," Wyndham Lewis both argued that "the particular qualities and characteristics that the sea always engenders in men are those that are [. . .] the most fundamentally English" and simultaneously credited the sea for "that unexpected universality [. . .] found in the completest English artists" (1914). Surveying the career of W. B. Yeats, T. S. Eliot similarly found that "in becoming more Irish, not in subject-matter but in expression, [Yeats] became at the same time more universal" (1940): as a "maturing artist," Yeats achieved the impersonality "of the poet who, out of intense and personal experience, is able to express a general truth; retaining all the particularity of his experience, to make of it a general symbol." In perhaps the most radical formulation, the separation of individual and universal was denied.

235

Universal

Predicting that "the next generations" would be characterized by a "new sense of life, this world sense, which goes towards a totality," Eugene Jolas nonetheless claimed, "By going towards this pure idea, we are individualists and universalists; subversive agents also whose vision is the synthesis of all the forces of life" (1929). Samuel Beckett explained Vico's construction of history as a similar rejection of dualism, one that refused to attribute history's course to either the achievements of "individual agents" or "the work of some superior force," offering instead "the spectacle of a human progression that depends for its movement on individuals, and which at the same time is independent of individuals in virtue of what appears to be a preordained cyclicism" (1929). Vico, in Beckett's reading, embraced and resolved the contradictions: "Individuality is the concretion of universality, and every individual action is at the same time superindividual. The individual and the universal cannot be considered as distinct from each other." Henry James, however, while acknowledging the ultimate unity of everything, considered the need to draw an arbitrary separating line: noting that "really, universally, relations stop nowhere," he nonetheless affirmed, "the exquisite problem of the artist is eternally but to draw, by a geometry of his own, the circle within which they shall happily *appear* to do so" (1907).

SEE ALSO: *Common Mind, Group Thinking; God, Gods; Personality, Impersonality; International; Primitive; Race; Unconscious; Words, Language*

References

(1922). "Universal Language." *Argus* (Melbourne) (October 26), 4.

Andrews, Stephen Pearl (1871). *The Primary Synopsis of Universology and Alwato: The New Scientific Universal Language*. New York: Dion Thomas.

Beckett, Samuel (1929). "DANTE. . . BRUNO. VICO . . JOYCE." *transition: An International Quarterly for Creative Experiment* 16–17 (June): 242–253.

Clark, W. J. (1907). *International Language: Past, Present and Future with Specimens of Esperanto and Grammar*. London: J. M. Dent.

Dalton, Annie Charlotte (1931). *The Future of Our Poetry*. Vancouver: W. Dalton.

De Witt, Marguerite E. (1925). "Our Americanadian Problem of the Spoken Word." *American Speech* 1.3: 170–180.

Eliot, T. S. (1930). "Baudelaire." In *Selected Essays*. London: Faber and Faber.

Eliot, T. S. (1940). "The Poetry of W. B. Yeats." *Purpose* 12.3–4 (July–December): 115–127.

Fenollosa, Ernest Francisco and Ezra Pound (1920). "The Chinese Written Character as a Medium for Poetry." 1919. In *Instigations of Ezra Pound*. New York: Boni and Liveright. 357–401.

Forster, E. M. (1924). *A Passage to India*. London and New York: Edward Arnold.

Garnett, Richard (1899). "The Use and Value of Anthologies." In *The Universal Anthology: A Collection of the Best Literature, Ancient, Mediaeval and Modern, with Biographical and Explanatory Notes* (eds. Richard Garnett, Leon Vallee and Alois Brandl). 33 vols.

London: Clarke Co.; New York: Merrill and Baker; Paris: Emile Terquem; Berlin: Bibliothek Verlag. Vol. 1: xiii–xxiii.

Greenberg, Clement (1939). "Avant-Garde and Kitsch." *The Partisan Review* 6.5 (Fall): 34–49.

Hogben, Lancelot (1943). *Interglossa: A Draft of an Auxiliary for a Democratic World Order, Being an Attempt to Apply Semantic Principles to Language Design.* Middlesex and New York: Penguin Books.

James, Henry (1907). "Preface to *Roderick Hudson.*" In *The Novels and Tales of Henry James.* New York Edition. 26 vols. New York: Charles Scribner's Sons. Vol. 1: v–xx.

Jolas, Eugene (1929). "Notes on Reality." *transition: An International Quarterly for Creative Experiment* 18 (November): 13–20.

[Lewis, Wyndham] (1914). "Manifesto [2]." *Blast* 1 (June 20): 30–43.

Molenaar, Heinrich (1906). *Gramatik de Universal.* Leipzig: Puttmann.

Ogden, C. K. (1929). "Basic England." *The Saturday Review of Literature* (July 20), 1193.

Ogden, C. K. (1930). *Basic English: A General Introduction with Rules and Grammar.* London: Kegan Paul, Trench, Trubner.

Ogden, C. K. (1932). "James Joyce's Anna Livia Plurabelle in Basic English." *transition: An International Quarterly for Creative Experiment* 21 (March): 259–262.

Pal, Bipin Chandra (1918). *Indian Nationalism: Its Principles and Personalities.* Triplicane, Madras: S. R. Murthy.

Pankhurst, E. Sylvia (1927). *Delphos; or, the Future of International Language.* To-Day and To-Morrow. London: Kegan Paul.

Phillips, Henry Albert (1916). *The universal plot catalog: an examination of the elements of plot material and construction, combined with a complete index and a progressive category in which the source, life, and end of all dramatic conflict and plot master are classified.* Springfield: Home Correspondence School; The Authors' Handbook Series. Larchmont: Stanhope-Dodge.

Propp, Vladimir (1958). *The Morphology of the Folk Tale.* [*Morfologiia skazi*, 1928]. Trans. Lawrence Scott. Austin: University of Texas Press.

Richardson, Dorothy (1932). "Continuous Performance: The Film Gone Male." *Close Up* 9.1 (March): 36–38.

Schele de Vere, M. (1887). "Volapük." *Modern Language Notes* 2.8 (December): 216–220.

Schleyer, Johann Martin (1885). *Grammar with Vocabularies of Volapük.* Trans. W. A. Seret. Glasgow: Thomas Murray and Sons.

Stead, W. T. (1902a). "Learning Languages by Letter-Writing." *The Review of Reviews* (August), 202.

Stead, W. T. (1902b). "Learning Languages by Letter-Writing." *The Review of Reviews* (May), 536.

Waugh, Arthur (1916). "The New Poetry." *The Quarterly Review* (October), 365–386.

Woolf, Leonard (1969). *The Journey not the Arrival Matters: An Autobiography of the Years 1939–1969.* London: Hogarth.

Zamenhof, Ludovic Lazarus (1889). *Dr. Esperanto's International Language: Introduction & Complete Grammar.* Unua Libro 1887. Trans. R. H. Geoghegan. Oxford: Balliol College.

Woman, New Woman

In *A Room of One's Own*, Virginia Woolf noted "how many books are written about women" and "how many are written by men"; woman, she concluded, must be "the most discussed animal in the universe" (1929). Men's obsession with defining the other sex, Woolf further observed, enshrined two recurrent tropes: the "Angel in the House" of the perfect but submissive wife and the ludicrous "dancing dog" of the woman who writes. Such definition, she also perceived, was relational. Consigning women to inferior roles helped create the illusion of the superiority that society expected of men: "women have served all these centuries as looking-glasses [. . .] reflecting the man at twice his natural size." Not surprisingly, modernist women's writing about women reveals a proliferation of ways to (re)write woman in her own terms. Converting from negative to positive images, however, involved more than simply replacing traditional views with the new.

Traditional constructs of women represented, for many, a depressing category. For Lyndall, in Olive Schreiner's *The Story of an African Farm*, "To be born a woman" is "to be born branded" (1883); for Edna St. Vincent Millay, it was to be "born [. . .] distressed" (1923). Women's limited possibilities were depicted with images of physical confinement: Lyndall asserts bitterly that women "fit our sphere as a Chinese woman's foot fits her shoe"; Miles Franklin imagined women as being "forced to sit with tied hands" (1901); and Elizabeth Bisland described woman's mind as "long cramped in the swaddling-bands of repression

ABCDEFGHIJKLMNOPQRSTUV**W**XYZ

Modernism: Keywords, First Edition. Melba Cuddy-Keane, Adam Hammond, and Alexandra Peat.
© 2014 Melba Cuddy-Keane. Published 2014 by John Wiley & Sons, Ltd.

and convention" (1894). Dora Marsden distinguished the revolutionary freewoman – the name of her journal – from the majority of "bondwomen," arguing that, for the latter, "ever waiting upon the minds of others" was destroying their "instinct for self-realization" and "achievement in their own person" (1911). New images of women, in contrast, were empowering and self-defining. W. T. Stead described the popular "novel of the modern woman" as "by a woman about women from the standpoint of Woman" (1894); noting a "flood of recent books written by the gentler sex," Elizabeth Bisland stated that woman "knows that she is in revolt against what has been," even though she "cannot yet say what is to replace it." The titles of books, some indeed written by men, further evidenced a progressive trend: Ursula Newell Gestefeld's *The Woman Who Dares* (1894), Ella Hepworth Dixon's *The Story of a Modern Woman* (1894), and Grant Allen's *The Woman Who Did* (1895).

Perhaps the strongest indicator of change was the coinage "New Woman," signaling the desire to remake the meaning of woman, indeed to make woman "new." The term first appeared in Sarah Grand's "The New Aspect of the Woman Question" (1894b), in which Grand roundly rejected the only two kinds of women men recognized – the passive and convenient "cow-woman" and the degraded and dangerous "scum-woman"; hailing the "new woman" of the "future" as "stronger and wiser," Grand declared that women "do not care to see life any longer in a glass darkly." The New Woman, however, was a target of fierce debate. The popular British novelist Ouida attacked Grand's "New Woman," alleging that "fierce vanity," "undigested knowledge," an "over-weening estimate of her own value," and a "fatal want of all sense of the ridiculous" made the "New Woman" a "menace to humankind" (1894). Eliza Lynn Linton castigated the rebels as "Wild Women" who flouted "conventional decencies and offend[ed] against all the canons of good taste" (1892). Grand, in turn, scoffed, "As if women had never been 'wild' or worse before there was any talk of emancipating them" (1894a). Some depictions of the New Woman, however, trod the path in between. In George Hall's *A Study in Bloomers, or, The Model New Woman* (1895), New Women abandon skirts for bloomers, ride bicycles, pole vault, and "Paddle Their Own Canoe," while – matching physical with intellectual freedom – the heroine delivers lectures on finance, prohibition, suffrage, hygiene, and race. Nonetheless, change in this novel by an Evangelical minister is not radical: the narrator posits that "new-woman" ideas need not clash with the "sacred interests of home and family," and – despite an unconventional marriage proposal – the plot ends in a conventional way. But fiction about the New Woman inspired imaginations, and in IC19, the New Woman novel became a popular craze, from detective fiction to romance. The turn from fiction to reality, however, prompted reaction; in 1910, Margaret Deland wrote that "the New Woman was becoming [. . .] something tangible" "outside the columns of the jocose newspaper," posing a threat to both "the family" and "the state." The New Woman is "almost ceasing to be 'new,'" she complained, "for there is something more than a joke in all this curious turning upside-down of traditions and theories in regard to women."

Such "upside-down" theories of women triggered debates about *where* woman should be, in the home or in the world; constructions of woman's nature became ways of arguing woman's place. Rejecting the notion that woman's only place was the home, Olive Schreiner asserted that "domestic labour" was "often the most wearisome and unending known to any section of the human race" and "not adequately recognised or recompensed" (1911). Supporting "voluntary motherhood" as "the key to the temple of liberty," birth control activist Margaret Sanger noted that it "seldom occurred to anyone to ask whether [women] would go on occupying [the home] forever" (1920). Alternative depictions of women supported their place in public life. The eponymous protagonist in Edna Ferber's *Fanny Herself* (1917), a successful young "American business woman," enjoys the "startled and defensive attentiveness" of male colleagues when she leaves "polite small-talk behind and soar[s] up into the cold, rarefied atmosphere of business"; ultimately rejecting the values of "big business," however, Fanny moves on to more liberating work in the newspaper world. In contrast, Grace Ellison argued that, hampered by her physique, "woman can only supplement, never replace man in the professions, the business world of the land" and proposed the careers of preaching and possibly politics instead (1922). The entrance of some women into the public realm occasioned different constructions of women according to class. An advertisement in *Good Housekeeping* for the White Star Line claimed the "modern and independent" "woman's place" to be "flying across the ocean, swimming the channel, running for mayor, writing the world's important books and doing the world's big jobs"; this "program of modernity," however, depended on assigning woman's traditional role to "our kindly stewardesses" who "watch over [the privileged traveler] with unobtrusive but maternal care" (1928).

Yet women also redefined the home by integrating it with the public sphere, agitating for political and social change to aid women's and children's lives. Cooperative women's organizations sprang up on both sides of the Atlantic, uniting the domestic sphere with public activist work. Margaret Llewelyn Davies, General Secretary of the Women's Co-operative Guild in England, spearheaded numerous publications, such as *Maternity: Letters from Working Women* (1915), in a campaign for improved maternity and infant care. An item on "Social Progress" in *The Crisis* reported on the first meeting of the Women's Cooperative League in Baltimore, citing its protests against segregation, "the unsatisfactory [conditions of] public school buildings," and the "lack of provision" for "delinquent and feeble-minded colored children." Women's domestic role was also invoked as a positive influence in national and international spheres. Clemence Dane suggested that women should "take their share of national housekeeping" (1926), and following WWI, Maude Royden called on "women whose husbands or lovers the war has slain, mothers now childless" to "birth a new world" and "make the nations a family," "the world a home" (1920). Rising nationalist agendas in the 1930s, however, returned the domestic to its restricted place. Quoting the British Fascist Oswald Mosley's call for "*men who are men and women who are women*," Winifred Holtby warned that Nazism and Fascism were reviving the "cult of the cradle," offering an "ingenious solution" to the problem of unemployment by "persua[ding] women to leave the labour market willingly, under a psychological pressure applied with formidable effect" while restoring the old myth of masculine superiority at the same time: "a world of hero-worshippers is a world in which women are doomed to subordination" (1934).

Women, however, were acquiring another place in the world through expanding global knowledge. The lists of books reviewed in the *TLS* on women between 1902 and 1950 range through Africa, Arabia, Bengal, China, France, Germany, India, Persia, and Soviet Russia. Yet, while such attention fostered the sense of a world-wide woman's movement, it also generated debates about women's identity, with Western writers strongly divided in opinion about societies that maintained woman's traditional role. Women's domestic life elsewhere could be used dogmatically to assert woman's proper "place" or it could be respected as a significant, even powerful influence in society. Novelist, poet, and Indianist Edward Thompson praised G. S. Dutt's memorial to his wife, Saroj Nalini Dutt, seeing her life – she founded Mahila Samitas (Women's Institutes) in Bengal – as representing the "energetic movements [. . .] working for the social liberation of India" (1929). John Bland, writing in the *TLS*, complimented Florence Ayscough's book on Chinese women for recognizing that they achieved the right to education more rapidly and with less struggle than their Western counterparts (1938); however, writing in *Pacific Affairs*, Olga Lang complained that Ayscough "dealt almost exclusively with Chinese Ladies" failing to examine "the life of farmer women and factory workers" (1939). The need to recognize diversity figured strongly in Esther Harwood's review of *African Women* (1939), which noted that "the Ibo woman has a shrewd head for business," and "the African woman has no very great idea of inferiority to the mere male" (1939). In light of global diversity, "a tidy mind," Harwood warned, "is sometimes a danger in an anthropologist." The Indian writer Cornelia Sorabji balanced female solidarity with awareness of cultural difference when she imagined a "Women's Highway" along which "women are travelling at different rates of progression" (1930). Noting that India achieved "in one night" what Great Britain took centuries to do (granting university degrees and allowing women to practice at the bar), Sorabji nonetheless respectfully acknowledged the purdah, noting that "those women of the shut door have a charm of their own – one does not want them to lose it. Since they cannot come out to take what awaits them, cannot we carry our gifts within?"

241

For African American women, a key question was how to balance racial and gender identity. While they shared in the worldwide struggle for female emancipation, they suffered both from racial discrimination in white culture and from being allotted a merely supporting role to black men. For Elise Johnson McDougald, "The Task of Negro Womanhood" was fighting both "sex and race subjugation" (1925). On one side, the leftist journal *The Messenger* published a "New Negro Woman Number" with an editorial defining women's task as "creat[ing] and keep[ing] alive, in the breast of black men," the determination to achieve "the stature of a full man, a free race and a new world" (1923); on the other, Anna Julia Cooper, while agreeing that "womanhood" was a "vital element in the regeneration and progress" of the black race, claimed the power of the black woman's voice to assert her own identity, since "only [she] can say 'when and where I enter, in the quiet undisputed dignity of my womanhood'" (1892). In "On Being Young, a Woman, and Colored," Marita Bonner claimed that being defined by her race made the "black woman" feel like "an empty imitation of an empty invitation. A mime; a sham; a copy-cat" (1925), whereas Zora Neale Hurston refused to be "tragically colored," celebrating instead her ability to be "the eternal feminine with its string of beads" (1928). Going beyond racial identity, Jessie Redmon Fauset emphasized all women's shared subjugation: in *Plum Bun*, Angela, who can "pass" as either black or white, finds that "men had a better time of it than women, coloured men than coloured women, white men than white women" (1929). W. E. B. Du Bois sought the middle way, endorsing the importance of choice for the "future woman" who, with access to education and "economic independence," could embrace the role of "motherhood at her own discretion"; Du Bois further advocated equality by declaring, "we will allow those persons to vote who know enough to vote, whether they be black or female, white or male" (1920).

242

As much as woman could be a unifying category, it was fraught with differences in age, appearance, class, and race. Generational differences could set women apart, as could society's assumptions about women's appearance: Miles Franklin's Sybylla complains that her mother treats her like a "piece of machinery" which she "winds up the wrong way" and that the "beautiful" woman is treated like the "dog on the top," whereas the "plain woman" will "have nothing forgiven her" (1901). Evelyn Sharp's suffragette story "The Woman at the Gate" presents gender imbricated with tensions between human solidarity and class divisions: watching a deputation, a working-class man shouts "Bravo" and wishes the "unemployed" had "half as much" of the protesting women's "pluck," but a "lady" calls it "terrible to see women going on like this" and wonders if any of them "are quite nice – like us, I mean" (1910). In Gertrude Colmore's *Suffragette Sally*, a "noble lord" bases his argument against suffrage on his claim that "women did not constitute a class" but "were a sex" who "must not be sullied by being dragged into all the hurly-burly of political conflict"; the suffragette wife of a sympathetic lord, however, disguises herself as working class to expose the differential treatments of women protesters in prison depending on their class (1911). Edna Ferber's *Fanny Herself* (1917) imagines solidarity and diversity combined: watching a "suffrage parade" coming up Fifth Avenue, Fanny sees "women, women, women! Hundreds of them, thousands of them, a river of them flowing up Fifth Avenue to the park," describing them further as "Artists. School teachers. Lawyers. Doctors. Writers. Women in college caps and gowns. Women in white, from shoes to hats. Young women. Girls. Gray-haired women. A woman in a wheel chair, smiling." Anaïs Nin made woman a term combining unity and difference, when she envisioned a novel expressing the "development of woman in her own terms" and in all her forms: "the masculine, objective one; the child woman of the world; the material woman; the sensation-seeker; the unconsciously dramatic one; the childish one; the cold egotistical woman. And the healing, intuitive guide-woman" ([1944]1971).

Even as woman was debated, redefined, and celebrated, the idea of a discrete gender category was being challenged, either with a view of men and women united or with doubts about any qualities of woman being innate. The woman's movement was cast as a cooperative endeavor for the good of all: Olive Schreiner imagined a "New Man" to stand "side by side" with the "New Woman" (1911), and Victoria Ocampo argued that the "emancipation of women" would better all humanity, not "separat[ing] her from man" but "bring[ing] her closer to him in the most complete, most pure, and most conscious way," noting, however, that accomplishing this feat would require "the combined heroism of two human beings" ([1936]1979). Woman was also understood as a gender identity that was constructed and performed: Joan Riviere described stereotypical performances of "Womanliness" as "Masquerade" and "mask" (1929), and like Edward Carpenter, she addressed the possibility of "intermediate types" who "display strong features of the other sex." Mathilde Vaerting, inventing a male alter ego, Mathieu, as a collaborating writer, differentiated between gender and sex: "what we call 'masculine' qualities are merely the qualities of a dominant sex, and feminine qualities those of a subordinate sex"; in a vast historical survey of "the peculiarities of man and woman," Vaerting showed how their characteristics changed when their social roles reversed (1923). Winifred Holtby agreed: "We do not know how much of sensitiveness, intuition, protectiveness, docility and tenderness may not be naturally 'male,' how much curiosity, aggression, audacity and combativeness may not be 'female'" (1934). In her children's stories, E. Nesbit imagined the possibility of girls and boys swapping their stereotypical gender qualities. In *The Magic City* (1910), a boy and girl enter a fantasy realm where "girls are expected to be brave and the boys, kind"; in "The Twopenny Spell" (1905), Lucy puts a spell on her brother Harry with the result that she becomes "saddled with her brother's boy-nature," while he, now "girlish inside," becomes "a mere milksop." By the end of the story, however, the siblings become more androgynous, Harry "kinder than before and Lucy braver" – "grow[ing] more and more alike," so that when "they are grown up," there will be little "difference . . . between them." Indeed, after exposing the inequalities in the distinctions imposed by society, Virginia Woolf concluded, "it is fatal to be man or woman pure and simple," and she proposed the hybrid categories of "woman-manly" and "man-womanly" instead. Imagining an "androgynous mind" formed through "collaboration" as crucial to "the art of creation," she ultimately rejected the binary woman/man: "to think [. . .] of one sex as distinct from the other is an effort. It interferes with the unity of the mind" (1929).

SEE ALSO: *Hygiene; Negro, New Negro; Sentimental, Sentimentality; Primitive; Unconscious*

References

(1917). "Social Progress." The Horizon. *The Crisis: A Record of the Darker Races* (May), 36–37.

(1923). "The New Negro Woman." Editorial. *The Messenger*, Special Issue: New Negro Woman's Number (July), 757.

(1928). Advertisement for the White Star Line. *Good Housekeeping* (New York) (February), 110; (March), 106; (July), 108.

Battiscombe, Christopher Francis (Esther Georgina Harwood) (1939). Rev. of *African Women* by Sylvia Leith-Ross. *TLS* (February 4): 76.

Bisland, Elizabeth (1894). "The Cry of the Women." *The North American Review* (June), 757–758.

[Bland, John Otway Percy] (1938). Rev. of *Chinese Women: Yesterday and Today* by Florence Ayscough. *TLS* (February 5), 85.

Bonner, Marits (1925). "On Being Young, a Woman, and Colored." *The Crisis: A Record of the Darker Races* (December), 63–65.

Colmore, Gertrude (1911). *Suffragette Sally*. London: S. Paul.

Cooper, Anna J. (1892). *A Voice from the South*. Xenia: Aldine Printing House.

Dane, Clemence (1926). *The Women's Side*. London: H. Jenkins.

Deland, Margaret (1910). "The Change in the Feminine Ideal." *The Atlantic Monthly* (March), 289–302.

Du Bois, W. E. B. (1920). *Darkwater: Voices from within the Veil*. New York: Harcourt, Brace and Howe.

Ellison, Grace (1922). *The Disadvantages of Being a Woman*. London: A. M. Philpot.

Fauset, Jessie Redmon (1929). *Plum Bun: A Novel without a Moral*. New York: Frederick A. Stokes.

Ferber, Edna (1917). *Fanny Herself*. New York: Frederick A. Stokes.

Franklin, Miles [Stella Maria Sarah] (1901). *My Brilliant Career*. Edinburgh and London: William Blackwell and Sons.

Grand, Sarah (1894a). "The Modern Girl." *The North American Review* (June), 706–715.

Grand, Sarah (1894b). "The New Aspect of the Women Question." *The North American Review* (March), 270–276.

Hall, George (1895). *A Study in Bloomers, or, The Model New Woman: a Novel*. Chicago: American Bible House.

Holtby, Winifred (1934). *Women and a Changing Civilization*. London: John Lane, The Bodley Head.

Hurston, Zora Neale (1928). "How it Feels to be Colored Me." *The World Tomorrow* (May 11), 214–216.

Lang, Olga (1939). Rev. of *Chinese Women: Yesterday and Today. Pacific Affairs* 12.2 (June): 212–214.

Linton, Eliza Lynn (1892). "The Partisans of the Wild Women." *The Nineteenth Century* (March 31), 455–464.

Marsden, Dora (1911). "Bondwomen." *The Freewoman* (November 23), 1–2.

McDougald, Elise Johnson (1925). "The Task of Negro Womanhood." In *The New Negro: An Interpretation* (ed. Alain Locke). New York: Albert and Charles Boni. 369–382.

Millay, Edna St Vincent (1923). "Sonnet XVIII." In *The Harp-Weaver and Other Poems*. New York: Harper and Brothers. 70.

Nesbit, E. (1905). "The Twopenny Spell." In *Oswald Bastable and Others*. London: Wells, Gardner, Darton, and Co. 167–180.

Nesbit, E. (1910). *The Magic City*. London: Macmillan and Co.

Nin, Anaïs (1971). "Diary entry, August 1944." [1944]. In *The Diary of Anaïs Nin* (ed. Gunther Stuhlmann). 7 vols. New York: Harcourt Brace Jovanovich. Vol. 4: 1944–1947: 25.

Ocampo, Victoria (1979). "Woman, Her Rights and Her Responsibilities." ["La mujer, sus derechos y sus responsabilidades," 1936]. Trans. Doris Meyer. In *Against the Wind and the Tide* (ed. Doris Meyer). New York: George Braziller. 228–234.

Ouida (1894). "The New Woman." *The North American Review* (May), 610–619.

Riviere, Joan (1929). "Womanliness as Masquerade." *International Journal of Psycho-Analysis* 8: 303–311.

Royden, Maude (1920). *Sermon Preached by A. Maude Royden in the Cathedral at Geneva on the Occasion of the Meeting of the International Alliance for Women's Suffrage Alliance, Sunday June 6th, 1920*. London: League of the Church Militant.

Sanger, Margaret (1920). *Woman and the New Race*. New York: Brentano's.

Schreiner, Olive (1883). *The Story of An African Farm*. London: Chapman Hall.

Schreiner, Olive (1911). *Women and Labour*. London: Fisher Unwin.

Sharp, Evelyn (1910). "The Woman at the Gate." In *Rebel Women*. London: A. C. Fifield; New York: John Lane.

Sorabji, Cornelia (1930). "The Women of India: Behind the Purdah." Education and Emancipation. *The Times* (London) (February 18), 46.

Stead, W. T. (1894). "The Book of the Month: The Novel of the Modern Women." *The Review of Reviews* (July), 64–74.

Thompson, Edward John (1929). Rev. of *A Woman of India* by G. S. Dutt. *TLS* (June 27): 504.

Vaerting, Mathilde and Mathais Vaerting [pseudonym] (1923). *The Dominant Sex: A Study in the Sociology of Difference*. Trans. Eden and Cedar Paul. New York: George H. Doran.

Woolf, Virginia (1929). *A Room of One's Own*. London: Hogarth.

Words, Language

Language – the very subject of this book – is a conduit carrying the past into the future, engaging the twin forces of continuity and change. As the modernists them-selves realized, every word uttered both echoes and alters words of the past. During the modernist period, the mutability, instability, and variousness of words became a focus of heightened attention, stimulated by expanding literacy, increasing cultural diversity, and the heightened scale of communicative technologies, global travel, and international conflicts and concerns. Perhaps nothing testifies to the modernist preoccupation with language so much as one of the great monuments of the modernist era: *A New English Dictionary on Historical Principles* (later the *Oxford English Dictionary* (OED)), conceived in 1857 and published in install-ments between 1884 and 1928. As the work progressed, the first editor James A. H. Murray and his colleagues not only discovered that it would take much longer than anticipated; they also realized that given the constant evolution of words and usage, the work would never be complete. A *Supplement* was added to the reissued dictionary in 1933, inaugurating a practice that has evolved into continuous updating today in electronic form. In itself, this great dictionary encap-sulates the tensions in the lives of words: identifying a word's origin offers a way of verifying and stabilizing meaning by recourse to semantic roots; at the same time, diversity in usage and ongoing historical evolution make definitive meaning impossible to ascertain and fix.

246

Given such diverse and changing usage, words, in the modernist period, were frequently thought to be in trouble. Many of our entries cite concerns that words were being used so casually and idiosyncratically that they had virtually lost any useful meaning: George Orwell's complaint, for example, that ``the word *Fascism*'' had been reduced to signifying merely ``something not desirable'' (see Fascism) or Richards's criticism that the words ``sincerity,'' ``truth,'' and even ``meaning'' itself ``discharge a cloud of heterogeneous missiles instead of a single meaning'' (see Form). A similar accusation came from Rose Macaulay, who, in an attack on *Catchwords and Claptrap* (1926), inveighed against words being used in ``not an individual, but a herd sense,'' overwhelmed by ``haloes'' reflecting ``some vague body of associations.'' Such debased usage, Macaulay argued, dis-credited words like ``Bolshevist'' and ``capitalist,'' which, like allusions to ``women and children'' and ``babies,'' functioned merely to ``excite general emotion''; she further professed outright bewilderment at ``the full aura of associations [. . .] which surround the name *woman*,'' arguing that ``this apparently simple and straightforward word has a considerable element of catchword about it, and has become surrounded by a good deal of claptrap.'' Sinclair Lewis's novel *The Job* (1917), in tracking the career of Una Golden from her initial work as a stenographer at ``one hundred words a minute,'' remarked the difference between words' vague emotional haloes and practical realities: "There is plenty of romance in business. Fine, large, meaningless, general terms like romance and business can always be related. They take the place of thinking, and are highly useful to optimists and lecturers." Writing at the end of WWII, George Orwell claimed that generally "the English language is in a bad way" but went further to link the "debasement of language" to "the present political chaos" (1946). Decrying the prevalence of "ready-made phrases" and "euphemism, question-begging and sheer cloudy vagueness," Orwell pointedly observed the way such obfuscation was "favourable to political conformity" and made possible "the defence of the indefensible" by covering up realities "which are too brutal for most people to face." Differing radically from Orwell in his politics, Ezra Pound similarly cast the ramifications of poor speech as political: arguing that "clear thought and sanity depend on clear prose," he conflated "the lack of representative government in Germany" with "the nonexistence of decent prose in the German language," charging that "the mush of the German sentence, the straddling of the verb out to the end" left the mind vulnerable to being "cheated or stampeded by national phrases and public emotionalities" (1917).

The desire to improve language frequently pushed words in the direction of greater consolidation of meaning, toward transparency and clarity of expression. In Macaulay's view, words needed a closer allegiance to dictionary definition: as she argued, "once you step outside precise dictionary values and depend on a nimbus of associations to carry your meaning across, you are on dangerous ground." Those whose minds were currently "excited, untrained, and confused" should be guided by "those with clear heads and good dictionaries" – those indeed with "dictionary minds." Orwell emphasized the pragmatic importance of linguistic clarity, arguing, "If one gets rid of these [bad] habits one can think more clearly, and to think clearly is a necessary first step toward political regeneration." This desire for clarity led him to advocate "driv[ing] out foreign phrases and strayed scientific words," but not to any prescriptive "setting up of a 'standard English'" or "avoidance of Americanisms"; his objective was to restore "language as an instrument for expressing and not for concealing or preventing thought."

Similar guidelines for using words were proposed by The Society for Pure English (1913–1930s), although preserving and developing the "English character" of the "national medium of expression" was this organization's goal (1919). Despite the regulatory sound of "pure," the group's "original prospectus" indicated that they were not against "foreign words" or against change; nonetheless, they believed that foreign words must be "assimilated" and "naturalized" into English, not simply "borrowed," and that "future development" should be guided by a knowledge of the history of the English language and "controlled by the forces and processes which have formed it in the past." Describing their ideals as both "conservative" and "democratic," they advocated "the preservation of 'dialects and local forms'''; believing that the "best wordmakers are the uneducated and not the educated classes," they opted for "vivid popular terms" over "the artificial creations of scientists." Above all, they advocated for "the living and popular character of our speech." H. L. Mencken, generally supportive of the Society's efforts and its focus on "the language that is in being," pursued similar work on American words, which he divided into the "two dialects" of "educated speech" and "vulgar speech" − noting, however, that one of his correspondents argued there were actually four kinds: "a language of the intellectuals, another of the fairly educated (business men, Congressmen, etc.), another of the great American democracy, another of the poor trash"(1921). While recognizing such differences within American usage, Mencken focused primarily on establishing "varieties of American English" as distinct from "standard English," citing such Americanisms as "loanwords" (*happy hunting ground, prairie, plaza, hamburger, smithereens, kowtow*), "artificial words" (*kodak, crisco*), and word "coinages" (*loan shark, bonehead, to light out, to hurry up, showdown, frame-up*). Like the work on the "English of England," Mencken's purpose was to establish, through attention to "spoken language," "national idiosyncrasies and ways of mind."

The goal of assigning to speech a national character clearly did not require a static language, and if one agenda sought to rescue words from pedantry, pretension, and obfuscation through greater clarification and categorization, another strain appreciated and indeed celebrated organic grassroots change. While jargon adopted from business or science was generally not well received, creative new coinages were broadly welcomed in vernacular speech. Concerned that the "importation of foreign words into the English language" had "weakened its ancient word-making powers," The Society for Pure English "encourage[d] those who possess the word-making faculty to exercise it freely." Reviewing the Society's Tract, the American critic Brander Matthews opined that "the atrophy of the word-making habit is less obvious in the United States than it is in Great Britain," citing "windjammer," "farm-hand," "that most delectable vocable pussy-footed," and, from the "electrical profession,'live wire'" (1920). Virginia Woolf similarly observed that "the Americans are doing what the Elizabethans did − they are coining new words," citing "poppycock, rambunctious, flipflop, booster, good-mixer" and adding that "all the expressive ugly vigorous slang which creeps into use among us first in talk, later in writing, comes from across the Atlantic" (1925). Zora Neale Hurston celebrated the word-coining power in African American speech, noting its distinctive use of "action words" that are always "dramatized" and "illustrated": the Negro's greatest contribution to language, she argued, appears in the invention of "rich metaphor and simile" ("like lawyers going to heaven" or "regular as pig-tracks"), double descriptives ("low-down" and "kill-dead"), and verbal nouns ("funeralize" and "jooking") (1934). Vernacular language was dynamic, vital, and alive.

With the growing diversity of speakers of English, linguistic mongrelization could of course be regarded with fear. Asserting the value of a national language's "particular character and genius" and its function as the "drapery of native atmosphere and circumstance," Henry James warned that "the vast contingent of aliens" who "have been artfully wooed and weaned" from their native speech will "play [havoc] with the English language," dumping a "mountain of promiscuous material into the foundation of the American" (1905). Yet James concurred that "language is a living organism" which must be capable of "new tricks, new experiments, new amusements"; at bottom, he feared not change but indifference and so urged "the conservative interest" "to respect, to confirm, to consecrate," hoping that the "music" of "formed and finished utterance" would become an object of "love." Against the "conservative interests," however, revolutionary approaches welcomed hybrid Englishes as a source of vitality. Mina Loy proffered a different version of national language in an America "where latterly a thousand languages have been born, and each one, for purposes of communication at least, English – English enriched and variegated with the grammatical structure and voice-inflection of many races." Loy considered "this composite language" to be truly expressive of America since, like Americans, "it grows as you speak": "while professors of Harvard and Oxford labored to preserve 'God's English,' the muse of modern literature arose, and her tongue had been loosened in the melting-pot." Words were productively mongrel for Virginia Woolf as well, overriding class, national, and ethnic difference: "Royal words mate with commoners. English words marry French words, German words, Indian words, Negro words," because words "do not live in dictionaries; they live in the mind" (1937).

249

The life of words "in the mind" impelled language toward expansion, complexity, and flux, taking words' associative haloes from obfuscating vagueness to illuminating diffusive light. When Eugene Jolas proclaimed the "Revolution of the Word" (1929b) and "the Revolution of Language" (1933), his goal was "a new and more pliable form of expression." Jolas's experience as a reporter – for, among other venues, the *Chicago Tribune* – turned him against "machine words" written to "a newspaper rhythm" ([1930s–1952]1998), and he championed "creative language as a pre-rational process" instead (1933). Yet, while fearful of the reigning "positivist metaphysics" and "the re-establishment of traditionalist rationalism" in which "the enigmatic or the pre-logical is ignored" (1929a), Jolas considered "the neo-romantic attitude" too one-sidedly focused on "irrationalism." Advocating "a new realism synthesizing two realities" – "subjective and objective," "reason and instinct," "the supernatural and the natural" (1928) – Jolas called for "experimental" uses of language to forge "a new composition [which] is polyphonic and on many planes" (1929a). Publishing works by the wordmongers James Joyce and Gertrude Stein in his journal *transition*, Jolas proclaimed, "THE LITERARY CREATOR HAS THE RIGHT TO DISINTEGRATE

THE PRIMAL MATTER OF WORDS IMPOSED ON HIM BY TEXT-BOOKS AND DICTIONARIES" and "THE RIGHT TO USE WORDS OF HIS OWN FASHIONING" (1929b).

For many writers, the literary touchstone for growing, living language was James Joyce. Emphasizing imagination's "ability to make words" and so "give created forms reality" (Williams, 1923), William Carlos Williams claimed that in a world where "all the words are dead or beautiful," Joyce achieved "truth through the breakup of beautiful words," "let[ting] the staleness out of them" (1927). Such "broken words" broke down the barriers in traditional language, and Williams extolled both the "fullness" of Joyce's humanity and "the universality of his growing language which is no longer english," since "Joyce uses German, French, Italian, Latin, Irish, anything." Canadian writer W. Eric Harris similarly heralded a revolution in language stimulated by "an Irishman" expatriate in Paris; quoting the opening words of Joyce's "Work in Progress" (later *Finnegans Wake*), Harris imagined the writer as inaugurating a new "American" speech – so-named because of its mongrelisms and iconoclasms – which, in a fantasized future, becomes the "world language" used by all (1929). For Wallace Stevens, Joyce's words signaled a turn in language to the "wholly connotative" – an indication of both "the tendency today" and "a use of language favorable to reality" (1942). Samuel Beckett wrote that Joyce had "desophisticated language," glossing "sophisticated" as "abstracted to death" (1949). In, for example, replacing the abstract "doubt" with the concrete "in twosome twiminds," Beckett argued, Joyce achieved "a quintessential extraction of language" with "the savage economy of hieroglyphics." Rejecting the idea that such words were "obscure," Beckett claimed instead: "Here words are not the polite contortions of 20th century printer's ink. They are alive." Ezra Pound similarly inveighed against the "anemia of modern speech," epitomized in the way "the universal copula 'is'" reduces concrete reality to "the abstractest state of all, namely, bare existence" (1920); Pound also championed Joyce for "the style, the actual writing: hard, clear-cut, with no waste of words, no bundling up of useless phrases, no filling in with pages of slosh" (1917).

While Joyce's iconoclastic word creations seemed thus to bring words closer to reality and universality, yet another modernist approach focused on the breakdown of connections between words and meaning, setting the falsity of language as a rational order against the irrational chaos of the world. In Joseph Conrad's *Lord Jim* (1990), Marlow wavers away from conventional assumptions of a meaningful universe, commenting, "I seemed to have lost all my words in the chaos of dark thoughts I had contemplated for a second or two beyond the pale"; for Marlow's skeptical self, language, like moral ideals and concepts of justice, boils down to a "convention," "one of the rules of the game, nothing more," shielding us from the "vast enigma" of existence: "for words also belong to the sheltering conception of light and order which is our refuge." In William Faulkner's *Absalom, Absalom!* (1936), Mr. Compson similarly refers to Quentin's "grandfather speaking the lame vain words, the specious and empty fallacies which we call comfort" and offers his own view of "the words, the symbols, the shapes themselves shadowy inscrutable and serene, against that turgid background of a horrible and bloody mischancing of human affairs." In E. M. Forster's *A Passage to India* (1924), the narrator remarks, "In the twilight of the double-vision, a spiritual muddledom is set up for which no high-sounding words can be found," and after her experience in the caves, Mrs. Moore thinks of "poor little talkative Christianity," feeling "that all its divine words from 'Let there be Light' to 'It is finished' only amounted to 'boum.'" Samuel Beckett's "Texts for Nothing" ([1950–1951]1955) paradoxically uses words to capture their emptiness: "The words too, slow, slow, the subject dies before it comes to the verb, words are stopping too," with relief only in ceasing to write – "what a blessing it's all down the drain, nothing ever as much as begun, nothing ever but nothing and never, nothing ever but lifeless words."

Alternatively, rather than duplicitously hiding chaotic disorder, words, in gesturing to what they cannot contain, could suggest rich plenitude. T. S. Eliot, calling the near impossible quest to fit words to human experience "a raid on the inarticulate," invoked a gestural dimension in language (in musical reverberations and pattern) to adumbrate experience at the edge of, or beyond, ordinary consciousness: "Words, after speech, reach/Into silence" (1943). In *A Passage to India*, in addition to emptiness, the inadequacy of words paradoxically implies spiritual vision: referring to his wife's and his brother-in-law's interest in Hinduism, Fielding explains that he "can't explain, because it isn't in words at all." The strange communications between people in *Absalom, Absalom!* take place where words are exchanged but on a deeper intuitive level behind them: in the opening scene, Quentin and Miss Rosa "tal[k] to one another in the long silence of notpeople in notlanguage," and Charles and Henry Bon communicate in "a dialogue without words." D. H. Lawrence propounded a positive divorce between intellectualized semantics and language as "sensuous gratification," expressing the difference through cultural contrast; whereas the Englishman seeks "to understand thoroughly and impersonally what is meant," the Italian responds to "speech which appeals to the senses and makes no demand on the mind": "like a child, hearing and feeling without understanding," he is "fulfilled" by "the physical effect of the language upon the blood" (1916). In Virginia Woolf's *Between the Acts* (1941), while others are attempting to explain aesthetic response, Mrs. Swithin protests, "We haven't the words – we haven't the words. Behind the eyes; not on the lips; that's all," and her brother muses, "Thoughts without words." For the playwright Miss La Trobe, however, the creative act begins in words without thoughts, reaching the senses before making sense: "Words of one syllable sank down into the mud. She drowsed; she nodded.

Words, Language

The mud became fertile. Words rose above the intolerably laden dumb oxen plodding through the mud. Words without meaning – wonderful words."

Modernists were haunted by words. The first published crossword puzzle, called a "Word-cross" and created by Arthur Wynne, appeared in *The New York World* on December 21, 1913, sparking the regular inclusion of such puzzles in *Pearson's Magazine* (1922), *The Times* (London) (1930), and *The New York Times* (1942). The public fascination with words fueled the popular BBC program "My Word," which ran from 1956 to 1990. A lighthearted game show posing questions about the meanings and origin of words and sayings, to which the answers were sometimes long punning shaggy dog stories, the program attracted a devoted audience around the world. Words also catapulted to prominence through a vigorous interest in historical semantics, a development that Owen Barfield attributed directly to the OED, "that unrivalled monument of imaginative scholarship" (1926). Barfield's title for his own work, *History in English Words*, also signaled a new approach: not a history *of* words, but history *through* words. Evocatively Barfield wrote, "In the common words we use every day the souls of past races, the thoughts and feelings of individual men stand around us, not dead, but frozen in their attitudes like the courtiers in the garden of the Sleeping Beauty." For Barfield, words record "the evolution of consciousness," revealing, over the centuries, a gradual alteration in subject/object relations: "the shifting for the centre of gravity of consciousness from the cosmos around him into the personal human being himself." While the new inner locus of meaning strengthened "the peculiar freedom of mankind," however, it weakened "the spiritual life and activity felt to be immanent in the world outside," and Barfield called for a reinvigoration of our spiritual connection to the universe through *Poetic Diction* (1928): the forging of "fresh meaning" through metaphor's "magic of new combinations," activating a "felt change of consciousness" in the reader. But it is Barfield's approach to historical understanding that perhaps is most relevant here. Discussing our difficulties in understanding even "our great grandfathers," Barfield distinguished between "trac[ing] the history of [words'] meanings" and "feel[ing] what different associations they must have called up" in earlier times (1926). Combining historical knowledge with the activity of "our own imagination, working introspectively," Barfield paved the way for investigating culture through keywords.

252

References

(1919). *SPE [Society for Pure English] Tract No. 1*. Oxford: Clarendon Press.
Barfield, Owen (1926). *History in English Words*. London: Methuen.
Barfield, Owen (1928). *Poetic Diction: A Study in Meaning*. London: Faber and Gwyer.
Beckett, Samuel (1929). "DANTE...BRUNO.VICO..JOYCE." *transition: An International Quarterly for Creative Experiment* 16–17 (June): 242–253.

Beckett, Samuel (1955). "textes pour rien." ("Texts for Nothing," [2 and 13]) [1950–1951]. In *Nouvelles et Textes pour rien*. Paris: Éditions de Minuit. 127–220.

Conrad, Joseph (1900). *Lord Jim*. Blackwood's Magazine 1899–1900. London: William Blackwood and Sons.

Eliot, T. S. (1943). *Four Quartets*. New York: Harcourt, Brace and Co.; London: Faber and Faber. 1944.

Faulkner, William (1936). *Absalom, Absalom!* New York: Random House.

Fenollosa, Ernest Francisco and Ezra Pound (1920). "The Chinese Written Character as a Medium for Poetry." 1919. In *Instigations of Ezra Pound*. New York: Boni and Liveright. 357–401.

Forster, E. M. (1924). *A Passage to India*. London and New York: Edward Arnold.

Harris, W. Eric (1929). *Achates, or, The Future of Canada*. To-Day and To-Morrow. London: Kegan Paul; New York: E. P. Dutton.

Hurston, Zora Neale (1934). "Characteristics of Negro Expression." In *Negro: An Anthology* (ed. Nancy Cunard). London: Lawrence and Wishart. 39–46.

James, Henry (1905). *The Question of Our Speech; The Lesson of Balzac. Two Lectures*. Boston and New York: Houghton Mifflin.

Jolas, Eugene (1928). "Notes." *transition: An International Quarterly for Creative Experiment* 14 (Fall): 180–185.

Jolas, Eugene (1929a). "Notes on Reality." *transition: An International Quarterly for Creative Experiment* 18 (November): 13–20.

Jolas, Eugene and signateurs (1929b). "Revolution of the Word." *transition: An International Quarterly for Creative Experiment* 16–17 (June): 11–14.

Jolas, Eugene (1933). "What is the Revolution of Language?" *transition: An International Quarterly for Creative Experiment* 22 (February): 125–126.

Jolas, Eugene (1998). *Man from Babel*. [1930s–1952]. Edited, Annotated, and Introduction by Andreas Kramer and Rainer Rumold. New Haven: Yale University Press.

Lawrence, D. H. (1916). *Twilight in Italy*. London: Duckworth.

Lewis, Sinclair (1917). *The Job*. New York: Harcourt, Brace and Co.

Macaulay, Rose (1926). *Catchwords and Claptrap*. London: Hogarth.

Matthews, Brander (1920). "A Campaign for Pure English." *The New York Times Book Review* (September 26): 46.

Mencken, H. L. (1921). *The American Language: An Inquiry into the Development of English in the United States*. 2nd rev. and enl. ed. New York: A. A. Knopf.

Orwell, George (1946). "Politics and the English Language." *Horizon* (April), 252–265.

Pound, Ezra (1917). "James Joyce: At Last the Novel Appears — Book Review of 'A Portrait of the Artist as a Young Man'." *The Egoist* 4.2: 21–22.

Stevens, Wallace (1942). "The Noble Rider and the Sound of Words." In *The Language of Poetry*, by Philip Wheelwright, Cleanth Brooks, I. A. Richards, and Wallace Stevens (ed. Alan Tate). Princeton: Princeton University Press. 91–105.

Williams, William Carlos (1923). *Spring and All*. Paris: Contact.

Williams, William Carlos (1927). "A Note on the Recent Work of James Joyce." *transition: An International Quarterly for Creative Experiment* 8 (November): 149–154.

Woolf, Virginia (1925). "American Fiction." *The Saturday Review of Literature* (August 1), 1–3.

Woolf, Virginia (1939). "Craftsmanship." *The Listener* (May 5), 868–869.

Woolf, Virginia (1941). *Between the Acts*. London: Hogarth.

253

Index of Modernist Authors

Abercrombie, Lascelles, 47
Acorn, George [pseud.], 28
Adams, Edward C. L., 152
Adams, Henry, 7, 31, 157–158, 216
Adams, James Truslow, 26, 28, 30
Adams, Mary, 57
Adams, William Edwin, 6, 28–29
A. E. R. See Randall, Alfred E. (A. E. R.)
Agronsky, Martin, 87
Aiken, Conrad, 228
Allen, Grant, 45, 239
Allen, Hervey, 17
Anand, Mulk Raj, 156
Anderson, Ethel, 144
Anderson, Margaret C., 181, 215
Anderson, Sherwood, 14, 22–23, 38,
    160, 201
Andrews, Stephen Pearl, 232, 236
Apollinaire, Guillaume, 2
Archibald, Norman, 218
Arnold, Matthew, 34–35, 99, 108
Auden, W. H., 38, 53–54, 65, 88, 122,
    180–181, 185, 201
Auden, W. H. (group), 173
Auerbach, Erich, 24, 199, 201
Austin, Mary, 206
Ayscough, Florence, 241

Babbitt, Irving, 60, 141
Bagley, Julian Elihu, 152
Ballinger, W. G., 81
Barfield, Owen, 252
Baring, Evelyn, 79–80
Baring, Maurice, 113
Barnard, Marjorie (See Eldershaw),
    M. Barnard
Barnes, Djuna, 100, 178
Barnes, J. S., 87
Barnes, Leonard, 185
Barney, Natalie, 51
Barrie, J. M., 102
Bartlett, F. C., 172
Bates, Daisy, 78
Battiscombe, Christopher
    Francis, 241
Bavin, T. R., 81
Beckett, Samuel, 41, 91–92, 100–101,
    139, 198, 236, 250–251
Bell, Clive, 51, 94, 204, 206
Bell, Julian, 131
Bellow, Saul, 155, 157
Benjamin, Walter, xiv, 200, 215
Bennett, Arnold, 23, 47–48, 50, 92, 112,
    192, 194, 196, 198, 210
Bentham, Jeremy, 129

Modernism: Keywords, First Edition. Melba Cuddy-Keane, Adam Hammond, and Alexandra Peat.
© 2014 Melba Cuddy-Keane. Published 2014 by John Wiley & Sons, Ltd.

Beresford, J. D., 95
Bergson, Henri, 73, 155, 224
Berreman, Joel V., 20(17)
Bertram, Anthony, 210
Betjeman, John, 121
Beveridge, Albert J., 35
Beverly Baxter, Arthur, 16
Beyer, Henry G., 119, 122
Beynon, Francis Marion, 82
Beynon Ray, Marie, 140
Bianco White, Amber, 171
Bierce, Ambrose, 198
Bigman, Stanley, 134
Billy, André, 2
Binyon, Laurence, 203
Bisland, Elizabeth, 238–239
Bland, John Otway Percy, 241
Blumenfeld, Harold, 86
Boas, Franz, 140, 163
Bogan, Louise, 93, 211
Bok, Edward, 31
Bolton, Thaddeus, 23, 205
Bonner, Marita, 242
Bowen, Elizabeth, xvi, 110
Bowen, J. W. E., 148
Boyd, Ernest, 30
Bradbrook, Muriel Clara, 108
Bradford, Gamaliel, 30
Bradley, Marion S., 215
Brande, W. T., 171
Brecht, Bertolt, 197, 198, 201
Breton, André, 137
Brieux, Eugène, 210
Brittain, Vera, 29
Broad, C. D., 228
Brooke, Rupert, 49, 51, 192
Brooks, Cleanth, 74, 91–94
Brooks, Van Wyck, 14, 49,
    53–54, 116
Brown, E. K., 112
Brownell, Baker, 211
Bryher (Annie Winifred Ellerman), 12
Buchan, John, 7
Bucke, Richard, 71
Bugg, Eugene G., 225
Burgess, Ernest W., 188
Burroughs, Edgar Rice, 166
Butler, A. G., 219

Butler, Nicholas Murray, 132
Butts, Mary, 28, 47, 50, 102–103
Byron, Milton, 27, 29, 49, 60

Caesar, Irving, 117
Callaghan, Morley, 67
Canby, Henry Seidel, 191, 193
Cargill, Oscar, 133
Carnevali, Emanuel, 74, 139, 211
Carpenter, Edward, 179, 243
Carpenter, William B., 224, 226
Carter, Elmer A., 151
Carter, Huntly, 205
Cary, Joyce, 67
Castagnary, Jules, 125
Cather, Willa, xvi, 103
Cecil, David, 31
Chakotin, Serge, 174
Chalmers-Mitchell, Peter, 89
Chamberlain, John R., 206
Chase, Richard, 13, 115
C. H. D. *See* Douglas, Clifford Hugh
    (C. H. D.)
Chéronnet, Louis, 1
Chesterton, Cecil, 185
Chesterton, G. K., 35, 75, 121
Cheyney, Ralph, 95, 143–145
Child, Charles M., 224
Childs, Harwood Lawrence, 171
Churchill, Winston, 61, 218
Clark, W. J., 232
Clifford, Carrie, 188
Cole, G. D. H., 58
Collingwood, R. G., 87, 172
Colmore, Gertrude, 242
Colton, Arthur, 27, 30–31
Connolly, Cyril, 117
Conrad, Joseph, xvi, 18, 22, 45, 78–79,
    126–127, 131, 142, 165, 168, 171,
    193, 194–195, 250, 253
Cooper, Anna Julia, 242
Copland, Aaron, 36
Corelli, Marie, 142
Cortot, Alfred, 167
Cox, R. G., 52
Cozzens, James Gould, 179
Crane, Frances (Kirkwood), 215
Crane, Hart, 182, 227

255

Crane, R. S., 74, 93–94
Crane, Stephen, 165
Crawford, Virginia M., 86
Cullen, Countee, 103, 149
Cummings, E. E., 67
Cunard, Nancy, 103, 188

Dalrymple, Leona, 18
Dalton, Annie Charlotte, 234
Dane, Clemence, 240
Darrow, Clarence, 15
D'Avenel, Viscount Georges, 216
Davidson, Carter, 65
Davidson, John, 142
Davies, Margaret Llewelyn, 240
Davies, William Henry, 29
Day Lewis, Cecil, 1
De Begnac, Ivon, 88
De Witt, Marguerite E., 232
Deland, Margaret, 239
Dell, Floyd, 211
DeVoto, Bernard, 31, 225, 228
Dewey, John, 57, 231
Dickinson, Goldie Lowes, 181
Dillon, George, 214
Dillon, John, 140
Dingle, Herbert, 70
Dixon, Ella Hepworth, 239
Dixon, Thomas, 187
Doob, Leonard, 171
Dos Passos, John, 131
Douglas, Clifford Hugh (C. H. D.), 58, 71
Douglas, Alfred, 177
Dreiser, Theodore, 165, 198
Du Bois, W. E. B., xvi, 57, 88, 153,
    172–173, 185, 187, 189, 226, 242
Duncan, Isadora, 167
Duncan, Lee, 180
Duncan, Robert, 180–182
Durkheim, Emile, 41
Durrell, Clement V., 70
Durrell, Lawrence, 160
Dutt, G. S., 241

Eagleson, Harvey, 73
Edgar, Pelham, 53
Edwards, Thomas C., 120
Eggleston, J. W., 81–82

Einstein, Albert, 70–75, 71–75
Eldershaw, Flora (*See* Eldershaw),
    M. Barnard
Eldershaw, M. Barnard, 60, 144
Eliot, Charles W., 122
Eliot, George, 111, 155
Eliot, T. S., xi, xvi, 8, 43, 50–53, 56–57,
    61, 63–67, 70, 73–75, 87, 92, 101, 104,
    109, 121, 140, 160, 164, 167, 194,
    204, 206–207, 214, 226, 234–235, 251
Elliot, W. Y., 86
Ellis, Havelock, 8, 179, 215
Ellison, Grace, 240
Ellison, Ralph, 152, 206
Erlich, Victor, 92–93
Ewart, John S., 80–81

Faber, Geoffrey Cust, 19
Fabre, Michel, 52
Fargue, Léon-Paul, 227
Farjeon, Eleanor, 107
Faulkner, William, xvi, 100, 103, 251
Fauset, Jessie Redmon, 149, 188, 242
Fearing, Franklin, 30
Fenollosa, Ernest Francisco, 96, 233–234
Ferber, Edna, 240, 243
Ferenczi, Sándor, 179
Fitzgerald, F. Scott, 3, 22, 45, 101, 156,
    187, 205
Fitzhugh, Percy Keese, 219
Flanner, Janet, 53
Flaubert, Gustave, 126, 133
Fleming, William H., 187
Flint, F. S., 137, 204
Flores, Angel, 181
Follett, Mary Parker, 43
Ford, Ford Madox, 31, 91, 109, 126, 128,
    133, 159, 172, 185, 212, 216, 219
Ford, Henry Jones, 80
Ford, Sewell, 114
Forster, E. M., 24, 35–36, 41, 47, 61, 92,
    94, 103–104, 116, 131, 156, 158, 188,
    204, 211, 234, 251
Fowler, H. W., 152
Frank, Waldo David, 187
Frankau, Gilbert, 112
Franklin, Miles (Stella Maria Sarah), 37,
    79, 238, 242

Fraser, Edward, 218
Frazer, James George (J. G.),
    163-16
Free, Edward, 7
Freud, Sigmund, 40, 108, 163, 179, 217,
    224–225, 228
Frierson, William Coleman, 126
Frost, Robert, 65
Fry, Roger, 41, 50–51, 88, 94, 167, 181
Frye, Northrop, 4, 174, 225

Galsworthy, John, 75, 91, 95, 104, 112,
    142, 185, 192–193
Galton, Francis, 186
Garnett, Richard, 232
Garvey, Marcus, 187
George, Walter Lionel, 48(46)
Gerould, Gordon Hall, 18
Gestefeld, Ursula Newell, 239
Gibbons, John, 218
Gide, André, 65
Gill, Eric, 173
Gilman, Charlotte Perkins, 120, 123
Glasier, John Bruce, 132
Goad, Harold E., 85–86
Golding, Louis, 87
Gollancz, Victor, 87
Goodman, Paul, 13
Gosse, Edmond, 30
Grand, Sarah, 239
Grant, Madison, 187
Grant, Robert, 121
Graves, Harold N., Jr., 174
Graves, Robert, 67, 143, 145, 192, 226
Gray, Cecil, 167
Green, Paul, 37
Greenberg, Clement, 12–13, 66, 235
Gregory, Horace, 65
Grew, E. S., 224
Grey, Zane, 21, 187
Grigson, Geoffrey, 173, 210
Gropius, Walter, 132

H. D. (Hilda Doolittle), 197
Haas, Robert B., 60
Haddon, Alfred C., 189
Hailey, Foster, 74
Haldane, Lord, 72

Hall, George 124(120), 245(239)
Hall, Radclyffe, 52, 178
Hamilton, Clayton, 49, 92–94, 96
Hamilton, E. W., 49
Hammett, Dashiell, 3
Harding, D. W., 225
Hardy, Thomas, 100, 139, 142–143
Harmsworth, Cecil Bisshopp, 185–186
Harris, Max, 144
Harris, W. Eric, 81, 250
Harrison, Jane Ellen, 23, 41
Harvey, W. F., 122
Harwood, Esther Georgina, *See*
    Battiscombe,
    Christopher Francis
Hastings, Beatrice, 211
Healy, William, 178
Heap, Jane (jh), 215
Hearn, Lafcadio, 142
Heilman, Robert, 112, 114
Hemingway, Ernest, 19, 88, 101, 178,
    195, 200, 205, 214
Henry, O., 15, 18
Hentoff, Nat, 205
Herbert, A. P., 112
Heyward, Dorothy, 166
Heyward, Edwin DuBose, 166
Hibbard, Addison, 64, 144
Hichens, Robert, 142
Hicks, Granville, 17
Hitchcock, Henry-Russell, 132
Hitler, Adolf, 54, 87, 123, 132, 134, 151,
    174, 186, 189
Hobson, John A., 79
Hogben, Lancelot, 232
Holmes, C. J., 203
Holtby, Winifred, 42, 78, 82, 211, 243
Hope, John Francis. *See* Randall,
    Alfred E.
Housman, A. E., 65
Howe, Julia Ward, 120
Howells, W. D., 103, 140
Hudson, W. H., 24–25, 165
Hughes, Langston, 149–150, 152, 166,
    181, 205–207
Hughes, William M., 81
Hulme, T. E., 101, 156
Hunter, Edward, 174

257

Index

Hurston, Katherine Cecil, 142
Hurston, Zora Neale, 101, 149, 152, 158,
    166, 242, 248
Huxley, Aldous, 3, 18, 37, 71, 102, 109,
    112, 114, 122, 188
Huxley, Julian, 189
Huxley, Thomas, 91

Irwin, Will, 171
Isherwood, Christopher, 31, 179, 201

Jabavu, D. D. T., 188
James, C. L. R., 79
James, Henry, 3, 18, 21, 45, 92, 96,
    126–127, 159
James, William, 23, 72, 226
Jameson, Margaret Storm, 35, 72, 200
Janis, Sydney, 163
Jaques-Dalcroze, Émile, 207
Johnson, Guy B., 141
Johnson, James Weldon, 95, 150
Johnson, Pamela Hansford, 65
Johnson, Philip, 132
Johnston, James Chapman, 26–27
Jolas, Eugene, 8, 52, 137, 197–198, 225,
    227–228, 236, 249
Jones, Gladys, 215
Jones, Gwyn, 52
Joyce, James, 4, 18–19, 42, 46, 49, 78,
    91–92, 102, 104, 233, 249–250
Jung, Carl, 42, 225, 228

Kallen, Horace, 219
Kaufman, George Simon, 115
Kaun, Alexander S., 131
Kennedy, Bart, 8
Kerfoot, J. B., 59
Kerr, Jean, 117
Kerr, Walter, 117
Keynes, John Maynard, 51, 53
Kilmer, Joyce, 59
King, Basil, 16
Kipling, Rudyard, 75, 78
Kohs, Samuel C., 157
Krafft-Ebing, Richard von, 179
Krutch, Joseph Wood, 36, 144
Kuhn, Helmut, 36
Lall, Chaman, 52–53

Lambert, Richard S., 172
Lang, Olga, 241
Langdon-Davies, John, 88
Larsen, Nella, 152, 206
Laski, Harold, 8
Lawrence, D. H., 8, 18, 43, 46, 71, 103,
    156, 159, 227
Le Bon, Gustave, 40
Leacock, Stephen, 71
League of Nations, 24, 77, 130, 171
Leavis, F. R., xi, 53, 65, 93, 109, 181
Leavis, Q. D., 2–3, 16–18, 116, 193
Lehmann, John, 138
Lerner, Max, 219
Leroy, Louis, 125
Levenson, Lew (pseudonym), 180
Levy-Bruhl, Lucien, 164
Lewis, C. S., 100
Lewis, Dorothy Roe, 3, 214
Lewis, Sinclair, 60, 62, 111, 246
Lewis, Wyndham, 2, 12, 50, 60, 65, 73–74,
    86, 137, 180, 186, 198, 205, 235
Lilly, W. S., 198
Linton, Eliza Lynn, 239
Lippmann, Walter, 61
Livesay, Dorothy, 53
Locke, Alain, 12, 51, 130, 149, 170,
    210, 213
Lodge, Oliver, 70
Lombroso, Cesare, 165
London, Jack, 22, 165
Lovecraft, H. P., 7
Low, A. Maurice, 78
Lowell, James Russell, 60
Lowes, James Livingston, 226
Loy, Mina, 23, 47, 58–59, 64, 137, 192,
    199, 206, 227, 249
Lubbock, Percy, 93–94, 195
Luce, Henry R., 34
Lukács, Georg, 198, 200
Lunacharsky, Anatoly, 75
Lustig, Theodore, 117
Lynes, Russell, 117

Macaulay, Rose, 100–101, 246–247
MacCarthy, Desmond, 41, 51
MacCarthy, Molly, 51
MacCurdy, John T., 40

Macdonald, Dwight, 53
Machen, Arthur, 102
Mack, Maynard, 108
Mackenzie, Alexander Johnston, 171–172
Mackenzie, Compton, 19
Mackenzie, J. S., 72
MacLeish, Archibald, 73, 109
MacLennan, Hugh, 107
MacLeod, Polly, 117
Macphail, Gunner, 218
Macpherson, Kenneth, 12, 64
Magil, Abraham, 87
Mahan, A. T., 130
Mais, S. P. (S.P.B.M.), 46
Malinowski, Bronislaw, 163
Mansfield, Katherine, 43, 158–159, 207, 211, 215
Margolis, Max, 186
Marinetti, F. T., 6–7, 12, 122–123, 136–138, 172, 197
Markino, Yoshio, 186
Marks, Jeanette, 71, 74
Marley, Dudley Leigh Aman, 90(87)
Marquand, John P., 169(165)
Marsden, Dora, 239
Marson, Una, 78
Maugham, Somerset, 47
Maurer, David, 178, 180
Maurois, André, 30–31
Mayes, Herbert R., 29
McAlmon, Robert, 178
McDougald, Elise Johnson, 242
McKay, Claude, 149, 153, 166, 206–208
McLuhan, Marshall, 4, 51, 75, 174
Mead, George Herbert, 157
Melcher, Frederic, 15
Mencken, H. L., 60, 117, 150–151, 248
Menner, Robert, 114
Menzies, R. G., 81
Michaud, Gustave, 187
Millay, Edna St. Vincent, 238
Miller, Arthur, 37
Miller, Kelly, 150
Miller, Henry, 36–37, 160
Molenaar, Heinrich, 232
Monroe, Harriet, 16, 24, 59, 142
Montgomery, L. M., 78
Moore, Jared Sparks (Jared S.), 225

Moore, Marianne, 46, 67, 72, 95, 145
Moran, Lord, 218
Morris, Harrison S., 17
Mosley, Oswald, 241
Moszkowski, Alexander, 73
Mott, Fred W. (Fredk. W.), 217
Mundy, Talbot, 9
Murdoch, Walter, 112–113, 116
Murphy, Emily, 34, 123
Murray, James A. H., 246
Murry, John Middleton, 141, 144, 203–204, 207
Mussolini, Benito, 36, 85, 86, 87, 88, 89
Myers, Charles Samuel (Charles S.), 216–217
Myers, Frederic W. H., 224

Nardal, Jane, 52
Nardal, Paulette, 50
Nash, Ogden, 71
Nathan, Walter, 165
Nesbit, E., 243
Nevinson, C. R. W., 12
Nicolson, Harold, 9, 29–31, 46, 73, 194
Nietzsche, Friedrich, 72, 99, 108
Nin, Anaïs, 42, 160, 243
Norris, Frank, 165, 198, 200

Ocampo, Victoria, 243
O'Faoláin, Sean, 200
Ogden, C. K., 232–233
O'Neil, David, 24
O'Neill, Eugene, 8, 226
Oppenheim, James, 185
Orage, A. R., 7
Orwell, George, 2, 36–37, 78, 82, 85, 89, 112, 121, 247
Ouida, 239
Overstreet, Harry, 219
Owen, Chandler, 149

Padmore, George, 78–79
Pal, Bipin Chandra, 81, 235
Pankhurst, Sylvia, 232–233
Park, Robert Ezra, 188
Partridge, Eric, 116
Pater, Walter H., 127–128
Paterson, Isabel (I.M.P.), 65, 67

Pattee, Fred Lewis, 46, 210
Peabody, Josephine Preston, 59–60
Pearson, Karl, 6
Pelham, Adrian, 167
Pelham, Edgar, 53
Penn, I. Garland, 148
Percy, Eustace, 57
Perham, Margery, 188
Perry, Lawrence, 23
Phelps, William Lyon, 2
Phillips, Henry Albert, 231
Phillips, William, 13, 53
Pickens, William, 149
Platt, Haviland Hull, 9
Ploetz, Alfred, 122
Popenoe, Paul, 146(140)
Porter, Eleanor H., 21
Pound, Elworth, 71
Pound, Ezra, 14, 38, 41, 47, 51, 58–59,
    66, 78, 86, 88, 91, 94, 96, 126, 137,
    192, 194, 204, 211, 226, 233–234,
    236, 247, 250
Pound, Roscoe, 215
Power, William S., 117
Powys, John Cowper, 181, 215
Priestley, J. B., 22
Progoff, Ira, 42
Propp, Vladimir, 231
Proust, Marcel, 24, 30, 65, 73–74, 96,
    128, 180–182, 198, 204
Pudney, John, 185

Radhakrishna, Sarvepalli, 61, 104
Randall, Alfred E. (A. E. R.), 71–72
Randolph, A. Philip, 149
Ransom, John Crowe, 142
Raverat, Gwen, 51
Read, Herbert, 72, 228
Repplier, Agnes, 170
Reynolds, Stephen, 31
Rhys, Jean, 4, 102
Rice, James, 70
Richards, I. A., 17, 64, 66, 91, 93–94, 204,
    212, 226, 246
Richardson, Dorothy, 50, 102, 126, 173,
    199, 201, 226, 234
Richardson, Henry Handel, 144
Rickword, Edgell, 137

Riding, Laura, 67, 143, 145, 192
Riley, James Whitcomb, 35
Rinehart, Mary Roberts, 227
Rivers, William H. R. (W. H. R.), 217, 225
Riviere, Joan, 243
R. M., 131
Robbins, Rossell Hope, 152
Roberts, Charles G. D., 144
Roberts, Michael, 173, 210
Robertson, Alexander, 85
Rogers, J. A., 166
Romains, Jules, 41
Romney, 35
Rose, Donald (F.), 115
Rosenblatt, Louise M., 195
Royden, Maude, 241
Russell, Bertrand, 71–72, 87, 163–164
Russell, George (AE), 212
Russell, Gilbert, 2
Russell, Sylvester, 151

Sackville-West, Vita, 86, 180
Saint Fiacre, 131
Sandburg, Carl, 21, 38, 206
Sanders, Emmy Veronica, 21
Sanger, Margaret, 123, 240
Sarton, May, 211
Sassoon, Siegfried, 218
Sayers, Dorothy L., 218
Schaller, Walter F., 218
Schele de Vere, M., 232
Schiaparelli, Elsa, 214
Schleyer, Johann Martin, 232
Schmidt, Paul, 123
Schreiner, Olive, 238, 240, 243
Schuman, Frederick, 87
Schuyler, George S., 151, 153
Scott-James, R. A., 142–144
Scudder, Vida Dutton, 216
Seccombe, Thomas, 26, 29
Selden, Elizabeth, 167
Seldes, George, 88, 171
Senghor, Léopold Sédar, 52
Sharp, Evelyn, 242
Shaw, George Bernard, 46, 86, 172
Shorer, Mark, 91
Sinclair, May, 91, 201, 226
Sinclair, Upton, 107

Sitwell, Edith, 9, 184
Slaughter, John Willis, 31
Smedley, Agnes, 78
Smith, A. J. M., 53
Smith, Nowell Charles, 26(24)
Smuts, Jan Christiaan (General the Right
    Hon. J. C.), 80–81
Snaith, Stanley, 50
Solomon, Israel, 46
Sorabji, Cornelia, 241
Southworth, James G., 30
Spender, Stephen, 2, 53, 173, 201
Spitzer, Leo, 2
Stannard, H. M., 191(186)
Stapledon, Olaf, 9
Stead, Christina, 79, 81
Stead, W. T., 216
Stein, Gertrude, 19, 31, 53, 64–65,
    67, 73–74, 95, 178, 180, 199,
    227, 249
Stein, Leo, 9
Steinberg, Milton, 187
Stekel, Wilhelm, 179
Stephensen, Percy Reginald, 144
Stern, Madeleine B., 73–74
Stevens, Wallace, 14, 101, 103, 197, 211,
    250
Stoddard, Lothrop, 166, 187
Stone, Alfred Holt, 187
Strachey, Lytton, 27–28, 30
Stuhlman, Frank, 215
Sumner, William Graham, 165
Sutton, E., 12
Swinnerton, Frank, 52, 112, 126
Symonds, Arthur, 195
Symonds, John Addington, 179

Tagore, Rabindranath, 24, 235
Tarkington, Booth, 22
Tawney, R. H., 58
Taylor, Bert Leston, 16
Thomas, Dylan (D. M. T.), 122, 173
Thomas, Edward, 107
Thompson, Dorothy, 8
Thompson, Edward John, 241
Thorpe, Edward, 8
Thurman, Wallace, 150
Tilley, Arthur, 198

Tönnies, Ferdinand, 40
Toomer, Jean, 149, 152, 184
Trent, Lucia, 95, 143–145
Trevelyan, R. C., 27, 66
Trilling, Lionel, 14
Trotter, Wilfred, 40
Tzara, Tristan, 136

Underhill, Evelyn, 102
Untermeyer, Louis, 59, 65

Vaerting, Mathilde, 243
Van der Post, Laurens, 168
Van Vechten, Carl, 151
Veblen, Thorstein, 36, 38

Walkley, Arthur (A. B.) 215
Wallace, Edgar, 122
Wallace, Henry A., 34–35
Walpole, Hugh, 216
Walters, Frank, 134
Ward, C. A., 8
Ward, Humphry, 142
Warren, Robert Penn, 94
Washington, Booker T., 33(29), 148
Watson, Lester Aglar, 151
Waugh, Arthur, 47, 199, 235
Waugh, Evelyn, 3, 37, 50–51, 91, 100,
    121, 216
Weaver, Harriet Shaw, 17
Webb, Beatrice, 61
Webster, Henry Kitchell, 219
Wedemeyer, Freda, 115
Wells, H. G., 2, 9, 35–36, 42, 50, 87, 92,
    96, 101, 111, 126, 163, 165, 171, 173,
    188, 215
Wescott, Glenway, 67
West, Nathanael, 122
West, Rebecca, 18, 41–42, 79, 100,
    199, 219
Weston, Jessie L., 66
Wharton, Edith, 18, 45, 47, 51, 121
Whelpley, J. D., 81–82
White, Ethel Lina, 120
White, Stewart Edward, 122
Whitman, Walt, 13, 21, 23, 59,
    139, 143
Whyte, William H., Jr., 41

261

Index

Widdemer, Margaret, 115
Wilde, Oscar, 165, 180–181, 196
Wilder, Thornton, 38
Williams, Iolo Aneurin, 29
Williams, William Carlos, 59, 64–65, 73, 95, 178, 189, 199, 250
Wilson, Betina, 214
Wilson, Edmund, 27, 73–74
Wilson, Woodrow, 61
Wiltshire, Harold, 217
Winters, Yvor, 211
Winwar, Frances, 28
Wood, Charles Erskine Scott, 21
Woolf, Leonard, 27, 40–41, 51, 57, 62, 80, 82, 112–113, 193
Woolf, Virginia, xvii, 4, 6–7, 11, 18–19, 19, 24, 27–28, 29, 31, 41–42, 46, 47–50, 53, 57, 67, 78, 80, 82, 86, 88–89, 93–96, 100, 102, 109, 113, 115–116, 120, 127, 138, 146, 159–161, 191, 194–197, 199–200, 205–207, 210–213, 216, 219, 228, 235, 238
Work, Monroe N., 154(150, 151)
Wylie, Elinor, 65

Yeats, W. B., 66, 86, 102, 205, 212, 235
Young, Michael, 23
Yourman, Julius, 174

Zamenhof, Ludovic Lazarus, 232
Zangwill, Israel, 187
Zimmern, Alfred (E.), 80–81, 133
Zola, Émile, 197–198, 200

Index of Modernist Keywords

The quotations in this book were chosen to illustrate modernist usages of the thirty-nine keywords (and their cognates) that constitute our main entries. These quotations do not offer a representative sampling of other keywords; however, when additional keywords do appear, we include them below, as the seeds for future entries on keywords. We do not index key concepts, but only words that are in some way being contested or in flux. In the case of variant spellings, we list only one.

abstract, abstraction(s), 114, 127, 138, 160, 164, 185, 235, 250

advertisement(s), advertising, **1–5**, 17, 20, 52, 101, 145, 172, 220, 226, 240

age, 9, 13, 27, 30, 47, 54, 59, 65, 87, 92, 137, 139, 185, 232

Age, 1, 5, 9, 35–36, 201

aristocracy, aristocrat(ic), 35–36, 60, 109, 187

atom(s), atomic, **6–10**, 28–29, 30, 32, 71, 76, 156

atmospher(e)(ric), 1, 11–12, 41–42, 46, 88, 121, 141, 205, 240, 249

audience(s), 53, 63, 67, 71, 151, 173, 194, 215 (*See also* reader)

authority, 12, 86, 100, 113, 141–142

avant-garde, advance guard, **11–14**, 64

average, 34, 37, 39, 59, 74, 192 (*See also* common)

barbarian(s), barbaric, barbarism, 45, 87, 88, 114, 121, 132, 165, 167, 186

beauty, 17, 22, 25, 35, 71, 94, 95, 128, 142, 198, 205, 212, 227, 234

best seller(s), 15–20, 75, 113, 116, 157

big, bigness, 17, **20–26**, 60, 117, 148, 169, 216, 240

biograph(y)(ies), **26–33**, 193

black(s), 55, 150, 152–154, 168, 172, 186–187, 189, 190–191, 226, 242

Bloomsbury, 32, 48, 50–51, 55 (*See also* coterie)

business, 4, 5, 60, 150, 216, 220–240, 241, 247, 248

chao(s)(tic), 36, 143, 203, 204–205, 247, 250

citizen(s)(ship)(ry), 8, 16, 38, 60–61, 78–79, 83, 111–112, 131, 150, 206

Modernism: Keywords, First Edition. Melba Cuddy-Keane, Adam Hammond, and Alexandra Peat.
© 2014 Melba Cuddy-Keane. Published 2014 by John Wiley & Sons, Ltd.

Index

civilization(s), 12, 44, 64, 75, 78, 80, 84,
  90, 106, 112, 114, 123, 134, 144,
  148–149, 163–164, 166, 176, 186, 245
civiliz(ed)(ing), 2, 41, 80, 88, 115, 132,
  149, 163–166, 168–169, 206
colo(u)red, 79, 83, 95, 147, 150–151,
  153–154, 158, 168, 187–188, 240, 242
common, 2, 6, 7, 23, 47, 52, 65, 81, 85,
  150, 156, 159, 182, 189, 208, 224,
  232, 252
common (communal) life, 159, 194, 234
common man, **34–39**, 112
common mind, **40–44**
common reader, 192–194
commonwealth, 80–83, 159
communis(m)(t)(tic), 64, 86, 124, 134,
  136, 141, 156 , 171
community, 35, 41–42, 44, 81, 130, 219
consciousness, 5, 21, 41, 71, 106, 108,
  133, 141, 143, 157, 160, 188, 224,
  227–228, 230, 235, 252
convention(s)(al)(ality), 27, **45–49**, 51, 74,
  115, 157, 199, 205, 211, 215, 239, 250
cooperat(ing)(ion), 43, 58, 81, 85, 91,
  130, 132, 148, 175, 188, 232, 240
cosmopolitan(ism)(ized), 50, 140,
  185–186, 233, 235
coterie, **49–55**
cultural, 13, 53, 137, 149, 189, 235
culture, 9–10, 12–13, 36, 43, 50, 53, 68,
  87–88, 115, 117, 120–121, 132,
  146–149, 163, 189, 235

democracy, 3, 8, 10, 38, **56–63**, 64, 80, 86,
  90, 121, 124, 142, 145, 174, 194, 221,
  248
democratic, **56–63**, 109, 112, 121, 139,
  217, 237, 247
difficult(y), 3, 29, 43, 47, **63–69**, 71, 74,
  114, 143, 174, 186, 193, 197, 214
  (*See also* obscure)
dream(s), 8, 75, 79, 104, 108, 110, 182,
  224–225, 228–229

education(al)(alist), xi, 10, 57, 58, 60–61,
  80, 95, 97, 114, 124, 131, 134,
  149–150, 172, 176, 208, 245
Einstein, **70–77**

elastic(ity), 31, 95–96, 142, 164
emotion(s)(al)(ally)(alities), 23, 41–42,
  47, 75, 78, 91, 94, 139, 142–143,
  160, 167, 171, 185, 199, 200, 205,
  211–212, 217–218, 246–247
empire(s), 4, **77–84**, 88, 96, 176, 187, 191
equal(s)(ity), 25, 28, 58–60, 73, 81, 132,
  203, 233
Everyman 34, 36, 38 (*See also* common
  man)
evolution, 8, 63, 81, 167–168, 252
experience(s)(d), 6, 42, 57–58, 61, 66,
  127–128, 141, 143, 156, 198–199,
  204, 207, 215–217, 225, 235

fascism(t)(ts), 62, 64, **85–90**, 156, 171,
  187, 219, 246
feeling(s), 16, 23, 30, 41, 59, 62, 64–65,
  115, 158, 160, 164, 175, 192, 195,
  210, 212, 251
form(s), 3, 47, 60, **91–98**, 141, 166–167,
  201, 204–206, 226, 233–234, 249
Formalist, 92

gay, 180 (*See also* queer)
God, god(s), 3, 4, 18, 22, 34, 50, 74,
  99–106, 141, 167, 249
group(s), 37, **40–45**, 50–53, 59, 133, 137,
  150–151, 157, 165, 184–185, 194,
  202, 205

Hamlet, 72, **107–111**, 156
herd(s), 3, 16, 37, 40, 116, 138, 246
highbrow(s)(ism), 17–18, 74, **111–119**,
  178, 193
histor(y)(ical), 28–29, 54, 92, 132, 144,
  150, 163, 170, 190, 252
home, 36, 124, 153, 179, 191, 208, 233,
  239, 240, 241
homosexual(ity), 178–181 (*See also*
  queer)
human, 8, 28, 31, 35–36, 60, 63, 75, 81,
  87, 103–104, 114, 121, 123, 129, 131,
  139, 141, 145, 155–156, 163, 167,
  180, 182, 186, 190, 198–199, 207,
  216, 219, 227, 230, 236, 251
human being(s), 30, 37, 57, 89, 149,
  235, 243

humanity, 8, 38, 53, 55, 82, 93, 102, 116, 123, 131–132, 167, 179, 235
human race, 92, 131, 134, 184–185, 189, 240
hygien(e)(ic), **119–124**, 136, 157, 239

imperial(ism)(ist), **77–84**, 134
impersonal(ity), 42, **155–162**, 194, 251
impression(s)(ism)(ist), 51, 94, 110, **125–29**, 159, 190, 201, 227–228
individual(s)(ity)(ism)(istic), 8, 23, 37, 40–41, 43, 53, 58–59, 62, 64, 65, 85–86, 100, 121, 131–132, 138, 141–142, 158, 161, 201, 206–207, 228, 235–236, 246, 252
intellectual(s), 13, 27, 40, 50, 55, 91, 108, 112–113, 130, 173, 193, 215, 219, 248
intelligentsia, 50, 53, 150
international(ism)(ity), 10, 38–39, 76, 80, 84, 86, 90, 119, **129–135**, 140, 175, 185–186, 190, 214, 232–234, 236–237, 245

jazz, 166, 170, 204, 206, 208
Jew(s)(ish)(ry), 123, 130, 134, 150, 174, 186–187, 191, 219

language, 38, 47, 53, 66, 90, 104, 118, 141, 143, 180, 189, 202, 232–234, 236, **246–253**
low(-)brow(s)(ism), **111–119**, 192

manifesto, **136–138**
mass(es), 12–13, 35–36, 43, 54, 78, 90, 110, 121, 175, 193, 235
middle(-)brow(s), **111–119**
mind, 6, 18, 67, 93, 115, 138, 142, 144–145, 156–157, 159, 162–164, 186, 193, 197, 207, 223, 225, 227–228, 241, 244, 247, 250 (*See also* common mind)
modern(s), 2, 4–6, 11, 23, 27, 30–32, 42, 44, 46, 53, 57, 59, 61–65, 73, 78, 93, 104, 107–108, 112, 129, 132, 138, **139–146**, 152, 155, 163, 193, 196, 199–201, 203, 213, 217, 221–222, 228–230, 234, 239–240, 244–245, 249–250

modernism, modernist(ic), 13, 67, **139–146**, 202–203, 207
multiple, multiplicity, 7, 81, 127, 157, 194, 204

national(ism)(ist)(ity), 16, 23, 29, 62, 83–84, 87, 101, 115, 119–120, 131–135, 144–146, 150, 202, 233–235, 240, 247–248
natural(ized), unnatural, 53, 116, 122, 158, 165, 167, 180, 203, 205, 207, 212, 234, 238, 243, 247, 249
naturalism(t), 13, 32, 145, 197–198, 200, 202
Negro(es), 12, 52, 58, 97, 103, 130, **147–154**, 158, 166, 169, 175, 182, 188, 190, 205–206, 242, 249
new, 3, 7, 9, 10–12, 22, 28, 44, 51, 59, 62, 64, 67, 73, 76, 79, 81, 87, 90, 92, 95, 111, 120, 123, 138, 141–146, 159–160, 166–167, 173, 193, 197, 199, 202, 208, 227, 234, 236–237, 241–243, 246, 248–249, 252
New Negro, **147–154**, 242
newspaper(s), 23, 193, 239, 249

obscur(e)(ity), 12, **63–69**, 193, 250 (*See also* difficulty)
ordinary, 3, 16, 29–30, 36–38, 59, 64–65, 98, 127, 141, 192–193, 204, 218

personality, 27, 30–31, 38, 148, **155–162**, 206, 217, 230, 235
press, the, 58, 61, 172, 194 (*See also* newspaper)
primitive, 37, 113, 131–132, 142, **162–170**, 207
progress(ion)(ive), 7, 22, 35, 81, 91, 112, 116, 137, 148–149, 236, 241, 241–242
propagand(a)(istic), 43, 78, **170–176**, 234
public, 2, 11, 16–18, 34, 58, 61, 66, 68, 80, 112, 119–120, 134, 171, 175, 181, 188, 192–194, 215, 240, 247
pure(ly), 3, 29, 45, 91, 103, 123, 141, 173, 187, 200, 207, 214, 236, 243–244, 247, 253

265

Index

queer(s), 36, 93, 96, **177–183**

race(s), 24, 36, 57–58, 80, 83, 87,
92, 101–102, 122–124, 131, 134,
148–151, 153, 163, **184–191**,
205–206, 240, 242
racial, 95, 123, 148, 151, 153,
184–191, 206
racism, racist, 89, 184, 187
reader(s), 16–17, 19, 38, 48, 53, 64–68,
74, 77, 94, 110, 115–117, 126, 146,
153, 179, **191–196**, 220–221
reading, 11, 16, 33, 66, 69, 76, 93, 98,
113, 174, **191–196**
realism, 25, **196–203**, 249
reality, 6, 8, 10, 25, 32, 41, 50, 126, 128,
196–203, 219, 228, 250
revolution(s)(ary), 8, 13, 47, 58–59, 88,
122, 137, 171, 175, 205, 249
rhythm(s)(ic), 28, 59, 65, 117, 142, 165,
167, 201, **203–209**, 249
romance, romantic(ism), 3, 66, 98, 105,
142, 188, 190, 198, 200, 247, 249

savage(ry), 79, 103, 164–167, 169, 186,
192, 250
scale, 7, 28, 73, 143, 211
self, 31, 35, 59, 91, 109, 141–142,
155–162 (*See also* personality)
sentimental(ity), 47, 114, 143, **210–214**
sex(ual)(ity), bisexual, 30, 32, 122–124,
166, 177–183, 215–216, 227, 238–
239, 242–245 (*See also* queer; woman)
sexes, 141, 227
shock(ing), shell(-)shock, 13, 75, **214–222**
simple, simplicity(ification), 3, 14, 65, 75,
83, 121, 141, 165–166, 244, 246
small(ness), 6, **20–26**, 28, 30, 36, 38, 52,
128, 133, 138, 151, 158, 233 (*See also*
bigness)
spiritual, 76, 88, 101, 106, 122, 139, 141,
143, 180, 186, 199, 206, 251–252

subconscious(ly), 30, 142, 150, 227–228
(*See also* unconscious)

taste, 16–17, 20, 29, 48, 68, 112,
115–116, 118–119, 192, 195, 215,
239
totalitarian(ism), 11, 53, 92, 121, 175,
219
tradition(s)(al), 17, 36, 47, 51, 55, 59, 62,
82, 95, 115, 137, 147, 161, 170, 189,
204, 223, 240, 249
truth(s)(ful)(ness), 27, 28, 31, 47, 64,
71–72, 92–93, 108–109, 114, 128,
143–144, 168, 174, 176, 196, 198–
200, 213, 215, 234–235, 250

unconscious, 30, 42, 46, 72, 108, 159,
221, **223–230**
understand(ing), 29–30, 59, 65–67, 71,
74, 81, 94, 113–114, 133, 164, 180,
208, 226, 251
unity, 7–8, 30, 43, 64, 78, 81, 131, 158,
188, 205, 244
universal(ity), 9, 42–43, 127, 145, 159,
160, 163, 225, **231–237**
universe, 7, 21–23, 71–72, 103, 127, 144,
207

woman, women, 45–46, 49, 55, 58, 90, 95,
98, 102, 106, 110, 118, 120, 126, 130,
138, 140, 165, 185–186, 212–215,
238–245, 246
words, 11, 60, 66–67, 96, 102–103, 116,
150, 164, 166, 178, 184, 203, 207,
212, 218, 221, 228, **246–253**
world (modern, new), 62, 65, 75, 124, 144,
160, 203, 216, 241–242
world (shared, united), 9, 24, 42–43, 61,
81, 101, 130, 173, 185, 188, 211, 225,
232–233, 235–237, 250
world (spiritual, physical reality), 7–8, 24,
41, 102, 128, 207, 252